A VISITOR'S GUIDE TO
A HISTORY OF BRITAIN

A VISITOR'S GUIDE TO
A HISTORY OF BRITAIN

LOCATIONS FROM FIVE THOUSAND YEARS OF HISTORY

Martin Davidson

ST. MARTIN'S GRIFFIN
NEW YORK

18077527
A

Commissioning editors: Khadija Manjlai & Sally Potter
Copy editor: Richard Rosenfeld   Researcher: Chris Childs
Art director: Linda Blakemore   Designer: Rachel Hardman Carter
Picture research: Rachel Jordan   Maps by Angela Wilson of All Terrain Mapping. © Maps in Minutes™ 2001. © Crown Copyright, Ordnance Survey & Ordnance Survey Northern Ireland 2001 Permit No. NI 1675 & © Government of Ireland, Ordnance Survey Ireland.

Set in Utopia & Franklin Gothic by BBC Worldwide
Printed & bound in France by Imprimerie Pollina s.a.
Colour separations by Kestrel Digital Colour, Chelmsford

First published in Great Britain by BBC Worldwide Limited

First St. Martin's Griffin Edition: 2002

10 9 8 7 6 5 4 3 2 1

Previous page: A view of the gardens at **Stourhead**, *Wiltshire.*

Contents

How to use this book 6   Introduction 8

ONE Ancient Stone and Wood 12

South-west 15   North-west 34
South-east 21   North-east 34
Eastern 25   Scotland 38
Central 27   Northern Ireland 41
Wales 32

TWO Norman Moats and Gothic Spires 42

South-west 45   North-west 78
South-east 50   North-east 80
Eastern 58   Scotland 91
Central 63   Northern Ireland 98
Wales 71

THREE Medieval Manors and Elizabethan Prodigies 100

South-west 103   North-west 136
South-east 109   North-east 137
Eastern 121   Scotland 140
Central 126   Northern Ireland 151
Wales 134

FOUR Stately Homes and Georgian Follies 152

South-west 155   North-west 193
South-east 160   North-east 194
Eastern 176   Scotland 198
Central 181   Northern Ireland 204
Wales 192

FIVE Grime, Soot, Steel and Glass 208

South-west 211   North-west 237
South-east 214   North-east 239
Eastern 229   Scotland 241
Central 230   Northern Ireland 249
Wales 233

Maps 250   Bibliography & websites 267   Index 268

How to use this book

The book is divided into five chapters, each of which focuses on types of buildings particularly characteristic of the era – for example, stone circles and Iron Age forts in chapter 1; castles and cathedrals in 2; manor houses in 3; stately homes in 4; and buildings associated with the industrial revolution and modern technology in 5.

Within each chapter the locations are divided into regions. Within each region, the sections have numbered main entries describing the most interesting and significant places. These are followed by additional entries that are also in the area and well worth visiting but are not numbered. The numbered main entries correspond to the numbers on the regional maps at the end of the book, on pages 259–68. You can see other main locations that are close by on these maps, and can, of course, also follow up the additional places in the same area listed within the chapters.

The maps give the approximate location of main entries and are meant as a guide only. When planning a trip, always use a good road atlas which will show much more local detail than is possible here.

Many of the locations were featured in the *A History of Britain* television series and these are indicated by an asterisk after their name.

There are roughly 800 locations listed here altogether. The information in the guide includes the full address, contact number when available, directions, website and email addresses if known, and opening times, as well as descriptions of the sites.

Properties often open, or summer opening times come into action, at the last weekend in March or the first in April, or at Easter; many close for the season, or change to winter opening times, on the last weekend of September or October, or the first weekend of the following month. As the dates for these change each year we have given months rather than dates. Many properties close in winter – if this is the case only summer months have been given, although it is always worth phoning as sometimes properties may be opened in winter for viewing by prior arrangement, especially if it is for a group.

Groups over a certain size can also often visit properties throughout the year on days when they are not normally open to the public by prior arrangement.

Properties often close for Christmas, Boxing Day and New Year's Day – check before going on these days as we have not given details for individual properties. Many properties are open at Easter (although not always on Good Friday) and at other bank holidays, particularly in summer. Some also have special opening times at half-term.

Many properties also close, or close early, on certain days for private and official functions, for concerts and festivals, and for other events. It is not possible to predict these dates far in advance which is another reason to check before setting out.

Properties often have the last admissions half an hour, or even an hour, before closing time, especially if there are tours. Make sure you don't arrive too late to get in.

It is worth noting that owners and organizations often adjust the visiting times each year; many of this year's times had not been finalized when we went to press.

If no days of the week are specified it means that the location is open every day. If no months are specified it means that it is open all year (apart from the possible exceptions mentioned above).

Parks and gardens are frequently open when the house itself is shut. Usually they close at dusk in winter if it is earlier than the stated closing time.

Unmanned sites are often described as open at 'Any reasonable time'. This means there is usually free access but for your own safety do visit at sensible times, for example in daylight hours. Some sites are manned by volunteers so their opening times may be erratic.

Cathedrals and churches restrict visitors walking around inside during services so check the times of services. Of course, if you would like to join in, you will be very welcome.

For admission fees, contact the sites.

We have indicated those sites managed or owned by the following: Welsh Historic Monuments (CADW), English Heritage (EH), Historic Scotland (HS), National Trust (NT) and National Trust for Scotland (NTS). Apart from these, the names of owners have not been given. Websites are given only when they are specific to the site or region. CADW, English Heritage, Histori Scotland, the National Trust and the National Trust for Scotland all have thei own websites which you can enter to find out details about specific propertie These websites are listed on page 267 near the end of the book.

Phone numbers given are UK dialling numbers. If you are phoning from the U.S., remember to add the international access code (011) plus the UK country code (44), followed by the number (but omitting the first 0 or 9 of the UK number).

Where no phone number has been given at all this is usually a site with free access. More information may be available from the relevant website.

There is nothing so frustrating as making a journey to a place of interest, only to arrive and find it closed. We have tried as hard as possible to supply up-to-date and accurate information about opening times and locations. But there are a million reasons why they might not apply on the day you choose to visit, so phone ahead to check.

Introduction

The BBC's *A History of Britain* was conceived right from the beginning as an epic television event. It was fired by great ambition: we would marry the latest technology to the oldest subject; we would bring alive as many of the great moments and turning points of British history as we could; we would try to rediscover, and then share with the widest audience possible as much of British history as we could. It would be a Bayeux Tapestry for the 21st century.

The series was born from a very simple observation – nobody had ever attempted before on television to tell the story of Britain from the earliest days to the present, and for a very good reason. The subject is huge, full of disagreement and controversy and, before the 20th century, there were no film archives of major events or even witnesses and participants to interview. The fear was that we could end up with nothing more than a lecture illustrated by slides. Yet the project nagged away at us so much that the doubts became challenges and not obstacles.

The first need was for a writer and a presenter, somebody to bring it all together, to provide the narrative power, to be our guide through 5000 years of history. After we had persuaded Simon Schama to write and present the series, and write the accompanying book, our minds turned to the tricky question, what would we actually see?

Of course we would have shots of Simon Schama appearing in or near certain key locations, but might this look a little stilted? And surely everyone knows what the greatest castles and houses in Britain look like. In the end, our fears were completely misplaced. We came to rediscover the sheer power and mystery exerted by British land-scapes and buildings, many of which are indeed extraordinary. Schama was adamant right from the beginning that location, location, location, would be the beating heart of the series. He was absolutely right.

We spent nearly four years making *A History of Britain*, and one of our most striking discoveries was that history is not just about *when* or *who* but *where*. Of course, all history is a leap of the imagination and a piece of detective work. We will never see it as it was, let alone as it looked to those who lived the events first hand. But the leap becomes very much easier to make when you stand and survey any one of the hundreds of historically significant sites that dot the country. They range from the largest, most imposing Norman castle to the tiniest worker's cottage; from great industrial shipyards to hidden stumps of Roman ruins; from turfed-over Neolithic burial mounds to royal mausoleums; from Scottish lochs to Cornish beaches. The history of Britain is written into the very fabric of the British Isles.

Even for those for whom the historical detail is only of passing or background interest, these locations are virtually, without exception, wonderful places to visit. The trouble is, which are the best and how do you find them? There is no problem with major sites, but what about the thousands of other less famous places, usually tucked away far from motorways?

In the course of researching and making *A History of Britain* we visited hundreds of such locations, many more than we could film. And for every one which we actually visited, we read descriptions of scores of others. So the total list of places considered for inclusion actually reached well over a thousand. While doing this research we realized that there does not exist in one volume a complete, or anything like complete, gazetteer covering British history. There are books touching on particular regions or periods or types of building. But many are out of print or are only available from specialist organizations. So we decided to compile our own, one that takes many of the locations we filmed and researched for *A History of Britain* as a central spine around which to list as many other historically interesting places as possible.

There is no doubt that the enormous success enjoyed by the series was in part proof that landscapes and historical locations do have a huge power to move and fascinate, even today. It is not just that there is a frisson when visiting, say, the **Banqueting House** in Whitehall, knowing that this was where Charles I was beheaded on 30 January 1649, powerful though that is. Look up to its extraordinary ceiling and you will see the great painted panels which Charles commissioned from the Flemish artist, Peter Paul Rubens, to celebrate the reign of his father James (VI of Scotland and I of England). What a picture this commission gives of a man whose idea of kingship was to catapult Britain into civil war. With their rich allegorical images, these panels look like the kind of court paintings which decorated the great Catholic courts of Europe – which is precisely the effect they had on 17th-century England. This was provocation of a high order, one in a series of many steps which led the King and Parliament to war. To stand in this exquisite place is to see major stories unravel right in front of you.

There are many, many pleasures to be enjoyed when visiting historical locations. Virtually all of them are visually pleasing. The great castle builders of the early Middle Ages chose their lofty vantage points for strategic reasons, but a happy consequence has been a network of forts which dominate and, to our eyes, enhance their surrounding landscapes. The 17th- and 18th-century country house builders knew only too well the importance of ravishing the eye, of constructing houses and gardens to seduce and astonish the senses of those who could afford to build and live in them.

Many have survived to this day, albeit often as ruins, thanks to the extraordinary work done by organizations like the National Trust and National Trust for Scotland, English Heritage, Historic Scotland, CADW (Welsh Historic Monuments), the Historic Houses Association, and the myriads of individual owners and institutions committed to preserving the material fabric of British history. I think it is fair to say that the impact these and similar organizations have had is beyond calculation. Those of us who worked on the series were totally impressed by our dealings with them all and hope, in some small way, that

the interest in history and historical locations provoked by the series, and the accompanying books will provide recompense for all the help which they gave us. So many have done so much work to preserve and protect the landscape of British history and their achievement deserves as much recognition and celebration as possible.

Even more exciting are those historical buildings which are still in daily use; perhaps they are lived in as private dwellings, are used as offices or, most significantly of all, are places of worship. Although they may have powerful associations with the past that does not mean that they are not living, vibrant places; they have a present and a future too.

We were continually struck by the sheer abundance of locations which have survived, testimony perhaps to the relative stability of large tracts of British history. When you consider, however, just how many castles and religious houses were damaged or 'slighted' during the Civil War, you realize just how destructive such times could be, and how much worse things could have been with more civil wars, more religious conflict, despots and invasions.

Most of what has survived has endured because it was built to last. Look at all those cathedrals, castles and grand houses. But they give a one-sided view of history because the cottages and hovels that housed most of the population are gone. Well, with exceptions. Just enough have survived to help round out the picture of the past and to remind us that not everyone lived in Palladian mansions or Norman castles. In fact, every type of building has survived in one form or another: the lighthouses, water-mills,

hotels, sewage works, schools, almshouses, grottoes and libraries... Visiting the past is not a repetitive experience.

There are tens of thousands of locations in Britain with considerable historical significance. Even a book as comprehensive as we hope this is can only hope to scratch the surface. It means that history in Britain is easy to find and yet also often has the feel of being a quest or adventure. There is every chance that you will make your own personal discoveries, and will stumble on places which are not familiar and make them your own. For every place which is easy to find there are ten which are not, which need that little bit of extra effort to find and explore, giving perhaps even greater satisfaction.

This book has three main purposes. First and foremost, it is designed to help you retrace some of the footsteps we took in preparing and then making the television series, just as we retraced the footsteps of those who went before us. Second, it is intended to form a companion to the series – an index to many of the fabulous places we filmed but which we were not able to include in the programme. And third, it is this: an invitation to as many people as possible to go out and savour British history in all its various guises.

Our series, when it ends, will have been an extraordinary journey covering thousands of years, thousands of miles and thousands of lives; from hard tough existences to the most cosseted and privileged. But the wonderful thing about history is that no sooner is one journey finished than it is time to embark on another. We hope this book will help you make many of your own.

The Banqueting House in Whitehall, with its ceiling by Peter Paul Rubens.

CHAPTER ONE

Ancient Stone and Wood

The first pressing question facing any large historical narrative is where to start. The television series, *A History of Britain*, was no exception. We called the first programme *Beginnings* because we wanted to cover a lot of ground quickly, to take the story up as far as we could. It was a shame, of course, because although early British history lacks the kind of documentation which comes later, the remains are among the most interesting of any period.

Eventually we decided to start our story 5000 years ago – and what shaped that decision was a location, and perhaps my favourite, **Skara Brae**, a Neolithic village in Orkney. Having grown up in Scotland, I was already familiar with the place – every Scottish school child is taught about their version of **Stonehenge**. What surprised me was how few people south of Carlisle had heard of it though. So it offered the perfect place to start – magical, slightly poetic and largely unheard of while being a Stone Age site which offered tantalizing insights into life thousands of years ago.

It is an extraordinary place, a small cluster of domestic interiors, perched on the western coast of Orkney's main island, which had lain covered by a sea of sand and grass for thousands of years until a vicious sea-storm uncovered it in 1850.

What is so striking about these tiny houses is that their interiors immediately make sense to 21st-century eyes. The main dwellings are all roughly equal in size; there are 'his' and 'her' beds on each side of the floor, a hearth, a tank for keeping sea food in and, most spectacular of all, great stone dressers, each given pride of place against the wall opposite the entrance. As far as we can tell, they were used just as you would imagine – as interior furniture, where a whole variety of decorative objects were laid out for display.

The houses were remarkably cosy. You would expect to find houses of many different sizes with big ones for the grand, the priests and lords, smaller ones for the farmers and providers of food, and hovels for the servants and slaves. But not at Skara Brae. A village with no hierarchy? Where everyone lived harmoniously together? Where there are no defensive walls? Obviously we will never know the full truth but, as far as we can tell, Skara Brae paints a fascinating and unexpectedly appealing picture of ancient life. The real sadness is that the sea is slowly eating away at the coastline, and there is nothing which can be done. Inevitably, these wonderful structures which have survived 5000 years will one day collapse into the Orkney brine.

Neolithic sandstone house at **Skara Brae**.

The great hill forts of the Iron Age, such as **Maiden Castle** in Dorset, speak of a time very different from the Neolithic centuries where we started. From the air, it is still possible to detect the outlines of ancient field systems which indicate how great an area of landscape was being used for agriculture. Our old picture of a forest nation with occasional clearings for villages has been shown, by recent research, to have been wide of the mark.

The jump in scale – in size, complexity and sophistication – to the new Roman buildings is still astonishing. The big, famous Roman locations are as impressive as ever. And **Hadrian's Wall** dramatically conveys a sense of frontier life which the intervening centuries have done nothing to diminish. Even if you did not know that this northern spine was, roughly, where Roman influence met its most serious northern challenge, a 20-minute walk along one of the ridges hints at this great divide. Of the smaller Roman sites, the charm of **Bignor Villa** in West Sussex, with its utterly captivating mosaics, was perhaps the most seductive. The Saxon Shore Forts tell their own story of the dangers felt by this most powerful of military empires. In fact the overall story of the Romans is the now familiar one of imperial expansion and resistance, and of acquiescence and slow consolidation. The mixture of military and civilian life provided a model for what came later.

The first programme also described the arrival of the Saxons and the Vikings and of Christianity, all of which profoundly influenced the shape Britain would take, not least architecturally in the form of churches, castles and domestic dwellings. The film ended on the eve of one of the most famous dates in British history, 1066.

Megalithic sarsen stones at **Avebury**.

South-west MAP 1

1 Avebury Stone Circles* EH & NT
☎ 01672 539250
Nr Marlborough, Wiltshire SN8 1RF
Email: wavgen@smtp.ntrust.org.uk
Website: www.avebury-stones.co.uk
6m W of Marlborough,
1m N of Bath road (A4) on A4361 & B4003
Open *Stone circle & Alexander Keiller Museum: Apr–Oct 10–6 (dusk if earlier), Nov–Mar 10–4*
One of the most important megalithic monuments in Europe, it is spread over a vast area, much of which is under National Trust protection. The great stone circle encompassing part of the village of Avebury is enclosed by a ditch and external bank and is approached by an avenue of stones. Many of the stones were re-erected in the 1930s by the archaeologist Alexander Keiller. West of Avebury, the Iron Age earthwork of Oldbury Castle and the conspicuous Lansdowne Monument crown Cherhill Down. This area of downland provides wonderful walking.

2 Carn Euny Ancient Village EH
Sancreed, nr Penzance, Cornwall
1m SW of Sancreed off A30
Open *Any reasonable time*
An Iron Age village once stood here, of which ten houses have been identified and excavated. At the heart of the village is a 'fogou' or underground chamber. Despite being fully excavated its purposes remain enigmatic, though the best guess is it must have served some kind of religious purpose unless, of course, it was just an old storage cellar.

3 Chysauster Ancient Village EH
☎ 07831 757934
Nr Penzance, Cornwall
3m N of Penzance off B3311
Open *Aug–Sept 10–6, Oct 10–5*
The remarkable Iron Age village has four pairs of houses, each facing out on to a central alley, one of the earliest high streets in Britain. The houses have circular rooms with thick walls and a central courtyard. The roofs are long gone. There is evidence that the houses had small walled back gardens. Like Carn Euny at Sancreed, there is also a 'fogou' or underground chamber.

4 Hod Hill*
Hod Hill, Dorset
3m NW of Blandford Forum on A350 above River Stour
The Iron Age hill fort covers an area of over 50 acres, with the remains of a later Roman fort covering about 11 acres. A legion of 600 men and a cavalry unit of 250 were thought to have been garrisoned at the hill fort, the largest in Dorset. Like most such sites, its real impact is evident when seen from the air.

5 King Alfred's Tower*

Athelney, nr Glastonbury, Somerset
SW of Glastonbury off A361
Open *Summer Tues Fri Sat & Sun pm*
This 18th-century folly, built as a
memorial to the great Saxon king Alfred,
stands near the swamps of Athelney
where he retreated from the Vikings and
gathered his forces before the battle of
Edington in 878. There are spectacular
views of the surrounding countryside
from the top. It stands as a great vertical
landmark at the end of a beautiful
avenue of trees. The most telling artefact
associated with the Alfred legend, the
Alfred Jewel, was discovered near
Athelney and is now on display at
the Ashmolean Museum in Oxford.

6 Maiden Castle* EH

Nr Dorchester, Dorset
2m S of Dorchester, off A354
Open *Any reasonable time*
Massive Iron Age fort, the finest of its
kind in Europe and the site of ferocious
battles with Vespasian's legionaries.
It was built over a Neolithic camp
around 600–500BC. When the site was
excavated in the 1930s and 1980s it
provided important information about
the way of life here, and dramatic proof
of British resistance to the Roman
invasion in AD43.

Near the eastern gateway are some
shallow graves of Roman casualties,
making this one of the earliest war graves
in the country. The north-east corner of
the fort even has the remains of a later
Romano-British temple, with a veranda.
The major finds from the site are now all
in the Dorchester County museum. They
include chilling evidence of the brutality
of 2nd-century conflict in the form of
the vertebrae of a defender, pierced by
a bolt which the Romans fired from their
powerful catapults or ballista.

7 Old Sarum* EH

☎ 01722 335398
Castle Rd, Salisbury, Wiltshire SP1 3SD
*Access to site only via slip road from A345;
paths to site from Salisbury are closed;
1½m N of Salisbury off A345*
Open *Apr–June & Sept 10–6, July–Aug 9–6,
Oct 10–5, Nov–Mar 10–4*
After a new cathedral was built in the
early 13th century at New Sarum, or
Salisbury as it is now known (p46), much
of Old Sarum was abandoned and fell
into ruin. It is hard now to realize that
these great earthworks, banks and
ditches were once part of a great and
powerful settlement lived in by Iron Age
peoples, Romans, Saxons and, lastly, the
Normans. It was here that William the
Conqueror received oaths of loyalty from
his nobles, and ordered the work
that culminated in the Domesday Book.
The old cathedral was demolished and
its stones used as a stone quarry for the
neighbourhood. But the castle remained
in use until the late 14th century.

8 Roman Baths*

☎ 01225 477785
Pump Rooms, Stall St, Bath,
Somerset BA1 1LZ
Website: www.romanbaths.co.uk
In centre of Bath
Open *Mar–June & Sept–Oct 9–6, July–Aug
9–10, Jan–Feb & Nov–Dec 9.30–5.30*
Despite the later 18th-century
accretions, the site still offers a perfect
window on the life lived by Roman
Britons following the arrival of the
legions; a world of socializing, gossip,
business and pleasure. Little remains
of the surrounding Roman town.

9 Silbury Hill* EH

Nr Avebury, Wiltshire
1m E of Avebury on A4
Open *Any reasonable time*

*The Great Bath, begun in the 1st century AD, part of the **Roman Baths** at Bath.*

Silbury Hill is an implausibly perfect cone of grass and soil. Many people climb to the top, although this is discouraged in order to protect the site from damage.

10 Stonehenge* EH

☎ Infoline 01980 624715;
Amesbury tourist info 01980 622833
Nr Amesbury, Wiltshire SP4 7DE
*2m W of Amesbury at junction of
A303 & A344/A360*
Open *Mid–Mar–May 9.30–6, June–Aug
9–7, Sept–mid-Oct 9.30–6, mid–late Oct
9.30–5, Nov–mid-Mar 9.30–4*
It has to be one of the great wonders of the world, and the most famous Neolithic stone monument on the planet. What we see now dates back to between *c*3000 and 1600BC, the latest phase in a whole series of monuments built on the site.

The 'henge' comprises an outer circle of huge standing stones, super-hard sarsens from the Marlborough Downs, topped by lintels making a continuous ring. Inside this was a horseshoe of still larger stones, five pairs of uprights with a lintel across each pair, known as trilithons. Inside the sarsens stood a circle of smaller blue stones which came from South Wales.

Debate has raged over the temple's purpose. It clearly involved a huge amount of time and labour getting the materials to the site, tremendous logistical sophistication and determination, and the ability to assemble it in precise alignment with the rising summer solstice sun. Stonehenge was the product of smart, elaborate thinking, and was of huge cultural or religious significance to those who conceived and built it.

11 West Kennet Long Barrow*
EH & NT

West Kennet, Wiltshire
1½m S of Avebury, ¾m SW of West Kennet
Open *Any reasonable time*

Barrows are the earliest surviving mausoleums found in the British landscape. They date from the early metal-working era of prehistory and represent a new and sophisticated attitude towards death, not least the willingness and ability to invest huge amounts of time, labour and manpower in the construction of these tombs. They tend to come in two shapes: long (burial chambers laid out one after the other) or round or disc (burial chambers laid out radially).

The West Kennet Long Barrow may be longer (at 330ft/100m) and cruder than the mausoleum of Maes Howe in Orkney, but it has an equally powerful allure. Even more intriguingly, its proximity to Silbury Hill creates an overwhelming sense that a whole landscape has been worked upon, not just individual structures. It is an unforgettable corner of the English countryside.

If you stand on the West Kennet Long Barrow and look behind you, you will see the fields that Steven Spielberg used in *Saving Private Ryan* in a scene where a Midwestern mother hears about the death of her sons. Having scoured the whole of the Midwest, Spielberg's scouts realized that here in Wiltshire of all places was the perfect replica of the American prairie; more Iowa than Iowa.

ADDITIONAL PLACES TO VISIT

Ballowall Barrow EH & NT

St Just, Cornwall
1m W of St Just, near Carn Gloose
Open *Any reasonable time*

Beautifully located Bronze Age tomb with a sophisticated layout of chambers.

Bant's Carn Burial Chamber and Halangy Down Ancient Village EH

St Mary's, Isles of Scilly
1m N of Hugh Town
Open *Any reasonable time*

Another Bronze Age burial mound located on a hill above the site of an ancient Iron Age village, complete with entrance tunnel and chamber.

Bratton Camp and White Horse EH

Nr Trowbridge, Wiltshire
2m E of Westbury off B3098
Open *Any reasonable time*

A large Iron Age hill fort with the Westbury White Horse on the side of the hill. The horse may have been cut in the Iron Age, but was re-cut and modified the 18th century. It looks much more naturalistic than the horse at Uffington (p29).

Cerne Abbas Giant

Nr Cerne Abbas, Dorset
8m N of Dorchester on A352
Open *Any reasonable time*

The most famous chalk-cut figure in Britain with his rib cage, nipples, balloon-shaped head and club. Resembling Hercules, he may date from the time of the Roman occupation of Britain.

Grimspound EH

Nr Moretonhampstead, Devon
6m SW of Moretonhampstead off B3212
Open *Any reasonable time*

This Late Bronze Age settlement has the remains of 24 huts in an area of 4 acres.

Halloggye Fogou EH

Nr Helston, Cornwall
5m SE of Helston off B3293
Open *Reasonable daylight hours Apr–Oct; take a torch & be prepared for dirt*

One of several strange underground tunnels associated with Iron Age villages unique to Cornwall.

Winterbourne Poor Lot Barrows EH

Long Bredy, nr Bridport, Dorset
2m W of Winterbourne Abbas,
S of junction of A35 with minor road
to Compton Valence; access via
Wellbottom Lodge off A35
Open *Any reasonable time*
Part of an extensive 4000-year-old
Bronze Age cemetery.

South-east MAP 2

12 Bignor Roman Villa

☎ 01798 869259
Nr Bignor, Pulborough,
W Sussex RH20 1PH
On minor road off B1238 SW of Pulborough
Open *Mar–Apr Tues–Sun & BH Mon,*
May–Oct daily, all 10–5
For a more intimate and personal look
at Roman interior life, there are few
more attractive Roman sites than the
villa at Bignor, beautifully situated
on the West Sussex Downs. The house
has no electricity, and is lit with
natural light. The floor mosaics offer
a wonderful contrast with those at
nearby Fishbourne (p22).

The first stone building here dates
from the early 3rd century. The principal
mosaic on display is that of a bust of Venus
in a medallion, with a strip of characters
underneath showing gladiators and their
trainers. Other mosaics include Ganymede
being carried off by Zeus disguised as an
eagle, the heads of Medusa and the Four
Seasons (Winter is the best preserved),
and various geometrical designs. The best
archaeological guess is that the house
fell into decay around the 5th century.
It was obviously the property of a family
of considerable wealth and standing.
It was certainly a private house rather
than a public palace, and historians

Mosaic from the 4th century AD at **Bignor Roman Villa**.

believe the mosaics were the work of native craftsmen which shows how quickly and well they had learnt this most Roman of arts.

13 Brading

☎ 01983 406223
Brading, Isle of Wight PO36 OEN
Website: www.brading.co.uk
3m S of Ryde on A3055
Open *Apr–Oct 9.30–5*
A superb villa with mosaics. They are somewhat enigmatic, the most impressive being one that depicts Medusa surrounded by diamond-shaped panels each containing mythological scenes. Whoever built it and lived here had great wealth and taste. The complexity of the iconography suggests a man with philosophical leanings.

14 Crofton Roman Villa

☎ Bromley Museum 01689 873826
Crofton Road, Orpington, Kent BR6 OHH
Open *Apr–Oct Wed Fri & Aug BH 10–1 2–5, Sun 2–5*
The reasonably well-preserved remains of the villa date back to the mid-2nd century, but it has many later additions. The whole structure is now protected within a larger museum building. The remains of 10 rooms are still visible, some with flooring, concrete or tiled. And there was a hypocaust (an ancient heating system with hot air circulating under the floor and between the walls).

15 Danebury*

Bury Hill, Hampshire
7m SW of Andover off A343
Open *Any reasonable time*
There was a timbered rampart built here dating back to probably the 4th century. Before that the great hill would have been home to a considerable settlement covering several acres, enclosed by a combination of ditch and 50ft(15m)-high rampart with streets and rectangular buildings facing it.

16 Dover Roman Painted House*

☎ 01304 203279
New St, Dover, Kent CT17 9AJ
In centre of Dover
Open *Apr–Oct Tues–Sun 10–5*
Dover boasts a number of key Roman remains because it was one of the important Saxon Shore Forts. Up on the hill within the Norman castle (p51), at the west end of the church of St Mary-in-Castro, is the *pharos* or Roman lighthouse, 62ft (21m) high, of which only the bottom 42ft (13m) are genuinely Roman. The fact that any of it survived is probably due to its being used by the adjacent church as a bell tower. It would probably have been nearer 80ft (24m) high in Roman times. Across the harbour are remnants of what would have been a sister beacon.

In the middle of Dover, in New Street, is something even more extraordinary. The remains of the so-called 'Painted House' which has, among the ruins, some of the best-preserved examples of Roman interior decoration you could hope to find. Apparently, this was the foyer of a 96-bedroom 'hotel', built to receive any Roman visitors newly disembarked from Gaul. Also fascinating are the foundations of a great Roman fort wall that was built right through what would have been the foyer – when Dover stopped being a place of welcome and became instead a major defensive stronghold against attack. The site is located within a museum enclosure, which includes other archaeological relics.

17 Fishbourne Roman Villa*

☎ 01243 785859
Salthill Rd, Fishbourne, Chichester,
W Sussex PO19 3QR

Email: adminfish@sussexpast.co.uk
Website: www.sussexpast.co.uk/fishbo/
1m W of Chichester off A27/A259
Open *Feb & Nov–mid-Dec 10–4,
Mar–July & Sept–Oct 10–5, Aug 10–6*
The famous Roman palace was found
completely by chance during digging
work in 1960, and is now one of the most
important Roman sites in Britain. The
site is justly famous for the mosaic floors,
which have survived in large fragments.
The earliest are simple black and white
geometric patterns but, within a century
or so, much more complex designs were
being executed. The north wing contains
the best-preserved mosaics, including
the famous cupid riding his dolphin, surrounded by sea horses and sea panthers.

It is reckoned that the original site
covered 4 acres, and there is a wonderful
model of what it might have looked like
in the museum foyer. The large formal
garden, around which the buildings were
set, is unique for a Roman site north of
the Alps. It seems there was a disastrous
fire sometime around the end of the 3rd
century from which the building never
recovered. There is also a good museum.

18 Lullingstone Roman Villa EH
☎ 01322 863467
Eynsford, Kent
*½m SW of Eynsford off A225,
8m NE of Sevenoaks*
Open *Apr–Sept 10–6, Oct 10–5,
Nov–Mar 10–4*
This Roman villa, first built *c* AD100 and
subsequently added to, has fine floor
mosaics. The main mosaic depicts
Bellerophon riding the winged horse
Pegasus, while fighting the Chimera. The
second myth illustrated is that of Europa
being abducted by Zeus, disguised as a
bull. It is accompanied by some lines
from Virgil, which suggests that the
original owners were educated and

wealthy. The villa also reveals the arrival
of Christianity in the form of a room
converted for use as a private chapel,
decorated with vivid plasterwork and
inscribed with Christian monograms. It
also has a shrine dedicated to the local
river nymphs.

19 Portchester Castle* EH
☎ 02392 378291
Portchester, Fareham, Hampshire PO3 5LY
On S side of Portchester off A27
Open *Apr–Sept 10–6, Oct 10–5,
Nov–Mar 10–4*
Visit Portchester and you will find the
best-preserved Saxon Shore Fort. Be
prepared to be astounded by the sheer
scale of the place. The massive walls,
with their great round towers,
look straight out of a Hollywood set.
Inside, dwarfed by the structure, is an
entire Norman castle (the Normans
recognized a good military location when
they saw one). You can climb to the top
of the keep – it really is worth it. The
view of the fortifications and Portsmouth
harbour bristling with warships and
dockyards (and the masts of *HMS Victory*)
is a powerful reminder of how little has
changed in 2000 years.

20 Richborough Roman Fort EH
☎ 01304 612013
Nr Sandwich, Kent
2m N of Sandwich off A256
Open *Mar Wed–Sun 10–4, Apr–Sept 10–6,
Oct 10–5, Nov Wed–Sun 10–4, Dec–Feb
Sat–Sun 10–4*
Richborough was the site of the Roman
Emperor Claudius' invasion of AD43,
and later became a Saxon Shore Fort
covering nearly 6 acres. A substantial
amount of encircling wall is still standing
20ft (6m) high. A complex series of
ditches and ramparts make this one
of the more impressive shore forts.

The triple ditches inside **Richborough Roman Fort**.

It guarded the south-east entrance to the Wantsum Channel. The foundations of a triumphal arch remain. A collection of Roman pottery and coins, among the most impressive found anywhere in Britain, was discovered at this site. Examples are on display in the museum.

21 St Albans Roman Theatre

☎ Museum 01727 751810
Gorhambury Drive, St Michael's St, St Albans, Hertfordshire AL3 6AH
Off A4147
Open *Mon–Sat 10–5.30, Sun 2–5.30*
One of St Albans' most impressive Roman remains (it is on the other side of the River Ver from the Roman site of Verulamium), it holds over 1500 spectators. This semi-circular structure dates from the mid-2nd century, and there is a museum next door with many of the finds on display.

22 Silchester's Roman City Walls and Amphitheatre EH

Silchester, Hampshire
Website: www.museumofreading.org.uk
1m E of Silchester on minor road
Open *Any reasonable time*
Scrutiny from the air has revealed one of the most complete Roman town plans discovered in Britain. Its significance is particularly great because it is one of the few Roman towns to have been abandoned after the departure of the Romans, so it was not built over. The surviving walls, enclosing over 100 acres, have the distinction of being the longest complete circuit in the country. Although the town's entire area was extensively excavated, little remains visible, except for the walls and two well-preserved gates. The Reading Museum Service (01189 399800) has the pick of the finds discovered on site.

ADDITIONAL PLACES TO VISIT

Flowerdown Barrows EH
Littleton, nr Winchester, Hampshire
2m NW of Winchester off A272
Open *Any reasonable time*
A disc barrow and bowl barrows remain as part of a Bronze Age burial site, and were once part of a larger group.

Kit's Coty House and Little Kit's Coty House EH
Nr Maidstone, Kent
2m N of Maidstone, W of A229
Open *Any reasonable time*
The ruins of two prehistoric burial chambers.

Littlecote House and Roman Villa
☎ 01488 682509
Nr Hungerford, Wiltshire RG17 OSS
3m NW of Hungerford off B4192
Open *Apr–Oct Wed & Sun 10–4*
The Tudor mansion (with a fine display of Cromwellian armour) has in its grounds the remains of a Roman villa. Its principal mosaic is of a scene from the Orpheus legend.

Reculver Towers and Roman Fort EH
Reculver, Kent CT6 6SS
3m E of Herne Bay
Open *Any reasonable time*
The twin towers of St Mary's Abbey have long been used as a landmark by boats navigating their way through Herne Bay. Indeed, the western façade was rebuilt for this purpose after the church was demolished. So there it stands within the battered remains of a Roman Saxon Shore Fort (Regulbium), like an abandoned movie set.

Roman Wall, Hertfordshire EH
St Albans, Hertfordshire
On S side of St Albans off A4147
Open *Any reasonable time*
Here are several hundred yards of the wall, built *c* AD200, which enclosed the Roman city of Verulamium. The remains of towers and the foundations of a gateway can still be seen.

Stockbridge Down NT
Stockbridge, Hampshire
1m E of Stockbridge off A30
There is a scattered group of round barrows, and a rampart of Woolbury Camp, an early Iron Age hill fort.

Eastern MAP 3

23 Colchester Castle*
☎ Museum 01206 282939
14 Ryegate Rd, Colchester, Essex CO1 1YG
Website: www.colchestercastle.co.uk
In town centre, off A12
Open *Mon–Sat 10–5 Sun 11–5*
In the middle of Colchester is the great Norman castle (one of the biggest keeps in Europe) where you can still see the remains of the original Roman foundations. Here stood a great Roman temple dedicated to the Emperor Claudius (similar to the one still standing in Nîmes, in France). This was the last refuge for those trying to flee the queen of the Iceni, Boudicca, as she bore down on the Romans in her great insurrection. Hundreds were burnt alive as she torched the place.

In the museum, you can still see what are believed to be a plate of grapes petrified in the flames. Other exhibits include the tombstones of Marcus Favonius Facilis, a centurion of the 20th Legion, and of Longinus Sdapeze, a cavalryman. There is also the Colchester Sphinx, an imposing Romano-Celtic sculpture, and the Colchester gladiator vase. On the edge of central Colchester you can see the remains of the Balkerne

St Peter-on-the-Wall, *one of the earliest surviving churches in the country.*

Gate; it is underneath, and adjacent to, the Hole in the Wall Inn. Well worth the quick detour.

24 St Peter-on-the-Wall Chapel, Bradwell-on-Sea*

☎ 01621 776203/776564
East End Rd, Bradwell-on-Sea,
Southminster, Essex CM10 7PX
Website: www.bradwellchapel.org
In Bradwell-on-Sea, follow signs
Open *Any reasonable time*
Stones from the 3rd-century Roman fort of Othona (later a Saxon Shore Fort) at Bradwell were used in 654 for this beautiful building, St Peter-on-the-Wall, one of the earliest surviving churches in the country. Of the original church, only the Saxon nave remains. It stands completely alone in the middle of a wheatfield, near the nuclear power station, standing guard over the Essex mudflats.

25 West Stow Anglo-Saxon Village

☎ 01284 728718
Icklingham Rd, West Stow,
Bury St Edmunds, Suffolk P28 6HG
Email: weststow@stedsbc.gov.uk
Website: www.stedmundsbury.gov.uk/
weststow.htm
5m NW of Bury St Edmunds off A1101
Open *Village: 10–5*
Park: summer 10–8, winter 10–5
Neolithic and Roman remains had the advantage of being built mainly out of stone, greatly increasing their survival chances. Virtually anything built of wood has disappeared though, and increasingly we have to rely on reconstructions. One of the best for giving a sense of Anglo-Saxon village life is here at West Stow in Suffolk. Built on the site of real remains, and using only the kind of tools used by the village's original inhabitants, it offers the best picture anywhere of Saxon village life.

ADDITIONAL PLACES TO VISIT

Burgh Castle EH
Breydon Water, nr Great Yarmouth, Norfolk
At W end of Breydon Water, SW of church
Open *Any reasonable time*
The second most northerly of the Saxon Shore Forts was built just inland of Great Yarmouth. It is believed to have been occupied between the 3rd and 5th centuries. Three of its four walls survive, rising to about 15ft (4.6m).

Caister Roman Site EH
Caister-on-Sea, Norfolk
Near Caister-on-Sea,
3m N of Great Yarmouth on A149
Open *Any reasonable time*
The remains of a Roman fort, including part of a defensive wall, a gateway and buildings along a main street.

Grimes Graves EH
☎ 01842 810656
Lynford, nr Thetford, Norfolk IP26 5DE
7m NW of Thetford off A134,
then minor road & track
Open *Apr–Sept 10–6, Oct 10–5, Nov–Mar Wed–Sun 10–4; closed 1–2 all year Children under 5 admitted at discretion of custodian*
This was the largest prehistoric flint mine in Europe with 350 shafts, which provided the materials for axes, tools and weapons 4000 years ago. The shafts are 30–40ft (9–12m) deep, with passages radiating out of their base. The flint was extracted from the walls of these shafts and passages, roughly shaped nearby, and traded far afield. Visitors can descend some 30ft (9m) by ladder into one excavated shaft and look along the radiating galleries where the flint, which was mined using picks made of red deer antler, was extracted.

Lexden Earthworks and Bluebottle Grove EH
Nr Colchester, Essex
2m W of Colchester off A604
Open *Any reasonable time*
Part of a series of Iron Age earthworks, once encompassing 129sq ft (12sq m), they protected Iron Age Colchester. The earthworks were subsequently expanded by the conquering Romans.

Central MAP 4

26 Chedworth Roman Villa NT
☎ 01242 890256
Yanworth, nr Cheltenham, Gloucestershire GL54 3LJ
Email: chedworth@smtp.ntrust.org.uk
Website: www.ntrustsevern.org.uk
4 miles SW of Northleach off A429
Open *Mar & first half of Nov 11–4, Apr–Oct 10–5, Tues–Sun & BH Mons*
Discovered by accident in the middle of the 19th century, Chedworth remains one of the best preserved of the Roman villas. Many of its original walls stand several feet high, and there is a local museum exhibiting many of the finds made on the site. The building was probably started in the 2nd century, but what we see today dates from the 4th century. There are patterned mosaics in the main west wing, laid to be viewed and enjoyed while reclining and eating. There is also a bath suite and hypocaust (an ancient heating system). There was also a pool, remnants of which are inscribed with Christian motifs, now in the museum.

27 Chester Roman Amphitheatre EH
Chester, Cheshire
In Vicars Lane beyond Newgate, Chester
Open *Any reasonable time*
The largest Roman amphitheatre in Britain has been partially excavated.

*Remains of the bathing complex at the Roman villa at **Chedworth**.*

It was used for entertainment and military training by the 20th Legion, based at the fortress they named Deva, at the head of the Dee estuary.

28 North Leigh Roman Villa EH

North Leigh, Oxfordshire OX8 6QB
2m N of North Leigh;
3m NE of Witney off A4095
Open *Exterior only: any reasonable time (viewing window for mosaic)*
Just to prove that extensive domestic remodelling was not exclusive to the 18th century, this fine courtyarded villa betrays all the signs of having been built on the site of earlier Roman dwellings. It is one of the larger villas to have been excavated, almost 300ft (90m) long with 60 rooms. The fine mosaic was probably the work of local craftsmen, possibly based in Cirencester. There are echoes of mosaics found at some of the other listed villas.

29 Offa's Dyke EH

Tidenham, Gloucestershire
Website: www.offa.demon.co.uk/offa.htm
3m NE of Chepstow off B4228; access via Forest Enterprise Tidenham car park
Open *Any reasonable time*

This is a 3-mile section of the great earthwork built by Offa, King of Mercia in AD757–96, as a defensive boundary for his kingdom between England and Wales. There is an impressive Iron Age fort defended by a series of five ramparts, with an elaborate western entrance and unusual earthworks.

The main Offa's Dyke Centre is at Knighton in Powys (01547 528753), halfway along the trail that runs some 80 miles along the Welsh-English border from the hills above Prestatyn to the Severn Estuary. It has an exhibition about the history of Offa's Dyke and information about the long-distance walk.

30 Uffington Castle, White Horse and Dragon Hill* EH & NT

Uffington, Oxfordshire
S of B4507, 7m W of Wantage
Open *Any reasonable time*

The most famous of the numerous chalk white horses cut into hillside turf – not least because it is the only one thought to date back to the Iron Age. It has a much more enigmatic design than the later more literal horse motifs (as at Westbury, p18). It comprises a number of bold strokes and shapes (which led to the legend that it was actually depicting the dragon killed by St George). It's the sort of animal that you imagine Picasso might have painted or a Japanese calligrapher – even if its use as the logo for the local district council has rather stripped it of its mystique. Particularly extraordinary is the fact that you can only see the whole design from the air, which makes you wonder whom the people that made it thought they were making it for. But just as lovely is the location – on a ridge with spectacular views of Oxfordshire laid out like a carpet and with curiously satisfying bowls and terracing underneath. Nearby are three sites of great interest – the

Aerial view of the **Uffington White Horse**.

ramparts of an Iron Age fort known as Uffington Castle, a mound called Dragon Hill where supposedly St George slew the dragon, and Wayland's Smithy, a Neolithic barrow (p32).

31 Wroxeter Roman City* EH

☎ 01743 761330
Wroxeter, nr Shrewsbury,
Shropshire SY5 6PH
5m E of Shrewsbury off A5 on B4380
Open *Apr–Sept 10–6, Oct 10–5,
Nov–Mar Wed–Sun 10–1 2–4*

Wroxeter, or Viriconium as it was then known, was at its peak the fourth largest town in Roman Britain, and is unusual because it was not built over by later towns. That has guaranteed the survival of some fairly substantial pieces of old Roman buildings, though the attentions of later builders have taken their toll. The most substantial remains are the so-called 'Old Work' which formed part of the entrance to the exercise area and baths. There is also a row of stumps that would have been a colonnade of a portico on the eastern side. Interesting is archaeological evidence of a later Saxon presence here, suggesting that the transition from Roman Britain to Anglo-Saxon Britain was a lot more gradual than we used to think.

ADDITIONAL PLACES TO VISIT

Arbor Low Stone Circle and Gib Hill Barrow EH

☎ 01629 816200
Upper Oldhams Farm, Monyash,
Bakewell, Derbyshire
2m S of Monyash, ½m W of A515
Open *Summer 10–6, rest of year 10–5*
A fine Neolithic monument, this 'Stonehenge of the North' comprises an inner stone circle in slabs of limestone all now lying flat and an outer henge consisting of a high bank and deep ditch. Gib Hill is a large round cairn about 18ft (5m) high.

Arthur's Stone EH

Nr Dorstone, Herefordshire
7m E of Hay-on-Wye off B4348
Open *Any reasonable time*
Although named after the king of medieval legend, these large blocks of stone comprise a burial chamber dating back to prehistoric times.

Belas Knap Long Barrow EH

Nr Charlton Abbots, Gloucestershire
2m S of Winchcombe, on Cotswold Way
Open *Any reasonable time*
A good example of a Neolithic long barrow, with the mound still intact and surrounded by a stone wall. The chamber tombs, where the remains of approximately 40 burials were found, have been opened up to let visitors see inside.

Cirencester Amphitheatre EH

☎ 01285 655611 (book for guided tours)
Cirencester, Gloucestershire
Email: martinwright@cotswold.gov.uk
Website: www.cirencester.co.uk
Next to bypass W of town; access from town or along Chesterton Lane
Open *Any reasonable time*
A large well-preserved Roman amphitheatre, earth covered.

Great Witcombe Roman Villa EH

Nr Gloucester, Gloucestershire
5m SE of Gloucester off A417
Open *Exterior only: any reasonable time*
There are the remains of a large villa with evidence of an under-floor heating system. The villa was built around three sides of a courtyard, and had a luxurious bathhouse complex.

Hob Hurst's House* EH

Nr Chesterfield, Derbyshire
9m W of Chesterfield,
from unclassified road off B5057
f**Open** *Any reasonable time*
A square prehistoric burial chamber with an earthwork ditch and outer bank.

Jewry Wall and Museum EH

☎ 0116 247 3021
St Nicholas Circle, Leicester LE1 4LB
Website: www.leicestermuseums.ac.uk/museums/jewwall.html
In St Nicholas St,
W of Church of St Nicholas
Open Wall: open access.
Museum: Mon–Sat 10–5.30 Sun 2–5.30
Built *c* AD125 is a 30ft(9m)-high remnant of wall, part of an old bathing facility, with hypocaust, drains and water channels adjacent. Luckily the wall was incorporated into a Saxon church, which helped ensure its survival. The museum alongside tells the story of Leicester's early history.

Lunt Roman Fort

☎ 02476 832381
Baginton, Coventry, Warwickshire CV8 3AJ
Website: http://www.exponet.co.uk/peter/lunt.htm
In the village of Baginton,
2m S of Coventry on A45
Open *BH weekends & Oct halfterm 10–5, summer hols 10–5 (except Wed); parties by arrangement at other times*

Remains of a cavalry training fort, with a reconstructed *gyrus* (a circular arena where the cavalrymen were actually trained).

Lydney
☎ 01594 845497
Lydney Park, Lydney, Gloucestershire GL15 6BU
Off A48 between Forest of Dean & River Severn; 20m from Gloucester
Open *Gardens, Temple site and museum: Apr–June Wed Sun & BHs 11–6*
The remains of a Roman temple dedicated to the Celtic god of healing, Nodens, lies within the precincts of Iron Age ramparts. This late 4th-century Roman settlement, as well as a museum which houses Roman artefacts, including the famous sculpture the 'Lydney dog', is set within secluded and beautiful gardens.

Mitchell's Fold Stone Circle EH
Nr Shrewsbury, Shropshire
16m SW of Shrewsbury, W of A488
Open *Any reasonable time*
An air of mystery surrounds this Bronze Age stone circle. It is set in dramatic moorland, over 1000ft (305m) up, and consists of about 30 stones, of which 15 are visible.

Nine Ladies Stone Circle EH
Nr Bakewell, Derbyshire
5m SE of Bakewell off A6, on minor road
Open *Any reasonable time*
This Early Bronze Age circle, once part of a burial site for 300–400 people, is 50ft (15m) across. It is adjacent to a Bronze Age cemetery.

Notgrove Long Barrow EH
Notgrove, Gloucestershire
1½m NW of Notgrove on A436
Open *Any reasonable time*
A Neolithic burial mound with chambers for human burials opens from a stone-built central passage.

Nympsfield Long Barrow EH
Nr Nympsfield, Gloucestershire
1m NW of Nympsfield on B4066
Open *Any reasonable time*
This Neolithic, chambered, long barrow is 90ft (27m) long, and contains the remains of 23 burials as well as tools and pottery.

Rollright Stones EH
Nr Chipping Norton, Oxfordshire
Website: www.rollright.demon.co.uk
Off unclassified road between A44 & A3400, 2m NW of Chipping Norton near villages of Little Rollright & Long Compton
Open *The King's Men stones: any reasonable time by courtesy of the owner (who may levy a charge). The King Stone & The Whispering Knights stones: any reasonable time, by footpath*
Three groups of stones, known as 'The King's Men', 'The Whispering Knights' and 'The King Stone', span nearly 2000 years of the Neolithic and Bronze Ages.

Uley Long Barrow EH
Uley, Gloucestershire
3½m NE of Dursley on B4066
Open *Any reasonable time*
Dating from around 3000BC, this 180ft(55m)-long Neolithic, chambered, burial mound is unusual in that its mound is still intact.

Wall Roman Site (Letocetum) EH & NT
☎ 01543 480768
Watling St, Wall, nr Lichfield, Staffordshire WS14 0AW
Off A5 at Wall near Lichfield
Open *Apr–Sept 10–6, Oct 10–5*
The small Romano-British town situated on Watling Street contained an official hotel or mansion. There are good remains

of what would have been the bathhouse, one of the best surviving examples in Britain, including the spaces that once contained the lockers where bathers would have left their clothes. There is also a small local museum.

Wayland's Smithy EH & NT

Nr Compton Beauchamp, nr Swindon, Oxfordshire
S of B4057, on the Ridgeway path
Open *Any reasonable time*
Near the Uffington White Horse lies this stunning Neolithic burial site, encircled by beech trees.

Windmill Hill NT

Avebury, Wiltshire
1½m NW of Avebury
Open *Any reasonable time*
Neolithic remains of three concentric rings of ditches, enclose an area of 21 acres.

Wales MAP 5

32 Caerleon Roman Fortress CADW

☎ 01633 422518
Caerleon, nr Newport, Monmouthshire
B4596 to Caerleon, M4 junction 25 or 26
Open *Apr–Oct 9.30–5, Nov–Mar Tues–Sun 9.30–5; closed Sun am in winter*
This was home to 6000 legionaries belonging to the Second Augustan Legion *c* AD75. Known as Isca (the name comes from the river Usk) and covering an area over 50 acres, it was at its peak in the years prior to 120, before the garrison was posted to the north to work on the Antonine Wall in Scotland. An inscription nearby suggests that some of the soldiers were involved in reclaiming waterlogged land. The fortress was finally abandoned in the 4th century.

There is an oval-shaped amphitheatre, the only one of its kind to have been properly excavated in Britain. It would have been big enough to seat the entire garrison. Other buildings excavated, with their remains visible, include barrack blocks, open-air swimming pool, kitchens, rows of ovens, covered exercise hall, heated changing rooms and a bathhouse. The Legionary Museum has hundreds of artefacts found at Isca.

33 The 'Hendy Head' *

01248 724444
Oriel Ynys Mon (Anglesey Heritage Gallery), Llangefni, Gwynedd, Anglesey LL77 7TW
½m from Llangefni on B5111
Open *Tues–Sun 10.30–5*
Of all the fascinating artefacts that were filmed for the television series, few were as haunting as this ancient stone head. It now lives in the Llangefni Museum on Anglesey. For many decades it survived being mortared on to a local farm wall before archaeologists decided the time had come to put it in a glass case. It now takes its place beside other exhibits that spell out Anglesey's long and colourful history.

ADDITIONAL PLACES TO VISIT

Brecon Gaer Roman Fort CADW

Nr Aberyscir, Powys
From Brecon via A40,
minor road to Aberyscir Farm
Open *Any reasonable time*
The fort has a commanding position at the top of the valley, and would once have housed a garrison of cavalry possibly 500 strong. There are remains of walls, gates and farm buildings, and a still impressive drainage channel.

The 'Hendy Head', *carved in sandstone probably during the pre-Roman Iron Age.*

Segontium Roman Fort CADW
☎ 01286 675625
Beddgelert Rd, Caernarfon LL5 2LN
Website: www.caernarfon.co.uk
On 4085 to Beddgelert just outside Caernarfon
Open *Mar–Oct Mon–Sat 10–5, Nov–Feb Mon–Sat 10–4; opens 2 on Sun*
The remains of a Roman fort established about AD77 with a good museum on site.

Tomen y Mur
Nr Ffestiniog, Gwynedd
In the mountains, on the E side of A470 about 5m S of Ffestiniog
Open *Any reasonable time*
This is the remotest of the Roman forts whose remains have survived. The outlines of the camp and its buildings are still very clear. It was built in the time of Agricola around AD78, and was presumably abandoned in the middle of the second century. There are also the remains of a Norman motte (mound) built on the location of what would probably have been the Roman west gate.

North-west MAP 6

34 Hardknott Roman Fort EH & NT
Nr Eskdale Green, Cumbria
9m NE of Ravenglass, at W end of Hardknott Pass
Open *Any reasonable time, but access possibly hazardous in winter*
One of the most dramatic Roman sites in Britain, it has stunning views across the Lakeland fells. Hardknott was the Roman fort Mediobogdum. Built between AD120 and 138, it controlled the road from Ravenglass to Ambleside. It was abandoned at the end of the 2nd century. There are visible remains of granaries, the HQ building and the commandant's house, with a bathhouse and parade ground outside the fort.

Ambleside Roman Fort EH & NT
Waterhead, Ambleside, Cumbria
Nr Waterhead car park
Open *Any reasonable time*
This 1st- and 2nd-century fort (now in ruins) would have guarded the Roman road from Brougham to Ravenglass.

Arthur's Round Table EH & NT
Eamont Bridge, nr Penrith, Cumbria
1m S of Penrith
Open *Any reasonable time*
The prehistoric circular earthwork is bounded by a ditch and an outer bank.

Castlerigg Stone Circle EH & NT
Nr Keswick, Cumbria
1½m E of Keswick
Open *Any reasonable time*
These 38 stones are possibly one of the earliest Neolithic stone circles in Britain.

Mayburgh Earthwork EH & NT
Eamont Bridge, nr Penrith, Cumbria CA10
1m S of Penrith off A6
Open *Any reasonable time*
An impressive prehistoric circular earthwork, with banks up to 15ft (4.5m) high, enclosing a central area of 1½ acres containing a single large stone.

North-east MAP 7

35 Arbeia Roman Fort*
☎ 0191 456 1369
Baring St, South Shields, Tyne & Wear NE33 2BB
Open *Easter–Sept Mon–Sat 10–5.30 Sun 1–5, Oct–Easter Mon–Sat 10–4*
In the middle of a large housing estate in South Shields, historians have built a perfect replica of a Roman Gate House. It stands on the site of the fort that stood at the eastern fringe of Hadrian's Wall

(though it was not part of the wall itself). There is a good museum on site too, with a number of fascinating exhibits, most notably the tombstone of a freed woman called Regina, a member of the Catuvellauni tribe, who married Barates of Palmyra (as recorded on another tombstone in Corbridge). There are plans to add a villa (the commander's house) and other structures, some built using original Roman tools.

36 Corbridge Roman Site and Museum EH

☎ 01434 632349
Corbridge, Northumberland NE45 5NT
½m W of Corbridge
Open *Apr–Sept 10–6, Oct 10–5, Nov–Mar Wed–Sun 10–1 2–4*
This depot, with granaries, supplied the forts behind Hadrian's Wall. It also guarded the main crossing point of the River Tyne. It was founded by the Emperor Agricola in the AD80s, and was rebuilt on a number of occasions. It evolved into an important Roman town and flourished into the 4th century. There is a small site museum displaying locally discovered finds, the best of which is the Corbridge Lion, a stunning piece of Romano-Celtic sculpture of a lion eating a stag. A good place to start an exploration of the Wall.

37 Hadrian's Wall* EH & NT

☎ Hexham tourist info 01434 605225;
Carlisle tourist info 01228 512444
Email: info@hadrians-wall.org
Website: www.hadrians-wall.org
Birdoswald, Chesters & Housesteads are all on B6318 off A68 between Newcastle & Carlisle

Birdoswald

☎ 01697 747602
Gisland, Brampton, Cumbria CA6 7DD
Open *Museum: Late Mar–Oct 10–5.30
Exterior: Any reasonable time*

Chesters Roman Fort (Cilurnum)

☎ 01434 681379
Chollerford, Humshugh, Hexham, Northumberland NE45 4EP
Open *Apr–Sept 9.30–6, Oct 10–5, Nov–Mar 10–4*

Housesteads Fort (Vercovicium)

☎ 01434 344363
Haydon Bridge, Hexham, Northumberland N47 6NN
Open *Apr–Sept 10–6, Oct–Mar 10–4*

No view of Roman Britain would be complete without a visit to Hadrian's Wall, once the largest curtain wall in the country. Built in the early 2nd century it runs nearly 70 miles from the Tyne near Newcastle to the Solway west of Carlisle. Despite centuries of being ransacked for building materials, there remain whole stretches of wall which are big enough to give a sense of its awesome purpose. Even today you can see why Hadrian built his outer wall here; the ridge separates two different landscapes; look to the north and you can almost feel the presence of barbarian hordes.

The trouble is, while it has every appearance of being a defensive wall designed, as one Roman said, 'to separate the Romans from barbarians', historians now view it primarily as a kind of customs zone cum military fortification. It is still utterly impressive in scale and ingenuity and feels completely at one with the landscape, more like a gigantic Andy Goldsworthy work of art than an ancient Berlin Wall.

There are the remains of several forts along the wall, hinting at the numbers once stationed here. One is *Birdoswald* (from the Latin for 'crooked bend'), the fort being above the River Irthing. Remains survive of the granary and the east gate, one of the best preserved on the wall.

Hadrian's Wall *winding down towards Housesteads Fort.*

Housesteads is the biggest of the surviving forts. Like many Roman ruins, there is little above waist-height, but the outlines are still very clear (especially from the air). It has well-preserved gateways, ramparts and HQ buildings, and one of the best preserved latrine blocks from the period in the country. It is also sited on a ridge, with tremendous views of the surrounding countryside. It has a lovely little museum with displays and exhibits taken from the wall, including models of the fort, altars and sculptured stones. Its most famous artefact is the carving of three deities who look like three housewives wearing duffel-coats.

Chesters is one of the most visited forts along the length of the wall. At its heart are the remains of a commandant's house with a hypocaust, and one of the best preserved bathhouses in Britain. Close by are the remains of a Roman bridge which once carried the Wall over the River Tyne, although the course of the river has changed over the centuries.

38 Jarrow Monastery and Church of St Paul's ✶ EH

☎ Bede's World museum: 0191 489 2106
Jarrow, Tyne & Wear NE32 3DY
7m E of Newcastle, in Jarrow off A19
Open *Museum: Apr–Oct Mon–Sat 10–5.30 Sun 12.30–5.30, Nov–Mar Mon–Sat 10–4.30 Sun 12.30–4.30*
Church: Mon–Sat 10–4 Sun 2.30–4
Monastery ruins: any reasonable time
Jarrow is the site of a monastery (now in ruins) where the Venerable Bede, a monk, wrote important works charting early English history in the 7th and 8th centuries. They include his *History of the English Church and People* and documents used in the later *Anglo-Saxon Chronicle*. The Anglo-Saxon chancel has been incorporated into the parish church which contains fascinating artefacts from the time of Bede, including an exquisite piece of Saxon stained glass. Across from the church is a group of reconstructed Saxon houses, including a 'hearth-hall' like the one

described in the poem *Beowulf.* The hall would have been the settlement's main meeting place, and the site of all the drinking, boasting, and story-telling that lies at the heart of *Beowulf.*

39 Lindisfarne Priory* EH and Lindisfarne Castle* NT
☎ Priory 01289 389200
Castle 01289 389244
Holy Island, Northumberland TD15 2RX
Website: www.lindisfarne.org.uk
13m SE of Berwick-upon-Tweed off A1; only reached at low tide across causeway
Open *Priory: Apr–Sept 10–6, Oct 10–5, Nov–Mar 10–4. Castle: mid-Mar–Nov open 4½ hrs a day, always open between 12–3; times depend on tides; closed Fri*
Lindisfarne, or Holy Island, on the north-east coast, approached over its causeway, is one of the most forlorn sites in Britain. One of the earliest centres for Christianity in Britain from 634, the monastery was ravaged by the Vikings in the 8th and 9th centuries after which the monks left. A Benedictine priory

was built *c*1070 but abandoned *c*1541.

The castle was built with stones from the priory in 1543–50 to protect the harbour from Scottish and French raiders but was destroyed during the Civil War. The Edwardian architect Edwin Lutyens converted the castle into a private home in 1903.

40 Vindolanda Fort and Museum*
☎ 01434 344277
Bardon Mill, Hexham,
Northumberland NE47 7JN
Email: info@vindolanda.com
Website: www.vindolanda.com
13m from Hexham off A69
Open *Chesterholm Museum: Mid-Feb– mid-Nov opens 10 daily; seasonal closure from 4 in winter to 6.30 July & Aug*
Besides the forts, Hadrian's Wall boasts another fantastic location. Chester-holm, or Vindolanda as the Romans knew it, is a privately owned archaeological site. It was originally one of the big Stanegate forts that would have housed garrisons to serve on the wall.

(The Stanegate was the original military road that ran from Carlisle to Corbridge; it predated the wall, but its forts and supply depots later supplied the wall.)

The best discovery at Vindolanda was made in the mid-1970s, when small strips of bark were found deep in the soil. Further inspection revealed writing on them. The bark turned out to be scraps and fragments of letters, drafts and jottings from the days of the Roman occupation. Now translated and published, the so-called Vindolanda tablets give us the voice of Roman Britain, loud and fresh, nearly 2000 years later. Among the most famous is an invitation to a birthday party, believed to be one of the earliest surviving examples of a letter written by a woman. The rest of the site offers some beautifully reconstructed defence structures to supplement the ruins, which have been excavated, including a stone turret, based on one of Hadrian's Wall's best towers, the Brunton Turret.

ADDITIONAL PLACES TO VISIT

Aldborough Roman Site EH
☎ 01423 322768
Aldborough, Boroughbridge,
N Yorkshire YO51 9EP
*Near Boroughbridge off B6265,
15m NW of York*
Open *Apr–Sept 10–1 2–6, Oct 10–1 2–5*
The remains of a Roman town (Isurium Brigantium) are still visible in the form of low walls, and 4th-century mosaic pavements. This was the principal town of the Brigantes, the largest tribe in Roman Britain. There is a small site museum. In the Church of St Andrew nearby, a long 14th-century church, a Roman sculpture with the figure of Mercury can be seen, taken from Isurium.

Blackstone Edge Roman Road*
Littleborough, Greater Manchester
1m E of Littleborough on A58
Britain's best-preserved section of Roman road runs over the Pennines between Rochdale and Elland, Halifax. It is paved with large kerb stones, has a groove running down the middle of it, and is about 16ft (4.8m) wide. The groove was once filled with turf to help give cart-pulling horses extra grip.

Stanwick Iron Age Fortifications EH
Forcett, Richmond, N Yorkshire
⁵n W of Darlington on B6274
Open *Any reasonable time*
These fortifications belonged to the tribal stronghold of the Brigantes, whose vast earthworks covered some 850 acres. Today you can see an excavated section of ditch, cut into the rock, and the rampart.

Wheeldale Moor Roman Road EH
Goathland, Whitby, N Yorkshire
S of Goathland, W of A169, 7m S of Whitby, in North York Moors National Park
Open *Any reasonable time*
A one-mile stretch of Roman road, still with its hardcore and drainage ditches, which runs across isolated moorland.

Scotland MAP 8

41 Broch of Gurness* HS
☎ 01856 751414
Mainland, Orkney
*At Aikerness, 14m NW
of Kirkwall on A966*
Open *Apr–Sept 9.30–6.30*
The Broch of Gurness (a broch was a dry-stone tower serving as a home) is now a ruin, and all that remains of that high, windowless tower built in the later Iron Age is a shattered stump of slate. The broch looks and feels much more like some kind of primitive castle,

Remains of the circular tower at the **Broch of Gurness**.

particularly as it guards a headland jutting out into the surrounding water, though recent research suggests it was a sanctuary from bad weather and not hostile tribes.

42 Jarlshof Prehistoric and Norse Settlement HS

☎ 01950 460112
Sumburgh, Shetland,
Shetland Isles ZE3 9JN
*At Sumburgh Head,
on A970 22m S of Lerwick*
Open *Apr–Sept 9.30–6.30*
The earliest remains are four Bronze Age houses, belonging to the 8th century BC. One is believed to have been lived in by a bronze-smith. There are also stone huts from the 5th century BC. 400 years later a broch (a dry-stone tower serving as a home) was built, only to make way later for so-called 'wheel houses' (similar to a broch but with dividing walls to create separate rooms). There are signs of later Viking and medieval habitation in the form of rectangular stone houses. There is a good visitors' centre.

43 Maes Howe* HS

☎ 01856 761606
Nr Clouston, Orkney KW17
9m W of Kirkwall on A965

Open *Apr–Sept 9.30–6.30, Oct–Mar 9.30–4; closed Sun am in winter*
Maes Howe is ancient Orkney's most spectacular burial mound. It was only re-discovered in the middle of the 19th century; the roof had collapsed centuries earlier and it had filled up with soil and turf. Thanks to the fine quality of the stone used in its construction it has been possible to restore it almost completely, making this the finest chambered tomb in north-west Europe. Most Stone Age sites are only ruined shadows of their former selves, but Maes Howe is now virtually intact.

Archaeologists estimate its date of origin to have been around a century or two either side of 3000BC, making it older than the Pyramids. It is over 112ft (35m) across and over 22½ft (7m) high. The stone slabs used in its construction weigh up to 35 tonnes. From a distance, it is no more than a pregnant hump of grass. But as soon as you approach the low entrance tunnel, you really feel you are entering an underworld. The main chamber is a high, coned space, with side vaults into which the bodies were laid.

And if you think tourism belongs only to the modern age, you are wrong. Some of its treasures are among the best preserved Viking runes found anywhere;

this is graffiti left 1000 years ago by visitors who had dug their way in from the top, and stood there as amazed as we are today. One inscription reads 'Ingiborg the fair widow, many a woman has walked stooping in here; a very showy person', a euphemism for something a lot more insulting. Another proclaims that they were the product 'of the most skilled carver of runes in the western ocean', and who could disagree?

44 Ring of Brodgar* HS
☎ 01856 841815
Mainland, Orkney
5m from Stromness
Open *All year*
The great stone circle of Brodgar is located on a narrow tongue of land. It is a double-entranced 'henge' (we still do not know why it was built) built between 3000 and 2000BC. Remains of 36 stones survive from an original total of about 60. Of all Orkney's sites, this is the one that exerts the most powerful pull on the surrounding countryside. You catch glimpses of it from far away. Once spotted, you cannot take your eyes off it. Up close, Brodgar is no less intriguing; each stone is so weathered that it now looks like modern sculpture.

45 Skara Brae Prehistoric Village* HS
☎ 01856 841815
Nr Stromness, Orkney KW16 3LR
8m N of Stromness off A967 & B9056
Open *Apr–Sept 9.30–6.30, Oct–Mar 9.30–4.30; closed Sun am in winter*
Skara Brae is important not just because it lay safely preserved under grass and sand till exposed once again in 1850 (after a storm had torn way the topsoil), but because both furniture and ornaments, as well as building structure, have survived. This is highly unusual. So not only can we peer into dwellings dating back thousands of years, we can also inspect the beds, hearths and ornament-laden dressers that helped to make life so bearable here, centuries before the Pyramids of Egypt or Stonehenge. This was obviously more than a loose collection of small houses, it was an integrated community – a village in fact. The houses cover two broad periods and suggest continuous habitation for some 600 years (from around 3100–2500BC). The later houses are more solid and substantial than the earlier ones.

There is a good replica built on the site allowing the visitor an even better glimpse of Neolithic domestic life. An absolute treasure, in every sense.

Part of the Stone Age circle known as the **Ring of Brodgar**.

Cairnpapple Hill HS

☎ 01506 634622
Bathgate, W Lothian EH47
3m N of Bathgate, near Torphichen, off A89
Open *Apr–Sept 9.30–6.30*
One of the most important prehistoric
monuments in Scotland, Cairnpapple
was used as a burial and ceremonial site
from about 3000BC.

Calanais (Callanish) Standing Stones HS

☎ 01851 621422
Callanish, Isle of Lewis PA86 9DY
12m W of Stornoway off A858
Open *Apr–Sept 10–7, Oct–Mar 10–4*
Thirteen standing stones in a circle date
back to around 3000BC. There are the
remains of stone avenues heading off
to the four main points of the compass.

Rough Castle

Bonnybridge, Falkirk
*1½m E of Bonnybridge
off B816 near Falkirk*
Open *All year*
The less glamorous twin of Hadrian's Wall
is the Antonine Wall, further to the north.
Built in the AD140s, it was intended to
replace Hadrian's Wall as the limit of
Roman power. Although less developed
as a fortified barrier, it too had forts and
this is the best preserved. About 1 acre
in size it has the remains of a rather
gruesome booby trap, a pit with stakes
that would have been covered with
bracken and branches to fool the unwary.

Northern Ireland MAP 9

46 Nendrum*

☎ 028 9754 2547
Mahee Island, Strangford Lough,
Comber, Co Down
*From Belfast take A20 towards New-
townards; then A22 to Comber; follow
signs from Comber for Mahee Island*
Open *All year*
The remains of this attractive monastery
of St Machaoi, a pupil of St Patrick, raised
on a hillside by the shores of Strangford
Lough, were discovered in 1845 and
further excavated in the 1920s. The result
is a remarkably complete plan of a
monastic enclosure, with its concentric
cashels (dry stone walled enclosures),
small buildings and cemetery. There is
also a small church with a nave and
sundial. The monastery itself was
destroyed near the end of the 10th
century; other interesting finds include
part of the bell, which was hidden for
safety; they are on display at the Ulster
Museum in Belfast.

47 Ulster History Park*

☎ 028 8164 8188
Cullion, Lislap, Omagh,
Co Tyrone BT79 7SU
Email: uhp@omagh.gov.uk
Website: www.omagh.gov.uk/
historypark.htm
7m N of Omagh on B48
Open *Apr–June & Sept–Oct 10–5.30,
July–Aug 10–6.30, Oct–Mar Mon–Fri 10–5*
This is a historical treasure trove, an
open-air museum located on the edge
of the beautiful Sperrin Mountains and
home to a wonderful set of full-size
reconstructions of historically significant
buildings. These date all the way back to
8000BC, and include Neolithic dwellings,
8th-century monastic 'bee-hive' cells of
the sort the earliest Irish monks would
have used, a 12th-century Anglo-
Norman motte-and-bailey, all the way to
a 17th-century Plantation house. To help
set these buildings in context, there is
a well-mounted exhibition in the
visitors' centre.

CHAPTER TWO

Norman Moats and Gothic Spires

Is it any wonder that the arrival of the Normans should be such a major turning point in British history? The Normans certainly thought it was, and they succeeded in making sure that others agreed by building structures which would last forever. Can there be any more enduring, time-defying testament to the will of the medieval mind than their castles and cathedrals?

Of course, the Normans were not the first to discover the power of fortifications or fortresses. The Romans knew a thing or two about the architecture of power. And recent excavations at Golthos in Lincolnshire have uncovered evidence of a fortified structure dating to the Anglo-Saxon 9th century. But the kind of castles with which we have become most familiar date from 1066, perhaps the most visible symbol to this day that the nine-hour battle of Hastings really did bring monumental change. Things were never the same again.

From the start, the Normans knew that while timber structures such as motte-and-bailey castles (ancient defences with a wooden tower on top of a mound enclosed by a ditch) got the job done, only stone promised real endurance. Castles like **Richmond** in Yorkshire, **Colchester** in Essex and, most famously, the **Tower of London**, were built of stone even in the earliest days

following William's successful conquest. Within a century or so stone became the rule rather than the exception, though not in Ireland where the invading Anglo-Normans made do with timber forts on raised earthworks.

After the conquest, despite William's ruthless genius, came years of anarchy and squabbling. It took one particular king to stop the rot and bring order to the country, and that man was Henry II. Like William before him, he did much of this by building castles, only his were even bigger and more sophisticated in their design and construction.

So we got castles which do not belong to the world of foreign invaders, but to the world which the invaders had helped to create. Designed to dominate and pacify the surrounding landscape (and often seascape), the best British castles are quite spectacular, such as **Bamburgh Castle** in Northumberland which has a near perfect silhouette, framed by the coastline and tide-hardened sands. At its heart is a Norman keep. Like virtually all successful castles it has been significantly added to, in this case in the mid-18th and late 19th centuries.

The dominant image of Britain after the Norman invasion is that of the medieval knight, an armoured aristocrat on a great horse trained to fight an enemy élite. And this was of course a flourishing

Warwick Castle *overlooking the River Avon.*

Christian world. People belonged to a faith which produced ever more spectacular churches, priories, abbeys and chapels. That faith also expressed itself in conquest, and especially in the great crusades to the Holy Land mounted by kings in the Middle Ages.

While the castles of this time are often partly destroyed – indeed we now find the idea of a totally pristine castle rather bizarre – the glory of many British cathedrals is that they are not ruins. Imagine that they had all been treated like the abbeys, monasteries and priories, and had been destroyed during Henry VIII's Dissolution of the Monasteries in 1536–40. Our whole knowledge of ancient faith would have to be constructed from ruins like **Fountains Abbey** in North Yorkshire. And we would be without some of our greatest buildings.

Visiting great cathedrals is as wondrous as ever. The hourly one-minute silence imposed at **Westminster Abbey** is still moving, even for the atheist or non-Christian. What they instil in you is a sense of the weight of the past through the effigies, chapels, altars and columns. But with weight goes also a sense of weightlessness. Cathedrals are about looking up and around, at great airy spaces filled with echoes and silence.

Cathedrals were buildings of enormous prestige. They were paid for by the wealthy in the Middle Ages who went in for the kind of competitive display shown by modern cities hoping to have the tallest skyscraper. Many cathedrals posed huge engineering and technical challenges which stretched and inspired their designers and builders to ever greater feats. They had to produce the biggest tower, strongest buttresses, inconceivably graceful spires and the tallest windows. Cathedrals such as **Salisbury**, **Wells**, **Durham** and **York** were completed in architectural styles which were the avant-garde of their day. It is hard now to look at those bastions of permanence and realize just how radical and daring they were when first seen.

The castles and cathedrals of this period are doubly historical. They are perfect microcosms of the worlds which created them and which they sustained. But they also transcend the moment of their creation, to outlast and dramatize it. That was their achievement.

*The ruins of **Fountains Abbey** on the banks of the River Skell.*

South-west MAP 1

48 Cleeve Abbey EH

☎ 01984 640377
Old Cleeve, nr Washford,
Somerset TA23 0PS
In Washford, ¼m S of A39
Open *Apr–Sept 10–6, Oct 10–5,*
Nov–Mar 10–1 2–4

It is one of the few pre-Reformation monastic sites to have survived the Dissolution of the Monasteries. Founded in 1198, it is a small, fascinating group of buildings with an authentic 13th-century feel. The 16th century saw the reconstruction of the refectory and the medieval hall with its great timber roof, one of the finest anywhere in the country to have survived. By the time of the Dissolution the monks were living in individual cubicles. Fortunately, the abbey was converted into a house and then a farm, just in time to avoid the fate of so many monasteries and abbeys liquidated to provide Henry VIII with land and money.

49 Corfe Castle NT

☎ 01929 481294
Nr Wareham, Dorset BH20 5EZ
Email: wcfgen@smtp.ntrust.org.uk
NW of Corfe village on A351
Open *Mar 10–5, Apr–Oct 10–6,*
Nov–Feb 10–4

Thanks to the Civil War, this medieval castle was turned into one of the country's most spectacular ruins, offering a fabulous silhouette on its lofty perch topping a steep humpbacked ridge. It began as a wooden Saxon tower on a hill standing guard over the road to Purbeck; Henry II built the stone tower and his son, John, added to it. In 1646 the

Corfe Castle, *destroyed during the Civil War.*

castle, defended by the Royalist Lady Bankes, was besieged by Cromwell, who later dismantled much of it stone by stone.

50 Exeter Cathedral

☎ 01392 255573/214219
Cathedral Close, Exeter, Devon EX1 1HS
Website: www.exeter-cathedral.org.uk
In city centre, between High St
& Southernhay
Open *Mon–Fri 7.30–6.15 Sat 7.30–5*
Sun 8–7.30

It is a cathedral that slightly conceals its glories. The exterior is fine but does not quite belong in the same class as the other great cathedrals; inside it is a totally different story. The ribbed vault, all 300ft (93m) of it, is a Gothic masterpiece. It is nearly 70ft (22m) off the ground and

supported by 16 shafts of Purbeck marble patterned like tree trunks. The whole effect has been likened to an avenue of stone palm trees.

The 14th-century cathedral is a good example of what is called Decorated Gothic. Some of the earliest carved misericords in England are on the choir stalls. The cathedral is unusual because it does not have a central tower; the towers it does have are over the transept, being the only surviving remains of an earlier Norman building. There is a particularly fine Bishop's throne, carved out of Devon oak between 1313 and 1317; there are few finer examples of medieval carving anywhere in the country. Also look for the more recent flag commemorating one of Captain Scott's Antarctic expeditions on display.

51 Restormel Castle EH

☎ 01208 872687
Lostwithiel, Cornwall PL22 0BD
1½m N of Lostwithiel off A390
Open *Apr–Sept 10–6, Oct 10–5*
One of the best surviving examples
of a classic shell-keep castle in Britain. Luckily, enough of the circular walls and internal partitions have endured to give a vivid picture of how this kind of castle functioned. Restormel was owned and occasionally lived in by the Black Prince (1330–76), who was also Duke of Cornwall. It was involved in one brief scrap during the Civil War, when the Royalists took control, but was spared being destroyed after the hostilities.

52 Salisbury Cathedral

☎ 01722 555120/555121/555123
The Close, Salisbury, Wiltshire SP1 2EJ
Email: visitors@salcath.co.uk
Website: www.salisburycathedral.org.uk
S of city centre
Open *7.15–6.15, June–Aug open until 8.15*

Apart from its astonishing spire, 404ft (123m) high, what makes Salisbury Cathedral unusual is that it was designed and built over a relatively short period, 1220–65. This gives a unity and harmony to its architecture in Early English style that other cathedrals do not share. The graceful spire was added a century later, *c*1320, and weighs over 6000 tonnes. The weight created extra problems, and Christopher Wren was called in to help reinforce the transepts with bands of iron.

The cathedral is enclosed by walls and medieval gateways that date back to the reign of Edward III. There is a Lady Chapel, with dark, dramatic, columns of Purbeck stone. Many of the surrounding houses date back to the Middle Ages; the best include the chapter house and cloisters (the largest of their kind anywhere in Britain), to the south of the cathedral.

Inside the cathedral there are a number of fascinating monuments and artefacts, among them the oldest surviving clock (1386) in the country that still works. One of the four surviving copies of Magna Carta is displayed in the chapter house. The cathedral was the subject of one of Constable's most famous and best-loved paintings.

53 Sherborne Old Castle* EH

☎ 01935 812730
Castleton, Sherborne, Dorset DT9 3SA
Website: www.sherbornecastle.com
½m E of Sherborne off B3145
Open *Apr–Sept 10–6, Oct 10–5,*
Nov–Mar Wed–Sun 10–4
The castle has lain abandoned since Oliver Cromwell besieged it for a fortnight during the Civil War. Originally built in the 12th century, it never had any real military importance. Its other historical claim to fame is that it was once owned by Sir Walter Raleigh.

54 Wells Cathedral

☎ 01749 674483
Cathedral Green, Wells, Somerset BA5 2UE
Email: visits@wellscathedral.co.net
Website: www.somerset.gov.uk/tourism
In city centre
Open *Mon–Sat 9.15–4.30, Sun 12.30–2.30*

Wells is one of the best-loved British
cathedrals, noted for its charm and
serenity, and was one of the first to be
built in the Early English style with
pointed arches throughout. The
elaborate nave was built in the late
12th and early 13th centuries.

Wells' crowning feature is the west
front façade, completed in 1282. It has
over 400 sculpted saints, bishops, popes
and kings arranged in ever ascending
rows and columns like a holy city of
stone (perhaps the most important collection of medieval sculpture anywhere
in Britain). They were originally brightly
painted but, like so much gaudy medieval
decoration, that effect has long since
vanished. Some of the statues were on
the hit list of Puritan iconoclasm during
the Civil War, but the majority survived
relatively unscathed.

There is the great octagonal chapter
house, with its triumphal windows and
soaring vaulted roof, supported by 32
ribs that radiate out of the central pillar,
which was built *c*1290–1306; the central
tower was added at this time too. Outside
there are wonderful old buildings, the
moated Bishop's Palace and cloisters.

ADDITIONAL PLACES TO VISIT

Bristol Cathedral

☎ 0117 926 4879
College Green, Bristol BS1 5TJ
Email: briscath@cwcom.net
Website: www.bristol-cathedral.co.uk
In city centre
Open *8–6*

More than half the cathedral is in fact
Victorian, and only the eastern half,
including the two Lady Chapels, is
medieval. Among the remnants of its
Norman origins as an abbey are the
chapter house, where the monks met to
discuss daily business, and a well-worn
midnight stair. This was the route taken
by the monks every night from their
dormitory to conduct the longest and
most important prayer of their day.

It was given cathedral status in 1542,
after the Dissolution of the Monasteries,
when it ceased being an abbey. Apparently, this delay was the price paid by
an earlier abbot who refused to accept
the body of Edward II who had been
murdered at nearby Berkeley Castle.
The illustrious corpse went to Gloucester
instead, and the resulting cult and crowds
of pilgrims helped create Gloucester's
rise in fortunes and status at the expense
of Bristol's.

Buckfast Abbey

☎ 01364 645500
Buckfastleigh, Devon TQ11 0EE
Email: enquiries@buckfast.org.uk
Website: www.buckfast.org.uk
2m from A38
Open *8.45–6.30*

Founded by King Cnut in 1018, and
allocated by King Stephen to Cistercian
monks in 1147, it was abandoned after
the Dissolution of the Monasteries
until 1882. Then exiled French Benedictine monks took it over, at which point it
was substantially and beautifully rebuilt.

Christchurch Castle and Constable's House EH

Christchurch, Dorset
In Christchurch, near the Priory
Open *Any reasonable time*

The Norman keep and constable's house
date back to the 12th century. The latter

was originally a domestic household, only later being fortified when a tower was erected.

Donnington Castle EH
Newbury, Berkshire
1m NW of Newbury off B4494
Open *Any reasonable time*
A victim to one of the Civil War's longest sieges, only the gatehouse and twin towers of this 14th-century castle survive.

Launceston Castle EH
☎ 01566 772365
Castle Lodge, Launceston, Cornwall PL15 7DR
In Launceston
Open *Apr–Sept 10–6, Oct 10–5, Nov–Mar Fri–Sun 10–4*
The ruined remains of the motte, shell keep and tower of the original castle which were built to guard the entry into Cornwall.

Malmesbury Abbey
☎ 01666 826666
Holloway Hill, Malmesbury, Wiltshire SN16 9BA
In centre of town
Open *Apr–Oct 10–5, Nov–Mar 10–4*
These are impressive remains: the Norman nave of a once mighty Benedictine church. There is some fabulous carving from the Norman period visible on the south porch, among the finest Romanesque carvings anywhere in the country. William of Malmesbury records one highlight in the abbey's history – man's first flight. In AD1000 a monk called Elmer apparently attached wings to his hands and feet, and launched himself off the roof, travelling a full furlong before plummeting to the

ground and breaking several bones. His heroic folly is celebrated in a modern stained-glass window. There is also the legend that this is where King Athelstan, grandson of Alfred the Great and the first Saxon king of all England, lies buried; his tomb is the abbey's proudest possession.

Marker's Cottage NT
☎ 01392 461546
Broadclyst, Exeter, Devon EX5 3HR
Off B3181 Exeter–Cullompton road
Open *Apr–Oct Sun–Tues 2–5*
A cob house (the walls were made of clay mixed with straw, gravel and sand) dating from the Middle Ages.

Muchelney Abbey EH
and Priest's House NT
☎ Abbey 01458 25066
Priest's House 01458 252621
Muchelney, Langport, Somerset TA10 0DQ
In Muchelney, 2m S of Langport
Open *Abbey: Apr–Sept 10–6, Oct 10–5*
Priest's House: Apr–Sept 2.30–5.30
A well-preserved religious settlement, it was a Benedictine abbey. The Priest's House, a medieval hall house across the road, is still used; there are also 17th-century painted panels in the roof and original medieval tiles.

Okehampton Castle EH
☎ 01837 52844
Okehampton, Devon EX20 1JB
1m SW of Okehampton town centre, off A30 bypass
Open *Apr–Sept 10–6, Oct 10–5*
An impressive ruin of a Norman castle which was the largest built in Devon by Baldwin de Brionne, shortly after the Norman Conquest, to protect travellers heading to Exeter. The castle was built

The scissors arch in **Wells Cathedral** *built to strengthen the crossing.*

along a ridge leading to a steep mound. When one of its owners, the 1st Marquis of Exeter, was found guilty of plotting against Henry VIII, he lost his head and his castle lost most of its walls. Okehampton later became the constituency of William Pitt, the Earl of Chatham .

Totnes Castle EH
☎ 01803 864406
Castle Street, Totnes, Devon TQ9 5NU
In Totnes, on hill overlooking town.
Access in Castle Street off W end of High St
Open *Apr–Sept 10–6, Oct 10–5,*
Nov–Mar Wed–Sun 10–1 2–4
The walled medieval town had four gates, of which this is the best preserved. The North Gate comprises a motte-and-bailey offering wonderful views over the River Dart.

South-east MAP 2

55 Battle Abbey* EH
☎ 01424 773792
Battle, E Sussex TN33 0AD
Off A2100, at top of Battle High Street
Open *Apr–Sept 10–6, Oct 10–5,*
Nov–Mar 10–4
Before fighting the Saxon army in October 1066, William of Normandy apparently made a promise to build an abbey in the event of victory, later dictating that it be built on the spot where Harold's body was found, even though the ground was boggy and steep. This he did, and the partial remains of the Benedictine abbey survive right next to the site where the battle occurred. In the 14th century an enormous fortified gatehouse was added which still dominates the end of the town's main street; ironically it was designed to protect the area from the French. After the Dissolution in 1538 the church was destroyed and the abbey adapted for secular use.

56 Canterbury Cathedral*
☎ 01227 762862
The Precincts, Canterbury, Kent CT1 2EH
Email: enquiries@canterbury-cathedral.org
Website: www.canterbury-cathedral.org
M2/M20, then A2; in city centre
Open *Summer Mon–Sat 9–7, winter Mon–Sat 9–5; check with cathedral for restricted times & Evensong details*
Crypt: all year Mon–Sat 10–7 (winter 10–5), Sun 12.30–2.30 4.30–5.30
The most important cathedral in the Church of England is the site of St Augustine's great mission to reconvert the southern parts of England to Christianity in AD597. The Saxon cathedral built here was destroyed by fire in 1067 but was rebuilt between the 11th and 15th century.

The Black Prince is buried here, but Canterbury is most notoriously associated with the 'murder in the Cathedral', the brutal slaying of Archbishop Thomas Becket by four of Henry II's knights. That he was murdered in the north transept shocked the whole of Christendom and it even traumatized Henry. He later visited the cathedral in an act of penitence, walking barefoot through Canterbury in 1174, being whipped by monks after arriving at the cathedral. As well he might because, even had he intended Becket's death, it backfired horribly. In 1173 Becket was canonized, becoming the pre-eminent martyr saint in the country. The fabulous stained-glass windows (1220–30) in the Trinity Chapel tell the story of his martyrdom and the miracles of St Thomas. The stained glass at Canterbury is among the finest and most complete in England.

One of the cathedral's most spectacular features is the 'transi' tomb of Archbishop Henry Chichele (in which he is figured both in his ecclesiastical

*Thomas Becket in a 13th-century stained-glass window at **Canterbury Cathedral**.*

spendour, and as a decomposing corpse).

Canterbury's transformation into a place of pilgrimage also brought the cathedral great riches, with monies from its estates; the chapter house was built, with its peerless barrel-vaulted ceiling, and Bell Harry, the great Gothic tower, was raised in *c*1498.

57 Dover Castle and Secret Wartime Tunnels * EH

☎ 01304 211068
Dover, Kent CT16 1HU
Easy access from A2 & M20. Signed from Dover centre & on E side of Dover
Open *Apr–Sept 10–6, Oct 10–5, Nov–Mar 10–4*
Given the location, overlooking the

English Channel at one of its narrowest points, it is not surprising that Dover has played a key strategic role over the centuries. It was the gateway to Britain for the Romans, Angles, Saxons, Normans and virtually anyone who arrived by sea. There is evidence of pre-historic fortifications on the site. Nearby are the remains of a Roman lighthouse or *pharos*.

The castle was originally a prefabri-cated fort brought to the site by William the Conqueror's half brother, Odo of Bayeux, and grew in importance in the centuries that followed. The main fortifications are from the 12th and 13th centuries, and the keep was constructed *c*1180. The castle is unusual in being one of the first to follow a concentric pattern, though the impact of the circuits of enclosing walls was drastically compromised during the Napoleonic Wars when many of the towers were dismantled and reconstructed as gun emplacements. The reinforcements continued during the two world wars of the 20th century. The castle's role during World War II is commemorated in the exhibitions in the underground tunnels which are full of audio-visual reconstructions.

58 Farnham Castle Keep EH

☎ 01252 713393

Castle Hill, Farnham, Surrey GU6 0AG
½m N of Farnham town centre on A287
Open *Apr–Sept 10–6, Oct 10–5*
Begun by Henry of Blois, Bishop of Winchester (Farnham was once a seat of the bishops of Winchester), much of the castle was destroyed by Henry II (Blois was the brother of Henry's great rival, Stephen). But the shell wall, gatehouse, court and keep still survive, though the great hall is much smaller now than in its heyday. The castle keep is the most impressive part of the remains. The castle swapped sides three times during the Civil War, ending up in Royalist hands in 1645, despite having had its gate blown up by the Parliamentary general, William Waller.

59 Pevensey Castle* EH

☎ 01323 762604

Pevensey, E Sussex PN24 5LE
In Pevensey off A259
Open *Apr–Sept 10–6, Oct 10–5,*
Nov–Mar Wed–Sun 10–4
Before the Normans built their defensive stronghold here, this was one of the largest Roman Saxon Shore Forts, built in the late 3rd century. It has an unusual 9-acre oval shape, due to the surrounding boggy terrain. A substantial portion of the enclosing walls survive, as well as a massive gateway and 10 of the bastions. The Anglo-Saxon Chronicle (first compiled in the late 9th century), describes an attack on the fort in 491 by the South Saxons who routed the Roman garrison. William the Conqueror landed here with his invasion fleet in 1066. He wasted little time, according to the Bayeux Tapestry, in building a temporary wooden fortification; later, it was strengthened with huge stone walls. It retained the unusual oval rather than rectangular shape, and continued to have major significance as a coastal defence. A keep was later built in the south-east corner, and a smaller inner bailey. Its importance receded, as did the sea, from the 15th century, though there was a Home Guard command post here during World War II.

60 Rochester Castle* EH

☎ 01634 402276

The Lodge, Rochester-upon-Medway, Kent ME1 1SX
By Rochester Bridge (A2),
M2 junction 1 & M25 junction 2
Open *Apr–Sept 10–6, Oct 10–5,*
Nov–Mar 10–4
There are few great Norman towers more impressive than Rochester, the last word in the architecture of intimidation. This was one of William the Conqueror's earliest motte-and-bailey castles, overlooking the River Medway and the main London–Dover road. It was later converted into stone, under the supervision of Bishop Gundulf. The rectangular Norman keep (by this time an utterly distinctive Norman feature) rises 120ft (36m) above the ground, and looks as though it will carry on standing until the end of time. The castle was the site of a later successful siege by King John.

St Augustine's Abbey, *founded by St Augustine in* AD*598.*

61 St Augustine's Abbey EH

☎ 01227 767345

Longport, Canterbury, Kent CT1 1TF

In Canterbury, ¼m E of Cathedral Close

Open *Apr–Sept 10–6, Oct 10–5,
Nov–Mar 10–4*

The second of Canterbury's great monasteries, the one that didn't become the cathedral, is too often missed in favour of its more famous and intact counterpart. This once powerful rival was founded in 598 by St Augustine, who is buried here along with other early archbishops. Now a ruin, its tallest surviving fragment is part of the north wall of the Norman nave. For nearly 20 years after the Dissolution of the Monasteries stone was being lifted from the site for use elsewhere, which took a huge toll on the remains visible today. A well-mounted exhibition displays many treasures dug up during excavations and presents a graphic picture of the abbey's history.

62 Tower of London*

☎ 020 7709 0765

Tower Hill, London EC3N 4AB

Website: www.hrp.org.uk

*Tube Tower Hill or London Bridge;
Tower Gateway Station (Docklands
Light Railway)*

Open *Mar–Oct Mon–Sat 9–6 Sun 10–6,
Nov–Feb Tues–Sat 9–5 Mon & Sun 10–5*

The Tower has been radically overhauled as a tourist destination (especially the Crown Jewels display), but behind it still stands one of the country's most important pieces of early medieval architecture. At the core is the White Tower, an immense Norman keep finished at the end of the 11th century, built by William I and II. It was only with the later addition of two encircling walls that it took on the appearance with which we are now familiar. It is much more famous as a prison and the site of high-ranking executions than as a fortress, and in this respect it retains a gloomy atmosphere. It is very hard to visit Tower Green and not be reminded of the curious mix of barbarism and elevated sentiment that defined so many of those executions. The list of those imprisoned or executed here is long and impressive. And there is still something chilling about Traitor's Gate, the watery entrance for those condemned for treason.

63 Westminster Abbey*

☎ 020 7222 5152; Info desk 020 7222 7110
Dean's Yard, London SW19 3PA
Email: info@westminster-abbey.org
Website: www.westminster-abbey.org
Tube Westminster
Open *Mon–Fri 9.30–4.45 Sat 9–2.45*
Built on the site of the previous structure erected by the Saxon king, Edward the Confessor, at a time when the whole site was an island surrounded by marshes. The present abbey was started by Henry III, the first of a number of monarchs buried here (including Edward I, whose tomb has the famous inscription in Latin, 'Hammer of the Scots'). Westminster also contains the tomb of Henry VII and his queen, Elizabeth of York, which is one of the finest monuments of the Renaissance era and the work of the Italian sculptor, Pietro Torrigiani. George II is the last of the many monarchs to have been interred here (since then, royal burials switched to Windsor Castle).

Henry wanted Westminster to inspire with its sheer loftiness. Even to this day, in a world dominated by office blocks and skyscrapers, no other type of building can match a cathedral for that ecstatic sensation of vertigo when craning the neck upwards. The nave was not finally finished until after 1375 but, because they never deviated from the original Gothic style, the final effect is of a building constructed in one go. The next

major addition was the Henry VII Chapel, in the early 16th century, crowned by a magnificent vaulted ceiling with the most elaborate tracery attempted anywhere in Britain. Work continued on the west front and the two main towers that were only finally finished between 1735–40 by Nicholas Hawksmoor.

The site of so many events of great historical significance right up to the present day, the abbey is not surprisingly much more than just the country's most famous medieval church. William the Conqueror was crowned here on Christmas Day 1066, anxious to be within sight of Edward the Confessor's tomb (granting a degree of legitimacy). Whatever the reason for choosing this as the place for coronations, the habit stuck; apart from Edward V (murdered in the Tower) and Edward VIII (who abdicated), all England's monarchs have been crowned here. The Coronation Chair lives in St Edward's Chapel, constructed in 1300 to house the Stone of Scone that Edward I filched during one of his Scottish campaigns (since returned). It is also the site of the Tomb of the Unknown Soldier. Technically, because the abbey was dissolved in the mid-16th century, the title Westminster Abbey survives only by convention.

64 Winchester Cathedral

☎ 01962 857202
The Close, Winchester,
Hampshire SO23 9LS
Email: cathedral.office@winchester-cathedral.org.uk
Website: www.winchester-cathedral.org.uk
In Winchester city centre
Open *8.30–5.30*
This is the second longest cathedral in Europe, at 556ft (169m) – only St Peter's in Rome is longer. Work started in 1079

on the site of earlier Christian buildings. The interior is more interesting than the exterior and is full of treasures. Look for the fine set of 14th-century misericords, and monuments going right back across the centuries. During the Middle Ages this was the Church's wealthiest see and William of Wykeham, twice Chancellor to medieval kings, was the one who most significantly remodelled it.

The cathedral is renowned for its chantry chapels with elaborate tombs for the local great and good (usually important benefactors), and they are among the finest in the country. Six are dedicated to bishops, and the one commemorating William Waynflete is particularly impressive. They make good companion pieces for the rows of mortuary chests containing the remains of various Saxon kings –

hardly surprising they are here because Winchester was a main city long before it was eclipsed by London. The best of the stained glass is Victorian, designed by Edward Burne-Jones.

Nearby is Wolvesey Castle (01962 854766) which was the official residence of the Bishops of Winchester, and was once one of the country's most magnificent medieval buildings. Now it is a ruin, thanks to Oliver Cromwell who ordered its destruction during the Civil War.

65 Windsor Castle*
☎ 01753 869898
Windsor, Berkshire SL4 1NJ
Email: windsorcastle@royalcollection.org.uk
Website: www.royal.gov.uk/palaces/windsor.htm
20m from central London, leave M4 junction 6 or M3 junction 3

Windsor Castle *is England's largest castle, built and rebuilt from the 11th to the 20th century.*

Open *Castle: Mar–Sept 9.45–5.15,
Oct–Nov 9.45–4.15. St George's Chapel:
closed Sun for services*
This is one royal residence which is still
open to the public, royal commitments
permitting. Its history goes right back to
William the Conqueror who established
it first. There is virtually no monarch or
age that has not added something to its
immensity. Originally a motte-and-
bailey, the wooden structure was
replaced by stone and fortifications were
added in the 12th and 13th centuries.
Royal apartments and a chapel were
added by Edward III, and significant
works of extension and restoration by
Charles II, George III, George IV and
Queen Victoria.

St George's Chapel, begun in 1475
by Edward IV, is the Chapel of the Order
of the Garter and a masterpiece of the
Perpendicular style. Much of what you
see inside is 16th century, eg the vault,
stalls, and most of the sculpture, although
the bare-breasted statue of Princess
Charlotte of Wales is the work of the
Victorian sculptor, M.C. Wyatt.

ADDITIONAL PLACES TO VISIT

Bayham Old Abbey EH
☎ 01892 890381
Lamberhurst, E Sussex
2m W of Lamberhurst off B2169
Open *Apr–Sept 10–6, Oct 10–5,
Nov–Mar Sat & Sun only 10–4*
The riverside ruins are set in a restored
18th-century landscape setting. The 13th-
century abbey was liquidated by Cardinal
Wolsey in 1525, a decade before most
abbeys, to help him raise funds to build
Christ Church in Oxford. Later renovations
were carried out in the spirit of a growing
Romantic love affair with old ruins, and
were the work of the fashionable garden
designer, Humphry Repton.

Beaulieu Abbey and Palace House
☎ 01590 612345
Beaulieu, Brockenhurst,
Hampshire SO42 7ZN
Email: info@beaulieu.co.uk
Website: www.beaulieu.co.uk
*From M27 take junction 2 to A326
& B3054, follow brown signs*
Open *May–Sept 10–6, Oct–Apr 10–5*
A Cistercian abbey founded by King
John, most of it is now in ruins, though
the old refectory serves as a local parish
church. The two-storey gatehouse was
used for a while as a private house in
the mid-16th century. The grounds
now accommodate the world-famous
Beaulieu National Motor Museum, with
its fantastic collection of a century's
worth of cars.

Boxgrove Priory EH
Boxgrove, Chichester, W Sussex
*N of Boxgrove, 4m E of Chichester
on minor road N of A27*
Open *Any reasonable time*
These ruins used to be the guest house,
chapter house and church (now func-
tioning) of a 12th-century priory.

Chichester Cathedral
☎ 01243 782595
West Sussex St, Chichester,
W Sussex PO19 1PX
Email: vo@chicath.freeserve.uk
Website: www.chichester-
cathedral.org.uk
Open *Summer 7.30–7, winter 7.30–5*
Right from the start, this building was
designed on a modest scale, Norman
with early additions. The retrochoir
(the large area of the chancel behind the
high altar) was rebuilt in the late 12th and
early 13th centuries. A separate bell tower
was added (highly unusual) because it
was obvious even in the 15th century that
the main tower would find it difficult to

support the weight. The central tower is a Victorian addition after one of many fires had taken a terrible toll, though pains were taken to reproduce the earlier tower as closely as possible.

The cathedral has two main treasures in its possession, the sculptured stone panels in the choir aisles dating from 1125–50 showing Christ arriving at the House of Mary at Bethany, and the Raising of Lazarus. They were discovered in 1829, minus their eyes which had been gouged out, though whether this was iconoclasm (attacking the eyes was a common form of vandalism of religious icons) or the theft of whatever precious stones had once been used, is open to question. There is a fine collection of modern art, including a huge tapestry designed by John Piper.

Jewel Tower EH
☎ 020 7222 2219
Abingdon Street, Westminster,
London SW19 3JY
Tube Westminster; opposite S end of Houses of Parliament (Victoria Tower)
Open *Apr–Mar 10–6, Oct 10–5, Nov–Mar 10–4*
A scrap of a building that has survived from the medieval Old Palace of Westminster, built in 1365 as a moated treasure house for Edward III. It is now the home of a museum, with a virtual reality tour of the Houses of Parliament.

Lewes Castle and Barbican House Museum
☎ 01273 486290
169 High St, Lewes,
E Sussex BN7 1YE
Email: castle@sussexpast.co.uk
Website: www.sussexpast.co.uk
Lewes town centre off A27
Open *Mon–Sat 10–5.30, Sun & BHs 11–5.30; closes at dusk in winter*

This massive castle dominates one end of the High Street. The barbican gate which protected the castle is now a local museum. The wall walk is a full 20ft (6m) above street level, supported on walls nearly 7ft (2m) thick; the 12th-century stonework is virtually intact.

Mottisfont Abbey Garden, House and Estate NT
☎ 01794 340757
Mottisfont, Hampshire SO51 0LP
4½m NW of Romsey, 1m W of A3057
Open *House: 1–5. Garden: mid-Mar–Oct Sat–Wed 11–6 (dusk if earlier)*
It was originally an Augustinian priory founded in 1201. Later a victim of the Dissolution of the Monasteries, the abbey fell into the possession of Henry VIII's Lord Chamberlain Lord Sandys who, needless to say, converted it into rather a fine house for himself. There are later Georgian touches. The medieval vaulting of the monks' cellarium is still in perfect condition. Today, the abbey takes pride of place in a large estate that includes grounds with walled gardens and magnificent trees and Mottisfont village. Inside are many notable paintings, a drawing room decorated by Rex Whistler and interesting pieces of furniture.

Rochester Cathedral
☎ 01634 843366
High Street, Rochester, Kent ME1 1JY
Signposted from M20 junction 6 & A2/M2 junction 3. Best access from M2 junction 3
Open *All year 7.30–6; closes at 5 on Sat & Sun*
One of the smaller cathedrals, and greatly altered over the centuries, it combines Norman and Early English architecture.The Norman west front, with its elaborate mid-12th-century doorway, is the most striking feature on

the exterior. On the choir wall there is a fragment of a painting of a 13th-century Wheel of Fortune, with a king on top, obviously about to be pitched off. The crypt, which is one of the largest and most beautiful in the country with splendid Early English vaulting and medieval graffiti on the piers, became an air raid shelter during one of the early Zeppelin raids over the coast during the First World War.

Titchfield Abbey EH
☎ 01329 842133
Titchfield, Fareham, Hampshire
½m N of Titchfield off A27,near Fareham
Open *Apr–Sept 10–6, Oct 10–5, Nov–Mar 10–4*
The ruins of a 13th-century abbey for White Friars, the last abbey of the order to be built in England. Its stones were taken by Thomas Wriothesley, later Earl of Southampton, during the reign of Henry VIII to build a substantial Tudor mansion. The chief survival today is the great four-storey Tudor gatehouse which was formed from the central bay of the monastic church. Most of the Tudor mansion was demolished in 1781.

Eastern MAP 3

66 Castle Rising Castle* EH
☎ 01553 631330
Castle Rising, King's Lynn,
Norfolk PE31 6AH
4m NE of King's Lynn off A149
Open *Apr–Sept 10–6, Oct 10–5, Nov–Mar Wed–Sun 10–4*
Castle Rising Castle is surrounded by enormous earthworks, but, amazingly, it was apparently never actually tested in battle. It became an open prison for Edward II's widow, Queen Isabella, the 'She-Wolf' of France, who died at Hertford Castle in 1358. The bridge and surrounding ditch are still formidable. It was built by William d'Albini who married Henry I's widow and became 1st Earl of Arundel.

67 Coggeshall Grange Barn NT
☎ 01376 562226
Coggeshall, Colchester, Essex CO6 1RE
Signposted off A120 Coggeshall bypass
Open *Apr–mid-Oct Tues Thurs Sun & BH Mons 2–5*

The 12th-century timber-framed **Coggeshall Grange Barn***.*

Thanks to restoration work in the 1980s, this oldest surviving timber-framed barn in Europe (dating back to c1140) is now open to visitors. It used to serve a Cistercian monastery.

68 Ely Cathedral*
☎ 01353 667735
Ely, Cambridgeshire CB7 4DL
Website: www.cathedral.ely.anglican.org
15m N of Cambridge off A10
Open *Summer 7–7, winter Mon–Sat 7.30–6 Sun & week after Christmas 7.30–5*
If cathedrals like Durham and Lincoln dominate their surrounding landscapes by virtue of their elevated situations, then Ely does it by being the highest point in a large area of flat fenland. During periods of flooding not unusual for this part of the country, Ely can take on the appearance of a ship.

It is one of the more instantly recognizable of English cathedrals, with its central octagon, western tower and four round corner towers, built on the site of one of the great rebellions, led by Hereward the Wake, against Norman rule. The cathedral was begun in 1083. The transept and east end were completed by 1106, and the nave c1189. Three doorways from around 1130 have survived, as has much of the cathedral's sculpture. The choir was rebuilt in the 13th century to provide St Ethelreda with a more sumptuous tomb.

The 14th century saw the building of an elaborate Lady Chapel, which has the widest medieval vault in the country, 46ft (14m), so delicate it could not support the weight of a single person. In 1322 the original central tower collapsed and was replaced by the central octagon and wooden lantern, reputed to be the only Gothic dome ever built.

The interior is especially impressive, austere and uplifting. The Norman nave and transepts are simple and powerful, while the interior of the octagon is just spectacular. The credit for this masterpiece belongs in particular to two men, Alan of Walsingham, a church official, and William Hurley, a master carpenter. They built the octagon out of eight large piers, rising up to create four 72ft(22m)-high arches. The resulting lantern is a miracle of medieval engineering, allowing light to pour right into the heart of the cathedral. It involved lifting eight enormous oak beams nearly 100ft (30m) straight up, to be attached to the body of the building by great struts. The resulting structure, weighing 200 tonnes, took 14 years to complete.

The magnificent Norman nave (208ft/63m long) had its ceiling painted in the 19th century which gives Ely a wonderful touch of exuberance. What is unusual about Ely is that it has a timber ceiling when the norm is a stone vaulted roof. It is well worth making the long climb up the tower for the breathtaking views of the rest of the cathedral and the flat, surrounding landscape of the Fens.

69 Framlingham Castle* EH
☎ 01728 724189
Framlingham, Suffolk 1PA 9BT
In Framlingham on B1116, NE of town centre
Open *Apr–Sept 10–6, Oct 10–5, Nov–Mar 10–4*
This is one of the best preserved castles in England. It was state of the art when it was constructed c1189 by Roger Bigod, 2nd Earl of Norfolk. This was when castle design took its great leap forward, away from the motte-and-bailey towards the more familiar pattern of a wall studded with towers encircling the inner fortifications. Framlingham's 13 towers are the older square shape. The castle was big

*The walls and towers of the 12th-century **Framlingham Castle**.*

enough to accommodate an entire army, and was the site from which Mary Tudor mounted her successful campaign to inherit the throne from Edward VI.

70 Hedingham Castle*

☎ 01787 460261
Castle Hedingham, nr Halstead,
Essex CO9 3DJ
Email: hedinghamcastle@aspects.net
Website: www.hedinghamcastle.co.uk
On B1058, 1m off A1017
between Cambridge & Colchester
Open *Week before Easter–Oct 10–5*
This square keep was built on the model of Rochester, but to only 75 per cent of the scale, though it is every bit as imposing. In its day it was considered the country's strongest castle. Its tower is four storeys high, and its walls up to 20ft (6m) thick. There are numerous passages running through the walls. It belonged to the de Vere family, Earls of Oxford. Despite one of their number helping Henry Tudor

defeat Richard III, it didn't stop him being fined £10,000 by Henry for allowing his servants to flaunt the family coat of arms. Henry had banned the practice to curb baronial powers.

The castle still has its great hall, minstrel's gallery and a magnificent Norman arch. It also had the first genuine castle chimneys concealed in a buttress. In the vicinity of the grounds you can see a Norman church and medieval village.

71 Lincoln Cathedral

☎ 01522 544544
Minster Yard, Lincoln LN2 1PX
Email: cev@lincolncathedral.com
Website: www.lincolncathedral.com
In city centre
Open *June–Aug Mon–Sat 7.15–8*
Sun 7.15–6, Sept–May Mon–Sat 7.15–6
Sun 7.15–5
For many, Lincoln probably is the finest cathedral in the country. It has a magnificent location on top of its limestone ridge,

and is a beacon for miles around. Its central tower is both lofty and imposing. It is most famous for its Angel Choir built between 1256 and 1280, designed to house the tomb of St Hugh. Other cathedrals are more austere; Lincoln is where you go to bask in ornamental carvings, in wood and stone, and to see stained glass, of which there is fabulous abundance. The most magnificent example of this is the Dean's Eye, a great circular stained-glass window at the north end of the great transept, dating from about 1220, and still possessing much of its original glass. The chapter house was built at this time, and has an octagonal form, the first to do so in England. Flying buttresses were added in the 14th century. As happened in a number of churches, the central tower collapsed, this one in 1237. Lincoln was the location for a number of Edward I's parliaments.

72 Orford Castle EH

☎ 01394 450472
Orford, Woodbridge, Suffolk IP12 2ND
In Orford off B1084,
5m E of Ipswich on A1214
Open *Apr–Sept 10–6, Oct 10–5,*
Nov–Mar Wed–Sun 10–4
Only the keep has survived, but it is a spectacular one. Orford was built for Henry II from 1165–73 by Maurice the Engineer, historians think, and it played a key part in Henry's regaining power over East Anglia, vital for its wool trade and ports, but which had no royal castle when Henry came to the throne. Henry wasted little time in remedying this by confiscating a number of castles, particularly those in the possession of the local nobleman, Hugh Bigod, 1st Earl of Norfolk. Then Henry commissioned his own castle.

Orford incorporated all the latest thinking in castle design, which was just

The 12th-century polygonal keep at **Orford Castle** *with its three towers.*

as well because it saw military action almost as soon as it was complete, helping Henry put down a local rising led by the now 80-year-old Bigod. Although it was never actually attacked, it provided Henry with a base to strike out over the Eastern counties. The inner courtyard was surrounded by curtain walls from which extended flanking turrets. The keep is an unusual shape; not rectangular as was norm, but circular inside and polygonal outside.

Orford remained of great strategic importance for the next 200 years, swapping hands on a number of occasions. It survived almost intact until the 1600s, but from then on serious decay set in, to which the surrounding walls succumbed in time, leaving only the keep.

73 Peterborough Cathedral

☎ 01733 343342
Peterborough PE1 1XS
Website: www.peterborough-cathedral.
org.uk
4m E of A1 in city centre
Open *Weekdays 8.30–5.15, Sat 8.30–5.45,
Sun 12–5.45*
Maybe not as famous as some of the
great cathedrals, but it is still one of the
finest Norman churches to have
survived. It is also one of the least
altered. It has an interior built of Barnack
limestone, and a wooden nave roof with
original medieval paintings (dating from
*c*1220) of bishops, saints and mythical
beasts. Work began around 1118 and it
took 120 years to build, being one of the
most impressive examples of Norman
architecture in the country.

The Early English west front, built
*c*1200–10, remains the cathedral's chief
masterpiece; it comprises three great
arches over 80ft (24m) high (though the
central one is narrower than the two
flanking it, for no very clear reason).
A porch was added in 1370 in the Perpendicular style, probably to lend stability
to the arch supports and prevent them
sagging. A fan-vaulted retrochoir was
built *c*1496–1509.

Catherine of Aragon, Henry VIII's
first wife, is buried here, which helped
protect the church during the Dissolution
of the Monasteries. Mary Queen of Scots
was buried here too, for a short time,
but her son removed her remains 25
years later to Westminster Abbey where
they now rest close to those of her
cousin, Elizabeth I. The cathedral
suffered during the Civil War at the
hands of the Parliamentarians, when
Catherine of Aragon's elaborate tomb
was demolished. Memorial tablets in the
Sanctuary mark where she and Mary
Queen of Scots once lay.

ADDITIONAL PLACES TO VISIT

Berkhamsted Castle EH

☎ 01442 871737
Berkhamsted, St Albans, Hertfordshire
Adjacent to Berkhamsted rail station
Open *Apr–Sept 10–6, Oct–Mar 10–4*
The original (now in ruins) 11th-century
motte-and-bailey were among the first
built in the country. The work was
completed after 1066 by William the
Conqueror's half-brother, Robert of
Mortaine. Thomas Becket later built a
second shell keep, only the motte-and-
bailey of which survived, though pretty
much as they would have been in the
11th and 12th centuries.

Bishops' Old Palace, Lincoln EH

☎ 01522 527468
Minster Yard, Lincoln LN2 1PU
S side of Cathedral in Lincoln
Open *Apr–Sept 10–6, Oct 10–5,
Nov–Mar Sat & Sun only 10–4*
These impressive remains are all that
is left of the medieval palace once
occupied by Lincoln's bishops.

Castle Acre Priory EH

☎ 01760 755394
Castle Acre, Norfolk PE32 2XD
*¼m W of village of Castle Acre,
5m N of Swaffham*
Open *Apr–Sept 10–6, Oct 10–5,
Nov–Mar Wed–Sun 10–4*
The village of Castle Acre, with its broad
street leading down to the River Acre, is
the site of several military and monastic
ruins. Of these, the castle and a motte-
and-bailey survive as part of a gatehouse
and earthworks. A polygonal shell keep
was built on the site of the original motte
in the 13th century.

The Cluniac priory is an impressive
ruin. Its chapel has a wooden ceiling
with 14th- and 15th-century murals.

The most imposing part of this building is the great west front which, miraculously, still stands.

Denny Abbey and the Farmland Museum EH

☎ 01223 860489
Ely Road, Chittering, Waterbeach, Cambridgeshire CB5 9TQ
Website: www.dennyfarmandmuseum. org.uk
6m N of Cambridge on A10
Open *Apr–Oct 12–5*
Remains of a 12th-century Benedictine Abbey with a farmland museum.

Grimsthorpe Castle

☎ 01778 591205
Grimsthorpe, Bourne, Lincolnshire PE10 0LY
Email: ray@grimsthorpe.co.uk
Website: www.grimsthorpe.co.uk
4m NW of Bourne on A151
Open *Castle: Apr–Sept Sun Thurs & BH Mons, Aug Sun–Thurs, 1–4.30. Park & gardens: 11–6*
13th-century castle that was considerably enlarged, first in 1540 and then, more triumphantly, in the 18th century, courtesy of Sir John Vanbrugh. The last round of alterations took place c1810. The castle contains paintings, tapestries, thrones and furnishings from the old House of Lords, and is surrounded by a huge park.

Lincoln Castle

☎ 01522 511068
Castle Hill, Lincoln LN1 3AA
Opposite west front of Lincoln Cathedral
Open *Mon–Sat 9.30–5.30 Sun 11–5.30*
Built on a Roman site by William the Conqueror in 1068. The gateway still survives, as does part of the barbican. A Victorian prison building was constructed here in the mid-19th century.

The Manor, Hemingford Grey

☎ 01480 463134
High St, Hemingford Grey, nr Huntingdon, Cambridgeshire PE18 9BN
Website: www.aboutbritain.com/ hemingfordgreymanor.htm
4m S of Huntingdon off A14
Open *House: all year (except Aug), by appointment only*
This is apparently one of the oldest continually inhabited houses in the whole of Britain. It is a moated, stone-built house dating back to the 12th century; two storeys high, it has a 16th-century fireplace and chimney stack. There is also a charming garden.

St Edmundsbury Cathedral

☎ 01284 754933
Angel Hill, Bury St Edmunds, Suffolk IP33 1LS
Website: www.stedmundsbury. anglican.org
In the town centre
Open *Jan–May Sept–Dec 8.30–6, June–Aug 8.30–7; opens at 9 Sat & Sun all year*
Suffolk's cathedral since 1914, it is one of three churches that have existed within the precincts of the old abbey. Particularly imposing is the Norman gateway, now used as the cathedral belfry.

Central MAP 4

74 Berkeley Castle*

☎ 01453 810332
Berkeley, Gloucestershire GL13 9BQ
By Berkeley village, 2m W of A38 midway between Bristol & Gloucester
Open *Apr–May Tues–Sun 2–5, June & Sept Tues–Sat 11–5 Sun 2–5, July–Aug Mon–Sat 11–5 Sun 2–5, Oct Sun 2–5*
Most famously, this was where Edward II met his grisly end in 1327; the dungeon where the brutal act occurred is open to

the public. But more than that, Berkeley is a giant among castles in every way. It is physically imposing, both in structure and in surrounding grounds (including Elizabeth I's bowling green). And it has a rich and varied story of its own, including the meeting of the barons prior to riding off to make King John put his seal to Magna Carta in 1215 and the siege by Oliver Cromwell in 1645.

This stronghold overlooking the Severn has been well preserved, and has been the home of the Berkeleys (of Berkeley Square fame) since 1153, from which time the hall, keep and kitchen date. There are lavish state apartments with paintings, tapestries and fine furniture dating from much more recent times.

75 Croft Castle NT
☎ 01568 780246
Nr Leominster, Herefordshire HR6 9PW
Email: croft@smtp.ntrust.org.uk
Website: www.ntrustsevern.org.uk/croft.htm
9m SW of Ludlow off B4362
Open *Castle: closed for repairs in 2002*
Gardens & Croft Ambrey: 11–5
A rendezvous point for Yorkist leaders in the Wars of the Roses, this is a 14th-century stone enclosure with corner towers. Later additions were made in the 17th and 18th centuries, but the majority of its pink stone exterior dates from the Middle Ages. The estate also includes a spectacular Iron Age hill fort, Croft Ambrey.

76 Gloucester Cathedral
☎ 01452 528095
College Green, Gloucester GL1 2LR
Website: www.gloucestercathedral.uk.com
Off Westgate St in city centre
Open *7.30–6.15*

This was once a Benedictine monastery that had fallen on hard times. Then William the Conqueror recognized the importance of its location guarding a crossing point on the River Severn and had it restored. But strangely it was the murder of Edward II at nearby Berkeley Castle that gave Gloucester's abbey a lift; the body was buried here, and his shrine drew crowds of pilgrims, many of them wealthy. The church was at this point massively remodelled in the new Perpendicular style. One of its finest features is the lavatorium, a long cloistered washing area used by the monks to clean their hands before meals. Above where they stood is some of England's earliest fan vaulting. The cathedral is particularly rich in tombs and memorials.

77 Goodrich Castle EH
☎ 01600 890538
Ross-on-Wye, Herefordshire HR9 6HY
5m S of Ross-on-Wye off A40
Open *Apr–Sept 10–6, Oct 10–5,*
Nov–Mar Wed–Sun 10–1 2–4
Overlooking the River Wye and satisfyingly high on an outcrop of red sandstone, this is one of the most beautiful ruined castles. The uniform appearance given by the sandstone makes it a particularly harmonious building. It stands guard on its high ridge, overlooking an old river crossing-point.

At its core is the Norman keep built in the middle of the 12th century. The walls were built later to improve its defensive capabilities. Major additions were made at the time of Edward I's conquest of Wales by Henry III's half-brother, William de Valence. The main tower has a startlingly modern appearance, with its round central turret

---

Fan vaulting in the cloisters of **Gloucester Cathedral**.

squared off at the ground with four corner darts. The castle as a whole is assembled from a wonderful array of geometric shapes, worthy of any sculptor. The three-storey tower is surrounded by walls and later drum towers. The remains of three separate halls with adjoining residential suites flank the central courtyard.

78 Great Coxwell Barn NT

☎ 01793 762209

Great Coxwell, Faringdon, Oxfordshire
Website: www.nationaltrust.org.uk/
regions/thameschilterns
2m SW of Faringdon
between A420 & B4019
Open *Any reasonable time*
For the great late-Victorian designer William Morris, this enormous barn was 'as noble as a cathedral'. Built in the 13th century by monks from Beaulieu Abbey in Hampshire, it is over 150ft (46m) long, and nearly 50ft (15m) high. Like ancient Rome, it is protected by its own small population of geese.

79 Hailes Abbey* EH & NT

☎ 01242 602398

Nr Winchcombe, Cheltenham, Gloucestershire GL54 5PB
2m NE of Winchcombe off B4632,
½m SE of B4632
Open *Apr–Sept 10–6, Oct 10–5*
There are the ruined remains of a 13th-century Cistercian abbey founded in 1246. Many of the monks and lay brothers became victims of the Black Death c1361. But it was the Dissolution of the Monasteries that finally destroyed Hailes; after it the abbey fell into ruin. Across the lane is a little Norman church with 15th-century glass and 14th-century wall paintings. There is also a small museum on site containing relics from various excavations.

80 Hardingstone Eleanor Cross*

London Road, Hardingstone, Northampton, Northamptonshire
On London Road, adjacent to Delapre Park
Open *Open access*
This was one of the 12 memorials erected by Edward I to mark the progress back to Westminster Abbey of his dead wife's (Eleanor of Castile's) funeral cortege. Geddington and Waltham Cross also each have one (the only three to have survived). They were erected between 1291 and 1294, built by John of Battle, with the statues sculpted by William of Ireland. The route taken was via Lincoln, Grantham, Stamford, Geddington, Hardingstone, Stony Stratford, Dunstable, Cheapside and Charing Cross. At Geddington (also in Northamptonshire) the tall cenotaph bears three statues of Eleanor, wearing a veil.

What is particularly touching about what otherwise would be just another (beautiful) piece of medieval memorializing is the sense we get that Edward I, the ruthless 'Hammer of the Scots', was a man utterly laid low by grief for the death of his wife. The three crosses make a powerful contrast, in stone and in sensibility, with the monuments more usually associated with him – Welsh castles and great siege engines.

81 Hereford Cathedral

☎ 01432 374202

Hereford HR1 2NG
Email: visits@herefordcathedral.co.uk
In city centre off A49
Open *Summer 10–5, winter 11–4*
As famous for some of its extraordinary artefacts as for its gorgeous pink sandstone appearance, Hereford Cathedral dates back to the earliest days of Christianity. It possesses the finest collection of brasses of any cathedral in the country. It boasts the Chained

Library, the largest of its kind in Britain, with nearly 1500 books, many of them unique. But pride of place goes to the *Mappa Mundi*, a map of the world drawn on vellum depicting the world as it was thought to be around 1290. Major rebuilding took place in the late 12th century, including the beautiful Lady Chapel in the Early English style (finished *c*1220). The central and west towers were added in the 14th century.

This was as nothing compared to the work done on the cathedral by James Wyatt 'The Destroyer' after 1786, when the west tower collapsed. He built an entirely new west front, shortened the nave, and replaced many of the original Norman features with his own. But his work too was to feel the cold hand of restoration, when his west front was transformed in the early years of the 20th century by a new west front.

82 Kenilworth Castle* EH
☎ 01926 852078
Kenilworth, Warwickshire CV8 1NE
In W end of Kenilworth, off A452
Open *Apr–Sept 10–6, Oct 10–5, Nov–Mar 10–4*
A spectacular ruin covering an enormous site, this was both a medieval castle and an Elizabethan palace. King John turned it into a formidable fortress, until forced to relinquish it by the Magna Carta. In 1266 Simon de Montfort and his rebel army held out in the castle during a nine-month siege by Henry III after the battle of Evesham. It later passed to John

*The great castle of **Kenilworth**, now an awe-inspiring ruin.*

of Gaunt who made it more of a palace and less of a fortress, a process completed by Robert Dudley, Earl of Leicester, who was given it by Queen Elizabeth I. The gatehouse was his most impressive addition. The great artificial lake was drained during the Civil War.

83 Ludlow Castle

☎ 01584 873355

Castle Square, Ludlow, Shropshire SY8 1AY
In centre of Ludlow on A49,
28m from Shrewsbury
Open *Jan weekends only 10–4,*
Feb–Mar & Oct–Dec 10–4,
Apr–July & Sept 10–5, Aug 10–7

One of the great 'Marcher' castles, it was built to protect the Anglo-Welsh border. It was founded by the so-called de Lacy lords (from Lassy, or Calvados, in Normandy). The gatehouse was later converted into a keep. It was from here in 1483 that the 12-year-old Edward V heard that he was the new king. He and his younger brother, Richard, left for London. The legend goes that they were intercepted by their uncle, Richard, Duke of Gloucester, who imprisoned them in the Tower, where they were later murdered, leaving their uncle free to become Richard III. There are many who dispute this utterly. It was also the location for the first performance of John Milton's *Comus*. Today the castle boasts a holographic exhibition to help bring all this to life.

84 Warwick Castle*

☎ General info 0870 4422000
Castle Lane, Warwick CV34 4QU
Email: customer.information@warwick-castle.com
Website: www.warwick-castle.co.uk
2m from M40 junction 15,
½m SW of town centre
Open *Apr–Oct 10–6, Nov–Mar 10–5*

There has been some kind of fortification on this site since the 10th century. The Norman castle then built here was caught up in the Barons Wars led by Simon de Montfort, and was duly sacked in 1264. The castle then saw massive reinforcements made to its defences, particularly to the east end which made it practically impregnable thanks to a vast gatehouse tower and two towers flanking it. One of these is the so-called Guy's Tower which has 12 sides, is nearly 130ft (39m) high, and has twin battlements.

Now a major tourist destination leading the way in the art of turning castles into living history, it plays host to lots of attractions. With its surrounding 'Capability' Brown landscaped gardens, this is one of the most entertaining castles anywhere in the country.

85 Wenlock Priory EH

☎ 01952 727466
Much Wenlock, Shropshire TF13 6HS
In Much Wenlock
Open *Apr–Sept 10–6, Oct 10–5,*
Nov–Mar Wed–Sun 10–1 2–4

The original Cluniac priory was founded by St Milburga, but was destroyed and rebuilt more than once. The remaining ruins are high-walled and atmospheric, surrounded by lawns and topiary. In 1685 the remains of a rare Norman lavatorium were discovered. A 13th-century church and Norman chapter house have also survived as substantial ruins.

86 Worcester Cathedral

☎ 01905 28854
College Green, Worcester WR1 2LH
Website: www.worcs.com/cathed.htm
Open *8.30–6.30*

A new cathedral was built here by the Severn by St Wulfstan in the Norman style in 1084–9, but only the crypt remains. Mainly Early English and

Norman Moats and Gothic Spires CENTRAL

Perpendicular style (especially its windows), the cathedral was remodelled in the 19th century, with the result that the exterior looks almost entirely Victorian. The choir is a masterpiece of the Early English style; the late Victorian choir stalls incorporate medieval misericords which have unique carvings on them of life in the Middle Ages, including scenes of a naked woman riding on a goat, a butcher killing a Carolingian ox, and knights jousting. Worcester's finest monument is the tomb built out of Purbeck marble to house the remains of King John, the oldest royal effigy in the country, which lies in the chancel by the high altar. There is also a fine 14th-century tomb, with painted effigies, for the Beauchamp family in the nave.

It is worth trying to visit in August when, for the purposes of cleaning, the nave is emptied of all its seats and pews, returning the space to something closer to its medieval condition.

ADDITIONAL PLACES TO VISIT

Buildwas Abbey EH
☎ 01952 433274
Ironbridge, Telford, Shropshire TF8 7BW
2m W of Ironbridge on A4169
Open *Apr–Sept 11–5*
The Cistercian abbey was founded in 1135. Broadly Norman, it is a well-preserved ruin but without a roof.

Bushmead Priory EH
☎ 01234 376614
Colmworth, nr Bedford, Bedfordshire MK44 2LD
2m N of Bolnhurst off B660
Open *July–Aug Sat Sun & BHs 10–1 2–6*
An Augustinian priory whose refectory still stands, complete with timber roof and a collection of fascinating wall paintings and stained glass.

Chester Cathedral
☎ 01244 324756
Abbey Square, Chester CH1 2HU
Website: www.chestercathedral.org.uk
In city centre
Open *8–6.30*
Started life as a Benedictine abbey, but survived the Dissolution of the Monasteries as an Anglican cathedral.

Clun Castle EH
Clun, Shropshire
In Clun off A488, 18m W of Ludlow
Open *Any reasonable time*
The fabulous setting for the ruins of a Norman keep once belonging to a border castle dating back to the 11th century. There is a large low motte (mound) with two baileys or open space courtyards. It was converted into a stone castle in the 12th century.

Deddington Castle EH
Deddington, Oxfordshire
S of B4031 on E side of Deddington, 17m N of Oxford on A423; 5m S of Banbury
Open *Any reasonable time*
The 12th-century castle was destroyed in the 14th century and is visible now only as extensive earthworks.

Dudley Zoo and Castle
☎ 01384 215300
2 The Broadway, Dudley DY1 4QB
Website: www.dudleyzoo.org.uk
On A461, 3m from M5 junction 2
Open *Daily Mar–Sept 10–4, Oct–Feb 10–3*
A 13th-century hilltop castle right in the middle of Dudley. Originally a motte-and-bailey castle, it was destroyed by Henry II during a rebellion led by one of his sons. It was then rebuilt by Roger de Somery and his son John. The Dudley family took it over during the reign of Henry VIII and spent lavishly on its refurbishment. It is believed they even

minted their own coins within the grounds. An impressive ruin in the midst of Dudley Zoo.

Haughmond Abbey EH
☎ 01743 709661
Uffington, nr Shrewsbury,
Shropshire SY4 4RW
3m NE of Shrewsbury off B5062
Open *Apr–Sept 11–5*
The 12th-century Augustinian abbey is now mostly in ruins, but the timber ceiling has survived, as well as pieces of medieval sculpture.

Hellens
☎ 01531 660504
Much Marcle, nr Ledbury,
Herefordshire HR8 2LY
4m S of Ledbury off A449
Open *Good Fri–Sept Wed Sat Sun & BH Mons for guided tours only at 2, 3 & 4*
A stone manor house dating from 1292, built by the Earl of March on the east side of Much Marcle. It contains a stone table at which the Black Prince is supposed to have once eaten. There is also a pigeon coop dating from 1641.

Langley Chapel EH
Acton Burnell, Shropshire
1½m S of Acton Burnell, on unclassified road 4m E of A49, 9½m S of Shrewsbury
Open *Any reasonable time*
There is a medieval chapel, set in a field. Also a collection of late 17th-century wooden fittings and furniture.

Lilleshall Abbey EH
Lilleshall, Oakengates, Shropshire
On unclassified road off A518, 4m N of Oakengates
Open *Any reasonable time*
This Augustinian ruin has the remains of the cloisters and a 13th-century church surrounded by lawns and yews.

Oakham Castle
☎ 01572 758440
The Marketplace, Oakham,
Rutland LE15 6HW
Website: www.rutnet.co.uk
Near town centre, E of the church
Open *Apr–Oct Mon–Sat 10–5 Sun 1–5, Nov–Mar Mon–Sat 10–4 Sun 1–4; closed weekdays all year 1–1.30*
The castle boasts a Norman great hall with the country's finest collection of horseshoes, forfeited by both royalty and peerage to the Lord of the Manor of Rutland over the centuries. There are also remains of the earlier motte.

Peveril Castle EH
☎ 01433 620613
Market Place, Castleton, Hope Valley,
Derbyshire S33 8WQ
S side of Castleton, 15m W of Sheffield on A6187
Open *Apr–Sept 10–6, Oct 10–5, Nov–Mar Wed–Sun 10–4*
Begun in the 1090s by William Peverel, a knight of William the Conqueror, it was later confiscated by Henry II, who was rightly paranoid about letting his barons build themselves powerful castles. In 1176 he added the square tower, which still stands almost to its original height. There are spectacular views from the castle of the surrounding Peak District.

Priory Cottages NT
☎ 01793 762209
1 Mill Street, Steventon, Abingdon,
Oxfordshire OX13 6SP
4m S of Abingdon on B4017, off A34 at Abingdon West or Milton interchange
Open *The Great Hall in South Cottage only; Apr–Sept Wed 2–6 by written appointment*
Two houses have been built out of what were former monastic buildings. In South Cottage are the remains of the great hall of the original priory.

St Briavel's Castle EH

☎ 01594 530272

YHA, The Castle, St Briavel's, Lydney,
Gloucestershire GL15 6RG

Email: stbriavels@yha.org.uk

Website: www.yha.org.uk

*In St Briavel's village, off B4228,
7m NE of Chepstow*

Open *Exterior: any reasonable time.
Bailey: Apr–Sept 1–4*

One 13th-century gatehouse with two
towers survives of this Norman fortress,
prison and court for the Forest of Dean.
It was where arrowheads were made
for Henry III, a local speciality in the
Middle Ages.

Stafford Castle

☎ 01785 257698

Newport Road, Stafford ST16 1DJ

On N side of A518, 1½m from town centre

Open *Apr–Oct Tues–Sun & BHs 10–5,
Nov–Mar Tues–Sun 10–4*

A Norman motte-and-bailey that was
demolished after the Civil War. A building
was reconstructed in the 19th century
but that, too, fell into rack and ruin.
The impressive castle remains are still
part intact.

Tamworth Castle

☎ 01827 709626

The Holloway, Tamworth,
Staffordshire B79 7LR

In town centre, off A51

Open *Mon–Fri 10–5.30 Sat & Sun 12–5.30*

The imposing Norman castle was built
on an earlier Saxon mound, originally
raised by King Alfred's daughter, and
within are Tudor and Jacobean buildings.
There are over a dozen rooms open to the
public. Tamworth was once the capital
of the Saxon kingdom of Mercia, where
Offa (757–96), one of their most famous
kings who built Offa's Dyke (p28) to consolidate his kingdom, held court.

Wales MAP 5

87 Beaumaris Castle* CADW

☎ 01248 810361

Castle Street, Beaumaris,
Anglesey LL58 8AP

*5m NE of Menai Bridge (A5) by A545,
7m from Bangor*

Open *Apr–May 9.30–5, June–Sept 9.30–6,
Oct 9.30–5, Nov–Mar 9.30–4; opens
11 on Sun*

With its beautiful moat, this was the last of
Edward I's 10-castle 'stone-collar' stranglehold over Wales. Never completed (the
money ran out) nor involved in a military
episode, it remains the best-preserved
example of a concentric castle, a design
inherited from the Byzantine Empire.

It was built to stand guard over the
Menai Strait back when this was actually
fordable at low tide. Designed in 1295
by Master James of St George, Edward's
genius of a military engineer, it is almost
perfectly symmetrical, something that only
really becomes obvious in photographs
taken from directly above. The point of
the symmetry was not to be aesthetically
pleasing but to maximize the defensive
capabilities, allowing the minimum
number of defenders the maximum
area of covering firepower, and to avoid
the weakness of the blind corners you
get in rectangular structures.

88 Caernarfon Castle* CADW

☎ 01286 677617

Castle Ditch, Caernarfon,
Gwynedd LL55 2AY

In Caernarfon, just W of town centre

Open *Apr–May 9.30–5, June–Sept 9.30–6,
Oct 9.30–5, Nov–Mar 9.30–4; opens
11 on Sun*

Begun in 1283, it was the most famous
of the castles which Edward I had built in
Wales. Its brutal military role is somewhat belied now by being so picturesquely

*The towers with bands of colour, inspired by the walls of Constantinople, at **Caernarfon Castle**.*

framed by the boats moored in front of it. Samuel Johnson described it as 'an edifice of stupendous majesty and strength'. The 18th-century Welsh antiquarian, Thomas Pennant, however, described it as 'the magnificent badge of our servitude'. They were both right.

Edward always intended that it should be a symbol of his conquest of Wales and a fortress guarding the Menai Strait. It was no coincidence that he chose this site for the castle: Caernarfon, or Segontium (p34) as it was then known, was where the Romans had administered Wales before him; it was perfect for a king who saw himself as a new Caesar rebuilding an imperial Britannia. For that very reason, he embedded waves of different coloured stone in the outer walls, to echo those of the walls built at Constantinople by the Emperor

Theodosius II in the 5th century, a site he saw as a crusader. To consolidate the idea of a new Rome, the year 1283 also saw the 'discovery' at Conwy of the bones of Emperor Magnus Maximus (the father of Constantine the Great), which Edward reburied at Segontium, another demonstration that a 'superior' civilization was now running Wales.

The castle adopted an hour-glass plan around an earlier Norman motte which the Welsh had occupied for more than a century until Edward drove them out. While the castle was only half-finished at the time of Edward's death in 1307, it was already a formidable place. Upper and lower shooting galleries gave the battlements their defensive power, from which missiles smashed on to attackers' heads. Caernarfon also has the most impressive towers (the Queen's

Tower and the Eagle Tower are the largest) giving amazing views of the surrounding town and countryside.

Edward was equally interested in cultural and military conquest. He was the first king to turn his eldest son into the new Prince of Wales. It was a brilliant tactic that still persists. In 1969, it was Prince Charles' turn to be invested with the title, at Caernarfon.

89 Caerphilly Castle CADW
☎ 02920 883143
Caerphilly CF8 1JL
Website: www.caerphillycastle.com
A468 from Newport; A470 from Cardiff; in centre of Caerphilly
Open *Apr–May 9.30–5, June–Sept 9.30–6, Oct 9.30–5, Nov–Mar 9.30–4; opens 11 on Sun*

In a country full of huge castles, it takes something pretty impressive to be the biggest, an honour that belongs to this stupefying immensity of stone towers and battlements. It was built on three artificial islands, and an entire 30-acre valley was flooded giving a combination of land and water defences that were among the most advanced of its day. No other British castle covers anything like the same area of ground.

The masonry is of a particularly high standard. It was one of the first castles to be built on a concentric design, a plan which then flourished in North Wales and further afield. It was never taken in war, and not even the Parliamentarians could 'slight' it during the Civil War. It has, most famously, a broken and dangerously leaning tower.

Caerphilly Castle, *built by the Anglo-Norman lord Gilbert de Clare in the late 13th century.*

90 Conwy Castle★ CADW

☎ 01492 592358
Rose Hill Street, Conwy LL32 8AY
In Conwy by A55 or B5106
Open *Apr–May 9.30–5, June–Sept 9.30–6, Oct 9.30–5, Nov–Mar 9.30–4; opens 11 on Sun*

Conwy Castle dominates the entire townscape at its feet. Sitting as it does at the end of the bridge over which you approach the town, you can appreciate Edward I's fortress from miles away; it is one of the most impressive in the country. Equally imposing are the city walls that girdle the entire town; they remain one of the best examples of such urban defences. Conwy demonstrates how castles were often integrated with the adjacent town; not all were isolated citadels of terror. The castle itself has a pattern similar to that of Caernarfon, being shaped to fit the rock on which it is built. It lacks the geometrical precision of castles like Beaumaris but its battlements are enormously impressive, and a circuit through the eight great drum towers is a thrilling experience.

91 Flint Castle CADW

☎ 02920 826185
Flint, Flintshire
Off A548 & short walk from edge of town
Open *10–4*

One of the earliest castles built by Edward I during his campaigns against Llywelyn ap Gruffydd ('the Last'), in 1277. It has an unusually strong and massive round tower placed outside one corner of its curtain walls, connected to the main structure by a drawbridge. The design was unique among Welsh castles, being based around a main central keep made up of two concentric shells. The structure strongly echoes the Tour de Constance in Aigues Mortes in Provence which, as a prince, Edward would have

Harlech Castle *sits spectacularly on a rocky outcrop, with Snowdonia's peaks beyond.*

seen on his way to fight in the Crusades. It was here, in 1399, that Richard II was captured by Henry Bolingbroke, the future Henry IV.The ruin, though impressive, is only a shadow of past grandeur.

92 Harlech Castle* CADW
☎ 01766 780552
Castle Square, Harlech,
Gywnedd LL46 2YH
On A496 coast road
Open *Apr–May 9.30–5, June–Sept 9.30–6, Oct 9.30–5, Nov–Mar 9.30–4; opens 11 on Sun*

Having established his control over Wales, Edward I did not relax his efforts. Instead, he engaged in building a second round of castles to help him strengthen that grip. They became four of his most ambitious creations, and are among the biggest castles built anywhere in Britain. They were at Beaumaris, Caernarfon, Conwy and Harlech. While Beaumaris took a leisurely 35 years to complete, Harlech was done at breakneck pace – finished in 8 years, at a huge cost.

It was designed and built by Master James of St George, who presumably supervised the work personally. It has a simple but formidable design, the classic box within a box designed with one purpose, to keep the enemy out. There was a high inner wall, huge round towers, a deep moat to the south and east, and a sheer drop to the west. On top of that, Harlech boasts a massive gatehouse tower in the east wall, a fortress in its own right. In the end it proved almost impossible to take by storm. In the great revolt of 1294, a garrison of barely 37 men held off the assault of an entire Welsh army. During the Wars of the Roses it was besieged for eight long years, a struggle that inspired the song 'Men of Harlech'. It was the last Royalist castle to fall to Parliament in the Civil War.

93 Pembroke Castle
☎ 01646 681510
Pembroke, Pembrokeshire SA71 4LA
Website: www.pembrokecastle.co.uk
10m E of Milford Haven off A477; in Pembroke at W end of the main street
Open *Apr–Sept 9.30–6, Mar & Oct 10–5, Nov–Feb 10–4*

A Norman castle which was founded in 1093 by Roger of Montgomery and almost completely rebuilt in the first half of the 13th century by William the Marshal and his family. Its great round tower, 75ft (23m) high, was built in 1204; it was remodelled around a triangular structure, protected by surrounding water. Later the castle was the birthplace of the future Henry VII (in 1457), the victor against Richard III at the Battle of Bosworth in 1485.

Pembroke had a bad Civil War thanks, in 1648, to a turncoat general who switched from the Parliamentarian side. The full wrath of Oliver Cromwell came crashing down on his head as cannon-fire reduced the outer walls to rubble. However, the inner tower surrendered only after an act of treachery resulted in the water supply being cut off, though it cost the traitor a one-way trip down the well when the defenders discovered his identity.

ADDITIONAL PLACES TO VISIT

Cardiff Castle
☎ 02920 878100
Castle Street, Cardiff CF10 3RB
In city centre
Open *Mar–Oct 9.30–6, Nov–Feb 9.30–4.30*

Founded by the Normans in the 11th century in the corner of what had been a Roman fortress, a 12-sided shell keep was added in the 12th century. Its most famous inhabitant was Henry I's elder brother, Robert Curthose, Duke of Normandy, imprisoned here until his death in his eighties, after losing a series of squabbles over who should be the next king of England. Further additions took place in the 13th century on the orders of the great de Clare family who divided it into an inner and an outer ward, with a great wall that joined the Black Tower to the keep. The biggest overhaul was completed in the Victorian period – to which we owe the ornate Clock Tower.

Castell y Bere CADW

☎ 02920 826185
Abergynolyn, nr Tywyn, Gwynedd
6m from Tywyn on B4405, signposted
Open *Access at all times*
It would be wrong to suppose that only the English built castles in Wales. Though they never had quite the same importance as they did for the Anglo-Normans, there were still a number built by Welsh princes and warlords, of which this is a particularly fine example and certainly the most dramatic. It was begun in 1221 by Llywelyn ap Iorwerth (Llywelyn the Great) to secure his southern border. All in all, he built five similar castles; the others are at Ewloe, Dolbadarn, Criccieth and Dolwyddelan. Ewloe (near Wrexham) is particularly well preserved.

It has two D-shaped towers, something characteristic of Welsh castles, but is now a ruin, albeit in a beautiful, remote setting. In 1283, Edward I paid it the supreme compliment when he laid siege and stormed it.

Chepstow Castle CADW

☎ 01291 624065
Chepstow, Monmouthshire NP16 5EY
In Chepstow off M48
Open *Apr–May 9.30–5, June–Sept 9.30–6, Oct 9.30–5, Nov–Mar 9.30–4; opens 11 on Sun*

This was the first great stone tower to be built after the Norman Conquest, and was occupied in 1071. It was located on a strategic ridge, along which the substantial castle extensions were all later built. The most important were begun in 1189 when William the Marshal built the wall that divides the middle and lower baileys (inner open spaces). It was he who carried out further major works. It later passed to Roger Bigod, Earl of Norfolk, and his son made further significant additions in preparation for a visit by Edward I in 1285. Despite falling to the Parliamentarians during the Civil War, it avoided the fate of so many other fortifications and was spared destruction. Henry Marten, one of the men who signed Charles I's death warrant, was imprisoned here after the Restoration and died here in 1680.

Chirk Castle NT

☎ 01691 777701
Chirk, Wrexham LL14 5AF
Email: gcwmsn@smtp.ntrust.org.uk
8m S of Wrexham off A483
Open *Apr–Oct Wed–Sun & BHs*
Castle: 12–5; closes at 4 in Oct
Gardens: 11–6; closes at 5 in Oct
This tough medieval fortress was built during the reigns of Edward I and II by the Mortimer family. It was besieged during the Civil War. One of the few castles of this era, complete with great round towers, still being lived in, it has been transformed into a stately home. Offa's Dyke ran through the grounds.

Cilgerran Castle CADW & NT

☎ 01239 615007
Nr Cardigan, Pembrokeshire SA43 2SF
3m SE of Cardigan
Open *Apr–Oct 9.30–6.30, Nov–Mar 9.30–4*
The 12th–13th-century castle ruins overlook the River Teifi, and are protected

on two sides by steep cliffs. The castle's position guaranteed, however, that it would be in the thick of things, and during the long period of warfare along the Anglo-Welsh border it swapped hands half a dozen times. The two huge cylindrical towers and the square gatehouse were built in the 13th century.

Coity Castle CADW
☎ 01656 664931
2 Morfa St, Bridgend CF31 1HA
3m from Bridgend off A4061
Open *Mon–Sat 11.30–11 Sun 12–10.30*
Originally a wooden palisaded castle, it was converted into a stone fortress in the 12th century. Later a second enclosure was added to the western side, just as well because it was besieged by Owain Glyndwr (whom it successfully resisted).

Criccieth Castle CADW
☎ 01766 522227
Castle Street, Criccieth, Gwynedd LL52 0DP
A497 to Criccieth from Porthmadog
Open *Apr–May 10–5, June–Sept 10–6, Nov–Mar open site*
This was a Welsh castle that had an English one added to it in 1292 by Edward I. During the Welsh rising of 1294 it needed only a tiny garrison to withstand an attack (a constable, 10 crossbowmen, and 4 maintenance men plus a chaplain), thanks to its proximity to its supply route across the sea. Its gatehouse resembles that of Harlech. The location is as spectacular as the castle.

Denbigh Castle CADW
☎ 01745 813385
Denbigh, Denbighshire
Denbigh via A525 or B5382
Open *Apr–Oct Mon–Fri 10–5.30 Sat & Sun 9.30–5.30*

A 13th-century castle ruin built in the reign of Edward I by Henry de Lacy (legend says he ceased work on it when his son fell into the well and drowned). This was what was called a 'lordship' castle, ie built by an aristocrat with royal permission and assistance. Like so many, Denbigh was built on confiscated Welsh land, and had a town attached to it. It saw action during the Welsh revolt of 1294, before being recaptured by the English. Further building work was done in the 14th and 15th centuries. Its most impressive structures are its hexagonal and octagonal towers, and its great gatehouse, comprising three octagonal towers arranged in a triangle. It later became a Royalist stronghold during the Civil War, and in 1646 endured a six-month siege, before finally surrendering.

Kidwelly Castle CADW
☎ 01554 890104
Kidwelly, Carmarthenshire SA17 5BG
Kidwelly via A484
Open *Apr–May 9.30–5, June–Sept 9.30–6, Oct 9.30–5, Nov–Mar 9.30–4; opens 11 on Sun*
Similar to Caerphilly in being constructed around a concentric design (although this one was completed later, in the 1270s). It played a full role in the skirmishes that characterized medieval life in this part of Wales, so full, in fact, that it is believed to be the most fought-over castle in Britain. It was designed to offer defence against attacks from the surrounding hills (it is situated on a plain), and was located near an estuary head to ensure a continual supply of food during a siege.

Manorbier Castle
☎ 01834 871394
Manorbier, Pembrokeshire SA70 7TB
SW of Tenby off A4139
Open *Easter weekend–Sept 10.30–5.30*

This well-preserved castle is the reputed birthplace in 1146 of Gerald of Wales, the 12th-century Welsh-speaking Norman historian and cleric who described very eloquently the pleasures of growing up here, with fishpond and orchards. Most of the contents appear to have been looted during local rioting in 1330.

Rhuddlan Castle CADW
☎ 01745 590777
Castle Street, Rhuddlan, Denbighshire LL18 5AD
SW end of Rhuddlan via A525 or A547
Open *Apr–Sept 10–5*
Another of Edward I's castles, built by his genius engineer, Master James of St George, from 1277–82. Its proximity to the sea was enhanced by a 2-mile-long channel diverting the Clwyd which protects the unmoated side. It was from here that Edward organized his administration of Wales. The concentric curtain walls and twin gatehouses enclose a square, and the moat is fed by the sea. It is now a ruin, thanks to Oliver Cromwell who besieged it towards the end of the Civil War. It is not as well preserved as the other great Edwardian Welsh castles.

St David's Cathedral
☎ 01437 720691
St David's, Pembrokeshire SA62 6QW
Email: tours@stdavidscathedral.org.uk
Website: www.stdavidscathedral.org.uk
A487 from Haverfordwest or Fishgaurd
Open *All year 7.30–6.30, Sun 12.30–5.30*
This gem of a cathedral is built near to the traditional birthplace of Wales' patron saint, St David, marked by the chapel of St Non. The cathedral was started around 1180 and work continued for three centuries. The nave is in the late Norman style, with rounded arches, and there is a wonderful 15th-century wooden roof. Nearby lie the ruins of the 14th-century

Bishop's Palace, built by Bishop Henry de Gower, which even in decay show the trappings of wealth and influence enjoyed by the bishops of St David's in the Middle Ages.

Valle Crucis Abbey* CADW
☎ 01978 860326
Abbey Rd, Llangollen, Denbighshire
B5103 from A5, 2m NW of Llangollen, or A542 from Ruthin
Open *Easter–Sept 10–5, winter any reasonable time*
Like so many abbeys, particularly the ruined ones, Valle Crucis enjoys a beautiful location, one of the finest in North Wales, deep in its enclosing valley. Another Cistercian abbey left to rot after the Dissolution in the 16th century, it is very well preserved.

White Castle CADW
☎ 01600 780380
Llantilio Crossenny, Monmouthshire NP7 8UD
6m NE of Abergavenny off B4233
Open *Apr–Sept 10–5, winter open access*
The castle once had white plastered walls, hence its name. Otherwise, it is an almost perfect example of a medieval castle with high walls, towers and moat.

North-west MAP 6
94 Brough Castle EH
Brough, Cumbria
7m SE of Appleby off A685
Open *Any reasonable time*
'If this castle does not yield, no one shall be let out alive when it falls.' This was the instruction given by William the Lion, king of the Scots (c1142–1214) and Scottish raider, as he laid siege to Brough in 1174. He got his castle in the end, though nobody knows what happened to those defending it. He was captured

in Alnwick Castle shortly after and had to submit to a humiliating peace. Another beautifully perched castle, it now stands guard over the A66. It was much restored in the 17th century by Lady Anne Clifford, who transformed the tower into a gracious residence.

95 Carlisle Castle* EH
☎ 01228 591922
Carlisle, Cumbria CA3 8UR
In Carlisle at N end of city centre
Open *Apr–Sept 9.30–6, Oct 10–5, Nov–Mar 10–4*
This is one of those castles that has everything: there is a bewildering network of staircases, passages, chambers, towers and ramparts; some of the medieval rooms have been furnished as they might have been in the Middle Ages;

and the castle was involved in all the conflicts that raged through the region. Robert the Bruce laid siege to it; Mary Queen of Scots was imprisoned here; it was captured by the Scots during the Civil War; and later, Bonnie Prince Charlie again seized it from English hands. One of his Scots stayed behind after he abandoned it, and the avenging Duke of Cumberland executed him, though not before he had penned the immortal song 'Loch Lomond' (the 'high road' being the gallows).

96 Furness Abbey EH
☎ 01229 823420
Barrow-in-Furness, Cumbria LH13 0TJ
1½m NE of Barrow-in-Furness
Open *Apr–Sept 10–6, Oct 10–5, Nov–Mar Wed–Sun 10–1 2–4*

The sturdy arches of the cloister within **Furness Abbey**.

The second largest Cistercian abbey in England was founded in 1123 by Stephen before he became king. Its proximity to the Scottish border meant it took a hammering from various raids but it still became a successful, wealthy base. The extensive ruins include the church's west tower, choir and transept.

97 Lanercost Priory EH
☎ 01697 73030
Lanercost, Brampton, Cumbria CA8 2HQ
Off minor road S of Lanercost,
2m NE of Brampton
Open *Apr–Sept 10–6, Oct 10–5*
This 1166 Augustinian priory was built largely from stone taken from nearby Hadrian's Wall. The guest house among the ruins was used by both Edward I and Robert the Bruce. The nave has survived well enough to be used as a parish church; adjacent are the ruined remains of the chancel, transepts and priory buildings.

98 Penrith Castle EH
Penrith, Cumbria
Opposite Penrith railway station
21m S of Carlisle on M6 & A592
Open *Park & castle: Apr–Sept 7.30–9,*
Oct–Mar 7.30–4.30
The 14th-century castle, set in a park, was built by the bishops of Carlisle to repel endless raids by the Scots. It was less fortunate in the Civil War when it was dismantled by the Parliamentarians.

ADDITIONAL PLACES TO VISIT

Beeston Castle EH
☎ 01829 260464
Beeston, Tarporley, Cheshire CW6 9TX
11 miles SE of Chester
on minor road off A49 or A41
Open *Apr–Sept 10–6, Oct 10–5,*
Nov–Mar 10–4

Built from *c*1226 by Ranulf de Blundeville, 6th Earl of Chester. Nobody could fault his choice of spectacular location. Perched on a 500ft (152m)-high rock of red sandstone, it has views of the surrounding terrain possibly unrivalled by any other castle in the country.

Brougham Castle EH
☎ 01768 862488
Penrith, Cumbria CA10 2AA
1½m SE of Penrith on minor road off A66
Open *Apr–Sept 10–6, Oct 10–5*
Built sometime between 1157–73 and passing into Lady Anne Clifford's possession. It was one of a number of castles that she paid to have restored, and it was here that she later died, in 1676, in her eighties. The ruins are themselves pretty impressive, and include the 13th-century keep.

North-east MAP 7

99 Alnwick Castle
☎ 01665 511100
Alnwick, Northumberland NE66 1NQ
Email: enquiries@alnwickcastle.com
Website: www.alnwickcastle.com
In Alnwick, 1½m W of A1
Open *Apr–Oct 11–5*
A Border castle in the possession of the Percy family since 1309, it is constructed from curtain walls around two baileys. For years, it occupied an exposed position between the English and Scottish borders; its alliances and loyalties swung north and south depending on prevailing circumstances.

There was considerable later restoration and embellishment, especially during the 18th century (by Robert Adam) and 19th (the Prudhoe Tower). Most fun are the stone soldiers placed on the battlements as decoys designed to fool enemy forces. (The present-day ones are 18th-century replicas of their medieval originals.) Featured in the movie version of *Harry Potter*, Alnwick stands in for the Hogwarts' School.

100 Bamburgh Castle*

☎ 01668 214515

Bamburgh, Northumberland NE65 7SP
Website: www.bamburghcastle.com
*20m S of Berwick upon Tweed, 6m E
of Belford by B1342 from A1 at Belford*
Open *Apr–Oct 11–5*

More photography prizes are awarded to pictures of Bamburgh than virtually any other English castle. This is due to the combination of its almost perfect silhouette, and its location on the horizon of a beautiful stretch of tide-hardened sand, especially stunning in the early light of dawn.

It was always a key defensive point on the north-east coast. There was an Anglo-Saxon fortification on this site when the Normans arrived at the end of the 11th century. William II found it a tough nut to crack when he laid siege to it in 1095. Later, in the Middle Ages, it fell into the hands of the Percys, who used it to menace generations of kings. In the 19th century it had to suffer some rather whimsical additions in a pseudo-baronial style, courtesy of arms millionaire Lord Armstrong.

Bamburgh Castle, *a centre of power for the Northern earls in the Middle Ages.*

101 Beverley Minster

☎ 01482 868540
Minster Yard North, Beverley,
E Yorkshire HU17 0DP
Email: minster@beverleyminster.co.uk
Website: www.beverleyminster.co.uk
In town centre, 4m N of Hull
Open *Summer 9–6, rest of year 9–5
(closes at 4 if very dark)*
Judging it by its size, you'd think this
was a cathedral. Actually, it's the largest
parish church in England. It was a place
of pilgrimage for many centuries for those
who shared a faith in the miracles of
St John of Beverley. It has a magnificent
Perpendicular-style west front, and
contains a wealth of carvings in wood
and stone, most notably, the 14th-century
Percy tomb. Records show that it was
a popular sanctuary for medieval
criminals: 469 tried to avoid justice by
coming here between 1478 and 1539.

102 Clifford's Tower* EH

☎ 01904 646940
Tower Street, York, N Yorkshire YO1 1SA
York city centre
Open *Apr–June 10–6, July–Aug 9.30–7,
Sept 10–6, Oct 10–5, Nov–Mar 10–4*
Constructed by William the Conqueror
to help hold York, this is the only
surviving tower on one of two mottes
(mounds), offering fabulous views of the
surrounding city. It dates to the 13th
century, the original wooden Norman
keep having been destroyed in the riots
against the Jews of 1190.

103 Conisbrough Castle EH

☎ 01709 863329
Conisbrough, Doncaster,
S Yorkshire DN12 3BU
Email: info@conisbroughcastle.org.uk
Website: www.conisbroughcastle.org.uk
4½m SW of Doncaster
Open *Apr–Sept 10–5 , Oct 10–4*

One of the oldest circular keeps in
England, Conisbrough also features
one of the earliest uses of round turrets.
It has survived as one of the country's
most forbidding fortresses. Its 100ft
(30m) great tower was built by Hamelin
Plantagenet, half-brother of Henry II,
in the 1180s, on a mound overlooking
the River Trent. It is four storeys high,
with six immense buttresses and walls
15ft (5m) thick. What must have made
living here so hard was that the tower
lacks virtually any windows; the entrance
chamber had no openings at all except
for the door, and the tower would have
filled with the smoke from the torches
needed to provide illumination.

Everything about its structure was
designed to make it impregnable, not
comfortable (what a contrast to nearby
Richmond Castle). There was an elaborate
system of outer walls, moats, portcullises,
and inner baileys. The chapel was ingen-
iously fitted into a hexagonal space
between the walls and one of the buttresses. However, it was still captured by
force in 1317 during fighting between
the owner John de Warenne, Earl of
Surrey, and Thomas, Earl of Lancaster.

104 Durham Castle

☎ 0191 374 3863
Palace Green, Durham DH1 3RW
Website: www.dur.ac.uk
City centre, adjacent to cathedral
Open *Mar–Sept 10–5, Oct–Mar 2–4*
Lying to the north of the famous cathedral,
and sharing the same dramatic outcrop,
its earliest buildings date from around
1072. There were many magnificent
buildings added later, but of the remains
nothing beats the main entrance to the
hall, perhaps the most ornate piece of
Norman work anywhere in the country.

The great hall belongs to the 13th
century. Much of the castle was restored in

the 19th century for use by the university. The castle and the cathedral together constitute arguably the finest Norman achievement in architecture in the country, if not Europe.

105 Durham Cathedral *

☎ 0191 386 4266
Palace Green, Durham DH1 3EH
Email: enquiries@durhamcathedral.co.uk
Website: www.durhamcathedral.co.uk
Durham city centre
Open *Oct–June Mon–Sat 10–5 Sun 12.30–3, July–Sept Mon–Sat 9.30–8 Sun 12.30–8; restricted access during services*
Norman cathedrals do not get any better than Durham's. It was begun in 1093, with most of it complete four decades later. You could not invent a better or more dramatic location for a cathedral. Once inside, it is the columns that you immediately notice not just for their immensity (22ft/6.7m in girth), but for their wonderful zig-zag patterns. The high rib-vaulted roof was ahead of its time (later to become a standard feature in Gothic construction). It has far fewer memorials and tombs than other cathedrals, but one of the more moving memorials is dedicated to generations of Durham miners. The cathedral interior doubled as Elizabeth's court in the recent film *Elizabeth*, starring Cate Blanchett.

The wonderful site for the cathedral, tucked inside a horseshoe bend in the River Wear, was used by monks fleeing the Viking raids on Lindisfarne (p37); they arrived here carrying the bones of their patron saint, Cuthbert. They brought him to his final resting place after much meandering in 995 when they founded a Benedictine monastery here. The saint's bones were moved to a place behind the altar when the Saxon church was swept away and replaced by the larger Norman cathedral. There is a Galilee Chapel (instead of the more usual Lady Chapel which was abandoned after several attempts to build it ended in failure). The chapel contains the bones of the Venerable Bede who died in 735; the bones were stolen from his tomb in Jarrow (p36) by a monk and brought here in 1022. Scottish prisoners of war, incarcerated here after the Battle of Worcester in 1650, burned many of the moveable wooden stalls to keep warm.

106 Finchdale Priory EH

☎ 0191 386 3828
Newton Hall, Co Durham DH1 5SH
3m NE of Durham off A167
Open *Apr–Sept 10–6*
Founded in 1237 on the site of St Godric's hermitage (he had been drawn to this site by a vision, and apparently lived here till the age of 105), it is now alas a ruin. For a while it served as a holiday home for the monks from Durham Cathedral but couldn't avoid becoming a victim of the Dissolution of the Monasteries. The remains are extensive and substantial enough to trace quite clearly its evolution through a number of different phases, from its earliest origins to its medieval heyday. It has a beautiful location too.

107 Fountains Abbey * NT

☎ 01765 608888
Ripon, N Yorkshire HG4 3DY
Email: info@fountainsabbey.org.uk
Website: www.fountainsabbey.org.uk
4m SW of Ripon off B6265, 8m W of M1
Open *Apr–Sept 10–6, Oct–Mar 10–4 (Nov–Jan closed Fri)*
One of the most spectacular of ecclesiastical ruins, Fountains was abandoned in 1540 after four centuries of use as a Cistercian abbey. The magnificent nave, and its site on the banks of the River Skell, have combined to make this one of England's great medieval landmarks.

Its origins belonged to the efforts of a small breakaway group of monks determined to live a life of ordered austerity. By the end of the 13th century it was the richest Cistercian establishment in the country, thanks to the monks' skill as farmers (of sheep mainly). It fell to the Crown with the Dissolution of the Monasteries.

108 Mount Grace Priory EH & NT
☎ 01609 883494
Osmotherley, Northallerton,
N Yorkshire DL6 3JG
12m N of Thirsk,
7m NE of Northallerton on A19
Open *Apr–Sept 10–6, Oct 10–5,*
Nov–Mar Wed–Sun 10–1 2–4
Founded for Carthusian monks in 1398. Instead of living a communal life the monks all lived as hermits in separate dwellings flanking the central cloister, each with its own living room, study and bedroom.

109 Norham Castle* EH
☎ 01289 382329
Norham, Northumberland
Norham village, 7m SW of
Berwick-upon-Tweed off A698
Open *Apr–Sept 10–6*
Right on the Anglo-Scottish border just south of the Tweed, this great ruined stronghold was right on the medieval front line. It was owned by the bishops of Durham. It was the site of a number of Scottish sieges by David I, Alexander II, Robert the Bruce (twice) and James IV. The walls stand to their original height (which is considerable, especially when viewed from the bottom of the now grassed-over moat), but the interior is all but gone.

110 Pickering Castle* EH
☎ 01751 474989
Pickering, N Yorkshire YO18 7AX
In Pickering 15m SW of Scarborough

Open *Apr–Sept 10–6, Oct 10–5, Nov–Mar Wed–Sun 10–4; closed 1–2 all year*
These well-preserved Norman ruins are built on the site of an earlier motte-and-bailey castle raised shortly after the Norman Conquest. Only the chapel, postern gate, dungeon and three towers of the curtain walls now survive. There are spectacular views of the surrounding landscape.

The castle was deliberately situated near a royal hunting forest to provide the king with protection and shelter while out hunting game; also, more menacingly, it would have been the site from which the draconian forest laws would have been enforced.

111 Richmond Castle* EH
☎ 01748 822493
Tower Street, Richmond,
N Yorkshire DL10 4QW
In town centre
Open *Apr–Sept 10–6, Oct 10–5,*
Nov–Mar 10–1 2–4
One of the earliest stone fortresses built in England. It was actually begun while William the Conqueror was still king, though it was not completed until the 1150s. William the Lion of Scotland was temporarily a prisoner within its walls, but despite the intimidatingly impressive nature of its architecture, it saw hardly any real military action. It still dominates its corner of the Swale valley, with its 100ft (30m) towers.

112 Rievaulx Abbey* EH
☎ 01439 798228
Rievaulx, Helmsley,
N Yorkshire YO62 5LB
2½m W of Helmsley off B1257
Open *Apr–July 10–6, Aug 9.30–7,*
Sept 10–6, Oct 10–5, Nov–Mar 10–4
Rievaulx Abbey, founded *c*1131, had the largest Cistercian community in

Richmond Castle, *an early Norman castle that has been little damaged over the centuries.*

Britain in the 12th century (as well as the largest Cistercian nave in Britain). By the time of the Dissolution, however, the number of monks living here was probably no higher than 22. The Cistercian order liked its architecture to be austere, and Rievaulx is a classic example of this, evident even in the ruins. Ruins do not come much more perfect, largely because of the fabulous setting deep in a wooded valley, girdled by beautiful Yorkshire hills.

113 Selby Abbey
☎ 01757 703123
The Crescent, Selby, N Yorkshire YO8 4PU
Email: SelbyAbbeyYorks@aol.com
Website: www.selbyabbey.co.uk
*Abbey adjacent to market place
in Selby town centre*
Open *10–4*
It is amazing that anything medieval is still standing here; at the east end

of the nave the Norman arches look very distorted, thanks to foundations that slowly sank while this spectacular church was being built. In 1690 the tower collapsed, as happened to so many larger churches, demolishing the whole south transept. It was rebuilt. A fire in 1906 inflicted more significant damage (the bells came crashing to the floor when the roof went up in smoke) which was also later repaired.

Today, Selby Abbey is in perfect condition, making it one of the three greatest churches in Yorkshire, along with Beverley and York Minster. Its greatest treasure is its stained-glass window depicting the Tree of Jesse, at the east end of the church. In a building that has known so many calamities it is particularly extraordinary that its medieval glass has survived at all. Apparently the 1906 fire spared it, thanks to a last-minute change in wind direction.

114 Skipton Castle
☎ 01756 792442
Skipton, N Yorkshire BD23 1AQ
Email: info@skiptoncastle.co.uk
Website: www.skiptoncastle.co.uk
In centre of town at N end of High Street
Open *Mar–Sept 10–6, Oct–Feb 10–4;*
opens at 12 on Sun
By the late 13th century this Norman
castle had become a formidable stronghold. It has a particularly imposing
gatehouse flanked by huge towers. It
was owned until 1678 by the powerful
Clifford family (of Clifford's Tower in
York). It escaped the ultimate fate, being
'slighted' (razed to the ground) by
Cromwell, after its owner promised to
make it impossible for cannon to be fired
from it. This saved the roof from almost
certain destruction, and has helped
future generations preserve it as one of
Yorkshire's finest medieval castles. Inside
the gatehouse is the Shell Room, which
accommodates a collection of shells and
Jamaican coral believed to have been
assembled by George Clifford, 3rd Earl of
Cumberland, in the early 17th century.

115 Whitby Abbey EH
☎ 01947 603568
Whitby, N Yorkshire YO22 4JT
On clifftop E of Whitby
Open *Apr–Sept 10–6, Oct 10–5,*
Nov–Mar 10–4
These remains of an 11th-century Benedictine abbey are gloriously perched
above Whitby, the fictional location of
part of Bram Stoker's chiller *Dracula* (it
seems quite fitting). It has one of the
most easily recognizable silhouettes in
the north of England. The chancel and
the north transept have survived. Excavations have uncovered evidence of a
much earlier building on the same
spectacular site; an earlier monastery,
where the Synod of Whitby took place in
664, was destroyed by Vikings in 867.

116 York Minster*
☎ 01904 557216
Deangate, York, N Yorkshire YO1 7HH
Email: info@yorkminster.org
Website: www.yorkminster.org
In city centre
Open *Jan–Mar Nov & Dec 10–6,*
Apr 10–6.30, May 10–7.30, June–Aug
9.30–8.30, Sept 10–8, Oct 10–7
This is technically a cathedral, although
it retains its old Saxon title of minster
(it is the seat of the Archbishop of York).
There were several false starts to the
Normans' attempt to build a mighty
church on the site of a Roman adminis-
trative fortress, but finally the central
crypt was built (1154–68). From 1220
construction began of the minster as we
now know it. The scene was set for two
centuries of work that created one of the
world's greatest Gothic masterpieces.

The minster boasts a particularly fine
eight-sided chapter house, three great
towers (completed *c*1480) and a central
lantern. The choir screen is studded with
statues of medieval kings from William
the Conqueror to Henry VI. But none
of this touches what is York's real glory,
its stained glass, among the finest and
most expansive in the country. There are
over 100 windows, with glass from
virtually every century from the 12th to
the 20th. Luckily, York was the home
town of General Thomas Fairfax, the Parliamentary commander, which helps
explain why the minster got off so lightly
during the Civil War. It was less lucky in
the 19th century when it was hit by two
major fires. There was another disastrous
fire in 1984 in the south transept.

Whitby Abbey *stands high on a windswept clifftop, overlooking the town below.*

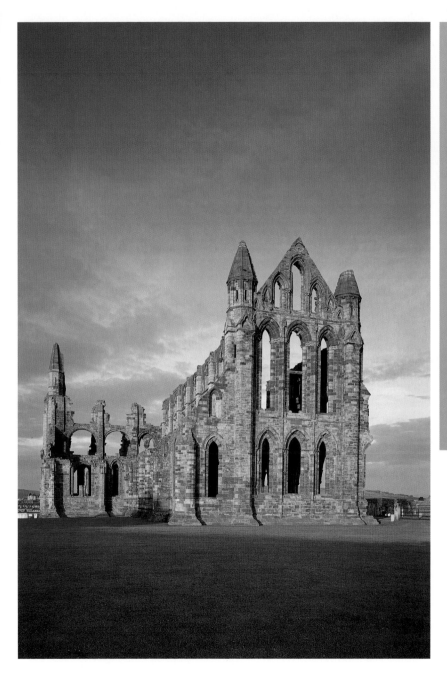

ADDITIONAL PLACES TO VISIT

Auckland Castle

☎ 01388 601627

Bishop Auckland, Co Durham DL14 7NR

Email: auckland.castle@zetnet.co.uk

Website: www.auckland-castle.co.uk

N end of town centre

Open *May–mid-July Fri & Sun,*
mid-July–Aug Sun–Fri, Sept Fri & Sun, also
BH Mons, all 2–5

Where the bishops of Durham have lived since Norman times (and continue to do so). A 12th-century banqueting hall became the chapel, making it reputedly the largest private chapel in Europe. A number of state rooms are open to the public, including the Throne Room, the Long Dining Room and the King Charles Dining Room. The medieval kitchens host an exhibition dedicated to the life of St Cuthbert.

Aydon Castle EH

☎ 01434 632450

Corbridge, Northumberland NE45 5PJ

1m NE of Corbridge off B6321 or A68

Open *Apr–Sept 10–6, Oct 10–5*

A fortified manor house, one of the finest in the country, dating from the 13th century. Luckily it was converted into a farmhouse in the 17th century which helped guarantee its survival.

Bolton Castle

☎ 01969 623981

Leyburn, N Yorkshire DL8 4ET

Website: www.boltoncastle.co.uk

Approx 6m from Leyburn,
1m NW of Redmire

Open *Apr–Sept 10–5, Oct–Mar 10–4*
(dusk if earlier)

This castle, begun in 1378 and now a fine ruin, once played host to Mary Queen of Scots, imprisoned here in 1569. Later, it received the attentions of Oliver Cromwell's cannons. Overlooking Wensleydale, there are magnificent views of the surrounding countryside.

Byland Abbey EH

☎ 01347 868614

Coxwold, Helmsley, N Yorkshire YO6 4BD

2m S of A170 between Helmsley & Thirsk,
NE of Coxwold village

Open *Apr–Sept 10–6, Oct 10–5; closed 1–2*

This 12th-century ruin was one of the great Cistercian abbeys of its time, but the Dissolution of the Monasteries did for it in 1536. It is famous for the medieval floor tiles in the church.

Chillingham Castle *

☎ 01668 215359

Nr Chillingham, Alnwick,

Northumberland NE66 5NJ

Email: info@chillingham-castle.com

Website: www.chillingham-castle.com

10m NW of Alnwick between A697 & A1,
2m S of B6348 at Chatton

Open *Easter, May–Sept Sun–Fri 12–5*

Fully restored in the 14th century, this 12th-century castle has had many later additions and embellishments. Like Alnwick, it played a central role in centuries of Border fighting and intrigue. Much of the surrounding grounds and gardens were added in the 19th century, giving the castle a lush, even extravagant feel. There are amazing views.

Chillingham Wild Cattle Park

☎ 01668 215250

Nr Chillingham, Alnwick,

Northumberland NE66 5NW

10m NW of Alnwick between A697 & A1,
off unmarked road S of B6348

Open *Apr–Oct 10–12 2–5 Sun 2–5;*
closed Tues

The park of over 350 acres is home to a unique herd of wild white cattle. They descend from a herd trapped in the park in the 13th century, and are the only pure breed of their kind. All visits have to be accompanied by a warden.

Easby Abbey* EH
Nr Richmond, N Yorkshire
1m SE of Richmond off B6271
Open *Any reasonable time*
The medieval abbey buildings are now substantial ruins on a beautiful site by the River Swale.

Egglestone Abbey EH
Barnard Castle, Co Durham
1½m SE of Barnard Castle on minor road off B6277
Open *Any reasonable time*
Picturesque ruins which are the remains of a 12th-century abbey on a remote spot near the River Tees. An imposing tomb of Sir Ralph Bowes (d1482) remains.

Helmsley Castle EH
☎ 01439 770442
Helmsley, N Yorkshire TO6 5AB
Near town centre
Open *Apr–Oct 10–6, Nov–Mar Wed–Sun 10–4; closed 1–2*
Only the square keep survives, all because it was on the wrong side during the Civil War when the Parliamentarian general, Thomas Fairfax, demolished most of it. It may have been begun by the man who founded nearby Rievaulx Abbey, Walter Espec, who died in 1154, but much of the earliest stonework dates from the 13th century.

Kirkham Priory* EH
☎ 01653 618768
Kirkham, Whitwell-on-the-Hill,
W Yorkshire YO6 7JS
5m SW of Malton on minor road off A64
Open *Apr–Sept 10–6, Oct 10–5; closed 1–2*
A magnificent carved gatehouse is all that remains of this Augustinian priory.

Knaresborough Castle
☎ 01423 556188
Knaresborough, N Yorkshire HG5 8AS
5m E of Harrogate off A59
Open *Good Fri–Sept 10.30–5*
Ruined 12th-century castle which fell foul of two turbulent moments in English history. Its great tower was demolished and replaced by a larger one in 1310, and it fell to the Parliamentarians in the Civil War. It contains a local history museum with a Tudor Court room and a gallery devoted to the Civil War.

Middleham Castle EH
☎ 01969 623899
Middleham, Leyburn, N Yorkshire DL8 4RJ
At Middleham, 2m S of Leyburn off A6108
Open *Apr–Sept 10–6, Oct 10–5, Nov–Dec 10–1 2–4, Jan–Mar Wed–Sun 10–1 2–4*
This is the castle that Richard III grew up in; from the massive 12th-century keep there are lovely views of Wensleydale.

Prudhoe Castle EH
☎ 01661 833459
Prudhoe, Northumberland NE42 6NA
Email: prudhoe@btinternet.com
In Prudhoe, on minor road N from A695
Open *Apr–Sept 10–6, Oct 10–5*
The castle passed into the hands of the Earls of Northumberland in 1381, having survived a number of Scottish sieges. Set on a beautiful wooded hillside, the gatehouse, curtain walls and keep survive. It had the first stone keep in the area, and the earliest oriel window in the country.

Ripon Cathedral
☎ 01765 602072
Minster Road, Ripon, N Yorkshire HG4 1QS
Email: postmaster@riponcathedral.org.uk
Website: www.riponcathedral.org.uk
5m W off A1, 12m N of Harrogate
Open *All year 8–6*

The only cathedral in England still with a Saxon crypt, originally built to house and display the bones of saints imported from Rome. It is home to St Wilfrid's needle, a tiny hole through which women accused of adultery were invited to crawl; to succeed proved your innocence, an example of what in the Middle Ages was called trial by ordeal, and we call Catch 22. The building was badly mauled during the Civil War, and fared little better in 1660 when its tower collapsed. Four years later, the cautious citizens removed the two remaining spires. The 19th century saw extensive restorations, and the church being granted cathedral status. There is a fine library with many medieval manuscripts and volumes, including a 12th-century copy of the Bible.

Roche Abbey EH
☎ 01709 813739
Maltby, S Yorkshire HG4 3JD
1m S of Maltby off A634
Open *Apr–Sept 10–6, Oct 10–5*
The ruin of a Cistercian monastery (1147) is sited in the beautiful, secluded valley of the River Ryton. The Gothic transepts, as well as some of the walls, are all that survive.

Scarborough Castle EH
☎ 01723 372451
Castle Road, Scarborough,
N Yorkshire YO11 1HY
E of town centre
Open *Apr–July 10–6, Aug 9.30–7, Sept 10–6, Oct 10–5, Nov–Mar Wed–Sun 10–4*
As you expect from a castle in such an important coastal position, the views of it, and from it, are spectacular. It is big and strong enough to have absorbed both Civil War cannon fire and First World War naval fire, and still stand. The major feature of the castle is its

keep, begun at the outset of the reign of Henry II and probably finished around the 1160s. It had enormous sums spent on it during the 13th century, the heyday for such castles, but fell into decline until funds were secured for its repair and restoration throughout the rest of the Middle Ages.

Thornton Abbey and Gatehouse EH
Thornton Curtis, Humberside,
N Lincolnshire
18m NE of Scunthorpe on minor road N of A160
Open *Gatehouse: Apr–Sept 1st & 3rd Sun 12–6, Oct–Mar 3rd Sun 12–4 Grounds: any reasonable time*
The three-storey-high 14th-century brick gatehouse once belonged to an Augustinian priory, founded in 1139 by William le Gros, Earl of Yorkshire, who is buried here.

Tynemouth Priory and Castle EH
☎ 0191 257 1090
North Pier, Tynemouth,
Tyne & Wear NE30 4BZ
In Tynemouth, near North Pier
Open *Apr–Sept 10–6, Oct 10–5, Nov–Mar Wed–Sun 10–1 2–4 Gun battery: Apr–Sept Sat–Sun & BHs 10–6*
A complete medieval settlement grew up on this headland jutting out into the mouth of the Tyne. There was a monastery, castle and several related settlements. The castle provided protection against incursions from across the Scottish border. The priory was built on the remains of an earlier 7th-century religious settlement. Both are now in ruins but are highly impressive especially with the sea panorama behind. When the Dissolution of the Monasteries ended the monastery's active ecclesiastical life, the castle was still in use as part of Henry VIII's coastal defences.

Scotland MAP 8

117 Aberdour Castle HS
☎ 01383 860519
Aberdour, Fife
In Aberdour on A921
Open *Apr–Sept 9.30–6.30, Oct–Mar
9.30–4.30; closed Thurs pm,
Fri & Sun am in winter*
The castle ruin, built on an L-shaped
plan, was once owned by one of the
noblemen who helped Lord Darnley
murder Mary Queen of Scots' secretary,
David Rizzio. It became even more of
a ruin when the keep collapsed in the
mid-19th century. But like many ruins it
has a pungent atmosphere, and a spectacular setting overlooking the Firth of
Forth across to the island of Inchcolm.

118 Bannockburn Heritage Centre* NTS
☎ 01786 812664
Glasgow Road, Stirling FK7 0LJ
Website: www.nts.org.uk/bannock-
burn.html
*Off M80 & M9/Junction 9,
2 miles S of Stirling*
Open *Site: all year. Heritage Centre: Mar
& Nov–23 Dec 10.30–4, Apr–Oct 10–5.30*
The exhibition celebrates Scotland's
most famous medieval victory, that of
Robert the Bruce over Edward II, the son
of Edward I, 'Hammer of the Scots', on
24 June 1314. The battle united the Scots
under Bruce and led to Scottish independence. The site of the real battle is
rather obscured now but this is a good
substitute.

Statue of Robert the Bruce at the **Bannockburn Heritage Centre**.

119 Blair Castle HS

☎ 01796 481207
Blair Atholl, Pitlochry,
Perth & Kinross PH18 5TL
Email: office@blair-castle.co.uk
Website: www.blair-castle.co.uk
7m NW of Pitlochry off A9
Open *Apr–June & Sept–Oct 10–6,*
July–Aug 9.30–6; winter by arrangement
A Scottish baronial-style castle, white-washed and turreted, with parts dating back to the 13th century. The castle was occupied during the 1745 Jacobite uprising which cost the Duke the temporary confiscation of his castle, after Bonnie Prince Charlie had abandoned it. He tried, unsuccessfully, to regain it by laying siege to the occupying government forces, possibly the last siege of a castle in Britain. Most of the castle dates from this later period, the interior being dominated by 17th- and 18th-century period pieces, with 30 rooms full of fine furniture, porcelain, paintings and historical artefacts. There is a particularly impressive main staircase lined with family portraits, and an outstanding collection of arms and armour. The previous owner, the Duke of Atholl, employed his own private army (the only man in Europe to do so), called the Atholl Highlanders. Queen Victoria had granted the Dukes of Atholl the right to have a private army after a visit in 1844.

120 Bothwell Castle* HS

☎ 01698 816894
Uddingston, S Lanarkshire
1 mile NW of Bothwell off B7071
Open *Apr–Sept 9.30–6.30, Oct–Mar 9.30–4.30; closed Thurs pm,*
Fri & Sun am in winter
A spectacular medieval building, perhaps the finest 13th-century stone castle in Scotland and one that saw more than its fair share of bitter fighting.

The solid red sandstone towers of **Bothwell Castle** with walls in places almost 16ft (5m) thick.

Its massive walls were nevertheless incapable of resisting one of Edward I's specialities – the endless siege, punctuated with attacks from one of his terrifying siege engines. It was recaptured by the Scots in 1314 after the Battle of Bannock-burn, though it once again fell into English hands when Edward III recaptured it, before the Scots got it back in 1337 for the last time. It was at this point that the castle's great tower, or donjon, was split in half and its masonry thrown into the Clyde to make sure that English marauders never used it again.

121 Caerlaverock Castle* HS
☎ 01387 770244
Glencaple, Dumfries & Galloway DG1 4RU
8m S of Dumfries on B725
Open *Apr–Sept 9.30–6.30, Oct–Mar 9.30–4.30; closed Sun am in winter*
Triangular in shape, with an impressive large round tower standing at its apex, this is one of those castles that looks as if it was simply dropped out of the sky into its moat. It is famous for its twin-towered gatehouse and Renaissance-era lodging, the Nithsdale Apartments. The castle was built in the second half of the 13th century during the reign of Alexander III, destroyed during the interminable Scottish Border conflicts of the 14th century as it was located slap bang in the middle of the main invasion route into Scotland from England, and was again rebuilt. It finally lapsed into irreversible decay after it was hammered by the Covenanters (Charles I's Scottish, Presbyterian opponents) in 1640.

122 Dirleton Castle* HS
☎ 01620 850330
Dirleton, E Lothian EH39 5ER
3m W of North Berwick on A198
Open *Apr–Sept 9.30–6.30, Oct–Mar 9.30–4.30; closed Sun am in winter*

The fine 13th-century castle ruin has surrounding gardens. Edward I besieged it, then lost it again; Cromwell destroyed it in 1650, after which it was never rebuilt.

123 Dryburgh Abbey* HS
☎ 01835 822381
St Boswells, nr Melrose,
Scottish Borders TD6 0RQ
5m SE of Melrose off B6404
Open *Apr–Sept 9.30–6.30, Oct–Mar 9.30–4.30; closed Sun am in winter*
It is one of the most beautiful of the Border abbeys (and that is saying something), where Walter Scott and Field Marshal Earl Haig lie buried. Founded by Hugh de Morville in 1150, and added to in the following centuries, it was a frequent victim of Border skirmishes, before being left to fall into decay in the 16th century. There is an obelisk commemorating James I and James II of Scotland, and de Morville, in the grounds.

124 Dunfermline Abbey and Palace* HS
☎ 01383 724586
St Margaret's St, Dunfermline, Fife
In Dunfermline off M90
Open *Church: Mon–Sat 10–4.30 Sun 2–4.30. Palace & ruins: Apr–Sept 9.30–6.30, Oct–Mar 9.30–4.30; closed Thurs pm, Fri & Sun am in winter*
Originally a large 12th-century Benedictine abbey it was, more importantly to Edward I, where the Scottish kings were buried, and so he destroyed it in 1303. Partially rebuilt, it was damaged again during the Reformation. The nave remains a stunning example of Norman medieval architecture. The east end was rebuilt 1818–21 and now serves as the parish church. The palace was once the guest house of the monastery, and was where Charles I was born. His son, Charles II, stayed here in 1650 when

Bruce's skull, discovered with his tomb in 1818 in the ruins of **Dunfermline Abbey**.

trying to raise Scottish support for his bid to regain the English crown from Cromwell's Commonwealth.

125 Edinburgh Castle* HS
☎ 0131 225 9846
Castlehill, Edinburgh EH1 2NG
At the top of Royal Mile
Open *Apr–Sept 9.30–6, Oct–Mar 9.30–5*
It is probably the best-known castle in the world, thanks to its utterly imposing position right in the middle of Edinburgh, overlooking the entire city. This is also where they fire the famous one o'clock gun every day, a bang which Edinburgh natives affect not to notice but which has visitors jumping out of their skins.

Apart from great views across Edinburgh, the Firth of Forth and deep into Fife, the castle is bursting with exhibits and history. It includes a gargantuan cannon called Mons Meg, the Stone of Scone, the Scottish Crown Jewels and the tiny St Margaret's Chapel. The Esplanade is where the annual Military Tattoo takes place.

126 Elgin Cathedral HS
☎ 01343 547171
Elgin, Moray
In Elgin on A96
Open *Apr–Sept 9.30–6.30, Oct–Mar 9.30–4.30; closed Thurs pm, Fri & Sun am in winter*
Elgin was known as 'The Lantern of the North', and was founded *c*1224 as the official establishment of the See of Moray. Nothing now survives but scattered ruins in an attractive meadow. Apart from St Andrews, this was once Scotland's finest medieval cathedral. Unfortunately Alexander Stewart, Earl of Buchan, fell out with the bishop who excommunicated him. The so-called 'Wolf of Badenoch' then 'with his wyld Wykked Heland-men burned ... the noble and highly adorned Church of Moray with all the books, Charters and other valuable things of the country therein kept.' Rebuilding did occur, but not enough to restore the cathedral to its former glory.

127 Huntly Castle HS
☎ 01466 793191
Huntly, Aberdeenshire
In Huntly on A96
Open *Apr–Sept 9.30–6.30, Oct–Mar 9.30–4.30; closed Thurs pm, Fri & Sun am in winter*
One of Scotland's most impressive baronial castles is now a ruin, partly thanks to Mary Queen of Scots who had it sacked after she defeated Lord Huntly.

He belonged to the Gordon family, and this was where the famous Scottish country dance, the Gay Gordons, was first named. A beautiful setting on the banks of the River Deveron.

128 Jedburgh Abbey HS
☎ 01835 863925
Abbey Bridge End, Jedburgh, Scottish Borders TD8 6JQ
In Jedburgh on A68
Open *Any reasonable time*
It is one of the most complete abbey ruins anywhere in Britain, thanks to late Victorian restoration work. Founded by David I in the 12th century, it is a wonderful mix of Gothic and Romanesque styles, built out of local red sandstone. It paid the price for its Border location, being repeatedly attacked in the endless conflicts that flared up along the Scottish-English border. Edward I's army ransacked it in 1297, and it was attacked in 1544–5. The abbey closed in 1560 with the Reformation. There is an excellent visitors' centre which displays many of the priceless artefacts uncovered in excavations.

129 Melrose Abbey HS
☎ 01896 822562
Melrose, Scottish Borders TD6 9LG
In Melrose off A7 or A68
Open *9.30–6.30; closed Sun am Oct–Mar*
Another of David I's abbeys, it belonged to the Cistercian order, and was at one time the wealthiest of them all. It survived the invasions of Edward I, but not of Richard II who destroyed it in 1385. The abbey was rebuilt, but a raid in 1545 by Edward Seymour, Duke of Somerset, finally finished it off. Much of its style reflects that of the great northern English churches, like York Minster. The site is dominated by the abbey church, where Robert the Bruce's heart lies buried.

130 St Andrews Castle HS
☎ 01334 477196
The Scores, St Andrews, Fife KY16 9AR
In St Andrews on A91
Open *Apr–Sept 9.30–6.30, Oct–Mar 9.30–4.30*
The castle began life as a fortress built for the Archbishop of Scotland and the bishops of St Andrews in the 12th century. It fell into Protestant hands during the Reformation. Catholic troops tried to retake it by boring a hole through solid rock up to the tower while the defenders were doing precisely the same thing, in the opposite direction, to counter them. The two tunnels never met, but you can inspect them to this day. John Knox, the firebrand Protestant preacher, was one of the defenders who then surrendered; it cost him a spell in the galleys. The castle fell into ruin in the 17th century.

131 Stirling Castle* HS
☎ 01786 450000
Castle Wynd, Stirling FK8 1EJ
At the top of Castle Wynd in Stirling
Open *Apr–Sept 9.30–6, Oct–Mar 9.30–5*
Thanks to its key position guarding the main point of access from the lowlands to the highlands of Scotland, Stirling Castle has played a pivotal role in Scottish history. It is probably the finest natural location for a defensive stronghold anywhere in the country. Mary Queen of Scots lived here as a child, and the key battles of Bannockburn and Stirling Bridge were both fought under its shadow. In 1304 it was the site of Edward I's longest and bloodiest siege. Much of what you see today belongs to the period between the 15th and 18th centuries. It was also involved in Cromwell's 1651 Scottish campaign and, later, Bonnie Prince Charlie tried in vain to capture it.

Tantallon Castle *overlooking the Bass Rock in the Firth of Forth.*

132 Tantallon Castle HS
☎ 01620 892727
By North Berwick, E Lothian EH39 5PN
3m E of North Berwick off A198
Open *Apr–Sept 9.30–6.30, Oct–Mar
9.30–4.30; closed Thurs pm,
Fri & Sun am in winter*
For anyone who loves castles that jut
out into the sea, Tantallon is a particularly
striking example. A coastal fort set on the
edge of cliffs, with the great Bass Rock out
in the Forth beyond it, there are few
castles that can compete with Tantallon
for the drama of their situation. It used
to be the Douglas family stronghold, and
has curtain walls that still look as though
they mean business. It has a particularly
imposing medieval gatehouse. There is a
good exhibition display.

133 Urquhart Castle* HS
☎ 01456 450551
Drumnadrochit, Loch Ness, Highland
On Loch Ness on A82 S of Drumnadrochit
Open *Apr–Sept 9.30–6.30, Oct–Mar
9.30–4.30; closed Thurs pm
& Fri in winter*

Loch Ness's second most famous attraction, though at least you can see this one.
This used to be one of Scotland's largest
castles, though the ruins belong to the
16th century rather than the earlier
Norman or medieval periods which saw
the construction of the site's first fortifications. It changed hands continually,
though it belonged principally to the
Macdonalds, the Lords of the Isles, who
used it as a base from which to mount
their endless raids. Stunning views of the
Loch and of you know what, should it
ever appear…

ADDITIONAL PLACES TO VISIT

Arbroath Abbey HS
☎ 01241 878756
Arbroath, Angus DD11 1EG
In Arbroath town centre on A92
Open *Apr–Sept 9.30–6.30, Oct–Mar
9.30–4.30; closed Thurs pm,
Fri & Sun am in winter*
A Tironensian (reformed Benedictine)
abbey founded in 1178 by King
William the Lion, it became one

of Scotland's most powerful and wealthy religious houses. It was here that the Declaration of Arbroath of 1320 was signed – a proclamation of national independence, still capable of raising the hairs on the backs of Scottish necks. Its links with Scottish nationalism continued into the 20th century when, in 1951, the Stone of Destiny (or Stone of Scone) was found here, after some students repatriated it from Westminster Abbey. The stone is now in Edinburgh Castle. There is a good example of an abbot's residence, now a ruin, but a substantial one.

Brodick Castle NTS

☎ 01770 302202
Isle of Arran, N Ayrshire KA27 8HY
Website: www.nts.org.uk/brodick.html
Ferries from Ardrossan, Claonaig (Kintyre)
Open *Apr–June & Sept–Oct 11–4.30,
July–Aug 11–5*
A salmon-coloured fortified house was converted from an earlier Viking fort in the 14th century into the L-shaped building we see today. But the real attraction are the gardens, one formal and walled, the other wild. The collection of rhododendrons is among the most impressive in Europe. It has a striking coastal setting.

Crossraguel Abbey HS

☎ 01655 883113
Maybole, S Ayrshire
2m S of Maybole on A77
Open *Apr–Sept 9.30–6.30*
The ruins are actually not that ruinous, and quite complete; there is an early Cluniac abbey, founded as a monastery in the 13th century, whose church, cloister, chapter house and domestic precincts are still visible. The abbey was rebuilt after damage sustained in the 1306 wars of independence.

Dunblane Cathedral

☎ 01786 823388
Dunblane, Stirling
Website: www.dunblanecathedral.org.uk
In Dunblane
Open *All year*
There are Norman elements that have survived but this is predominantly a church built between the 13th and 15th centuries. It had no roof for 300 years, but it was restored in the late 19th century to its Gothic splendour.

Dunstaffnage Castle HS

☎ 01631 562465
By Oban, Argyll & Bute PA37 1PZ
3m N of Oban on A85
Open *Apr–Sept 9.30–6.30,
Oct–Mar 9.30–4.30*
The 13th-century castle is built on a rock on a promontory extending into the Firth of Lorne with curtain walls nearly 10ft (3m) thick. Flora MacDonald, of Bonnie Prince Charlie fame, was briefly imprisoned here before being taken south to the Tower of London though she was later released. The castle was owned by the Campbells who had astutely switched allegiance from the Stuarts to William III.

Dunvegan Castle

☎ 01470 521206
Isle of Skye IV55 8WF
Email: info@dunvegancastle.com
Website: www.dunvegancastle.com
NW corner of Skye
Open *Apr–Oct 10–5.30, Nov–Mar 11–4*
The Isle of Skye's only great castle is now as renowned for its glorious gardens, filled with azaleas and rhododendrons, as for its rocky setting and 13th-century remnants. It has a wonderful loch-side location, and boasts being Scotland's longest inhabited-by-the-same-family house; home to the Clan Macleod.

Hailes Castle HS

☎ 0131 668 8800
East Linton, E Lothian
1½m SW of East Linton, off A1
Open *Any reasonable time*
It is the castle to which Mary Queen
of Scots was abducted by the Earl of
Bothwell in 1567 (the dungeon where
she was lodged is still there). Though
a ruin it is beautifully located.

Inchcolm Abbey HS

☎ 01383 823332
Inchcolm Island, Fife
*On island in Firth of Forth; reached by
ferry from South Queensferry*
Open *Apr–Sept 9.30–6.30*
A well-preserved ruin dating back to
the days of Alexander I, who founded
the abbey in 1123 after, the story goes,
landing on the island during a storm
and being fed by a hermit. It is now
known as the 'Iona of the East'. There is
a splendid octagonal chapter house.
Few monastic buildings from this era are
better preserved.

Inchmahome Priory HS

☎ 01877 385294
Port of Menteith, Stirling SK8 3RA
*On island in Lake of Menteith;
take ferry from Port of Menteith;
4m E of Aberfoyle off A81*
Open *Apr–Sept 9.30–6.30*
An Augustinian priory built on the
shore of an island in the middle of
Scotland's only lake, Lake Menteith
(it is not a loch). Much of the building
survives despite dating back to the 13th
century. And yes, Mary Queen of Scots
stayed here too, though only as a child
when in 1547, after the Scottish defeat
at the battle of Pinkie, she was spirited
away to prevent her being taken by
the English and married off to the
victorious Edward VI.

Whithorn Priory HS

☎ 01988 500508
Whithorn, Dumfries & Galloway
At Whithorn on A746
Open *Apr–Oct 10.30–5*
The ruins are of the 12th-century
St Ninian's priory. St Ninian, Scotland's
first Christian missionary, landed on
the Isle of Whithorn. The priory church
nearby, used as a parish church until
the 19th century, has the pre-Act of
Union Scottish coat of arms carved in
a 17th-century doorway called the 'pend'.

Northern Ireland MAP 9

134 Carrickfergus Castle*

☎ 028 9335 1273
Carrickfergus, Co Antrim BT38 7BG
Website: www.carrickfergus.org
5m NE of Belfast on Belfast Lough
Open *Mon–Sat 10–5 Sun 12–5.30*
Carrickfergus Castle is widely regarded
as one of the first true castles to be built
anywhere in Ireland, and it is among
the largest there. Situated on a rocky
peninsula projecting out into Belfast
Lough, it was built between 1180 and
1205 by John de Courcy, one of the first
Anglo-Norman lords to invade Ulster,
after Richard de Clare, 'Strongbow', had
landed in Leinster in 1169. The keep
survives in pretty good shape as does
much of the inner ward or courtyard
(and, almost uniquely, its original
portcullis). The four D-shaped towers
were added at a later date.

135 Dunluce Castle*

☎ 028 2073 1938
Bushmills, Co Antrim BT57 8UU
Off A2 between Bushmills & Portstewart
Open *Apr–Oct Mon–Sat 10–6 Sun 2–6,
Nov–Mar Mon–Sat 10–4 Sun 2–4*
The roofless, clifftop castle ruins are
on the way to the Giant's Causeway.

Built by Richard de Burgh c1300, few castles anywhere in Ireland can rival its location. Its precarious position did not come without a price though. The kitchen was blown into the sea during a particularly vicious storm in 1639, killing a number of servants sleeping in their quarters. Two cylindrical towers remain, as does its 16th-century gatehouse with its Franco-Scottish turrets. It was the stronghold of the MacDonnells, chiefs of Antrim.

136 Rathlin Island*
☎ Ballycastle tourist info 028 2076 2024
6m off Ballycastle, 14m from Mull of Kintyre; boats from Ballycastle daily in summer & in winter depending on weather

Rathlin is actually more famous for a Scot than an Irishman. The island gave birth to the Robert the Bruce spider legend, because it was here, apocryphally, that he was forced to find refuge in a cave having fled Scotland in 1306, and where a spider's perseverance spinning its web inspired him to try, try and try again. He raised fresh forces, returned to Scotland, and eight years later at Bannockburn he beat the English army and regained the crown of Scotland.

The island is a 50-minute ferry ride from Ballycastle. About 30 families live here, and there is a minibus to take tourists to the side of the island with the famous cave. The island is heaven for birdwatchers.

*The massive four-storey keep of **Carrickfergus Castle** overlooking the harbour.*

CHAPTER THREE

Medieval Manors and Elizabethan Prodigies

The late medieval and Tudor periods offer the English particularly the locations and landscapes for which they have most affection. The great castles of the Norman period are spectacular and forbidding, but who would want to live in one? And the great country houses of the 18th century are stunning too, but they put most of us in our place which is definitely *somewhere else.*

For the first time we are in the presence of structures and styles which seem authentically native, and even desirable, and which are not the imposition of outsiders. Enough has survived of the more ordinary houses and parish churches to give us a tantalizing, if rose-tinted, glimpse of how we would have lived had we been born 500 years ago. At last we see a world that extends beyond the lords and the bishops.

It is not surprising that for those with more conservative tastes in architecture, this is the period which is most ardently praised, with its moated manor houses, parish churches and half-timbered village streets. Lavenham in Suffolk is an especially good example and we filmed its **Guildhall** and other buildings at the end of programme 5 about the Black Death. At last we found interiors that felt lived in, a very distinct feeling replicated in large numbers of rooms and halls roughly from this period. Ones which

really stood out were the great hall at **Penshurst** in Kent, the dining area of **Cotehele** in Cornwall and the stairwell of **Gladstone's Land** in Edinburgh.

But there was also evidence of social trauma. The Black Death, which first struck in 1348, killed up to a third of the population and changed forever the ways in which the classes interacted. The many deserted villages up and down the country, especially **Wharram Percy** in Yorkshire, speak of the pathos of things which have vanished. The tiny outlines of now-deserted houses and streets clearly show how fragile and precarious life was.

This period was marked by plenty of rapture and rupture. The dominant style was now the Decorated and the Perpendicular. Great religious buildings of unsurpassed quality and character, of real genius, began to be erected in Britain. This is the benchmark of what the sublime looks like in stone. The ribbed vaulting and flying buttresses are exuberant and almost unbelievable, and they transcend all manner of engineering problems. One of the best examples is **King's College Chapel** in Cambridge where the Perpendicular reached a magnificent flowering. These styles now exert a stranglehold on the national imagination, alive and powerful even in the 21st century.

*The south wing and gatehouse of **Little Moreton Hall**.*

Holy Trinity Church *at Long Melford in Suffolk, built from the profits of the wool trade.*

But behind this vision of harmony and continuity lies another story of huge religious and social dislocation. The Lady Chapel in **Ely Cathedral**, whose light and acoustics make it one of the country's most beautiful interiors, is full of religious statues that have lost their heads. They were decapitated during the 150 years of religious spasm which marked the Reformation which took a pick-axe to the coloured world of the Catholic Church. What is strange is just how invisible that act of vandalism has now become. You simply do not notice how broken those images are, and how colourless so many churches have become.

That was why we went to so much trouble in programme 6 to re-create the sensation of entering a Catholic church as it would have looked before the whitewash and the hammers did their work. The church we filmed was **Holy Trinity** at Long Melford, a great Suffolk church built from the profits of the wool trade. A detailed description exists of what it used to look like, and with the help of computer technology we turned the clock back 500 years.

The impact of the Dissolution of the Monasteries, which was done as much for wealth and stone as for issues of religious uniformity, was another great blow in this period. Its most visible consequence was to bequeath us so many ecclesiastical ruins.

This, then, is the moment which saw Britain cut off from Europe on matters of religion, and war and diplomacy too. But one thing did arise which helped to bridge the gap – the desire to impress. In an age where the need for fortification was fast shrinking, when castles were becoming more decorative and more about luxury than impregnability, the impulse for the aristocracy to display the glamour of wealth and patronage became irresistible. The so-called 'Prodigy Houses' were often, like **Longleat** in Wiltshire, built from the smashed or plundered stone of the dissolved monasteries, and they created a new addition to the historical landscape – the non-royal palace. **Hardwick Hall** in Derbyshire, **Burghley House** in Lincolnshire and **Hatfield House** in Hertfordshire were but three of many, huge essays in continental style and swagger, with plenty of panache.

South-west MAP 1

137 Bath Abbey*
☎ 01225 422462
13 Kingston Buildings, Bath BA1 1LT
Email: office@bathabbey.org
Website: www.bathabbey.org
*In centre of Bath, near Roman Baths
& Pump Room*
Open *Mon–Sat 9–6 Sun 1.30–3;
closes at 4.30 Oct–Easter Mon–Sat*
Overlooking the Roman Baths, this
Benedictine abbey church, the so-called
'Lantern of the West', had its construction
drastically disrupted by the Dissolution
of the Monasteries. Elizabeth I commissioned the repair work, which carried
on for nearly a century. It was only in the
latter half of the 19th century, under the
guidance of one particularly energetic
rector, Charles Kemble, that the abbey
was really finished. The west front has
carved on its exterior a memento of the
dream vision that was supposed to have
inspired the abbey's foundation – angels
climbing and descending ladders
coming out of an olive tree.

138 Corsham Court
☎ 01249 701610
Corsham, Wiltshire SN13 0BZ
*4m W of Chippenham
off M4 at junction 13*
Open *20 Mar–Sept Tues–Sun & BH Mons
2–5.30, Oct–20 Mar Sat & Sun 2–4.30*
The Elizabethan manor house, with
Georgian additions, was built in 1582
by 'Customer' Smythe (so-called because
he was Collector of the Customs of
London). In 1760 'Capability' Brown
remodelled both the house and garden;
he adapted the house so that it could
accommodate its wonderful collection
of Old Masters, most notably the
Annunciation by Renaissance painter Fra
Filippo Lippi. He also built a cold bathhouse in the gardens, with a plunge pool.
There is Georgian furniture, and mirrors
designed by Chippendale and Adam.

139 Cotehele NT
☎ 01579 351346; Infoline 01579 352739
St Dominick, nr Saltash,
Cornwall PL12 6TA
Email: cctlce@smtp.ntrust.org.uk

Cotehele, *the perfect example of a late medieval manor house.*

*1m W of Calstock by steep footpath;
8m SW of Tavistock*
Open *House: Mid-Mar–Sept 11–5,
Oct 11–4.30; closed Fri but open Good Fri
Garden: All year 10.30–dusk*
Set at the top of a steep Cornish valley,
it is one of the finest medieval manor
houses anywhere in Britain. The
Edgcumbe family have lived in it for
600 years, and its great attraction comes
from the way it has been preserved –
parts are unlit by modern lighting giving
the unique collection of tapestries,
furniture and armour the aura of a
house, not a museum. There are also two
dining areas, one for the family and the
other for the servants, whose great table
still stands in the hall. This is definitely
a new point in the history of domestic
architecture; previously, the household
would have eaten together.

Cotehele is richly adorned in tapestries, as much for insulation and draught
protection as for decoration. The beds
are all heavily curtained and still have
the original hangings. Luckily for Cotehele
the family began to build a second home,
Mount Edgcumbe on Plymouth Sound,
leaving the first stuck in its wonderful
16th-century time-warp, a place for
occasional family visits, not adapted
or modernized in any way. The house
is surrounded by woods, and there
is a lovely hillside walk.

140 Longleat
☎ 01985 844400
Warminster, Wiltshire BA12 7NW
Email: enquiries@longleat.co.uk
Website: www.longleat.co.uk
Between Warminster & Frome off A362
Open *House: Apr–Oct 11–5.30, Nov–Dec
11–4. Park: Mon–Fri 10–4 Sat & Sun 10–5*
Now as famous for its lions as its
eccentric owner, this is generally consid-
ered the earliest true Renaissance house

in Britain. It has a complicated history
because fire destroyed much of the
house in the 1560s. The subsequent
restoration work was then covered by
a new façade in the late 1570s, designed
by Robert Smythson who went on to
build Hardwick Hall (p128).

Longleat is a more squat, horizontal
building than some of the other great
houses built at the same time; it has none
of the towers or obelisks of Burghley in
Lincolnshire, for example. What is characteristic of the period, however, is its
extravagant use of glass, in hundreds of
windows, many in a bay window configu-
ration. Nothing better distinguishes the
16th-century house from its predecessors
than this new love affair with daylight.
In 1757 'Capability' Brown helped create
a 900-acre park. For those interested in
art there is an impressive collection of
paintings, tapestries and furniture.

141 Montacute House* NT
☎ 01935 823289
Montacute, Somerset TA15 6XP
Email: wmogen@smtp.ntrust.org.uk
4m W of Yeovil on S side of A3088
Open *House: Late Mar–Oct 11–5 (closed
Tues). Garden: Late Mar–Oct 11–5.30
(closed Tues), Nov–Mar Wed–Sun 11.30–4*
Built from 1588–1601 for Sir Edward
Phelips, who became Speaker of the
House of Commons in 1601, this is a particularly fine example of an Elizabethan
mansion built during the era when houses
were being constructed not so much to
keep their owners safe, as to impress
visitors. It is particularly celebrated for
many Renaissance features, eg plasterwork, chimneys, stained glass and
panelling, and for its fine collection of
portraits and attractive gardens, including
an original walled garden, with two domed
pavilions. Lord Curzon lived here during
World War I, and you can still see his bath.

142 Pendennis Castle EH
☎ 01326 316594
Falmouth, Cornwall TR11 4LP
1m SE of Falmouth
Open *Apr–Sept 10–6, Oct 10–5,*
Nov–Mar 10–4

Like St Mawes in Cornwall, this is one of Henry VIII's coastal defence castles, and is constructed in the same sort of way with a central circular keep and semi-circular bastions enclosed by curtain walls, with gun positions. It was a victim of its own success when it held out against Cromwell's troops for months (St Mawes fell in days), and took a terrible pounding. Its clover-leaf shape (common to all these coastal forts) indicates the new priority given to artillery in castle design, compared to the earlier types of fortification.

Athelhampton House and Gardens
☎ 01305 848363
Dorchester, Dorset DT2 7LG
Email: pcooke@athelhampton.co.uk
Website: www.athelhampton.co.uk
5m NE of Dorchester off A35
Open *Mar–Oct Sun–Fri 10.30–5; open*
Easter Sat & Aug BH weekends 10.30–5;
Nov–Feb Sun only 10.30–dusk

A medieval house fortified with battlements, it has a range of beautiful gardens, with courts, pavilions, dovecote, coachhouse and toll house. The great hall, with a timber roof, brass chandeliers and minstrel's gallery, is bettered only by Penshurst in Kent as an example of late medieval interior architecture. The crest in the windows, of a chained monkey

Medieval Manors and Elizabethan Prodigies SOUTH-WEST

The circular keep of **Pendennis Castle** *facing St Mawes across the mouth of the River Fal.*

looking in the mirror, belonged to the man who built it, Sir William Martyn, a lord mayor of London. The east wing, destroyed by fire, was restored in the early 1990s.

Barrington Court NT

☎ 01460 241938
Barrington, nr Ilminster,
Somerset TA19 0NQ
Email: wbagen@smtp.ntrust.org.uk
5m NE of Ilminster, on B3168
Open *Mar & Oct Thurs–Sun 11–4.30,
Apr–June & Sept 11–5.30 closed Fri,
July–Aug 11–5.30 (Fri gardens only)*
A fine 16th-century Tudor manor house in the Gothic style believed to have been built by William Clifton, with stables added in the 17th century.

Berry Pomeroy Castle EH

☎ 01803 866618
Totnes, Devon TQ9 6NJ
2½m E of Totnes off A385
Open *Apr–Sept 10–6, Oct 10–5*
This great Tudor mansion was built within the walls of a Norman castle by the brother of Jane Seymour, Henry VIII's third wife. Both parts are now in ruins, though they are extensive and impressive, particularly in terms of their location on top of a wooded hillside. Originally the mansion was a quadrangular building with an unusual gatehouse of twin towers built in the 12th century. It was never really restored after being severely damaged during the Civil War.

Bradford-on-Avon Tithe Barn EH

Bradford-on-Avon, Wiltshire BA15
Just S of town centre off B3109
Open *10.30–4*
The stone barn has a roof built of slate and is supported on wooden beams, making it one of the most impressive survivors from the Middle Ages.

Bradley Manor NT

☎ 01626 354513
Bradley, Newton Abbot, Devon TQ12 6BN
½m from town centre on A381
Open *Apr–Sept Wed & Thurs 2–5*
Virtually unaltered, this 15th-century manor house is one of the finest in this region. It has a great hall, buttery, solar (private residence) and chapel.

Branscombe Manor Mill, Old Bakery and Forge NT

☎ Old Bakery 01297 680333
Manor Mill 01392 881691
Branscombe, Seaton, Devon EX12 3DB
In the village of Branscombe off A3052
Open *Old Bakery: Easter–Oct daily
& Sat–Sun in winter 11–5. Manor Mill:
Apr–Oct Sun, July–Aug Sun & Wed 2–5.
Forge: daily, phone for times*
A mill, bakery and forge are all on the same site, which has been recently restored and is in full working order.

Buckland Abbey NT

☎ 01822 853607
Yelverton, Devon PL20 6EY
11m N of Plymouth off A386
Open *Late Mar–early Nov 10.30–5.30
closed Thurs, Nov–Feb Sat & Sun 2–5;
closed 24 Dec–mid-Feb*
This old Cistercian monastery was founded in 1278. It fell into secular hands in 1541 when Henry VIII granted it to Sir Richard Grenville. His grandson Richard Grenville converted it into a private home, turning the nave into a great hall. He sold the house to Sir Francis Drake. There is a medieval tithe barn in the gardens.

Cadhay

☎ 01404 812432
Ottery St Mary, Devon EX11 1QT
Email: cadhay@eastdevon.net
Website: www.eastdevon.net/cadhay

1m NW of Ottery St Mary off B3176
Open *July–Aug Tues–Thurs, spring*
& late summer BH Suns & Mons all 2–6
Beautiful mid-16th-century house,
with gardens, long gallery, and an
earlier surviving great hall.

Compton Castle NT
☎ 01803 875740
Marldon, Paignton, Devon TQ3 1TA
3m W of Torquay, 1m N of Marldon
Open *Apr–Oct Mon Wed & Thurs*
10–12.15 2–5
This was once the home of the man who
founded Newfoundland, Sir Humphrey
Gilbert, a half-brother of Sir Walter
Raleigh. He modified a house dating
from the early 14th century into the
fortified manor we see today, as protection against the French raids that
were frequently made along the south
Devon coast. The great hall and
gatehouse have been fully restored.

Cothay Manor
☎ 01823 672283
Greenham, nr Wellington,
Somerset TA21 0JR
M5 junction 26 or 27,
Greenham 2m off A38
Open *Gardens: May–Sept Wed Thurs*
Sun & BHs 2–6. House: all year by
appointment only to groups of over 20
You would have to look long and hard
to find a better and more enchanting
example of the middle-sized manor
house. It is virtually untouched since
it was built *c*1480. There are beautiful
gardens too.

Dartmouth Castle EH
☎ 01803 833588
Castle Road, Dartmouth, Devon TW6 0JH
1m SE of Dartmouth off B3205
Open *Apr–Sept 10–6, Oct 10–5,*
Nov–Mar Wed–Sun 10–1 2–4

The castle has been exceptionally well
preserved, and is bristling with naval and
military history. This was the point from
which an international fleet gathered in
the mid-12th century to embark on the
second crusade. Later castles were added
to provide much-needed defensive protection at the mouth of the River Dart,
from where a number of ships sailed to
take on the Spanish Armada. Unlike
many other castles, Dartmouth was built
with cannons in mind, and has a particularly advanced design for its time. The
castle offers spectacular views.

Farleigh Hungerford Castle EH
☎ 01225 754026
Nr Bath, Somerset BA3 6RS
9m SE of Bath,
3½m W of Trowbridge on A366
Open *Apr–Sept 10–6, Oct 10–5,*
Nov–Mar Wed–Sun 10–1 2–4
It was built in 1383 by Sir Thomas
Hungerford, Speaker in the House of
Commons. In the 14th century the
right to build fortifications was strictly
controlled by the crown, for obvious
reasons. Sir Thomas clearly had not got
planning permission for his because
there is a record of his being pardoned
for the offence. It changed hands during
the Civil War, when one brother, a
Parliamentarian, took it from another,
a Royalist.

Godolphin House
☎ 01736 763194
Godolphin Cross, nr Helston,
Cornwall TR13 9RE
Email: godo@euphony.net
On minor road from Breage to
Townshend 5m NW of Helston
Open *May–Sept Thurs Fri & Sun &*
BH Mons, July–Sept Tues also, all 10–5
(opens at 2 on Sun). Groups by appoint-
ment all year

This early Tudor house, with Elizabethan and Stuart additions, is the former home of the Earls of Godolphin, one of whom owned one of the three Arab stallions from which all the British racing blood-stock is descended. A façade of columns was added in the mid-17th century.

Great Chalfield Manor NT

☎ 01225 782239
Nr Melksham, Wiltshire SN12 8NJ
3m SW of Melksham off B3107
Open *Apr–Oct Tues–Thurs guided tours only at 12.15, 2.15, 3.45 & 4.30*
This 15th-century manor house was one of the first in the country to try its hand at a symmetrical design, which dominated the construction of great houses later in the century and beyond. The E-shaped plan became particularly popular in later house design.

The manor was built by the Member of Parliament, Thomas Tropnell, and completed in 1480. A portrait of him, the earliest ever of an MP, was discovered hidden behind whitewashed walls. There are hidden peepholes in the 'solar' (private residence) that are disguised as the eyes of three grotesque masks that allowed the ladies of the house to scrutinize events in the great hall below. There are some beautiful oriel windows, a moat and a gatehouse, and the gardens are charming too.

Horton Court NT

☎ 01249 730141
Horton, nr Chipping Sodbury, Gloucestershire BS17 6QR
3m NE of Chipping Sodbury off A46
Open *Apr–Oct Wed & Sat 2–6 (dusk if earlier)*
Cotswold manor house; only the Norman hall and an ambulatory are open to visitors.

Powderham Castle

☎ 01626 890243
Kenton, Exeter, Devon EX6 8JQ
Email: Powderham@eclipse.co.uk
Website: www.powderham.co.uk
6m SW of Exeter off M5 at junction 30, off A379 in Kenton village
Open *Apr–Oct 10–5.30; closed Sat*
Built in the last years of the 14th century by Sir Philip Courtenay, the castle was heavily damaged during a Civil War siege when it fell to Parliamentarian forces, but was greatly restored in the 18th and 19th centuries. It is still the home of the Courtenay family, Earls of Devon. It has a beautiful dining hall and a good collection of portraits, and is regarded as one of the finest mansions in the country. It is surrounded by gardens and a deer park.

St Mawes Castle EH

☎ 01326 270526
St Mawes, nr Truro, Cornwall TR2 3AA
in St Mawes on A3078
Open *Apr–Sept 10–6, Oct 10–5, Nov–Mar Wed–Sun 10–1 2–4*
On the other side of the estuary from Pendennis Castle (p105), St Mawes shared the same purpose, being part of Henry VIII's chain of coastal defences. It is the best preserved of those that remain.

Wolfeton House

☎ 01305 263500
Nr Dorchester, Dorset DT2 9PN
1½m from Dorchester on A37
Open *Mid-July–mid-Sept Mon Wed & Thurs 2–6; groups over 10 by appointment only*
A splendid example of a great Elizabethan manor house complete with plaster ceilings, fireplaces and panelling. There is also a great hall, chapel and cider house. The gatehouse towers are especially impressive.

South-east MAP 2

143 Arundel Castle*

☎ 01903 882173 & 01903 883136
Arundel, W Sussex BN18 9AB
Website: www.arundelcastle.org
4m N of Littlehampton on A27
Open *Apr–Oct Sun–Fri 12–5*

Built as part of the Normans' South Coast defences, the castle's original fortifications were much damaged by Cromwell's cannon fire. Henry II built a stone shell keep on the original motte in the 12th century, but little of that early structure has survived either. Still, the castle remains one of the most impressive in Britain, partly because of its distant views from its commanding situation overlooking the Arun valley.

It is now the home of the Duke of Norfolk whose family history was intimately interwoven with many of the great kings and queens of England, especially Richard III and the Tudors. Many historical documents and artefacts attest to this, including the death warrant of the 4th Duke of Norfolk who was convicted of treason and executed during the reign of Elizabeth I.

144 Bodiam Castle* NT

☎ 01580 830436
Robertsbridge, E Sussex TN32 5UA
10m N of Hastings off A21 at Hurst Green
Open *Mid-Feb–Oct 10–6 (dusk if earlier), Nov–mid-Feb Sat & Sun 10–4*

With so many later accretions and modifications, there are few castles that bear much resemblance to what

Bodiam Castle *reflected in the waters of the moat.*

they originally looked like when first lived in, but Bodiam, with its great circular towers and girdle of water, is an exception. Interestingly, the interior lacks many passage ways and connecting doors because, by the mid-14th century, the main danger facing castle life was mutiny or insurrection from within, and not a siege from without.

The castle looks like a compact version of Harlech, but the living quarters were less haphazardly thrown together than was customary with older, more military castles. The towers are arranged symmetrically around a wide central court. The apartments are spread around the sides of the quadrangle rather than, as would have been usual with a medieval keep, being built one upon the other in a tower. Luckily Bodiam was never attacked or besieged, hence its almost pristine condition. It is one of the country's most loved medieval castles.

145 Church of St Leonard

☎ 01303 262370/266217
Oak Walk, Hythe, Kent CT21 5DN
Website: stleonardschurchhythe.co.uk
Open *Church: daylight hours*
Crypt: May–Sept 10–30–12 2.30–4
The church is in one of the original Cinque Ports, which provided the early Navy with ships in return for favoured trading status. To savour the church's most memorable possessions you need to visit the crypt, which has one of the country's finest collections of skulls and bones, known as an ossuary. There are 8000 thigh bones and 2000 skulls to look at, all beautifully stored on shelves, packed together like a wall of death.

Archaeological work carried out here and elsewhere broadly points to what we all suspect about medieval life: to cite the 17th-century philosopher Thomas Hobbes, it was nasty, brutish and short.

Probably fewer than 10 per cent of people lived beyond the age of 50 or 60. Barely one child in three made it through childhood. Once you had survived those first few years, chances were you would not make it much past your early 30s. It is particularly chastening to look at all those bones, and realize that the majority belonged to people younger than you.

146 Church of St Mary

☎ 01491 837823
Ewelme, Wallingford,
Oxfordshire OX10 6HP
S of Oxford on A4131
Open *Daylight hours*
Here is a perfect microcosm of medieval life laid out in front of you. Not just a church, but an almshouse and school too, a trio of medieval buildings all built at the behest of Geoffrey Chaucer's grand-daughter, Alice, and her husband, William de la Pole, Duke of Suffolk.

The church reciprocated by building her a 'transi' monument after her death, featuring the Duchess rendered in alabaster surrounded by adorable little stone angels wearing trousers made of feathers, a huddle of monks, and other mourners, some sitting on her pillow. More morbidly it is still possible to see another figure, again in alabaster, representing the corpse within the tomb, with withered breasts and decaying flesh. The church's other great tomb is that of Thomas Chaucer, the Duchess's father (and son of the poet, Geoffrey), who owned the manor and fought at Agincourt. It has 24 heraldic devices painted on it.

The 1437 almshouse cloister, built round a quadrangle, is also fascinating. Almshouses were established to educate local, deserving, poor men. The school, built at the same time, is made of brick and is still used as a primary school, perhaps the oldest such building in the country.

147 Deal Castle EH

☎ 01304 372762

Victoria Road, Deal, Kent CT14 7BA
SW of Deal town centre
Open *Apr–Sept 10–6, Oct 10–5,
Nov–Mar Wed–Sun 10–4*

The castle was built in the 1540s by
Henry VIII as part of his coastal defences.
They were considered necessary after
he broke away from the Church of Rome,
leading to fears of continental crusades
of revenge sanctioned by the Pope. From
the air it looks like a set of gear wheels
and still has a formidable air, but it feels
very different from earlier generations of
castles. This had no pretence as a place
of residence, and was completely geared
to providing a solid base for defensive
cannon fire.

Like St Mawes and Pendennis, both
in Cornwall, this has much more the
shape of a blossoming flower than the
more rigid design of earlier castles. They
were built entirely for defence, and there
is no attempt to marry this requirement
with living quarters of any size at all.
This was more like a huge bunker than
a royal fortress. It was home to a garrison
not a lord, and was built for artillery
not banquets.

148 Hampton Court Palace*

☎ 020 8781 9500

Hampton Court, Surrey KT8 9AU
Website: www.hrp.org.uk
*From M25 junction 13 A30/A308,
junction 10 A3/A307, or from A3 take
A309 at Hook junction*
Open *Mid-Mar–late Oct Mon 10.15–6
Tues–Sun 9.30–6, late Oct–mid-Mar
Mon 10.15–4.30 Tues–Sun 9.30–4.30*

Although virtually every British
monarch has made some alteration
or left some significant mark, Hampton
Court will always be most closely
associated with Henry VIII. He did
not actually build it: that was done
from 1515–29 by Cardinal Thomas
Wolsey, the second most important man
in the kingdom after the king. Henry
confiscated the palace in 1529 when
Wolsey was rapidly and desperately
sliding out of favour. You can see why
Henry was so keen to get his hands on
it. Even before major additions were
planned, it had 1000 rooms, miles of lead
plumbing, and had taken an army of
labourers years to build.

Henry enlarged it still further, adding
the tilt yard for jousting, the great hall
for banquets, and the real (or royal)
tennis court in which to work up a sweat.
Small was not in his vocabulary. The
kitchens could cater for 500 diners at one
sitting. He enjoyed three honeymoons
here and built lodgings for his second
wife Anne Boleyn, but by the time they
were finished she was dead and Jane
Seymour (wife number three) had moved
in. Edward VI, Henry's only son, was
born here.

James I presided at Hampton Court
over the committee later to produce the
Authorized Version of the Bible in 1611.
Charles I had his honeymoon here, and
it was the first place he ran to from
London as the country tipped into Civil
War. William and Mary commissioned
Christopher Wren to rebuild much of it
from 1689. William Talman completed
some of the interior apartments between
1699 and 1702 and helped to lay out the
gardens. And, finally, it was opened to
the public by Queen Victoria to celebrate
her accession in 1838. Inside there are
priceless works of art including many of
the Queen's Renaissance paintings. The
Chapel Royal is stunning, and the great
hall still contains Henry's Flemish tapestries. It is also home, of course, to the
famous maze – not to be attempted
if you are in any way tight for time.

*The south-west front of **Hatfield House**.*

149 Hatfield House *

☎ 01707 287010

Hatfield, Hertfordshire AL9 5NQ

21m N of London off M25 junction 23

Open *House: late May–late Sept Tues–Thurs 12–4 guided tours only, Sat & Sun 1–4.30, PH Mons 11–4.30. Gardens: Tues–Sun 11.30–6*

This is the house where Elizabeth I, who had been kept here as a virtual prisoner during her half-sister Mary's reign, was told that Mary had died and that she was now queen. According to legend, she was sitting under an oak tree here at the time.

Much of the original Tudor building was torn down and replaced by the surviving Jacobean structure that we see today; most of this was done around 1605 by Robert Cecil, James I's Secretary of State and son of Lord Burghley. It has been the family home of the Cecils ever since. There are a number of different styles at work in Hatfield's many façades, suggesting more than one architect. Cecil himself had a hand in its conception, as did Robert Lyminge, a carpenter-cum-architect, and Inigo Jones. The south front has a particularly appealing Italian graciousness.

The house contains a host of important historic objects including letters between Elizabeth and Mary Queen of Scots, Mary's death warrant and Charles I's cradle. The most impressive painting is the famous *Rainbow Portrait of Elizabeth I*, attributed to Isaac Oliver, one of a series of semi-allegorical paintings of the Faerie Queene when at the height of her national cult. Here, the details seem powerfully and wilfully obscure – what do all those eyes and ears symbolize? The image has a powerful mystique giving a sense of charisma and the real person, unlike the more straightforward pictures of powerful males like Henry VIII with his bloated physique and well-filled codpiece. The portraits of Elizabeth had to work harder, and more obliquely, in their quest to depict female power.

There is also fine furniture from the 16th, 17th and 18th centuries, rare tapestries and historic armour in the state rooms. The west gardens contain a formal and wilderness area, a scented garden, and a knot garden planted with the kinds of plants and bulbs grown in the 15th–17th centuries.

150 Herstmonceux Castle

☎ 01323 834444
Herstmonceux, Hailsham,
E Sussex BN27 1RN
Website: www.herstmonceux-castle.com
2m S of Herstmonceux off A271
Open *Apr–Sept 10–6, Oct 10–5*
One of England's most picturesque
castles has a ravishing assortment of battlements, towers and moat. Built from
brick during the 15th century, there are
echoes of nearby Bodiam in its design
and construction. The thin walls and
abundance of windows suggest that there
were no real defensive intentions in its
design; many of its other features, like its
gatehouse, are more symbolic than real.

151 Hever Castle

☎ 01732 865224
Edenbridge, Kent TN8 7NG
Email: mail@HeverCastle.co.uk
Website: www.HeverCastle.co.uk
3m SE of Edenbridge off B2026
Leave M25 junction 5 or 6
Open *Mar–Nov 12–5. Gardens: 11–5*

Inextricably linked to the story of Henry
VIII and at least two of his wives, it had
been long owned by the Boleyn family,
but was confiscated after Anne Boleyn's
execution. It was later given to Henry's
fourth wife, Anne of Cleves, in compen-
sation for the annulment of their hasty
marriage after seven months in 1540.
Hever is a moated castle with formal,
Italianate gardens and topiary hedging.

152 Ightham Mote NT

☎ 01732 811145
Ivy Hatch, Sevenoaks, Kent TN15 0NT
6m E of Sevenoaks off A25
Open *Apr–Oct 10–5.30; closed Tues & Sat*
The word 'mote' derives from the
old word for 'moot' as in 'moot court',
a place of discussion and decision-making,
not moat as in watered defence, although
Ightham has one over which visitors
have to pass. Once crossed, you are in
perhaps the best-preserved house of
its period in Kent; the great hall dates
to 1340, the entrance tower to 1480,
and the chapel to 1520.

Ightham Mote, *one of the most perfect moated manor houses in the country.*

153 Knole NT

☎ 01732 462100; Infoline 01732 750608
Sevenoaks, Kent TN15 0RP
In Sevenoaks, just off A225 at end of High St
Open *Late Mar–Oct Wed–Sun*
& BH Mons & Tues 11–5

A jumble of medieval buildings were transformed into one of the most spectacular 15th-century palaces by Thomas Bourchier, Archbishop of Canterbury, from 1456 to his death in 1486. Henry VIII needless to say 'persuaded' a later owner, Archbishop Thomas Cranmer, to add it to Henry's already groaning collection of lavish palaces, but in fact he is only known to have stayed there once.

Knole was given by Elizabeth I to her cousin Thomas Sackville in 1566, and it was he who added the family emblem (a leopard) to the curved gables. The house has stayed with the Sackville family ever since. The suite of rooms on the first floor, approached by the great hall and Painted Staircase, were unashamedly designed to impress. There are fabulous wooden long galleries, and collections of peerless 17th-century fabrics. Although the largest private house in Britain, Knole is not just an intimidating exercise in aristocratic hauteur. The house is very proud of being rather random in its elements, reminiscent of a self-sustaining village rather than an imposing palace, and it still retains that feel.

154 Leeds Castle *

☎ 01622 765400
Maidstone, Kent ME17 1PL
Email: enquiries@leeds-castle.co.uk
Website: www.leeds-castle.co.uk
7m E of Maidstone off M20 junction 8
Open *Mar–Oct 10–5, Nov–Feb 10–3*

No, it is not in deepest Yorkshire but Kent. Its name comes from the nearby village of Leeds, and derives from the Saxon word *esledes*, meaning slope or hillside. The structure of the castle is basically Norman; do not be misled because some of its most medieval-looking sections are Victorian.

It was the favourite home for a number of English queens, starting with Eleanor of Castile (it was part of her dower). Her husband Edward remodelled the gatehouse, and he equipped the walls with their D-shaped towers. Being on an island, the castle had both a beautiful setting and an effective ready-made defence. Today it is used as a conference centre, and hosts all kinds of attractions and events.

155 Penshurst Place and Gardens

☎ 01892 870307
Penshurst, Kent TN11 8DG
Email: enquiries@penshurstplace.com
Website: www.penshurstplace.com
Off M25 junction 5 to Tonbridge on A21
Open *House: Mar Sat & Sun, Apr–Oct*
daily 12–5.30. Grounds: daily 10.30–6

This was the birthplace of the Elizabethan poet and soldier Sir Philip Sidney. It is a house whose gardens, furniture and art are all capped by its most spectacular asset, the 14th-century great hall. Built on the proceeds from the wool trade (the North Sea oil of the Middle Ages), the house was considerably extended and modified through the Elizabethan age and beyond, and much has been added, including paintings, decorations and artefacts.

The house had an H-plan, and originally no defences, though a stone wall with towers were later added. It remains, however, one of the best places to savour what medieval life offered the wealthy. The great hall was the communal heart of the house. This was where everybody ate (we are not yet in a world with separate dining arrangements for the grand and the humble).

The old central louvre, or roof opening, for the smoke to escape has long gone, but the roof is particularly impressive. It has a span of over 60ft (18m), its great curved braces resting on beautifully carved wooden corbels (projecting support blocks) representing human figures. Instead of using traditional oak, they are made of chestnut with its much mellower colour. It is probably the finest surviving example of a 14th-century hall anywhere in the country. The garden is well worth visiting too.

156 Upnor Castle EH
☎ 01634 718742
Nr Upnor, Kent ME2 2XG
2½m NE of Strood off A228
Open *Apr–Sept 10–6, Oct 10–4*
This fort was designed to defend the River Thames, the gateway to London, but was still unable to protect Charles II from perhaps his gravest humiliation –

a raid by the Dutch when they towed away the very ship that had brought him back from exile. This happened in 1667 after the Plague and the Fire of London had done so much to darken the early years of the Restoration. No wonder then that much effort was invested in reinforcing the capital's naval defences. Later, Upnor served as an arsenal for the Royal Navy.

157 The Vyne NT
☎ Infoline 01256 881337
Sherborne St John, Basingstoke, Hampshire RG24 9HL
Email: svygen@smtp.ntrust.org.uk
Website: www.nationaltrust.org.uk/ southern
4m N of Basingstoke off A340
Open *House: Late Mar–Oct. Grounds: Feb–Oct Sat–Wed & Good Fri, all 11–5*
A house with a bit of everything. Built in the early 16th century for William

*The north front and classical portico of **The Vyne** seen across the lake.*

Sandys, later Lord Sandys, Henry VIII's Lord Chamberlain, it has a Tudor chapel with Renaissance glass, considered one of the finest in the country. The house has some significant later additions. They included a classical portico, the first of its kind in England, probably designed by John Webb, and a Palladian staircase. Both Henry VIII and Elizabeth visited the house. It became a Parliamentarian stronghold during the Civil War. The 18th-century Strawberry Parlour was named after Horace Walpole's Gothic-style masterpiece, Strawberry Hill (p176), in Twickenham. The surrounding gardens contain herbaceous borders, a wild garden, lawns, lakes and woodland walks.

ADDITIONAL PLACES TO VISIT

Alfriston Clergy House NT
☎ 01323 870001
Alfriston, Polegate, E Sussex BN26 5TL
Email: ksdxxx@smtp.ntrust.org.uk
4m NE of Seaford just E of B2108
Open *Mar Sat & Sun 11–4, Apr–Oct 10–5; closed Tues & Fri but open Good Fri, Nov–Dec 11–4*
14th-century timber-framed and thatched 'hall house' characteristic of the Wealden vernacular style.

Anne of Cleves House
☎ 01273 474610
52 Southover High Street, Lewes, E Sussex BN7 1JA
Email: anne@sussexpast.co.uk
Website: www.sussexpast.co.uk
Off A27/A275/A26, close to town centre
Open *Jan–mid-Feb Tues Thurs & Sat, mid-Feb–Oct daily, 10–5 (opens 12 Sun), closed Mon in Nov & Dec*
One of the luckier wives of Henry, Anne of Cleves received a divorce settlement in 1541 which included this

16th-century timbered Wealden hall house, although she never actually lived in it. Now owned by the Sussex Archaeological Society, it offers a fascinating glimpse of 16th- and 17th-century life.

Boarstall Tower NT
☎ 00844 239339
Boarstall, nr Aylesbury, Buckinghamshire HP18 9OX
Email: rob.dixon@boarstall.com
2m W of Brill off B4011
Open *Apr–Oct Wed & BH Mons 2–6*
The 14th-century gatehouse belongs to a long-demolished fortified house.

Brenchley
3m NE of Tunbridge Wells, Kent
The village boasts some lovely half-timbered houses and an avenue of yew trees leading to the 13th-century church.

Calshot Castle EH
☎ 02380 892023
Calshot, Fawley, Southampton, Hampshire SO45 1BR
2m SE of Fawley off B3053
Open *Apr–Oct 10–4*
Henry VIII's coastal fort now houses an exhibition and pre-World War I barracks.

Camber Castle EH
☎ 01797 223862;
Reserve Manager 01797 223862
Camber, nr Rye, E Sussex TN31 7RT
1m S of Rye off A259, access by delightful 1m walk across fields
Open *July–Sept Sat 2–5; monthly guided walks round Rye Harbour Nature Reserve including Camber Castle – phone Reserve Manager for information*
One of Henry VIII's coastal defences now in ruins. It was built to offer protection for the joint harbour of Rye and Winchelsea. It now lies one mile further back from the sea thanks to silting.

Charleston
☎ 01323 811265
Nr Firle, Lewes, E Sussex BN8 6LL
Email: charles@solutions-inc.co.uk
Website: www.charleston.org.uk
6m E of Lewes off A27 near Firle
Open *May–June Sept–Oct 2–6,
July–Aug 11.30–6, Sun & BH Mons 2–6*
With its own tithe barn, it is a good
example of a Norman house greatly
extended during the Tudor and Georgian
periods. In the early 20th century it
became the home of Vanessa Bell and a
focal point for the Bloomsbury set, who
decorated the house and garden.

Chenies Manor House
☎ 01494 762888
Chenies, Rickmansworth,
Buckinghamshire WD3 6ER
*N of A404 between Amersham
& Rickmansworth;
3m from junction 18 on M25*
Open *Apr–Oct Wed Thurs & BH Mons 2–5*
The manor house with its beautiful
old brickwork dates from the 15th and
16th centuries, and has a full complement of furniture and tapestries. It is
surrounded by re-created period gardens,
among them a Tudor sunken garden.
There is a fabulous show of tulips
each spring.

Dorney Court
☎ 01628 604638
Windsor, Berkshire SL4 6QP
Email: palmer@dorneycourt.co.uk
Website: www.dorneycourt.co.uk
*2m W of Eton, W of B3026,
2m SE of Maidenhead*
Open *May BHs, Aug Mon–Fri & Sun
1.30–4, guided tours only;
rest of year by appointment*
An outstanding Tudor manor house, it is
timbered and built out of pale red brick.
The furniture and fittings date back

through its long history as a family
home. There is a church close by and,
all in all, it is quite idyllic.

Englefield House
☎ 01189 302221
Englefield, Theale, Reading,
Berkshire RB7 5EN
Email: benyon@netcomuk.co.uk
Website: www.englefield-est.
demon.co.uk
6m W of Reading off A340
Open *House: by appointment only.
Gardens: Apr–Sept Mon–Thurs, Oct–Mar
Mon only, all 10–6*
An Elizabethan house added to in the
Victorian period, still surrounded by
gardens and park.

Eton College
☎ 01753 671177
Windsor, Berkshire SL4 6DW
Email: visits@etoncollege.org.uk
Website: www.etoncollege.com
*Vehicle access from Slough 2m N;
access from Windsor by foot only*
Open *Mar–early Oct; phone Visitors' Office
to confirm times*
Within spitting distance of Windsor Castle
(p55), stands another great bastion to the
power of the English establishment
– Eton College, the world's most famous
'public' school, modelled on Winchester
College. Founded by Henry VI in 1440
(a statue of whom stands in the main
court), its most distinctive feature – apart
from the otherworldly uniform of the
boys, all pinstripes, tails and stiff collars –
is the chapel, a masterpiece of the Perpendicular style built from 1449–82.

Glynde Place
☎ 01273 858224
Glynde, nr Lewes, E Sussex BN8 6SX
Email: hampden@glyndeplace.co.uk
Website: www.glyndeplace.co.uk

Off A27 between Lewes & Eastbourne
Open *June–Sept Wed Sun & BH Mons,*
July–Aug Thurs also, all 2–5
Built of flint and brick and with great views across the South Downs, this is a good example of 16th-century architecture. Richard Trevor, Bishop of Durham, lived here in the early years of the 18th century, and rebuilt much of it. There is a fine long gallery with some impressive paintings.

Great Dixter House and Gardens
☎ 01797 252878
Northiam, nr Rye, E Sussex TN31 6PH
Email: office@greatdixter.co.uk
Website: greatdixter@compuserve.com
Signposted off A28 in Northiam
Open *Apr–Oct Tues–Sun 2–5.30*
The half-timbered manor house dates from the mid-15th century and is now famous for the gardens, and the restoration work by Edwardian architect, Edwin Lutyens. The owner and plantsman Christopher Lloyd is responsible for the colourful planting.

Loseley Park
☎ 01483 304440
Loseley Park, Guildford, Surrey GU3 1HS
Website: www.loseley-park.com
Leave A3 S of Guildford, taking B3000
Open *House tours & garden:*
May–Aug Wed–Sun & BH Mons 1–5
The beautiful 16th-century Elizabethan house was built by a relative of Sir Thomas More. There are extensive grounds, and a fine collection of furniture and art, including a series of panels that may have once been in Henry VIII's tent during his mock medieval tournaments. Other fine pieces include George IV's coronation chair, a Hepplewhite four-poster bed, a unique chimney piece carved from local chalk, and tapestries.

Lullingstone Castle
☎ 01322 862114
Eynsford, Kent DA4 0JA
1m S of Eynsford on W side of A224
Open *May–Aug Sat Sun & BH Mons 2–6*
A fine example of a medieval manor house with significant Tudor additions, in particular the brick gatehouse.

Maison Dieu (Medieval Hospital) EH
☎ 01795 534542
Ospringe, Faversham, Kent ME13 8TW
½m W of Faversham on A2
Open *Mid-Apr–Oct Sat Sun & BH Mons 2–5*
Fall ill in the 16th century, and if you were lucky this is where you might have ended up. A precursor to the modern hospital, Maison Dieu still retains many of its original features.

Mapledurham House and Watermill
☎ 01189 723350
Mapledurham, nr Reading, Oxfordshire RG4 7TR
Email: mtrust1997@aol.com
Website: www.mapledurham.co.uk
4m NW of Reading; 1½m W of A4074
Open *Easter–Sept Sat Sun & BH Mons 2–5*
This is a beautiful house dating from the Elizabethan period, offering a fascinating glimpse into the troubled life of the Blounts, a Catholic family in post-Reformation England. Catholics were not ennobled or allowed to serve in the army or navy. The nearby church is split in two, one part being for Protestant worship, the other being a small Catholic chapel.

Medieval Merchant's House EH
☎ 02380 221503
58 French St, Southampton, Hampshire SO1 0AT
¼m S of Bargate off Castle Way
Open *Apr–Sept 10–6, Oct 10–5*

*The half-timbered house at **Great Dixter** seen from the gardens.*

Based in 58 French Street, which would have been one of medieval Southampton's busiest thoroughfares, this is one of the earliest merchants' houses still standing in the country. Dating back to c1290, it was built by a successful merchant called John Fortin who had trading interests in Bordeaux. He lived and worked here. The house has been fully restored to its 14th-century appearance, with a number of replica furnishings added to complete the facsimile of life familiar to many of Chaucer's pilgrims.

Milton Chantry EH
☎ 01474 292257
New Tavern Fort Gardens,
Gravesend, Kent
Off A226 in New Tavern Fort Gardens,
E of central Gravesend
Open *Mar & Oct–23 Dec Sat 12–4 Sun*
10–4, Apr–Sept Wed–Sat 12–5 Sun & BH
Mons 10–5; closed Jan–Feb
This used to be a leper colony's chapel, though later it was amalgamated into a fort. Dating from the 14th century, it includes artefacts from the area.

Nether Winchendon House
☎ 01844 290199
Aylesbury, Buckinghamshire HP18 0DY
2m N of A418 between Thame & Aylesbury
Open *May & Aug BH Sun & Mon*
2.30–5.30; groups by appointment
The medieval and Tudor manor house has 18th-century Gothic-style alterations, and a surrounding garden.

Netley Abbey EH
☎ 02392 581059
Netley, Southampton, Hampshire
4m SE of Southampton, in Netley
facing Southampton Water
Open *Any reasonable time*
The ruins of a Cistercian abbey which was later converted into a Tudor house.

Oakhurst Cottage NT
☎ 01428 684090
Hambledon, nr Godalming,
Surrey GU8 4HF
Email: swwgen@smtp.ntrust.org.uk
Phone for directions
Open *Late Mar–Oct Wed Thurs Sat Sun &*
BH Mons 2–5. By appointment only
Tiny but full of delights, this is a 16th-century timber-framed cottage with a cottage garden lovingly restored.

Old Soar Manor EH & NT
☎ 01732 810378; Infoline 01732 811145
Plaxtol, Borough Green, Kent TN15 0QX
2m S of Borough Green (A25)
Open *Apr–Sept 10–6*
These are the highly impressive private dwellings of a medieval knight, although the hall dates to a much later period. There is a beautifully preserved 'solar' (or private) wing.

Parham House and Gardens
☎ Infoline 01903 744888
Nr Pulborough, W Sussex RH20 4HS
Email: Parham@dial.pipex.com
Website: www.parhaminsussex.co.uk
Between Pulborough & Storrington on A283
Open *Apr–Oct Wed Thurs Sun & BH Mons*
House: 2–6. Gardens: 12–6
An Elizabethan building that was started by Sir Thomas Palmer, who had sailed with Sir Francis Drake on his daring raid on Cadiz. The great hall has impressive, high mullioned windows, and a fine collection of Elizabethan, Georgian and Jacobean portraits. The stylish, colourful, huge gardens with long borders are well worth visiting in their own right.

Stoneacre NT
☎ 01622 862871
Otham, Maidstone, Kent ME15 8RS
3m SE of Maidstone, 1m S of A20
Open *Late Mar–mid-Oct Wed & Sat*

& *BH Mons & Tues 2–6*
A yeoman's house dating from the late
medieval period, there is half-timbering,
a great hall, and a newly restored garden.

Sutton House NT

☎ 020 8986 2264
2 & 4 Homerton High St, Hackney,
London E9 6QJ
Email: tshslh@smtp.ntrust.org.uk
Website: www.nationaltrust.org.uk/
thameschilterns
Tube Bethnal Green; rail Hackney Central
Open *Mid-Jan–Dec Fri–Sun &
BH Mons 2–5*
How incongruous – a Tudor redbrick
house in the middle of Hackney in East
London. Recently restored, it is a fasci-
nating example of the kind of house in
which one of Henry VIII's principal
secretaries lived. It has beautiful
panelling and wall paintings.

Wolvesey Castle
(Old Bishop's Palace) EH

☎ 01962 854766
College St, Wolvesey, Winchester,
Hampshire SO23 8NB
*¾m SE of Winchester Cathedral,
next to the Bishop's Palace*
Open *Apr–Sept 10–6, Oct 10–5*
The see of Winchester used to be the
wealthiest in England, and these are the
remains of the palace where its bishops
used to live. The castle, founded by
Bishop Henry of Blois, was built between
1130 and 1140. The last great occasion
celebrated here was the marriage of
Mary Tudor to Philip of Spain in 1554.
Like so many buildings the castle was
'slighted' by Cromwellian troops during
the Civil War on Cromwell's personal
orders. A new bishop's palace was built
in the 1680s next to the ruins, which
are today surrounded by school
playingfields.

Eastern MAP 3

158 Binham Priory EH*

Binham-on-Wells, Norfolk NR21 OAL
¼m NW of Binham-on-Wells off B1388
Open *Any reasonable time*
This is one of those churches that
astonishes the visitor, even though it is not
in the front rank of cathedrals or abbeys.
But it has a sense of scale which, as eloquently as some of the grander church
buildings, speaks of a time when religion
underwrote the whole of worldly life.

The west front is an unusual example
of the Early English style in East Anglia
and was built by the prior Richard de
Parco between 1226 and 1244. There are
haunting glimpses of the impact of the
Reformation – in particular, examples of

A panel from the rood screen at **Binham Priory**
*shows a painting of Christ as the Man of Sorrows
superimposed with text from Cranmer's Bible
of 1539.*

Biblical texts superimposed on top of earlier religious images suddenly regarded as blasphemous. The abbey was dissolved in 1540 and the site and possessions were granted to Thomas Paston. The original nave of the abbey church now serves as the local parish church.

159 Burghley House
☎ 01780 752451
Stamford, Lincolnshire PE9 3JY
Email: info@burghley.co.uk
Website: www.burghley.co.uk
1½m from Stamford
Open *Apr–Oct 11–5*
The largest Elizabethan house in Britain was built for William Cecil (who became Lord Burghley in 1571), Elizabeth I's principal secretary, then Lord High Treasurer and her most trusted advisor for four decades. The house took nearly as long to build. It was begun in *c*1555 and completed in the same year that Mary Queen of Scots was executed, 1587.

It remains perhaps the most spectacular of the great 'Prodigy Houses' of the period, with particularly impressive windows and a Byzantine landscape of chimneys on the roof. Its great courtyard has an Italianate colonnade and an imposing three-storey tower dating from 1585. It is a monumental building, especially in its huge pyramid-like obelisk, flanked by two smaller towers over the second courtyard. It has echoes of a French château. This was the house to which Burghley retreated when he escaped life at court. Apparently he would arrive, remove his cloak and command it, 'Lie thou there, Lord Treasurer'.

The interiors were reworked in the late 17th century by the 5th Earl of Exeter who was a voracious art collector. All the great names of interior decorating from his lifetime are represented here – Antonio Verrio, Grinling Gibbons and Louis Laguerre. The masterpieces are the so-called Heaven Room and Hell Staircase, which look as though they were beamed right out of the Louvre, with sensational murals by Verrio. There is a great collection of 17th-century Italian paintings. Outside are 300 acres landscaped by 'Capability' Brown.

160 Caister Castle *
☎ 01493 720267
Caister-on-Sea, Norfolk
4m N of Great Yarmouth off A1064
Open *Late May–Sept Sun–Fri 10–4.30*
With its tall, slender and actually well fortified tower, this is an especially attractive example of the later kind of fortified house. It was built by Sir John Fastolf (immortalized by Shakespeare rather unfairly as the fat buffoon Falstaff), and is unusual for being constructed in brick and not stone. John Paston inherited the house and it became the home of the Paston family, famous for their collection of letters, one of the most vivid pictures of 15th-century domestic and national life to have survived. There is now a motor museum here too.

161 Church of the Holy Trinity *
☎ 01787 310845
Long Melford, Suffolk CO10 9DL
Website: www.longmelford.co.uk
3m N of Sudbury off A134
Open *Mar–Oct 10–4, Apr–Sept 10–5, Nov–Feb 11–3*
This huge 15th-century church has magnificent windows and a three-gabled Lady Chapel. The interior is illuminated by a wealth of 15th-century stained glass, much of it reassembled during the 19th century. A great deal was lost, however, during the stormy, iconoclastic years of the mid-17th century. The best

window is over the north door, and depicts the Virgin Mary holding the body of Christ with his crown of thorns. A long and lavish description was left by one Roger Martyn of what this church looked like before the whitewash purge of the Reformation – a hymn to colour and spectacle long since vanished from its Anglicized interior.

162 Fotheringhay Castle*

Nr Oundle, Northamptonshire
1m N of A605 on River Nene
Open *Any reasonable time*
Nothing much exists now of the castle in which Mary Queen of Scots was executed except a barren, rather bleak mound. But nearby is the beautiful Church of St Mary and All Saints built 150 years before Mary's execution. Intended as a mausoleum for the Plantagenet family, it has a tower three storeys high, with tall triple lights. Inside there is a monument to Richard, Duke of York, and his wife Cicely and son Edmund. It has a painted master-piece of a pulpit.

163 King's College Chapel

☎ 01223 331212
King's Parade, Cambridge CB2 1ST
Website: www.kings.cam.ac.uk
In city centre
Open *Term time Mon–Fri 9.30–3.30 Sat 9.30–3.15 Sun 1.15–2.15 & 5–5.30; out of term Mon–Sat 9.30–4.30 Sun 10–5. Services: daily 5.30, Sun 10.30 & 6 (1st Sun of month); public welcome*
We have Henry VIII to thank for the magnificent fan-vaulting, completed in 1515. Henry VI, who founded King's College in 1441, stipulated that the chapel should be plain and spare of ornament, but the later Henry suffered no such restraint, thank goodness. The chapel remains firmly lodged at the top

of most people's lists of beautiful buildings in England. If you are lucky enough to attend a concert or recital, you will be struck by the purity of the acoustics.

164 Lavenham: The Guildhall of Corpus Christi* NT

☎ 01787 247646
Market Place, Lavenham,
Suffolk CO10 9QZ
In centre of village, 6m NE of Sudbury
Open *Mar Sat & Sun 11–4, Apr May & Oct Wed–Sun & BH Mons 11–5, June–Sept daily 11–5, Nov Sat & Sun 12–4*
The whole town is rightly celebrated for its 15th-century survivals, notably the Church of St Peter and St Paul which is one of the most impressive in the whole of Suffolk thanks to all that wool money. But nothing tops the Guildhall, a spectacular piece of early 16th-century architecture which was originally built as a social and business centre for the wool magnates, although it was later used briefly as a jail.

165 Longthorpe Tower EH

☎ 01733 268482
Thorpe Rd, Longthorpe,
Cambridgeshire PE1 1HA
2m W of Peterborough on A47
Open *Apr–Oct Sat Sun & BH Mons 12–5*
Though it's a fortified manor house, what makes it really worth visiting is its unique collection of art, particularly 14th-century wall paintings, as good as any in Northern Europe. The paintings are in the tower's principal chamber; their Biblical and secular subjects share one theme, how to live your life well. The scenes depicted include the Seven Ages of Man, the Labours of the Months, the Three Quick and the Three Dead and, most delightfully, the Wheel of the Five Senses with a different beast for each one.

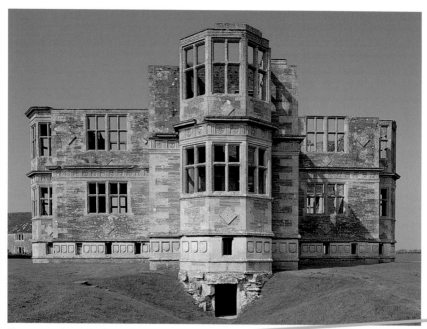

*The spectacular shell of **Lyveden New Bield**.*

166 Lyveden New Bield* NT
☎ 01832 205358
Nr Oundle, Peterborough,
Northamptonshire PE18 5AT
4m SW of Oundle via A427
Open *Apr–Oct Wed–Sun & BH Mons
10.30–5, Nov–Mar Sat & Sun 10.30–4*
Begun in 1595 by Sir Thomas Tresham,
one of the Gunpowder Plot conspirators,
who decided to make his house speak for
his beliefs. He incorporated the shape
of the Cross in the ground plan and
windows, and venerated the Passion in
the stone frieze round the exterior walls.
The house was never completed.

167 Tattershall Castle NT
☎ 01526 342543
Tattershall, Lincolnshire LN4 4LR
Email: etcxxx@smtp.ntrust.org.uk
15m NE of Sleaford on S side of A153

Open *Apr–Sept Sat–Wed 11–5.30 (also
open Thurs in Aug), Oct Sat–Wed 11–4,
Nov–mid-Dec Sat & Sun 12–4*
The castle is famous as one of the
country's best examples of a Norman-
style keep made of brick and not stone.
Built in the mid-15th century, it was
part of an expansion to the site dating
back to the late 13th century. Although a
purely defensive structure, it is still very
imposing. Look for the 15th-century fireplaces saved from destruction by Lord
Curzon just before the First World War.

168 Walsingham Abbey*
☎ 01328 820259
Common Place, Little Walsingham,
Norfolk NR22 6BP
5m N from Fakenham on B1105
Open *Grounds: Feb daily, Mar & Oct–Dec
Sat & Sun, Apr–Sept daily, all 10–4.30*

The site of the famous Shrine of Our Lady of Walsingham was one of the most important pilgrimage destinations from the Middle Ages until the Reformation. An annual revival of this pilgrimage takes place every spring.

169 Waltham Abbey Church and Gatehouse* EH
☎ 01992 702200
Church 01992 767897
Highbridge St, Waltham Abbey, Essex EN9 1XQ
Off A112, junction 25 on M25
Open *Gatehouse: any reasonable time Church: Mon–Sat 10–4 (opens 11 on Wed) Sun 12–6*

Dating from the 14th century, the surviving gatehouse sits alongside a number of other remains from one of the most important monastic sites in Britain. The abbey church was founded c1030, rebuilt by King Harold, and consecrated in 1060. Harold was buried here after the Battle of Hastings thanks to his wife who found his corpse among the heaps of dead on the battlefield. It has a massive nave begun by Harold, a Lady Chapel of 1316 and an Elizabethan west tower. Much of the abbey was destroyed by Henry VIII, though the nave has become the parish church. Later additions date from the Victorian period (supervised by William Burges from 1859–76). Most notable are the stained-glass windows by Edward Burne-Jones.

ADDITIONAL PLACES TO VISIT

Bourne Mill NT
☎ 01206 572422
Bourne Rd, Colchester, Essex CO2 8RT
1m S of centre of Colchester, off B1025
Open *All BH Suns & Mons, June–Aug Sun & Tues 2–5*

This was originally built as a fishing lodge in 1591. Much of the mill machinery is still intact.

Doddington Hall
☎ 01522 694308
Doddington, Lincoln LN6 4RU
5m W of Lincoln on B1190, off A46
Open *House: May–Sept Wed Sun & BH Mons 2–6. Gardens: as house & Mar–Apr Sun 2–6*

One of the masterpieces of the Elizabethan architect, Robert Smythson. There is a gabled gatehouse, and the hall is crowned with a fabulous array of belvederes and cupolas. Built from 1593–1600, it contains a good collection of furniture, porcelain and tapestries.

Gainsborough Old Hall EH
☎ 01427 612669
Parnell St, Gainsborough, Lincolnshire DN21 2NB
In Gainsborough opposite Library
Open *Easter Sunday–Oct Mon–Sat 10–5 Sun 2–5.30, Nov–Easter Mon–Sat 10–5*

The original hall was ruined during the Wars of the Roses. What you see today, built out of brick and half-timbering, dates from the early years of the 16th century. Later that century a number of key religious dissenters (the Pilgrim Fathers) used to congregate here. John Wesley, the founder of Methodism, preached here on several occasions. There is a reconstructed medieval kitchen as well as a great hall.

Helmingham Hall Gardens
☎ 01473 890363
Stowmarket, Suffolk IP14 6EF
Email: helminghamestate@aol.com
Website: www.helmingham.com
9m N of Ipswich
Open *Gardens: May–mid-Sept Sun 2–6, groups by appointment on Wed 2–5. House: closed to public*

Set in the middle of a 400-acre deer park, Helmingham is a quadrangular moated Tudor hall. Its 16th-century half-timbering has been rather obscured by later Georgian and Victorian alterations (the battlements are by Thomas Nash). The home of the Tollemache family, they still raise the drawbridge every night, a tradition going back four centuries.

Landguard Fort EH

☎ 01394 277767 or 01473 218245
Felixstowe, Suffolk IP11
Website: www.landguard.com
1m S of Felixstowe
Open *Mid-Apr–May Oct–Nov Sun & Wed, June–July & Sept Tues Wed Sat & Sun, Aug daily, all 1–5*
A fort built in the 18th century, on the site of one built by Henry VIII, it has additions made in the 19th and 20th centuries.

Melford Hall NT

☎ 01787 880286
Long Melford, Sudbury, Suffolk CO10 9AA
3m N of Sudbury on A134
Open *Apr & Oct Sat Sun & BH Mon, May–Sept Wed–Sun & BH Mon 2–5.30*
Despite the 18th-century additions, this is still primarily a brick-built, turreted Tudor manor house where Elizabeth I was entertained in 1578.

Row 111 House, Old Merchant's House and Greyfriars' Cloisters EH

☎ 01493 857900
Great Yarmouth, Norfolk NR30 2BQ
In Great Yarmouth, make for South Quay along riverside & dock, ½m inland from beach
Open *Apr–Oct 10–1 2–5*
These two 17th-century town houses have original fittings. They survived a World War II bombing raid, and remain one of Great Yarmouth's most valued

sites. When carrying out repairs after the bomb damage, the remains of a Franciscan friary were discovered.

St George's Guildhall NT

☎ 01553 764864
27–29 King Street, King's Lynn, Norfolk PE30 1HA
Website: www.west-norfolk.gov.uk
On W side of King St, close to Tuesday Market Place
Open *Mon–Fri 10–2; closed Good Fri & BHs & during performances*
One of the largest surviving guildhalls from the medieval period is now used as an arts centre.

Central MAP 4

170 Ashby de la Zouch Castle EH

☎ 01530 413343
South St, Ashby de la Zouch, Leicestershire LE65 1BR
SE of town centre; 12m S of Derby on A511
Open *Apr–Sept 10–6, Oct 10–5, Nov–Mar Wed–Sun 10–4*
The ruined Hastings Tower survives and is a good example of the 15th-century idea of what a castle tower should look like (and from which there are fine panoramic views). Ashby also shows signs of the attempts made by later medieval castle builders to incorporate more expansive and comfortable living quarters, so that it did not just provide accommodation for a lord and a military garrison. It was initially a Norman manor house, but was later fortified by Lord Hastings in the reign of Edward IV. It fell into disrepair during the Civil War.

171 Compton Wynyates

Upper Tysoe, Warwickshire
N from village of Upper Brailes off B4035 Shipston–Banbury road, near Upper Tysoe
Open *Not open to the public*

*The ruined Hastings Tower of **Ashby de la Zouch Castle** built in 1474–83.*

It might be closed to the public, but it is magnificently visible from the nearby road. One of the finest Tudor-era houses, it was built in the years of relative peace that followed the Wars of the Roses, and was later enlarged in the 1520s. It was the home of the Compton family who later fought on Charles I's side during the Civil War; it cost them £20,000 in fines to get the house back from the Parliamentarians who had confiscated it.

Apart from some mock-Gothic windows added in the 19th century, this is a house bristling with beautiful Tudor and Elizabethan touches, especially the plasterwork, furniture and great hall. Tall decorated chimneys rise from its many fireplaces, and there are mullioned windows which let the light pour in. Henry VIII stayed here with Catherine of Aragon, and their emblems are painted on glass in the room in which they slept. The surrounding topiary hedging is very ornate.

172 Haddon Hall
☎ 01629 812855
Bakewell, Derbyshire DE45 1LA
Email: info@haddonhall.co.uk
Website: www.haddonhall.co.uk
1½m S of Bakewell on E side of A6,
Open *Easter–Sept daily 10.30–5,*
Oct Mon–Thurs 10.30–4.30
A fine 16th-century manor house with Norman origins, it really came into its own when it passed into the hands of the Dukes of Rutland. The estate was originally part of a settlement bequeathed to William I's illegitimate son. It is now frequently used as a movie location (*Elizabeth*, with Cate Blanchett, was partly filmed here in 1997) because, despite a long history of additions – many done as recently as the 20th century – little of substance has changed since late medieval times. There is a 14th-century galleried banqueting hall, medieval kitchens, buttery and bakehouse, and an Elizabethan rose garden.

173 Hardwick Hall NT

☎ 01246 850430
Doe Lea, Chesterfield, Derbyshire S44 5QJ
Email: ehwxxx@smtp.ntrust.org.uk
9m SE of Chesterfield, leave M1 junction 29
Open *Hall: Late Mar–Oct Wed Thurs
Sat Sun BH Mons & Good Fri 12.30–5
Gardens: Apr–Oct daily (closed Tues)
11–5.30*
Possibly one of the most interesting, it
is certainly one of the most characterful
houses of the Elizabethan period. It was
built by Elizabeth, Countess of Shrewsbury (Bess of Hardwick), a redoubtable
woman in possession of a fine fortune
thanks to three dead husbands. She
invested it in building this gorgeous house
with the help of the great Elizabethan
architect, Robert Smythson. You can see
her initials (ES) on the towers. Inside is
a stark but opulent palace remarkably
pristine because, unlike so many other
houses of the period, the family moved
on to a new site (at nearby Chatsworth).
It was not expanded and transformed
by later generations. The tapestries
are particularly impressive, as are
the surrounding gardens.

174 Kirby Hall* EH

☎ 01536 203230
Deene, nr Corby,
Northamptonshire NN17 5EN
4m NE of Corby off A43
Open *Apr–Sept 10–6, Oct 10–5,
Nov–Mar Sat & Sun 10–4*
This Elizabethan house was begun
in 1570 by Sir Humphrey Stafford and
completed by Sir Christopher Hatton,
who commissioned Inigo Jones to do
the work between 1638 and 1640. It is a
very fine example of a large Elizabethan
mansion. Today it is a ruin, but still
spectacular. There are hundreds of acres
of grounds which are frequently used
for historical displays.

175 Little Moreton Hall NT

☎ 01260 272018
Congleton, Cheshire CW12 4SD
Email: mimsca@smtp.ntrust.org.uk
3m SW of Congleton on E side of A34
Open *Apr–Oct Wed–Sun & BHs 11.30–5
(dusk if earlier), Nov–Dec Sat & Sun 11.30–4*
Built between 1559–80, this is generally
regarded as the finest timber-framed,
moated manor house in the country. It is
endlessly used as a television location,
partly for its fabulous long gallery,
cobblestone courtyard, and lovely
setting. It is a refreshing contrast to the
ordered symmetry of so many stately
homes with its cheerful anarchy
of shapes and decoration. Each of three
generations of the Moreton family helped
add to it and had very distinct, possibly
irreconcilable, ideas about how it should
look. The result is the most famous black
and white house in England, and
a genuine, eccentric delight.
The house testifies to the abundance
of wood in the 15th century, which was
used as much as plaster in constructing
the external walls. The house has
wonderful bow windows, proudly
inscribed by the man who put them in;
'Richarde Dale Carpeder made thies
windows by the grace of god'. Little
Moreton is an unforgettable exuberance
of pattern and geometry.

176 Stanton Harcourt Manor

☎ 01865 881928
Main Rd, Stanton Harcourt, nr Witney,
Oxfordshire OX8 1RJ
5m SE of Witney off B4449
Open *Selected days from Apr–Sept;
phone for opening times*
A manor house with very little in the
way of fortifications, it instead has nearly
12 acres of gardens, wild borders, paths,
ponds, and the very impressive, cruciform
Norman Church of St Michael, with its

Early English tower and a lovely private chapel. There was once a great medieval house on the site, but it was demolished in the 18th century.

Two delightful medieval buildings have survived though. One is Pope's Tower (named after the poet Alexander Pope who often stayed and wrote at Stanton Harcourt) which contains a late 15th-century chapel on the ground floor, and the other is the great kitchen. The latter has that exhilarating quality of still completely belonging to the medieval world. This kitchen is quite different to those in later stately homes. It is square with a high octagonal, pyramidal roof and no opening for the smoke and heat from its three open fire 'ovens'. It gives the most graphic sense of what a completely different experience the communal preparation of food was in the Middle Ages.

Stanton also has a wonderful and miscellaneous collection of medieval statues and memorials to the Harcourt family. This is one of those locations that really is more than the sum of its parts, a perfect little oasis.

177 Stokesay Castle * EH

☎ 01588 672544
Craven Arms, Shropshire SY7 9AH
7m NW of Ludlow off A49
Open *Apr–Sept 10–6, Oct 10–5, Nov–Mar Wed–Sun 10–1 2–4*
Built by a rich medieval merchant Lawrence of Ludlow, Stokesay has few rivals in the country for its picturesque setting. With 12th- and 13th-century fabrics still evident, this fortified manor house had major additions (the timber-framed Jacobean gatehouse and some fortifications) in the 16th and 17th centuries. It is acknowledged to be one of the most attractive smaller fortified houses in Britain, an opinion shared by one of its 17th-century owners who could not bear to see it destroyed by the

The 13th-century fortified manor house **Stokesay Castle**, *with 16th- and 17th-century additions.*

Medieval Manors and Elizabethan Prodigies CENTRAL

Parliamentarians in the Civil War, and who therefore promptly surrendered. Without question that spared it from being 'slighted' (razed to the ground). His loss of dignity maybe, but our gain, no doubt.

178 Sudeley Castle *
☎ 01242 602308
Winchcombe, nr Cheltenham, Gloucestershire GL54 5JD
Email: marketing@sudeley.org.uk
Website: www.stratford.co.uk/sudeley
8m NE of Cheltenham on B4632
Open *Castle: Apr–Oct 11–5*
Gardens: Mar–Oct 10.30–5.30
The house has quite a history. Henry VIII's last wife, Catherine Parr, lies buried here. Charles I's nephew, Prince Rupert, used it as his Royalist headquarters during the latter years of the Civil War. It underwent major redevelopment during the Victorian period, with many pieces of furniture bought from Horace Walpole's Strawberry Hill (p176). There is a ruined banqueting hall dating back to 1450. Surrounding the house are acres of award-winning gardens and landscape.

ADDITIONAL PLACES TO VISIT

Ancient High House
☎ 01785 619131
Greengate St, Stafford ST16 2JA
Website: www.staffordbc.gov.uk
Email: tic@staffordbe.gov.uk
In town centre
Open *Mon–Sat 10–5*
The largest timber-framed house in England dating back to 1595. King Charles stayed here in 1642. It is now a museum.

Arbury Hall
☎ 02476 382804
Nuneaton, Warwickshire CV10 7PT
2m SW of Nuneaton, 1m W of A444

Open *Easter–Aug Sun & Mon BH weekends only 2–5.30; groups by arrangement only*
Beneath the 18th-century cladding lies a Tudor mansion, but the interior styling is so striking that the house reveals little of its earlier origins The chapel contains a magnificent plaster ceiling laden with flowers, fruit and foliage, the work of Edward Martin in 1678. The final 50 years of the 18th century saw the completion of the hall's transformation into a fully fledged Gothic Revival gem. The novelist George Eliot was born on the estate.

Ashleworth Tithe Barn NT
☎ 01684 855300 (Regional office)
Ashleworth, Gloucestershire
Email: sevinfo@smtp.ntrust.org.uk
Website: www.ntrustsevern.org.uk
6m N of Gloucester on A417, on W bank of the Severn
Open *Apr–Oct 9–6 or sunset if earlier, closed Good Fri; other times by appointment*
A fine 15th-century tithe barn with a huge stone-tiled roof.

Baddesley Clinton NT
☎ 01564 783294
Rising Lane, Baddesley Clinton, Knowle, Solihull, Warwickshire B93 0DQ
Email: baddesley@smtp.ntrust.org.uk
Website: www.ntrustsevern.org.uk/baddesley.htm
¾m W of A4141 Warwick–Birmingham road at Chadwick End
Open *House: Mar–Oct Wed–Sun & BH Mons 1.30–5, May–Sept open till 5.30*
Gardens: open at 12, closed mid-late Dec
It is one of the most romantic moated manor houses still in existence, dating from the 15th century but with later additions. Inside everything is present and correct, including the portraits and priest holes, while outside are gardens, ponds and lakeside walks.

Benthall Hall NT
☎ 01952 882159
Broseley, Shropshire TF12 5RX
Email: mlajlc@smtp.ntrust.org.uk
*1m NW of Broseley on B4375, 4m NE
of Much Wenlock, 1m SW of Ironbridge*
Open *House & garden: Apr–Sept Wed Sun
& BH Mons 1.30–5.30; parties by prior
arrangement*
The 16th-century stone house has
mullioned windows and moulded
chimneys. It has a particularly fine oak
staircase, decorated plaster ceilings and
oak panelling despite being damaged
during the Civil War. It was originally
owned by a Catholic family which
explains the presence of some particularly
interesting insignia on the south wall
of the entrance porch: there are four
stone discs, with a conspicuously
missing fifth one – an allusion to the
stigmata (the Crucifixion 'wounds' on
Christ's body) which signalled sanctuary
to any fugitive Catholic. It was later
owned by the man who designed Coalbrookdale Iron Bridge (p231), Thomas
Pritchard, and after him the Victorian
botanist George Maw. It has some
carefully restored gardens.

Broughton Castle
☎ 01295 276070
Banbury, Oxfordshire OX15 5EB
Website: www.broughtoncastle.
demon.co.uk
*2m SW of Banbury Cross on B4035
(leave M40 at junction 11)*
Open *Easter, BH Suns & Mons May–Aug,
late May–mid-Sept Wed & Sun, July–Aug
Thurs also 2–5; groups by appointment*
Used as the secret meeting place for a
cabal of anti-Royalist leaders in the lead
up to the Civil War, this house stands on
a moated island. The house dates back
to about 1300 and still has many remains
of its medieval origins. There are later

embellishments and additions including
paintings, fireplaces, ceilings and
panelling. It is still in private ownership.

Charlecote Park NT
☎ 01789 470277
Warwick, Warwickshire CV35 9ER
Email: charlecote@smtp.ntrust.org.uk
Website: www.ntrustsevern.org.uk/
charleco.htm
*5m E of Stratford-upon-Avon,
6m S of Warwick, on N side of B4086*
Open *Late Mar–Nov Fri–Tues house 12–5,
grounds 11–6, Nov–Dec Feb–late Mar
grounds only Sat & Sun 11–4*
The house was built in 1558 by Sir
Thomas Lucy. Although much of the
interior reflects major changes made
in the Victorian period, the outside still
powerfully evokes the Tudor world. It is
also where Shakespeare was reputedly
caught trying to catch deer. The deer park
was landscaped by 'Capability' Brown.

Coughton Court
☎ 01789 400777
Alcester, Warwickshire B49 5JA
Website: www.coughtoncourt.co.uk
2m N of Alcester on A435
Open *Apr–Sept Wed–Sun
& BH Mons 11.30–5*
The long-held family home of the
Throckmortons (of Gunpowder Plot fame)
was where relatives and co-conspirators
anxiously awaited news of the outcome
of the plot to blow up the Houses of
Parliament. It was later damaged during
the Civil War, but the main features are
untouched – namely two half-timbered
Elizabethan wings and a battlemented
gatehouse dating back to 1509.

The Greyfriars NT
☎ 01905 23571
Friar Street, Worcester WR1 2LZ
Email: greyfriars@smtp.ntrust.org.uk

Website: www.ntrustsevern.org.uk/
greyfria.htm
In centre of Worcester
Open *Apr–Oct Wed Thurs & BH Mons 2–5*
It was due to be demolished after World
War II but won a reprieve. The National
Trust has since restored this fabulous
late 15th-century house, which has
additions from the 17th and 18th
centuries.

Leigh Court Barn EH
☎ 0121 625 6820 (Regional office)
Leigh, nr Worcester, Worcestershire
5m W of Worcester off A4103
Open *Apr–Sept Thurs–Sun 10–6*
The largest barn of its kind in Britain,
this is a magnificent, timber-framed,
14th-century barn, which was erected
for the monks of nearby Pershore Abbey.

Minster Lovell Hall and Dovecote EH
☎ 02392 581059
Minster Lovell, nr Witney, Oxfordshire
*Adjacent to Minster Lovell church,
3m W of Witney off A40*
Open *Any reasonable time*
As beautiful for its setting as for its
ruined remains, this is a beautiful and
quiet Cotswolds destination.

Moreton Corbet Castle EH
☎ 01604 730320
Moreton Corbet, Shrewsbury, Shropshire
7m NE of Shrewsbury off B5063
Open *Any reasonable time*
One of those ruins with an almost
archetypal historical record: it has
Norman origins, became a great Elizabethan mansion house, and was badly
damaged in the Civil War.

Owlpen Manor
☎ 01453 860261
Nr Uley, Gloucestershire GL11 5BZ
Email: sales@owlpen.com

Website: www.owlpen.com
1m E of Uley off B4066
Open *Easter–Sept Tues–Sun
& BH Mons 2–5*
The stone Cotswold manor from the
15th century has a barn, mill and court-
house. The gardens have particularly
well-clipped yew trees. More recently
the manor gained a number of Arts
and Crafts associations. It has a lovely
wooded setting deep in the Gloucestershire countryside.

Rockingham Castle
☎ 01536 770240
Market Harborough,
Leicestershire LE16 8TH
Website: www.rockinghamcastle.com
1m N of Corby
Open *Castle: Apr–Sept Sun & BH Mons,
July–Aug Tues & Thurs also 1–5
Grounds: as castle, open from 11.30*
Granted by Queen Elizabeth I to Edward
Watson, this Norman castle was later
frequented by Charles Dickens, who
used it as the model for Chesney Wold in
Bleak House. Although mentioned in the
Domesday Book, and the site of
a number of key medieval councils, it is
very much a Tudor building, though the
Norman gateway has survived. Good
access to nearby Rockingham forest
made it an ideal hunting lodge for the
Tudor monarchs. Rockingham was
slightly Gothicized in the 19th century,
but not to its detriment. Inside there
are fine furniture and paintings.

Rushton Triangular Lodge EH
☎ 01536 710761
Rushton, nr Kettering,
Northamptonshire NN14 1RP
3m E of Desborough off A6
Open *Apr–Sept 10–6, Oct 10–5*
Like Lyveden New Bield, this fell into the
hands of Sir Thomas Tresham, who made

extensive additions from 1590–1600. And Like Lyveden the design has a religious significance. The triangular shape represents the Holy Trinity, each side is 33ft (10m) long, and there are a number of three-sided features and motifs.

Rycote Chapel EH

☎ 02392 581059

Milton Common, Oxfordshire OX9 2PE

3m SW of Thame off A329

Open *Apr–Sept Fri–Sun & BH Mons 2–6*

The chapel (Church of St Michael and All Angels) dates back to the 1400s, when it was built as a domestic chapel with a west tower. The interior contains some fine early 17th-century woodwork, a musician's gallery, and a two-storey family pew with an organ.

Shakespeare Houses

Shakespeare's Birthplace, Anne Hathaway's Cottage, Nash's House and New Place, Hall's Croft and Mary Arden's House

☎ 01789 204016

The Shakespeare Birthplace Trust, Henley St, Stratford-upon-Avon, Warwickshire CV37 6QW

Email: info@shakespeare.org.uk

Website: www.shakespeare.org.uk

In centre of Stratford except for Anne Hathaway's Cottage which is 1m W of town and Mary Arden's house which is 3½m N of town

Open *Mid-Mar–mid-Oct 9–5 (opens 9.30 Sun), mid-Oct–mid-Mar 9.30–4 (opens 10 Sun). Nash's House and Hall's Croft open half an hour later all year*

No, we do not have Shakespeare's shoes or diaries or any of those possessions left by other great historical figures. But there are the Stratford houses and museums. They have their charm, but you will have to get there early to beat the crowds in order to appreciate them.

Snowshill Manor NT

☎ 01386 852410

Snowshill, nr Broadway, Gloucestershire WR12 7JU

Email: snowshill@smtp.ntrust.org.uk

Website: www.ntrustsevern.org.uk/snowshill.htm

3m SW of Broadway off A44

Open *Apr–Oct Wed–Sun & BH Mons 12–5*

With its collection of clocks, toys and musical instruments, among other things, this 16th- and 17th-century manor house is a treasure trove. It is the former home of Charles Paget Wade, who did most of the collecting. So great was his mania for collecting that he was forced to live in an outbuilding for lack of space.

Tutbury Castle

☎ 01283 812129

Tutbury, Staffordshire DE13 9JF

W side of Tutbury off A50

Open *Easter–mid-Sept Wed–Sun & BH Mons 11–5*

Overlooking the Dove Valley are the remains of a large motte-and-bailey. There have been fortifications here since Saxon times, but the surviving buildings date from the days of Mary Queen of Scots. She was imprisoned here on various occasions during her 19-year confinement in England before her execution.

Wingfield Manor* EH

☎ 01773 832060

Garner Lane, South Wingfield, Derbyshire DE5 7NH

11m S of Chesterfield on B5035

Open *Apr–Sept Wed–Sun 10–6, Oct Wed–Sun 10–5, Nov–Mar Sat & Sun 10–1 2–4*

High on a hill above South Wingfield, this is one of the most spectacularly located houses in which Mary Queen of Scots found herself after escaping to England. It is in ruins today.

Wales MAP 5

179 Cosmeston Medieval Village *
☎ 02920 701678
Nr Penarth, Vale of Glamorgan CF6 5UY
On B4267 coast road towards Barry
Open *Apr–Oct 11–4, Nov–Mar 11–3*
This deserted village has become the
site of a fascinating reconstruction project.
Much archaeological work has been
done to reconstruct the medieval
buildings that once stood here, giving
visitors a vivid sense of what they might
have looked like and fleshing out the
experience of medieval village life.

180 Plas Mawr CADW
☎ 01492 580167
High St, Conwy LL32 8EF
Open *Apr–May & Sept 9.30–5, June–Aug
9.30–6, Oct 9.30–4 Tues–Sun & BH Mons*

Plas Mawr, the 'Great Hall', was built
in 1576–85 for an influential Welsh
merchant Robert Wynn. It is possibly
the finest example of an Elizabethan
town house anywhere in Britain; note
the wonderful plasterwork ceilings and
friezes, the plaster overmantel in the hall
which has been repainted in its vivid
original colours. Look out for the initials
R.W. in the crests and coats of arms.

181 Powis Castle and Garden NT
☎ 01938 551920
Infoline 01938 557018
Welshpool, Powys SY21 8RF
Email: ppcmsn@smtp.ntrust.org.uk
1m S of Welshpool
Open *Castle & museum: Apr–June
& Sept–Oct Wed–Sun & BH Mons 1–5,
July–Aug Tues–Sun & BH Mons 1–5.
Garden: as castle & museum 11–6*

*The west front of **Powis Castle**, with a statue of Fame riding Pegasus by Andries Carpentière, c1705.*

Raglan Castle, *begun in 1435 and completed more than a century later.*

The castle is perched high on a rock above the garden, and has quite beautiful views. Within is Wales' best collection of paintings and furniture, and outside one of the best gardens in the country, largely thanks to its setting. There are long thinnish borders in terraces running down the side of the hill, immaculately and imaginatively planted, with superb pot arrangements and plenty of boisterous hothouse colours.

182 Raglan Castle CADW
☎ 01291 690228
Raglan, Monmouthshire NP5 2BT
½m N of Raglan off A40,
7m SW of Monmouth
Open *Apr–May & Oct 9.30–5, June–Sept 9.30–6, Nov–Mar 9.30–4 Sun 11–4*
Raglan is one of the very best examples of late medieval fortress architecture in Britain, let alone Wales. It was begun by Sir William ap Thomas, and completed by his son, Sir William Herbert, later the Earl of Pembroke. The castle was severely damaged during the Civil War (being besieged in 1646), but large parts do still survive, in particular parts of the keep, walled enclosures, round courts, gateways and the surrounding moat. The outstanding quality of the design and workmanship are still evident.

ADDITIONAL PLACES TO VISIT

Aberconwy House NT
☎ 01492 592246
Castle St, Conwy LL32 8AY
At junction of Castle St & High St
Open *Apr–Oct Wed–Mon & BHs 11–5*
A merchant's house from the mid-14th century with furnished rooms.

Cochwillan Old Hall
☎ 01248 335853
Talybont, Bangor, Gwynedd LL57 3AZ
3½m SE of Bangor off A55
Open *By appointment only*
The medieval castle has a house dating from the late 15th century, and is considered one of the best of its kind in Wales. Its first owner, William ap Gruffydd, fought at Bosworth. For many years it was used as a barn until it was restored in the 1970s.

Gwydir Castle
☎ 01492 641687
Llanrwst, Gwynedd LL26 OPN
Email: info@gwydircastle.co.uk
Website; www.gwydir-castle.co.uk
½m W of Llanrwst on B5106
Open *Mar–Oct 10–5*
A Tudor mansion built *c*1550 and owned by the Wynn family, the descendants of the great Welsh prince, Owain Gwynedd. It is one of the best examples of a Tudor manor house design anywhere in North Wales. There are later additions, most notably in the mid-17th century, with dining room panelling which was returned from loan to the New York Metropolitan Museum. Badly damaged by fire, it was fully restored in the 20th century.

St Mary's Priory Church
☎ 01873 853168
Monk Street, Abergavenny,
Monmouthshire
Website: www.stmarys-priory.org
Off A449 & A40
Open *10–4*
In addition to the castle in Abergavenny, which is a William the Conqueror-era motte-and-bailey, there is the Priory Church. It has one of Britain's most impressive pieces of medieval carvings – an enormous reclining Jesse (the father of David) – on a scale which is startling. This is actually, though you would not guess it from its rather shabby setting, one of the most important pieces of medieval carving anywhere in the country, and well worth a visit.

North-west MAP 6

183 Gawsworth Hall*
☎ 01260 223456
Church Lane, Gawsworth,
Cheshire SK11 9RN
Email: gawsworth@compuserve.com
Website: www.gawsworthhall.com
3m S of Macclesfield on A536
Open *Apr May & Sept Sun–Wed, June–Aug daily, all 2–5*
The half-timbered Elizabethan manor house is a classic example of the black and white Tudor exterior. The former home of the Fitton family, one member was Mary Fitton, Elizabeth I's maid of honour in 1595 and a one-time candidate among scholars as Shakespeare's Dark Lady of the sonnets.

184 Sizergh Castle NT
☎ 015395 60070
Nr Kendal, Cumbria LA8 8AE
Email: Ntrust@sizerghcastle.fsnet.co.uk
3½m S of Kendal off A590
Open *Castle: late Mar–Oct Sun–Wed 1.30–5.30. Garden: as house 12.30–5.30*
For 700 years this has been the home of the Strickland family; it comprises a pele tower from *c*1350, which was built to provide protection against raids from the border Scots. There are many later additions. One of its owners, Sir Walter Strickland, agreed (according to surviving documents) to provide the local earl with an army for whatever purpose he required. The castle contains particularly fine examples of Elizabethan carved wooden overmantels as well as period furniture and paintings. Substantial gardens surround the castle.

Rufford Old Hall NT
☎ 01704 821254
Rufford, nr Ormskirk, Lancashire L40 1SG
Email: rrufoh@smtp.ntrust.org.uk
7m N of Ormskirk, in Rufford
Open *House: late Mar–Oct Sat–Wed 1–5*
Garden: as house 12–5.30
Presented to the National Trust in the
mid-1930s, this is a medieval, timber-
framed manor house with a particularly
fine hammerbeam roof (with an inset,
ornamental arch) and screen. The great
hall is early 16th century and the east
wing – an impressive example of late
Jacobean architecture – dates back to
the Restoration period. There is a huge
variety of historical artefacts on display
from virtually all periods, including
some beautiful Georgian dolls houses.

Speke Hall NT
☎ 0151 427 7231; Infoline 0345 585702
The Walk, Speke, Liverpool,
Merseyside L24 1XD
Email: mspsxc@smtp.ntrust.org.uk
Website: www.spekehall.org.uk
8m SW of Liverpool off A581 & M62
Open *Apr–mid-Oct Wed–Sun & BH Mons
1–5.30, mid-Oct –Dec Sat & Sun 1–4.30*
A distinctive, and rightly famous half-
timbered house, it contains a Tudor great
hall, and wallpapers designed by the
Victorian designer, William Morris. Speke
is surrounded by gardens and woods.

North-east MAP 7

185 Burton Agnes Hall
☎ 01262 490324
Burton Agnes, Driffield,
E Yorkshire YO25 OND
Website: www.burton-agnes.co.uk
Between Driffield & Bridlington off A614
Open *Apr–Oct 11–5*

An Elizabethan mansion with particularly impressive ceilings, it was built
between 1598 and 1610 in the standard
style of the period, except for its bow
windows. It now houses a fine collection
of art, particularly paintings from the
Impressionist and Post-Impressionist era
by Renoir, Cézanne, Corot and Gauguin.
It has splendid ceilings and a great hall
with elaborate plasterwork. There is also
a lovely surrounding garden with topiary.
And then we come to the ghostly bit.

Anne Griffith, one of the original
owner's daughters, was murdered, but
begged (with seconds to go) that her head
be allowed to stay in the house (that's
ghost stories for you). She was buried in
the churchyard, and her unhappy ghost
rose up in horror but it promptly vanished
as soon as her skull was disinterred and
lodged in the house walls!

186 Dunstanburgh Castle EH & NT
☎ 01665 576231
Craster, Alnwick, Northumberland
9m NE of Alnwick off A1
Open *Apr–Oct 10–6, Nov–Mar Wed–Sun
10–4 (dusk if earlier)*
Brave the coastal walk and you will be
rewarded with a breathtaking silhouette
of the perfect coastal castle ruin with
gatehouse and keep. Originally built in
1316, it was enlarged by John of Gaunt
but was largely destroyed during the
Wars of the Roses. This is one of those
castles that is worth visiting as much for
the exhilarating walk to it as for the
atmospheric ruins.

187 Etal Castle EH
☎ 01890 820332
Etal, Northumberland
In Etal village, 10m SW of Berwick
Open *Apr–Sept 10–6, Oct 10–5*
Given its location near the battle
zone that was the England/Scotland

border, there is little wonder that this 14th-century house should have been transformed from a family dwelling into an impressive castle. This was the work of Robert Manners who began it in 1341. However, it was powerless to resist a full Scottish army that came pouring over the border and captured it in 1513. This triumph was short lived because the Scots were brutally defeated at Flodden. The castle has an award-winning exhibition which tells the full story. The castle's slide into decay began at the end of the 16th century.

188 Wharram Percy (deserted medieval village)* EH

Wharram le Street, N Yorkshire
½m S of Wharram le Street off B1248; park at Bella Farm, then ½m by foot
Open *Any reasonable time*
One of the most famous of the several deserted medieval villages still visible in Britain. About 3000 villages are thought to have been abandoned between the 11th and 18th centuries. There have been major excavations here over many years, providing historians with some of their best clues about medieval village life.

It was abandoned (this is the best guess) for a combination of factors which struck English rural life in the decades after the Black Death, when the population rapidly declined and those who survived often moved home tempted by higher wages elsewhere. The major monument in the site is the parish church, a ruin, but still clearly the focal point to what was once a thriving community. There are also the remains of farm cottages and over 30 peasant homes. The structure of the village is best seen from the air which was how we filmed it in our programme on the Black Death, still beautiful and poignant.

*The ruins of St Martin's Church in the deserted village of **Wharram Percy**.*

Belsay Hall, Castle and Gardens EH

☎ 01661 881636

Belsay, nr Ponteland,
Northumberland NE20 ODX
*In Belsay, 14m NW of Newcastle on A696,
7m NW of Ponteland*
Open *Apr–Sept 10–6, Oct 10–5,
Nov–Mar 10–4*

At the centre of the estate lies a 14th-century castle, a 16th-century manor house and the New Hall, a 19th-century pastiche of Greek classical architecture built by the owner Sir Charles Monck to his own designs of 1810. The castle predates the surrounding town and was built on top of a bluff by a crossing point of the River Tees. At the heart of the New Hall is a stunning atrium, the Pillar Room, constrcted from two storeys of Greek columns. It is exactly 100ft (30m) square, and all the main rooms radiate from it. The quarry that provided the honey-coloured stone for the house is now itself a particularly fine garden. Surrounding Belsay Hall are 30 acres of 19th-century landscaped park which are largely the work of Sir Charles Monck and his grandson Sir Arthur Middleton.

Berwick Barracks EH

☎ 01289 304493

The Parade, Berwick-upon-Tweed,
Northumberland TD15 1DF
In Berwick town centre
Open *Apr–Sept 10–6, Oct 10–5,
Nov–Mar Wed–Sun 10–4*

Anyone interested in the details of early 18th-century military life will love these barracks, among the first to be purpose-built, designed by Nicholas Hawksmoor and begun in 1717. A good exhibition recreating the life of British infantrymen has been mounted to help bring it back to life.

Bessie Surtees House EH

☎ 0191 269 1200

41–44 Sandhill,
Newcastle upon Tyne NE1 3JF
On quayside near Tyne Bridge
Open *Mon–Fri 10–4; closed BHs*

Actually two houses, with rooms open to the public, they offer a rare example of Jacobean town architecture and interior design.

Nunnington Hall NT

☎ 01439 748283

Nunnington, N Yorkshire YO62 5UY
Email: yorknu@smtp.ntrust.org.uk
In Ryedale, 4½m SE of Helmsley
Open *Late Mar–May & Sept–Oct Wed–Sun
& BH Mon, June–Aug Tues –Sun & BH
Mon, 1.30–5 but closes 4.30 Apr & Oct*

The 17th-century manor house has a panelled hall and staircase. The west wing dates from 1580. It also contains the Carlisle collection of miniature rooms fully furnished to reflect different periods.

Spofforth Castle EH

☎ 0191 2691200

Nr Harrogate, N Yorkshire
3½m SE of Harrogate off A661
Open *Apr–Sept 10–6, Oct–Mar 10–4*

Like Warkworth Castle this was once owned by the all-powerful Percy family who had been given permission to build a defensive home in 1308. The great hall has 15th-century window tracery and a moulded doorway. The kitchens were part of the undercroft (a vaulted room below an upper room such as a chapel).

Warkworth Castle EH

☎ 01665 711423

Warkworth, Morpeth,
Northumberland NE66 0UJ
In Warkworth, ½m S of Alnwick on A1068
Open *Apr–Sept 10–6, Oct 10–5,
Nov–Mar 10–1 2–4*

This used to be the ancestral home of one of the great Northumberland families, the Percys, the most famous of whom was Harry 'Hotspur'. It was built as the last word in fortified homes for the nobility, and still dominates the local town. The Percys took it over in 1332 and later built the keep using an unusual pattern – not a square or rectangle but the plan of a cross inscribed on a square. Later additions have survived, most notably the Lion Tower which forms the entrance porch.

Scotland MAP 8

189 Borthwick Castle
☎ 01875 820514
North Middleton, Gorebridge, Midlothian EH23 4QY
1½m SE of Gorebridge off A7
Open *Now a hotel; phone to confirm times*
It is the castle to which the newly wed Mary Queen of Scots and the Earl of Bothwell came to stay three weeks after their marriage. They only stayed a few days before being forced to flee an approaching army and that was the beginning of the end of her story, one which took her to England, 19 years of imprisonment and execution in 1587. Borthwick is still immense, with machic-olated towers (ie with a projecting parapet on the outside of the castle walls with openings in the floor through which boiling oil, molten lead and missiles were dropped), and a great hall with vaulting and a fireplace.

190 Burleigh Castle HS
☎ 0131 668 8800
Kinross, Perth & Kinross
1½m N of Kinross off A911, near Loch Leven
Open *Any reasonable time*
This 16th-century Scottish castle was once the seat of the Balfours. Much was

lost when it fell into ruins, but it is still clear that there was once a tower at the heart of a castle with curtain walls and moat. Only two of the towers now remain.

191 Castle Menzies
☎ 01887 820982
Aberfeldy, Perth & Kinross PH15 2JD
1½m from Aberfeldy on B846 off A827
Open *Apr–mid-Oct Mon–Sat 10.30–5 Sun 2–5*
Built on the plan of a Z (rather than the more usual H or L), this is the seat of the chiefs of the Menzies Clan. Bonnie Prince Charlie stayed here in 1746 on his way to catastrophic defeat at Culloden. As a design, it has clearly moved away from the sole requirements of war towards those of a stately home, open and spacious instead of being cramped and contained. The turrets and gables are particularly attractive and, although there are defensive features like an iron yett (or gate), gunloops, turrets and a single, defendable entrance, you can tell it was built for style too. There have also been Victorian additions.

192 Craignethan Castle HS
☎ 01555 860364
Nr Lanark, S Lanarkshire ML11 9PL
5½m NW of Lanark off A72
Open *Apr–Sept 9.30–6.30*
Set in spectacular countryside, this was Tillietudlem Castle in Sir Walter Scott's novel *Old Mortality*. It boasts a stone-vaulted artillery chamber that is apparently unique in Britain. It was built to counter a new tactic in castle warfare – tunnelling under the walls instead of blowing them up with cannon fire. The castle provided ground-level defensive fire to deter the enemy.

It is now a well-preserved ruin, a great stone box with some surrounding walls and defensive ditches, high above the

River Nethan. But in the 16th century it saw quite a bit of action, being in the possession of the fearsome Hamilton family, fervent supporters of Mary Queen of Scots. This earned it considerable trouble – it suffered much damage in 1579.

193 Crathes Castle NTS
☎ 01330 844525
Banchory, Aberdeenshire AB31 3QJ
Website: www.nts.org.uk/crathes.html
3m NE of Banchory on A93,
15m W of Aberdeen
Open *Apr–Sept 10.30–5.30, Oct 10.30–4.30;*
other times by appointment
A fantastic example of a Scottish Baronial-style castle, it was built in the mid- to late 16th century and is immaculately preserved. A later wing was added in the time of Queen Anne. It has the archetypal features of this kind of castle with corbelled turrets (ie with projecting blocks), stepped gables and lovely conical roofs. The solitary entrance has a weighty iron grille, a sharp reminder of the kind of defences you needed in the 16th century when life got tricky. Look for the particularly impressive Jacobean painted ceilings, especially those in the Chamber of the Nine Worthies, and in the long gallery. There is a fine early 18th-century garden packed with topiary.

194 Crichton Castle HS
☎ 01875 320017
Crichton, Pathhead, Midlothian
2½m SW of Pathhead off A68
Open *Apr–Sept 9.30–6.30*
The castle was owned by the Earls of Bothwell, one of whom famously

Crathes Castle: *a view of the garden with the Scottish Baronial-style castle beyond.*

persuaded Mary Queen of Scots to marry him. Largely ruined now, its most striking feature, apart from its strategic location, is its 16th-century Italianate stone façade, the work of Francis Stewart, a later Earl of Bothwell, who was given the castle by James VI. It is strongly reminiscent of the Palazzo del Diamante in Ferrara, north-east Italy. Bothwell, who had spent some years in exile in Italy, obviously liked what he saw. The castle dominates the rather bleak, bare hillside on which it stands.

195 Eilean Donan Castle

☎ 01599 555202
Dornie, by Kyle of Lochalsh,
Highland IV40 8DX
Email: info@eileandonancastle.com
Website: www.eileandonancastle.com
8m E of Skye Bridge on A87
Open *Mar & Nov 10–4.30, Apr–Oct 10–5.30*
Eilean is so ludicrously scenic you would think it was a hologram. It has become the ultimate poster castle thanks to its impossibly beautiful loch-side setting, but be careful choosing your angle of vision because the road behind can disrupt the romantic idyll.

Eilean is named after an early Celtic saint who made the islet, on which the castle is built, his home. The islet is now linked to the shore by a stone bridge (they used to have to rely on boats). Unfortunately, the castle's slightly ruined appearance is not due to weathering but a Royal Navy broadside in 1719. They were firing at a small garrison of Spanish soldiers holed up inside, who had come to support the 'Old Pretender', James Stuart. It was two centuries before anyone undertook the necessary restoration work. Today it is the headquarters of the Macrae Clan.

196 Falkland Palace NTS

☎ 01337 857397
Falkland, Fife KY15 7BU
Website: www.nts.org.uk/falkland.html
11m N of Kirkcaldy off A912
Open *Apr–May & Sept–Oct Mon–Sat 11–5.30 Sun 1.30–5.30, June–Aug Mon–Sat 10–5.30 Sun 1.30–5.30*
Falkland Palace belongs to the sovereign, though no monarch has actually lived here since the days of Charles II. Built during the first half of the 16th century by James IV and James V on the site of an earlier palace, it became a hunting lodge, a favourite with the Stuarts, with whom it is now deeply associated. The Chapel Royal is still in use and is the only wholly surviving original interior in the Palace. The King's Bedchamber has been reconstructed to show where James V died. His daughter Mary Queen of Scots spent much of her childhood here, returning later when queen to go riding or to embroider tapestries. There is also, unique to Scotland, a royal tennis court that is still in use. The game is played in a large open-air chamber with four sides, two of which are angled, and is actually more like squash or fives than lawn tennis. (Hampton Court has Britain's oldest royal, or real, tennis court.)

The palace has a distinctly French feel, thanks to the continental masons brought over to help build it, and the fact that James V had two French wives. Much careful and effective restoration work has been done.

197 Gladstone's Land NTS

☎ 0131 226 5856
477B Lawnmarket, Edinburgh EH21 2NT
Website: www.nts.org.uk/gladstone.html
At top of Royal Mile, near the castle
Open *Apr–Oct Mon–Sat 10–5 Sun 2–5*

Eilean Donan Castle, *strategically built where three lochs meet.*

For anyone curious about what the old Edinburgh looked like, the one that the middle classes started to abandon in the 18th century in favour of their Georgian masterpiece, the New Town, then come and have a look. This has been rescued from centuries of neglect and been beautifully restored by the NTS, opening a fascinating window on traditional Edinburgh life.

Situated on the Royal Mile (and perfect to combine with a visit to Edinburgh Castle and the nearby Camera Obscura), it is one of the city's best historic locations. The one thing it cannot do is convey just how unsanitary, filthy and overcrowded it must have been. That has to be imagined.

Gladstone's Land is named after Thomas Gledstane, who lived in the house in the early 17th century with his wife, Bessie Cunningham. He added rooms to the property, and it is unique in Edinburgh for having retained its arcade of two ground-floor arches to provide shelter for customers, a feature once common in several Scottish cities. The tall, narrow architecture, six storeys high, is typical of Edinburgh, the city which built some of the world's first tenements in the 15th and 16th centuries.

198 Hermitage Castle HS

☎ 01387 376222
Hermitage, Newcastleton,
Scottish Borders
5m N of Newcastleton on B6399
Open *Apr–Sept 9.30–6.30*

For those who like their castles bleak and forbidding, Hermitage is unbeatable. Nicknamed the 'Strength of Liddesdale', it had a satisfyingly turbulent history. It was owned by the Earl of Bothwell, Mary Queen of Scots' third and most disastrous husband, and played a key role in the long period of border wars. The ride there and back from Jedburgh undertaken by Mary Queen of Scots to visit Bothwell, after he had been injured in a brawl, all but killed her (much later, she used to lament that it had not). The site has now been extensively restored. It remains a pre-eminent example of medieval fortification, relying as much on its location, surrounded by boggy ground making siege engines impossible to move into position, as on its impregnable walls.

199 Holyroodhouse Palace *

☎ 0131 556 7371
Canongate, Edinburgh EH8 8DX
Email: holyroodhouse@royalcollection. org.uk
Website: www.royalresidences.com/ holyrood.htm
At E end of Royal Mile,
opposite Scottish Parliament
Open *Apr–Oct 9.30–6. Nov–Mar 9.30–4.30*

The present-day royal palace, which sits at the foot of Arthur's Seat, grew out of an Augustinian abbey founded by David I in 1128. James IV established the palace of Holyrood as the official residence of the kings of Scotland. He extended the abbey guest house in the late 15th century and his work was continued by James V. What we see today, however, is largely the work of Charles II, who reconstructed much of Holyroodhouse in the 1670s, although he never actually lived here.

The James V Tower houses the apartments where Mary Queen of Scots lived when in Edinburgh during her tempestuous years as Queen. Here in this tower David Rizzio, her Italian secretary, was brutally murdered; his bloody body was dragged through her bedchamber by her enraged and jealous husband Darnley, aided and abetted by a large group of Scottish nobles.

The 15th-century royal **Linlithgow Palace** *burnt down soon after the rebellion of 1745.*

200 Linlithgow Palace* HS
☎ 01506 842896
Linlithgow, W Lothian
Halfway between Edinburgh & Stirling, off A803
Open *Apr–Sept 9.30–6.30, Oct–Mar 9.30–4.30; closed Sun am in winter*
The birthplace of both James V and his daughter, Mary Queen of Scots, is now a magnificent ruin set by the banks of the loch. Bonnie Prince Charlie stayed here during the 1745 rebellion. A year later a fire destroyed the palace.

201 Lochleven Castle* HS
☎ 017778 040483
By Kinross, Perth & Kinross KY13 7AR
On island in Loch Leven, 1m E of Kinross
Open *Apr–Sept 9.30–6.30 (or last sailing)*
The castle played a dramatic part in the life of Mary Queen of Scots. The island castle in the middle of the loch seemed the perfect place for her Scottish Protestant enemies to imprison her in 1567. The brutal regime did work; she was

subject to endless petty torments at the hands of Sir William Douglas, and finally abdicated the Scottish throne in favour of her son, James, making the (Protestant) Earl of Moray Regent. Eventually she escaped, legend has it, thanks to the lovelorn younger brother of her jailer who hid a key for her under a napkin. Today only the central tower remains, but at least this is pretty well preserved, although it has no roof. It is one of those historical buildings that the imagination cannot improve upon.

202 Rosslyn Chapel
☎ 0131 440 2159
Roslin, Midlothian EH25 9PU
Email: rosslynch@aol.com
Website: www.rosslynchapel.org.uk
6m S of Edinburgh off A701
Open *Mon–Sat 10–5 Sun 12–4.45*
Founded in 1446, this is a super ornate chapel set in beautiful woodlands, a favourite location for Sir Walter Scott's walks. Its most famous feature is its

legendary 'Prentice Pillar', a column with beautifully carved, curling detail spiralling up its length. Apparently, it was completed by the master's apprentice during his absence, for which impudence the young man had his head smashed in by a mallet. Whoever did finish it, did a very good job.

203 Scone Palace

☎ 01738 552300
Perth, Perth & Kinross PH2 6BD
Email: visits@scone-palace.co.uk
Website: www.scone-palace.co.uk
Just outside Perth to N on A93
Open *Apr–Oct 9.30–5.30*

A post-Reformation palace on the site of an earlier abbey and bishop's palace, it occupies one of Scotland's most historic locations, the place where the ancient kings of Scotland were crowned. This was also where the Stone of Destiny lived until Edward I took it south to Westminster Abbey (it is now in Edinburgh Castle, returned to Scotland after 700 years). Edward shrewdly calculated that taking away a conquered nation's cultural treasures was a good way to demoralize it. Today Scone has a good collection of historical artefacts, and fine, wooded grounds.

204 Threave Castle HS

☎ 07711 223101
River Dee, Dumfries & Galloway DG7 1RX
3m W of Castle Douglas on A75
Open *Apr–Sept 9.30–6.30*

Now a ruin, this used to be a stronghold of the infamous Black Douglases, the Lords of Galloway. Built by the fabulously named Archibald the Grim in the late 14th century, it later housed a Royalist garrison during the Civil War and was wrecked by the Covenanters. The 15th-century walls were no mere decorative afterthought, and are 70ft (21m) high, and over 8ft (2.4m) thick. Access to the castle, then, as now, is by boat which would dock at a movable wooden bridge. Most ghoulish of all is the Gallows' Knob from with Archibald would hang his enemies; he once noted rather blackly that it was rarely 'without a tassel'.

205 Tolquhon Castle HS

☎ 01651 851286
Tarvis, Aberdeenshire AB41 0LP
15m N of Aberdeen on A920
Open *Apr–Sept daily 9.30–6.30,
Oct–Mar Sat 9.30–4.30 Sun 2–4.30*

The original keep was built by the Prestons of Craigmillar, but the rest of the castle was built by the Forbes family. And 'all this warke, excep the auld tour, was begun be William Forbes 15 April 1584 and endit be him 20 October 1589'. Few would begrudge him the pleasure he took in the many improvements he wrought on a castle his family had owned since 1420. The result is among the finest examples of Renaissance architecture anywhere in Scotland. There is a particularly impressive gatehouse, large courtyard, two lovely drum towers, gables and large courtyard windows. It is also beautifully situated on rising ground.

206 Traquair House

☎ 01896 830323
Innerleithen, Scottish Borders EH44 6PW
Email: enquiries@traquair.co.uk
Website: www.traquair.co.uk
Just S of Innerleithen off A803 on B709
Open *House: Apr–May & Sept 12.30–5.30,
June–Aug 10.30–5.30, Oct 12.30–4.30
Grounds: Easter–Oct 10.30–5.30*

This house has touched virtually every chapter of Scotland's past. It has particular

*The richly decorated late Gothic interior of the **Rosslyn Chapel**.*

*The handsome whitewashed façade of **Traquair House**.*

associations with the royal Stuarts, the Catholic Church in Scotland and the Jacobite Risings. With a stunning setting close to the River Tweed, it also boasts its own brewery that makes beer to die for.

ADDITIONAL PLACES TO VISIT

Balvenie Castle HS

☎ 01340 820121

Dufftown, nr Keith, Moray AB55 4DH
11m SW of Keith, at Dufftown on A941
Open *Apr–Sept 9.30–6.30*

The fabulous 13th-century ruin of a fortress was first the home of the Comyn family, one of the claimants to the throne of Scotland at the time of Edward I. Later the renegade Douglas clan and the Atholls lived here. The castle was visited by Edward I and later by Mary Queen of Scots. It has a magnificent yett (iron gate) of enormous size which guards the entrance to the tower, and surviving curtain walls. The later additions, including a round tower, came in the late 16th century as the Atholls tried to turn it into a stately mansion. Their family motto is carved on the 15th–16th-century front. The castle was abandoned in 1746.

Blackness Castle HS

☎ 01506 834807

Blackness, Linlithgow,
W Lothian EH49 7NH
*4m NE of Linlithgow
on Firth of Forth, off A904*
Open *Apr–Sept 9.30–6.30, Oct–Mar
9.30–4.30; closed Thurs pm, Fri
& Sun am in winter*

This huge and imposing stronghold is stuck out in the middle of the Firth of Forth on a rocky promontory. Built in 1440, it was much reinforced over the following two centuries to withstand artillery assault. Blackness looks a bit like a ship and always had a military purpose, as is evident from its fabulously grim dungeon, a black rocky pit. Happily, for those who like their castles to be rather forbidding, much of the 19th-century additions have been stripped away, returning Blackness Castle to something like its former state.

Castle Campbell HS & NTS
☎ 01259 742408
Dollar, Clackmannanshire FK14 7PP
10m E of Stirling on A91
Open *Apr–Sept 9.30–6.30, Oct–Mar 9.30–4.30; closed Thurs pm, Fri & Sun am in winter*
Although most Scottish Baronial castles have an attractive domestic appearance compared to their grimmer medieval predecessors, that does not mean that the style cannot intimidate. Castle Campbell, built by Colin Campbell, 1st Earl of Argyll, takes the form of a tall, oblong tower house dating back to the 15th century. It was nicknamed 'Castle Gloom' because its sheer bulk dominates the surrounding countryside and the town of Dollar. At its heart is the tower, 60ft (18m) high and predating most of the other surviving buildings. There is a 1/4 mile steepish walk from the road.

Cawdor Castle
☎ 01667 404615
Nairn, Highland IV12 5RD
Email: info@cawdorcastle.com
Website: www.cawdorcastle.com
12m E of Inverness on B9090
Open *May–mid-Oct 10–5.30*
For the location of Shakespeare's *Macbeth*, Cawdor is altogether too romantic. And it post-dates the Thane of Cawdor by some 300 years. With many layers of Scottish vernacular architecture added in the 16th and 17th centuries and later, as well as its lovely gardens, the medieval nightmare of murder and guilt seems far away. It is very picturesque, and has a central tower dating from 1454, moat, drawbridge and iron gateway grille.

Claypotts Castle HS
☎ 01786 431324
Dundee, Angus
3½m E of Dundee at junction of A92 & B978
Open *House: July–Sept Sat & Sun phone for details. Exterior: any reasonable time*
Quite extraordinary, not just because the castle has survived so well over the centuries but because it is the last kind of building you would expect to find half-hidden in the suburban outskirts of Dundee. It was built between 1569 and 1598 to an unusual design, with a rectangular central block and two circular blocks on a Z-pattern. The decoration inside is sparse, and there is a gun port in the kitchen; even at this period you had to expect armed trouble. However, the internal layout, with a stairwell ascending uninterrupted right the way up through the storeys, which no castle owner seriously expecting trouble would ever have built, suggests that comfort rated more highly than war.

Craigmillar Castle HS
☎ 0131 661 4445
Nr Edinburgh
2½m SE of Edinburgh off A68
Open *Apr–Sept 9.30–6.30, Oct–Mar 9.30–4.30; closed Thurs pm, Fri & Sun am in winter*
Another castle featuring in the roller-coaster life of the tragedy queen, Mary Queen of Scots. This, the less famous of Edinburgh's two castles, was where she fled after the murder of her Italian secretary, David Rizzio, in her apartments in Holyroodhouse and here the plot was hatched to murder her husband Lord Darnley. At the castle's heart is a great central tower built in the shape of an L in the 15th century. Later, curtain walls were added, as well as provision for the use of artillery.

Delgatie Castle

☎ 01888 563479

Delgatie, Turriff, Aberdeenshire AB53 5TD
Email: jjohnson@delgatie-castle.freeserve.
co.uk
Website: www.delgatiecastle.com
12m S of Banff off A947
Open *Apr–Oct 10–5*
The castle dates back to the 11th century,
but many of its most interesting features
come from the 16th century, including
the inevitable Mary Queen of Scots
slept-here bed-chamber. There are late
16th-century painted ceilings and a wide
turnpike stair (the widest in Scotland);
Delgatie is surrounded by woodland
and countryside. The home of Clan Hay,
it also has fine collections of paintings
and armour.

Doune Castle HS

☎ 01786 841742

Doune Castle Road, Doune,
Stirling FK16 6EA
8m SE of Callander on A84
Open *Apr–Sept 9.30–6, Oct–Mar 9.30–4.30;
closed Thurs pm, Fri & Sun am in winter*
This incredibly impressive 14th-century
castle was built by Robert Stewart,
1st Duke of Albany, the younger son of
Robert II and regent of Scotland from
1406 to 1420. Guarding one of the main
routes north out of Edinburgh, Doune
was a castle of huge strategic significance. You can see that just by looking at
the size and bulk of its main tower,
nearly 100ft (30m) high, with 9ft (2.7m)-
thick walls. The machinations that
Robert and then his son indulged in cost
his family the castle for many generations, though they did eventually get it
back. It was taken by the Jacobites and
used as a prison in 1746 after the battle
of Falkirk. The castle later became royal
property and is now one of the best-
restored castles in Scotland.

Edzell Castle HS

☎ 01356 648631

Edzell, nr Brechin, Angus DD9 7UE
At Edzell 6m N of Brechin on B966
Open *Apr–Sept 9.30–6.30, Oct–Mar
9.30–4.30; closed Thurs pm, Fri
& Sun am in winter*
The 16th-century tower house is now
in ruins, but is the site of one of the most
spectacular 17th-century walled gardens
in the country. Set into the 12ft (3.6m)-
high walls are a number of stone panels
with allegorical illustrations advocating
the Cardinal Virtues, the Liberal Arts, and
various Celestial Deities. The family motto
of the Lindsays (the earliest owners) is cut
into a trimmed hedge – *Dum spiro spero*
(While I breathe I hope). And then they
lost the house through bankruptcy in the
early 18th century. There is a bathhouse,
and a summerhouse constructed like
a mini-gatehouse tower.

Glamis Castle

☎ 01307 840393

Glamis, by Forfar, Angus DD8 1RJ
Email: enquiries@glamis-castle.co.uk
Website: www.glamis-castle.co.uk
6m W of Forfar on A94
Open *Easter–June & Oct 10.30–5.30,
July–Aug 10–5.30*
Childhood home of the Queen Mother
and birthplace of Princess Margaret,
Glamis Castle is also the legendary
setting for Shakespeare's *Macbeth*,
although there is little of the early Middle
Ages on view. Most of the building dates
from the 15th century, but it has many
later additions, including billiard rooms,
barrel-vaulted state rooms and royal
apartments. From the outside, it has the
classic appearance of Scottish baronial
architecture with pointed round towers.
Surrounded by spectacular parkland,
its pink sandstone gives a lovely glow in
the sunshine.

Huntingtower Castle HS
☎ 01738 627231
Huntingtower, nr Perth,
Perth & Kinross PH1 3JL
3m NW of Perth off A85
Open *Apr–Sept 9.30–6.30, Oct–Mar
Mon–Sat 9.30–4.30; closed Thurs pm,
Fri & Sun am in winter*
Taking the form of two tower houses from
the 15th and 16th centuries, and joined
by a third (built later), this well-restored
house is celebrated for its painted ceilings.
It used to belong to the Ruthven family,
the Earls of Gowrie. There is the story of a
lover's leap between the two towers when
the first Earl's daughter vaulted out of the
arms of her disapproved lover, back to
the other tower and safety, when about
to be confronted by her raging father.

Kellie Castle NTS
☎ 01333 720271
Pittenweem, Fife KY10 2RF
3m NW of Pittenweem on B9171
Open *Castle: mid-Apr–Sept 1.30–5.30,
Oct Sat & Sun 1.30–5.30
Gardens: all year 9.30–sunset*
With 14th-century origins, this is a
particularly fine example of a large
domestic residence. Much restored and
added to in the 19th century, it also
features some high-quality plaster
ceilings and painted panelling.

Lennoxlove House
☎ 01620 823720
Haddington, E Lothian EH41 4NZ
Email: fayangus@dial.pipex.com
Website: www.lennoxlove.org
1m S of Haddington
Open *Easter–Oct Wed Thurs & Sun 2–4.30*
It used to be known as Lethington Tower,
and was the home of Mary Queen of
Scots' secretary and counsellor, William
Maitland. The house still has a death mask
said to be that of the executed queen, as

well as her letters and a ring. The house's
origins go back to the 14th century.
There is an excellent museum on site.

MacLellan's Castle HS
☎ 01557 331856
Kircudbright, Dumfries & Galloway
In Kirkcudbright on A711
Open *Apr–Sept 9.30–6.30*
A ruin since the mid-18th century,
it was originally built in 1577 as a fine
castellated mansion.

Preston Mill NTS
☎ 01620 860426
East Linton, E Lothian EH40 3DS
23m E of Edinburgh off A1
Open *Apr–Sept 11–1 2–5 (opens 1.30
on Sun), Oct Sat & Sun 1.30–4*
A favourite subject for local artists,
this was a working mill until it finally
ceased in the late 1950s.

Northern Ireland MAP 9
207 Springhill House NT
☎ 028 8674 8210
20 Springhill Road, Moneymore,
Magherafelt, Co Londonderry BT45 7NQ
Email: uspest@smtp.ntrust.org.uk
1m off Moneymore–Coagh road, B18
Open *Easter daily, mid-Mar–June & Sept
Sat Sun & BH Mons, July & Aug Mon–Fri,
all 12–6*
A classic example of a 17th-century
'Planter' house (though with many
later additions) that was lived in by ten
generations of the one family originally
hailing from Ayrshire in Scotland. Much
of the house's contents reflects directly
on that family and their experiences
living here, including paintings, fine
furniture and 18th-century hand-blocked
wallpaper. There are a number of
exhibitions and displays accommodated
in various outhouses.

CHAPTER FOUR

Stately Homes and Georgian Follies

It is hard for us, conditioned by two centuries of empire and post empire, to recognize just how insignificant Britain was in the seventeenth century: a rocky archipelago somewhere off the north-west coast of the European superpowers, the object of endless suspicion, but in the end largely irrelevant. In the 150 years following the Civil War an explosion took place, catapulting these rain-lashed islands into one of the greatest global powers the world has ever seen.

At home, power moved decisively away from the court to country, from church to city, from God to money, and from the inward looking to the imperially expansive. It was as though all the violence and energy directed inwards during the Civil War was now projected out into the world at large, driven by a new and irresistible urge – profit.

The most visible evidence for this extraordinary transformation was a whole new Britain with buildings to match. At the top, of course, were the great country houses, like **Wilton** in Wiltshire and **Blenheim** in Oxfordshire, which still have the power to take your breath away. Unlike the more modestly proportioned houses of the earlier Elizabethan and Tudor periods, these houses do not really evoke nostalgia or envy: what they do is astonish.

The sheer wealth required to build these houses and fill them with art culled from all over the Continent, particularly from Italy, was awesome. Their saving grace was that they were at least designed as homes, to be inhabited by a family. They definitely were not mausoleums.

Competition with the French encouraged their owners to create another great feature, the landscaped gardens. In conscious rejection of the model offered by a palace like Versailles, whose gardens were dictated by symmetry, design, hierarchy and stultifying formality, the English chose a new direction. They wanted the rolling pseudo-natural parkland of artificial lakes, acres of rough grass, avenues of trees and ha-has (barriers invisible from the house which kept sheep and cows off the main lawns). No wonder we now regard these houses as the ultimate symbol of man and nature, not man over nature, where the rural became the cutting edge of national self-esteem and not, as in France, an anchor tying us to the past, to be despised and escaped from as quickly as possible.

The sense of a new national dawn accounts for more than the size and the staggering extravagance of these houses; it also explains how they were built and why. This is the time when architecture for the first time became

*The classical façade by William Talman at **Chatsworth**.*

An aerial view of the Georgian squares, circuses, terraces and crescents of **Edinburgh New Town**.

manifesto. The styles, and the works of art inside, may all have come from abroad, but they came together to produce something indisputably British.

There is also, of course, a closer relationship between these houses and the empire which they symbolized because it was largely sugar and slavery which paid for them. The rolling acres in Hampshire did not end somewhere just beyond the horizon, but in Antigua or Barbados. The desire for profit under-wrote the houses and the empire. The former may be tranquil hideaways, but tranquillity did not create them.

This is also the era of town planning, where the style and panache of the great Palladian mansions was imported into the cities. Interestingly, it was often the city house that was built after the country home, and not vice versa. No matter, because in Bath and in Edinburgh, and parts of London, the eighteenth century produced its greatest extended master-pieces, especially the **Royal Crescent** in Bath and **Edinburgh New Town**. The latter, in particular, offers dramatic evidence of a middle class no longer willing to suffer the privations (and privies) of squalid

medieval life, especially with Scottish culture by then at the forefront, not the rearguard, of British life.

This is the moment that the city – particularly London – really entered national life. The metropolis was both a world in itself and an underworld. It would dominate the new art forms of the 18th century – the novel and the printed engraving. Both would depict crowds, humanity as a seething mass, obsessed by shopping and promenading, a world of incessant noise, chatter, social life, assemblies, salons, taverns, pleasure gardens, newspapers, politics, factions, money and poverty. And the new types of building reflected this – there would be banks, inns, courts of law, temples, prisons, excise houses, parks and suburbs.

It was also the moment when, for the first time, the British started exporting, not importing, their architecture. From Madras to Savannah, from Minorca to Melbourne, for the next 150 years British styles would crop up all over the globe. **Kedleston Hall** would be rebuilt in Calcutta as the Governor General's palace. The British home had stopped being his castle and had now become his empire.

South-west MAP 1

208 Dyrham Park NT

☎ 0117 937 2501

Dyrham, S Gloucestershire SN14 8ER
Email: wdymxa@smtp.ntrust.org.uk
8m N of Bath, 12m E of Bristol;
2m S of M4 junction 18, off A46
Open *House: Apr–Oct Fri–Tues 12–5.30*
Garden: as house 11–5.30 (dusk if earlier)
Park: daily 12–5.30 (dusk if earlier)
& opens 11 when garden opens
Winter opening for domestic rooms:
mid-Nov–mid-Dec Sat & Sun 12–4
Classic William III era mansion. The
estate surrounding it took its name as a
corruption from the Anglo-Saxon for
deer enclosure – *deor-hamm* – and it is
recorded in the Domesday Book. The
house is surrounded by parkland with
deer, and was built for William's Secretary
for State, William Blathwayt, in the 1690s.
There are many Dutch furnishings, and
in the great hall there is a pair of oak
presses, the earliest kind of bookcase
known in England, replacing the lidded
chest. The rooms have been kept almost
exactly as they would have been,
including the Balcony Room, one of the
country's finest Baroque interiors.

209 Kingston Lacy NT

☎ 01202 883402 (Mon–Fri), 01202 842913
(Sat & Sun); Infoline 01202 880413
Wimborne Minster, Dorset BH21 4EA
Email: wklgen@smtp.ntrust.org.uk
1½m W of Wimborne Minster,
on B3082 Blandford–Wimborne road
Open *House: Apr–Oct Wed–Sun*
& BH Mons (closed Good Fri) 12–5.30
Garden & park: Feb–Mar Sat & Sun 11–4,
Apr–Oct daily 11–6, Nov–Dec Fri Sat
& Sun 11–4
This is the only surviving house designed
by architect Sir Roger Pratt (his other
four were destroyed). He was one of the
key figures who helped restore London
following the Great Fire of 1666. Originally conceived as a perfect example of
the Restoration style, Kingston Lacy was
greatly altered in the 1830s by Sir Charles
Barry (who designed the Houses of
Parliament). The house is full of
paintings and Egyptian relics.

Kingston Lacy, *built for Sir Ralph Bankes after the destruction of Corfe Castle in the Civil War.*

Royal Crescent *in Bath, designed by John Wood the Younger in 1767.*

210 No 1 Royal Crescent

☎ 01225 428126
Bath, Somerset BA1 2LR
Website: www.bath-preservation-trust.
org.uk
½m NW of city centre
Open *Mid-Feb–Oct Tues–Sun 10.30–5,
Nov 10.30–4*
Like the Georgian House (p200) in
Charlotte Square in Edinburgh, this is a
perfectly restored 18th-century Palladian
town house with all the appropriate
furniture, art and domestic accoutrements. You get an immediate sense of
why the Georgian period represents
the unbeatable high point of domestic
architecture. Outside is John Wood the
Younger's Royal Crescent, a semi-circle of
terraced houses which, with Charlotte
Square, is widely acknowledged as one of
the finest achievements of the era.

211 Saltram House NT

☎ 01752 333500
Plympton, Plymouth, Devon PL7 3UH
*3½m E of Plymouth city centre,
between A38 & A379*
Open *House: daily (closed Fri)
Apr–Sept 12–4.30, Oct 11.30–3.30
Garden & Chapel Art Gallery: daily
(closed Fri) Apr–Oct 11–5, Nov–Feb 11–4*
Dr Johnson's friend Fanny Burney wrote:
'The house is one of the most magnificent in the kingdom; its view is noble.'
How true! It was originally a Tudor
mansion, with later Georgian façades
added to conceal the fact; Robert Adam
then decorated much of the interior,
including the saloon, in the Neoclassical
style to complete its transformation.
Saltram boasts a number of portraits by
Reynolds (he was a friend of the owner)
and others by Angelica Kauffmann. The

kitchens are wonderful, complete with antique cockroach traps, so are the surrounding gardens, with their exquisite orangery and several follies.

212 Sherborne Castle*

☎ 01935 813182
Sherborne, Dorset DT9 3PY
Website: www.sherbornecastle.com
1m SE of Sherborne town centre
Open *Apr–Oct Tues Thurs Sun
& BH Mons 12.30–5 Sat 2.30–5*
Built in 1594 by Sir Walter Raleigh, in the 1630s the castle was owned by George Digby, a staunch Royalist, and it was here that Charles I planned his coup to snatch back power from the rebel Parliamentarians who had enraged him with their truculence and intransigence. The result was his botched attempt to arrest five of their key members, followed by his famous quip that the 'birds' had 'flown'. But of even greater historical significance, this was where William of Orange issued his proclamation to the English people having landed his 20,000 troops in 'the Glorious Revolution' of 1688. There are later additions to the castle, most notably a Victorian solarium and extensive, beautiful grounds.

213 Stourhead* NT

☎ 01747 841152
Stourton, Warminster, Wiltshire BA12 6QD
Email: wstest@smtp.ntrust.org.uk
At Stourton, off B3092, 3m NW of Mere (A303), 8m S of Frome (A361)
Open *House: Apr–Oct Sat–Wed 12–5.30 or dusk. Garden: daily 9–7 (dusk if earlier) King Alfred's Tower: Apr–Oct Tues–Fri 2–5.30 Sat Sun & BH Mons 11.30–5.30*
One of the two or three best examples of the great 18th-century English garden. It is landscaped into the contours of the countryside, and has temples, follies, statues, and a sequence of beautifully

framed vistas. Designed by Henry Hoare (the son of the man who built the house in 1721–4) and laid out between 1741 and 1780, the garden was inspired by his trips to Italy. It was meant to create the effect of walking through a landscape oil painting and is wonderfully effective, even if the rhododendrons planted in the 19th century make it sometimes feel like a crematorium garden. Unlike Stowe (p186), these gardens are built round a central lake giving it a more watery feel.

The genius of the 18th-century landscape garden designer was his ability to create subtle views every few paces, offering glimpses framed by trees, and a constant promise of something new around the corner. The effect is not of walking through a garden, but of moving in and out of a thousand different vignettes. No wonder that the English style was then regarded as far superior to anything that the French could achieve. After you have tackled the garden, there is a fine Palladian mansion to inspect.

214 Wilton House

☎ 01722 746729
Wilton, Salisbury, Wiltshire SP2 0BJ
Website: www.wiltonhouse.com
3m W of Salisbury on A30
Open *Mid-Apr–Oct 10.30–5.30*
Wilton is one of those houses that caters for everyone. It is noted for its long, perfectly proportioned south front set off by wide lawns, ancient cedars, and an exquisite Palladian bridge designed by Roger Morris. There are plenty of playgrounds for children. The architectural story of the house involves a number of contributing hands, fire damage and restoration, but for most people the house stands as tribute to one architect in particular, Inigo Jones, who enjoyed a long association with it. The 4th Earl

of Pembroke commissioned the Italianate south front in the 1630s, apparently at Charles I's instigation. Inigo Jones largely shaped it, with the help of Isaac de Caus and John Webb, Inigo Jones's nephew and assistant.

Jones was also responsible for the proportions of Wilton's two finest rooms, the Double and Single Cube rooms. The former was used by film director Stanley Kubrick in his masterpiece *Barry Lyndon*. They are called cubes because the smaller of the two is 30 × 30 × 30ft (9.1 × 9.1 × 9.1m) and the larger is 60 × 30 × 30ft (18.2 × 9.1 × 9.1m). What really stands out is the huge and wonderful family portrait by Van Dyck, one of his finest pictures. So many portraits simply vanish into the room in which they hang in a kind of heritage fog, but this comes straight at you, animating and inhabiting the house. The rest of the house is a goldmine of art. There are works by Reynolds, Gainsborough, Van Dyck and Brueghel in particular. There is much fine furniture, some designed by William Kent and Thomas Chippendale.

From 1801 to 1814 the architect James Wyatt made some significant additions, particularly to the west range and the north front, which he turned into the main entrance. For many, the gardens and parkland are as much an attraction as the paintings and saloons, and nobody leaves disappointed.

ADDITIONAL PLACES TO VISIT

Antony House and Garden NT
☎ 01752 812191
Torpoint, Plymouth, Cornwall PL11 2QA
Email: canmva@smtp.ntrust.org.uk
5m W of Plymouth via Torpoint car ferry, 2m NW of Torpoint
Open *Apr–May & Sept–Oct Tues–Thurs & BH Mons 1.30–5.30, June–Aug*

daily except Mon Fri & Sat (open BH Mons) 1.30–5.30; Bath Pond House can be seen when the house open by written application to the Custodian. Woodland Garden (not NT): Mar–Oct 11–5.30 (closed Mon & Fri but open BHs)
The early 18th-century mansion, with its distinct, lustrous grey Pentewan stone, is a real contrast to the redbrick used to build the wings. Inside, there is a fine collection of paintings and furniture, and outside a Humphry Repton-inspired garden with a dazzling variety of plants and flowers. There is also an 18th-century bathhouse.

Assembly Rooms and Museum of Costume, Bath NT
☎ 01225 477789
Bennett St, Bath, Somerset BA1 2QH
Email: costume_enquiries@bathnesgov.uk
Website: www.museumofcostume.co.uk
Near city centre
Open *All year 10–5*
Here you can now see the fashionable, public side of 18th-century Bath life. The Assembly Rooms, which opened in 1771, were designed by John Wood the Younger for 'assemblies', evening entertainments where you could also strut and be seen. The museum, in the basement, contains an enormous exhibition of historical costumes.

Bowood House and Gardens
☎ 01249 812102
Calne, Wiltshire SN11 0LZ
Website: www.bowood.org
7m from Chippenham off A4, leave M4 junction 17
Open *Apr–Oct 11–6*
A beautifully proportioned Georgian mansion with a wing designed by Robert Adam, gardens by 'Capability' Brown (few are more beautiful), and a lavish collection of works of art including the Lansdowne Sculpture Collection.

Dunster Castle NT
☎ 01643 821314; Infoline 01643 823004
Dunster, Somerset TA24 6SL
Email: wdugen@smtp.ntrust.org.uk
In Dunster, 3m SE of Minehead
Open *Castle: Apr–Oct Sat–Wed,
Apr–Sept 11–5, Oct 11–4. Garden &
park: Apr–Sept 10–5, Oct–Mar 11–4*
Dominating the surrounding market town
is this house that has metamorphosed
over the centuries. It began as a motte-
and-bailey, later gaining a 13th-century
gatehouse flanked by semi-circular towers
which survive, each tower containing
a dungeon needing eight keys. Most of the
house was remodelled by Anthony Salvin
in the 19th century, but an oak staircase
and plasterwork survive from the
17th-century. It played a stormy role in
the Civil War, when Thomas Luttrell
surrendered it to the Royalists in 1643;
it was in turn besieged for six months
by the Parliamentarians before being
surrendered back again.

Old Wardour Castle EH
☎ 01747 870487
Nr Tisbury, Wiltshire
2m SW of Tisbury off A30
Open *June–Sept 10–6, Oct 10–5,
Nov–Mar Wed–Sun 10–1 2–4; closed Apr*
An impressive example of a castle that
did not survive the Civil War. It is the
setting, though, that helps make this one
of Britain's most attractive ruins. The
hexagonal shape of the building perfectly
echoes the oasis of grass it was built on,
right next to a dreamy little lake. It had
been heavily adapted by the great Elizabethan architect, Robert Smythson, but
was later abandoned after suffering at the
hands of the Parliamentary army. A later
Palladian-style mansion was built nearby
(now a girl's boarding school), and the
castle sits in a landscape designed by
'Capability' Brown.

Pencarrow
☎ 01208 841369
Bodmin, Cornwall PL30 3AG
Email: pencarrow@aol.com
Website: www.pencarrow.co.uk
4m NW of Bodmin off A389 at Washaway
Open *House: Apr–Sept Sun–Thurs 1.30–5,
May–Aug BH Mons open from 1;
Oct–Mar pre-booked groups only.
Gardens: Mar–Oct dawn to dusk*
This is the 18th-century Georgian house
at its most sublime. The family who built
it, the Molesworths, are commemorated
by nearly a dozen portraits of themselves
by Reynolds in the house. The garden, a
stunning masterpiece, was the product
of Sir William Molesworth, and was created
(apparently) to console himself for losing
his Parliamentary seat in 1836. There is an
extensive network of walks in the 50 acres
of parkland, lawns and hanging woods.

Royal Citadel EH
☎ 01752 775841
The Hoe, Plymouth, Devon P11 2NZ
Email: bluebadge@plymouth-
chamber.co.uk
Open *May–Sept 2.30, by guided tour only*
Coastal fortress, dating from the late
17th century, built to ward off the Dutch.

Trewithen
☎ 01726 883647
Grampound Rd, nr Truro,
Cornwall TR2 4DD
Email: gardens@trewithen-estate.demon.
co.uk
Website: www.trewithengardens.co.uk
S of A390 between Grampound & Probus
Open *Mar–Sept Mon–Sat 10–4.30,
Sun in Apr & May only*
A fine early Georgian house with
world-famous gardens known for their
camellias, magnolias and rhododen-
drons, with plenty of rare trees and
shrubs. A 'must' for keen gardeners.

South-east MAP 2

215 Banqueting House*

☎ 020 7930 4179
Whitehall, London SW1A 2ER
Website: www.hrp.org.uk/bh/
indexbh.htm
*Tube Westminster, Embankment
or Charing Cross*
Open *Mon–Sat 10–5; closed BHs & for
official functions often at short notice*
Commissioned by James I and designed
by Inigo Jones, it was built between
1619 and 1623 and cost nearly £15,000.
It was built to replace the antiquated
Whitehall Palace as a grand setting for
court functions, and for the popular
court masques, colourful plays and
pageants written by Ben Jonson with
costumes and sets by Inigo Jones that
became increasingly elaborate. The
practice was stopped, however, after
the ceiling panels by Rubens were put
in place in order to protect the paint
from the smoke of the actors' torches.

The ceilings consist of panels commissioned by Charles I to celebrate the reign
of his father, James, and illustrate his own
theory about the nature of kingship. Each
of the three main panels (of a total of
nine) dramatizes one of James's supposed
great attributes as king: the provider of
peace and prosperity; his rise to the
heavens, apotheosized after his death,
to take his place among the immortals;
and, above the entrance, James accept-
ing the crowns of Scotland and England
in a gesture of national beneficence
(pretty ironic since the principle of union
was the first victim of the Civil War).

The building was also the location for
a far more gruesome piece of royal history.
Here on 30 January 1649 Charles I was
beheaded. He had been condemned a few
days earlier in Parliament Hall where a
tiny plaque in the floor marks the spot
where he sat for his trial. He was marched
here from St James' Palace on a freezing
January morning. After being held a few
hours in the private apartments, he was
led across the floor of his great building.
Since the windows were boarded up, he
was spared the sight of the ceiling whose
allegory was now so pathetically ironic.

Today the Banqueting House seems
a bit of an anomaly. There it stands,
rather unsure of itself, opposite the more
familiar Horse Guards Parade; it is not
very clear what sort of building you are
entering. The space has lost a lot of
atmosphere, and it is no surprise to
discover that it is used for corporate
functions. In fact, if it were not for the
ceilings, you would be hard pushed to
bother going in. Even the ceilings do not
quite belong here; it is as though they had
migrated down the road from the
National Gallery. And this is quite significant. The ceilings show the extent to
which that type of art – grandiose,
sensuous and allegorical – has been
expelled from the canon of British taste.
They are also a powerful image of the
distance that separated Charles I from
the life of his subjects. In the end, it is
rather a relief that this place stands
slightly outside the London tourist trail.
You have to work quite hard to savour it
but it is worth it. The Banqueting
House gives you a real frisson.

216 Basing House

☎ 01256 467294/817618
Redbridge Lane, Basingstoke,
Hampshire RG24 7HB
2m E of Basingstoke town centre
Open *Apr–Sept Wed–Sun & BHs 2–6*
Perhaps the most spectacular of the ruins
created by the Civil War, even if it is the site
of one of the most vicious episodes in a
series of vicious wars with more casualties
being inflicted in sieges than in set battles.

The house was a 1530 Tudor mansion (built on the site of previous Saxon and Norman structures). It just survived one of Elizabeth I's famous, and ruinously expensive, visits (part of the house had to be demolished to help pay for it). It survived Parliamentary seizure for over 3 years, before finally falling in 1645. It was completely razed by Cromwell.

his fate. He was later moved to Hurst Castle in Hampshire. Charles' daughter Elizabeth, however, died here in 1650, a victim of pneumonia contracted while playing in the rain on the bowling green that had been constructed for his exercise (his children were imprisoned here after his death). The castle dates back to Norman times.

217 Carisbrooke Castle EH
☎ 01983 522107
Newport, Isle of Wight PO30 1XY
1¼m SW of Newport, Isle of Wight
Open *Apr–Sept 10–6, Oct 10–5,
Nov–Mar 10–4*
Charles I was held here from 1647 till shortly before he was executed in January 1649. It was here that he planned what became the second Civil War which, even more than the first, sealed

218 Chiswick House EH
☎ 020 8995 0508
Burlington Lane, Chiswick,
London W4 2RP
*In W London, off A316 or westbound A4
just beyond Hogarth roundabout*
Open *Apr–Sept 10–6, Oct 10–5,
Nov–Mar Wed–Sun 10–4*
Built by Lord Burlington in 1723–9, it was designed as a showcase for Palladian-style architecture, a role it brilliantly succeeded

Chiswick House, *Lord Burlington's elegant Palladian villa.*

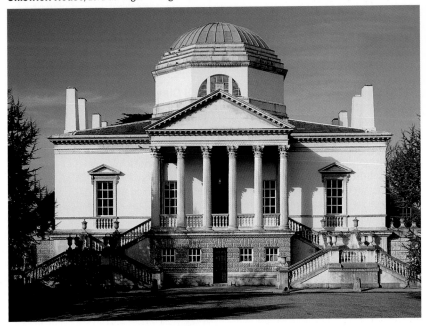

The front of **Claydon House**, *remodelled in the 1760s and 1770s for Ralph, 2nd Earl of Verney.*

in achieving. Unlike so many of even the finest 18th-century houses, Chiswick House (also known as Burlington House) remains powerfully idiosyncratic, an architect's house, as interesting for the uncompromising lines of its design as for its window on the lives of the wealthy. The garden, remodelled by William Kent, was one of the first to adopt the 'natural' style and depart from the strict geometry of the previous era. Temples, columns and follies create gentle surprises and allusions to classical literature and landscape paintings. In this respect the house plays a pivotal role in the direction taken by later 18th-century houses and gardens.

219 Claydon House* NT

☎ 01296 730349; Infoline 01494 755561
Middle Claydon, nr Buckingham,
Buckinghamshire MK18 2EY
Website: www.nationaltrust.org.uk/
regions/thameschilterns
In Middle Claydon 13m NW of Aylesbury; signposted from A413 & A41
Open *House: Apr–Oct Sat–Wed 1–5 Grounds: as house, 12–6*
The house has belonged to the Verney family since the late 15th century. They were a poignant example of a family split by the Civil War; Sir Edmund Verney fought for the Royalists while his son, Ralph, swore allegiance to the Parliamentarians.

Family letters still survive. In one Edmund wrote, 'for my part I do not like the quarrel and do heartily wish that the king would yield and consent to what they desire; so that my conscience is only concerned in honour and gratitude to follow my master. I have eaten his bread and served him near thirty years and will not do so base a thing as to forsake him and choose rather to lose my life (which I am sure I shall do) to preserve and defend those things which are against my conscience to preserve and defend...' Edmund was Charles' standard bearer at Edgehill where he was killed in 1642. Poor Ralph had to take his seat in the Commons and listen to a report gloatingly describe the fate of his father.

The house saw large extensions and alterations in the mid-18th century to what was originally a 16th-century manor. A new south front was built in the Victorian period. Florence Nightingale was the sister of one Lady Verney, and often stayed there; her bedroom is on display. The house is wonderfully light and airy; tucked away in a beautiful corner of Buckinghamshire it feels incredibly remote from London and Oxford. In the grounds is a beautiful chapel, with a family monument bearing the figures of Edmund and his son Ralph.

220 Ham House* NT

☎ 020 8940 1950
Ham, Richmond, Surrey TW10 7RS
Email: shhgen@smtp.ntrust.org.uk
Website: www.nationaltrust.org.uk/
regions/southern
*On S bank of Thames, W of A307
at Petersham*
Open *House: Apr–Oct Sat–Wed 1–5
Garden: all year Sat–Wed 11–6
(dusk if earlier)*
The elegant 17th-century home of the Duke and Duchess of Lauderdale

has magnificent interiors and gardens, and is a perfect showcase for period style. Built right on the banks of the Thames it is one of the great Stuart/Jacobean houses. Architecturally little has changed since the 1670s, with many of its original furnishings intact. The sequence of rooms has a pleasing progression from the grand to the intimate. The garden has been restored to its original 17th-century design, complete with knot garden and topiary. Right underneath the Heathrow flight path, it is harder than in most stately homes to expel modern life but it is still very impressive.

221 Kenwood House* EH

☎ 020 8348 1286
Hampstead Lane, London NW3 7JR
*On N side of Hampstead Heath,
on Hampstead–Highgate road*
Open *House: Apr–Sept 10–6, Oct 10–5,
Nov–Mar 10–4; opens 10.30 Wed & Fri
all year. Grounds: Apr–Sept 8–8.30
(or dusk if earlier), Oct–Mar 8–4.45*
Located at the northern end of Hampstead Heath, it was remodelled in the mid-18th century by Robert Adam. It now contains a fabulous art collection including Vermeer's *The Guitar Player*, a self-portrait by Rembrandt and, for many, Thomas Gainsborough's masterpiece, his portrait of *Mary, Countess Howe*. It provides a powerful contrast with the portraits by Reynolds, also on display, which tend to involve aristocratic sitters playing at being classical goddesses. They are beautifully done, but you cannot imagine falling in love with his subjects. The *Countess Howe* is different. It is a portrait by somebody who knows what it is to be ravished by a woman's beautiful neck, or a haughty half-smile. The park is the site of the famous open-air summer concerts.

222 Old Royal Naval College, Greenwich*

☎ 020 8269 4747
King William Walk, Greenwich,
London SE1D 9NN
On south bank of Thames at Greenwich
Open *Mon–Sat 10–5 Sun 12.30–5*
The college was built by Charles II on the site of one of Henry VIII's favourite palaces, the Placentia, which was demolished in 1662. The new buildings were designed in two stages. The first – the King Charles Block – was designed by John Webb. The second stage fell to the great architect Christopher Wren and his assistant Nicholas Hawksmoor, who drew it all together in a single, coherent design. They were given to the Royal Naval College in 1873.

The interior is dominated by the Painted Hall which boasts a magnificent ceiling painted by William Hogarth's uncle, Sir James Thornhill, a rich and fulsome allegorical tribute to William and Mary, with a host of what were then happily considered uniquely British virtues. There is also a lovely chapel.

223 Osterley Park* NT

☎ 020 8568 7714; Infoline 01494 755566
Jersey Rd, Isleworth, Middlesex TW7 4RB
Email: admin@osterleypark.org.uk
Website: www.nationaltrust.org.uk/regions/thameschilterns
Follow signs on A4 between Gillette Corner & Osterley Tube Station; M4 junction 3
Open *House: Mar–Oct Wed–Sun 1–4.30; closed Good Fri but open BH Mons. Jersey Galleries: as house. Grand stables: Sun pm in summer. Park: all year 9–7.30 (or dusk)*
Osterley was once a Tudor mansion owned by the then wealthiest man in the country, Sir Thomas Gresham, the founder of the Royal Exchange in 1565–7.

The building was completely reworked by Robert Adam from 1761–80. The result is a fascinating hybrid of the Elizabethan and Georgian periods. Some of its most spectacular features are the ceilings: the drawing room, for example, has a pattern of ostrich feathers radiating out of a golden sunflower, surrounded by rich stucco. The use of colour for ceilings was something which Adam was particularly adept at, bored as he was with the endless use of white. The interior represents Adam at his peak, and is one of the most complete to have survived. The style is much more delicate and subtle than is usual for the period. Horace Walpole called it 'the palace of palaces'.

Much of the furniture is original, and there are many fine paintings and tapestries. The house is now surrounded by one of the largest gardens in greater London, familiar to anyone looking out the aircraft window as they approach Heathrow (usually it is on the right).

224 Petworth House NT

☎ 01798 342207; Infoline 01798 343929
Church St, Petworth, W Sussex GU28 0AE
Email: spegen@smtp.ntrust.org.uk
Website: www.nationaltrust.org.uk/regions/southern
In centre of Petworth
Open *Apr–Oct Sat–Wed 11–5.30 & Good Fri. Park: all year 8–dusk*
A fantastic twin package consisting of one of the most beautiful 17th/18th-century stately homes ever built and a world-class collection of art. The art on display is not the usual combination of Old Masters, rounded off by dutiful English portraits and landscapes (though the Old Masters are here, in spades, with great paintings by Claude, Holbein, Van Dyck, Gainsborough, Reynolds, Blake

*The west front of **Osterley Park**, remodelled in the Neoclassical style by Robert Adam.*

and Titian among them). Petworth's real masterpieces are the sequence of paintings by Turner, which are among his most sublime. Turner lived here for a while, under the hospitality of Petworth's then owner, the 3rd Earl of Egremont. He had a real feel for the place. The combination of 'Capability' Brown's landscape and Turner's love of colour and space produced some of his best paintings.

On display in the house is Turner's famous painting of the parkland, with a herd of deer and a cricket match. It is an incredible study of light and immensity. There is comfort too in the fact that so little has changed there to this day. Not all of Turner's Petworth pictures are so elevated; one is a little watercolour painted as an apology for spilling cream at the breakfast table over his hostess's dress depicting the sorry scene.

The house is a Baroque masterpiece, and was built from 1688–96 by the 6th Duke of Somerset on the site of an old manor house (only the chapel and cellars of which survive). Since trade with the Orient was booming at the time, there are plenty of expensive, exquisite Chinese furniture and artefacts, for which the then Duchess had great enthusiasm, and much is still displayed. The Carved Room was decorated by Grinling Gibbons, who was also responsible for a pair of stunning picture frames. A fire in 1714 resulted in much remodelling, including the staircase which is now decorated with floor-to-ceiling murals by Louis Laguerre. There is a large collection of antique statues assembled in Italy for the 2nd Earl of Egremont, now housed in their own gallery, presenting a powerful window on the mind of the 18th-century collector obsessed by the grandeur of imperial Rome and its relevance to England. Further changes were made early in the 19th century.

225 Queen's House, Greenwich

☎ 020 8858 4422
Part of National Maritime Museum, Romney Rd, Greenwich, London SE10 9NF
On south bank of Thames at Greenwich
Open *Daily 10–5*
In the early 1600s Greenwich Palace – or Placentia as it was known – was a jumble of royal buildings straddling the Woolwich–Deptford road and facing on to the south bank of the Thames. In 1616 James I commissioned Inigo Jones to build a house for his queen, Anne, in the newly fashionable Palladian style. Unfortunately she never moved in. She died in 1619 and James did not have the heart to go on. Work was only completed after a long interruption and it was Henrietta Maria, Charles I's queen, who got the keys. The great hall is a perfect cube (like Inigo Jones's other cube room, at Wilton House), exactly 40ft (12m) in all dimensions. The house is built of brick with Portland stone dressings.

Close by, in Greenwich Park, is the Old Royal Observatory, designed by Christopher Wren and built in 1675–6 by order of Charles II. It is the location of the longitude zero line.

226 St Andrew's Church, Didling*

Nr Treyford, W Sussex
On minor road 2m W of Cocking on A286
Open *Any reasonable time*
This tiny little shepherds' church is buried in the Sussex countryside. It is the perfect example of a plain and simple place of worship. It still has its Laudian communion rails – a low barrier built to separate the altar from congregation, named after Archbishop William Laud, who introduced them to many churches in the 1630s and 1640s. They seem harmless enough, but to Puritans the feature smacked of Popery.

St Paul's Cathedral, *seen from the south.*

227 St Paul's Cathedral*

☎ 020 7236 4128
Ludgate Hill, London EC4M 8AD
Email: chapter@stpaulscathedral.org.uk
Website: www.stpauls.co.uk
Tube St Paul's, Bank or Mansion House
Open *Cathedral: Mon–Sat 8.30–4.30;*
closed for special services. Ambulatory,
crypt & galleries: Mon–Sat 9–4.15
Probably the greatest monument from
the 17th century in England, it was
designed by one of the luminaries of
the period, Sir Christopher Wren. The
famous inscription '*Lector, si monumen-*
tum requiris, circumspice' ('Reader, if you
seek a monument, then look around
you'), located in the crypt under the
dome, is brilliantly apt. There had been a
church on this spot since Saxon times,
and the original was the first of five to be
destroyed by fire, the last in the Great
Fire of 1666, memorably described by

diarist Samuel Pepys. It was Wren, the
Surveyor General, who persuaded
Charles II to pull down the smouldering
wreck of St Paul's, with its Gothic tower,
and start again. The aim? To build a great
central masterpiece for a whole new city.

The cathedral took 35 years to
complete, and the design went through
a number of key modifications as Wren,
and his clients, argued over the proper
form that a great Protestant church
should take. Wren lived long enough to
see his son lay the final stone in 1710.
This was the first cathedral in Britain
to be conceived, designed, built and
completed under the supervision of the
same man.

The crowning feature is the dome,
sitting on a colossal stone drum. Actually
there are three domes: the inner one,
visible from inside the church; a middle
one made of brick which supports the

stone cupola; and the outer dome made of timber and covered in lead. They allowed Wren to build a structure this size safely, and with a proportionally correct shape.

The trip to the top is arduous, but really worth it. The views over the roof of the cathedral are spectacular, and while up there the sheer scale and panache of the design becomes very clear. The cross that you can see at the very top of the dome is exactly 365ft (111m) above ground level, 1ft for every day of the year. Other features include the famous Whispering Gallery with its uncanny ability to transmit barely audible whispers around its circumference. To get to it there is a climb of 259 steps up between the two skins of the dome. And of course there is the mausoleum in the crypt for the nation's heroes, such as Nelson and Wellington, as well as Wren himself. Still on display in the library is the fabulous oak model that he constructed, at enormous expense, to help sell his radical designs to the king.

228 Syon Park

☎ 020 8560 0883
Brentford, Middlesex TW8 8JF
Email: info@syonpark.co.uk
Website: www.syonpark.co.uk
Between Brentford & Twickenham, off A4
Open *House: mid-Mar–Oct*
Wed Thurs Sun & BHs 11–5
Gardens: daily 10–5.30 or dusk

With its dramatic black and white marble hallway and long corridors and galleries, this is one of the great stately homes in the London area. Originally it was a nunnery founded by Henry V in 1415, the year of Agincourt. After the Dissolution of the Monasteries, the building passed to the Duke of Somerset (brother of Jane Seymour, third wife of Henry VIII). He converted it into a castellated mansion.

Syon came into its own in the 18th century when that formidable duo, Robert Adam and 'Capability' Brown, got their hands on it. Adam's interior is characterized by brilliant colours, stucco panels and gilt. As you would expect, it is full of fine furniture and works of art. 'Capability' Brown's landscaped park is extensive and exquisite.

229 Uppark NT

☎ 01730 825415; Infoline 01730 825857
South Harting, Petersfield,
W Sussex GU31 5QR
Email: supgen@smtp.ntrust.org.uk
Website: www.nationaltrust.org.uk/ regions/southern
1½m S of South Harting,
5m SE of Petersfield on B2146
Open *House: Apr–Oct Sun–Thurs 1–5,*
opens 12 on Sun in Aug. Grounds: 11–5.
Print room: open first Mon of each month

The Wren-style house is situated high on the crest of the South Downs, and is surrounded by pastures that, unusually, go right up to the building. Castles have long been built on rocky outcrops or high ridges, but for stately homes the setback of such a lofty position was inaccessible water. The problem was solved here by the pump that was invented by the first owner's grandfather.

The house was designed by the same man responsible for Chatsworth, William Talman. The house was full of beautiful Italian works of art and fine furniture, most of it gathered by Sir Matthew Fetherstonhaugh, one of its first owners, while doing the Grand Tour with his young wife. The flock wallpaper, damask curtains, and other fabrics would normally have been the first victims of a 19th-century clear out, but thanks to the dedication of the two women who lived here then, nothing was altered. H.G.Wells spent a lot of time here as a young man because his mother was the housekeeper; he left a vivid description of how lively life was below stairs in his autobiography. A devastating fire in 1989 destroyed much of the house and its contents but they have now been meticulously restored.

230 Wallace Collection

☎ 020 7935 0687
Hertford House, Manchester Square, London W1U 3BN
Website: www.the-wallace-collection. org.uk
Tube Bond Street or Marble Arch
Open *Mon–Sat 10–5 Sun 2–5*
Buried in the heart of a rather anonymous bit of Marylebone, in central London, is this extraordinary art collection. The building is a large, 18th-century town house originally built for the 4th Duke of Manchester in the late 1770s and 1780s. The interior is devoted to the Wallace Collection, probably the biggest and most valuable single gift of an art collection made by an individual to the nation. Sir Richard Wallace's widow handed over the contents of Hertford House, the family home, in 1897. There are some superb 18th-century French paintings,

including Fragonard's *The Swing* which looks like innocent froth until you learn that, apparently, the frolicking Marie Antoinette-type figure is not supposed to be wearing any underwear – but who knows? Frans Hals' famous *Laughing Cavalier* is also here. There is a priceless collection of 18th-century French furniture, sculpture, porcelain and arms and armour.

231 West Wycombe Park NT

☎ 01494 513569
West Wycombe, Buckinghamshire HP14 3AJ
Website: www.nationaltrust.org.uk/ regions/thameschilterns
At W end of West Wycombe, S of A40
Open *House: June–Aug Sun–Thurs 2–6 (weekdays: entry by guided tour every 20 mins). Grounds: as house, & Apr–May Sun–Thurs & BHs 2–6*
In the 18th century this was the site of the notorious Hellfire Club, famous for its black magic rites and orgies, organized by Sir Francis Dashwood. The house is a riot of Italianate swagger and excess, its façades disguised as classical temples. A two-storeyed Tuscan and

*The west front of **West Wycombe Park** seen from across the lake.*

Corinthian colonnade extends between the wings of the south front. The Ionic portico at the west was designed by Nicholas Revett around 1770. The house contains painted ceilings by Borgnis, tapestries, pictures and fine furniture. The grounds are modelled by Humphry Repton, and contain a swan-shaped lake and temples. There is a mausoleum at the top of the hill. It is a hexagonal, roofless monument decorated with vases and plastered columns. There are caves in the hill associated with the Hellfire Club's activities.

232 Woburn Abbey

☎ 01525 290666
Woburn, Bedfordshire MK17 9WA
Email: enquiries@woburnabbey.co.uk
Website: www.woburnabbey.co.uk
*10m NE of Waddesdon on A4102;
or follow signs from M1 junction 13*
Open *House: Apr–Oct Mon–Sat 11–4 Sun
& BHs 11–5, Jan–Mar Sat Sun & BHs 11–4*
Built on the site of a dissolved monastery, it was greatly modified during the 18th century by the Russell family (created Dukes of Bedford, and one of the grandest families to rise to prominence during the Tudor period). Much of the early money required to launch the house into the big league came from the 4th Earl.

It now houses a magnificent and varied art collection including a series of Canaletto paintings of Venice, and the famous *Armada Portrait* of Elizabeth I. Also look out for work by Van Dyck, Hals, Rembrandt, Tintoretto, Murillo, Claude, Poussin and Velazquez, and the two great bookends of 18th-century British art, Reynolds and Gainsborough. The furniture is also of amazingly high quality.

Notable rooms include the saloon, known as the Star Chamber because of the stellar gold decorations on the walls.

The north wing has a wonderful grotto, the Fountain Room, full of shells, designed by an assistant of Inigo Jones, Isaac de Caus, and is groaning with pearly Mannerist excess.

The family was once again at the forefront of British politics in the 18th century, being powerful players in the Whig period. That necessitated yet more work on the house, this time by Henry Flitcroft who created the state rooms, an exotic Chinese Room, a state bedroom, dining room, breakfast room and long gallery. A huge amount of urgent restoration was done after the Second World War turning Woburn Abbey into one of the country's most popular stately homes. The house is surrounded by thousands of acres of parkland, with great herds of deer, landscaped by Humphry Repton. There is a dramatic safari park too.

ADDITIONAL PLACES TO VISIT

Ascott NT

☎ 01296 688242
Wing, nr Leighton Buzzard,
Bedfordshire LU7 0PS
Email: info@ascottestate.co.uk
Website: www.ascottestate.co.uk
2m SW of Leighton Buzzard, S of A418
Open *House & garden: Apr & Aug–mid-Sept
2–6; closed Mon. Garden: May–Aug every
Wed & last Sun in each month*
This began life as a half-timbered Jacobean farmhouse, but once bought by the Rothschild family it quickly expanded. They injected fine paintings, furniture and porcelain. The surrounding gardens are varied and delightful.

Ashdown House NT

☎ 01488 72584
Lambourn, nr Newbury,
Oxfordshire RG16 7RE
Email: tadgen@smtp.ntrust.org.uk

*2m S of Ashbury, 3m N of Lambourn,
on W side of B4000*
Open *Hall, staircase & roof: Apr–Oct
Wed & Sat by guided tour only at 2.15,
3.15 & 4.15. Garden: Apr–Oct Wed & Sat
2–5. Woodland: all year daily except Fri,
dawn to dusk*
Set in beautiful gardens, this four-storey
Dutch-style white house on the Lambourn Downs belonged to James I's
daughter, Elizabeth, Queen of Bohemia
('The Winter Queen'), when she and
her husband Frederick of the Palatinate
fled to Jacobean England. Much of the
interior is taken up by a huge staircase.

Avington Park
☎ 01962 779260
Winchester, Hampshire SO21 1DB
Email: Sarah@avingtonpark.co.uk
Website: www.avingtonpark.co.uk
*4m N of Winchester; leave M3 junction 9,
on B3047 to Itchen Abbas*
Open *May–Sept Sun & BHs 2.30–5.30;
other times by arrangement*
A redbrick country house dating from
the Jacobean and Restoration period,
in the Wren style, with its own Georgian
church, St Mary's, in the grounds. The
wings and central portico were added
in the 1670s.

Basildon Park NT
☎ 0118 984 3040;
Infoline 01494 755558
Lower Basildon, Reading,
Berkshire KG8 9NR
Website: www.nationaltrust.org.uk/
regions/thameschilterns
*Between Pangbourne & Streatley,
7m NW of Reading on A329;
leave M4 at junction 12*
Open *House: Apr–Oct Wed–Sun 1–5.30;
closed Good Fri but open BH Mons
Park, garden & woodland walks:
as house, 12–5.30*

The lovely Palladian mansion was
designed by John Carr and built in
1776–83 from money made in India by
Sir Francis Sykes, the first owner. Its most
beautiful rooms are the Octagon Room
and the Shell Room. Elsewhere there is
an abundance of plasterwork, art and
furniture thanks to the efforts of later
owners who rescued the house from decay
(it had lain empty for nearly 40 years). The
grounds are in the 19th-century style, and
are in the process of being fully restored.

Bembridge Windmill NT
☎ 01983 873945
NT Office, Longstone Farmhouse,
Strawberry Lane, Mottistone, Newport,
Isle of Wight PO30 4EA
Website: www.nationaltrust.org.uk/
regions/southern
½m S of Bembridge on B3395
Open *Apr–end June & Sept–Oct daily
except Sat (but open Easter Sat),
July–Aug daily, all 10–5*
Very well preserved windmill, with
original wooden machinery, dating
from the early 18th century.

Christ Church, Spitalfields
☎ 020 7247 7202
Commercial St, London E1 6LY
Email: admin@ccsfields.fslife.co.uk
Tube Aldgate East
Open *Mon–Fri 12–2.30 Sun 1–4*
After a diet of London's earlier churches,
Hawksmoor's masterpiece comes like a
revelation. Built over 15 years from 1714
to 1729, this is one of the city's most
imposing and idiosyncratic churches.
It is still in the throes of a massive
restoration project.

Clandon Park NT
☎ 01483 222482; Infoline 01483 223479
West Clandon, Guildford, Surrey GU4 7RQ
Email: sc/sea@smtp.ntrust.org.uk

Website: www.nationaltrust.org.uk/regions/southern
3m E of Guildford on A247;
from A3 follow signposts to Ripley,
join A247 via B2215
Open *House & Garden: Apr–Oct*
Tues–Thurs & Sun, Good Fri, Easter Sat &
BH Mons 11–5. Museum: as house 12–5
Built *c*1730 by Venetian architect
Giacomo Leoni, this is a Palladian
masterpiece. The house, not surprisingly,
contains high-quality plasterwork, wallpapers, paintings and furniture. There
are also fascinatingly detailed accounts
recording all the salaries paid to the
servants in the late 19th century. 'Capability' Brown softened and naturalized
the original, more formal gardens.

Nearby is Hatchlands Park, built in
1758, with Robert Adam interiors, naval
feel (it was built for an admiral), and a
collection of early keyboard instruments.

Cobham Hall

☎ 01474 823371
Cobham, Kent DA12 3BL
Email: Cobhamhall@aol.com
Adjacent to A2/M2 4m W of Strood,
8m E of M25 junction 2 between
Gravesend & Rochester
Open *Through the year on a variety*
of days, phone to check
A beautiful house with Tudor origins,
but many later additions, making
it a wonderful hybrid of Elizabethan,
Jacobean, Carolinian and 18th-century
styles. The ornate decorations in the
Gilt Hall are the product of Inigo Jones's
great pupil, John Webb; it is considered
one of the most beautiful rooms of its
kind in England. The gardens were
designed by Humphry Repton. Although
now a girls' school, it is open to visitors
on certain days.

Danny

☎ 01273 833000
New Way Lane, Hurstpierpoint,
W Sussex BN6 9BB
1m SE of Hurstpierpoint,
S of Hassocks road
Open *May–Sept Wed & Thurs 2–5; groups*
at other times by prior arrangement
The redbrick Elizabethan mansion
was built in the 1590s in a distinctive
E-shape and with a fine great hall, one of
the last great halls to be built. A wing was
added by Henry Campion in 1728.
During the First World War the house
was rented by Lloyd George for War
Cabinet meetings and the Armistice was
drawn up here.

Goodwood House

☎ 01243 755048;
Infoline 01243 755040
Goodwood, Chichester,
W Sussex PO18 0PX
Email: housevisiting@goodwood.co.uk
Website: www.goodwood.co.uk
4m NE of Chichester, off A27, A286
or A285
Open *May–Sept Sun & Mon 1–5*
The elegant Georgian mansion with
its appealing corner towers topped by
shallow copper domes was built by the
architect James Wyatt for the 3rd Duke of
Richmond, who pulled down most of an
earlier 17th-century house. His grandfather had bought the estate for hunting.
It has a wonderful collection of 17th-
and 18th-century British and European
paintings including works by Stubbs,
Van Dyck, Romney, Lely and Canaletto.
There is also a fine collection of French
furniture, porcelain and tapestries. In
the garden, there is a statue of a lion
over the grave of a real one which had
been the start of an early menagerie.

The entrance front of **Goodwood House** *with its double portico and corner towers.*

*The gabled exterior of **Greys Court**.*

Greys Court NT
☎ 01491 628529;
Infoline 01494 755564
Rotherfield Greys, Henley-on-Thames,
Oxfordshire RG9 4PG
Email: tgrgen@smtp.ntrust.org.uk
*W of Henley-on-Thames. From Nettlebed
mini-roundabout on A4130 take B481*
Open *House (part of ground floor only):
Apr–Sept Wed–Fri & BH Mons 2–6.
Garden: Apr–Sept Tues–Sat & BH Mons 2–6*
Where did 18th-century houses draw
their water? From a well, of course, but at
Greys Court the job of lifting the buckets
belonged to a donkey treading the inside
of a large wheel. The system only stopped
in 1914, but you can still see the workings.
The house retains other elements of
16th-, 17th- and 18th-century life, like an
ice-house. It even has a modern maze,
completed in 1980. In all, it is a charming
house (with medieval origins) whose
rooms still contain excellent 18th-
century plasterwork.

Groombridge Place Gardens
☎ 01892 863999
Tunbridge Wells, Kent TN3 9QG
Email: office@groombridge.co.uk
Website: www.groombridge.co.uk
4m SW of Tunbridge Wells, just off A264
Open *Garden only: Apr–Oct daily 9–6*
A Restoration-era country house built in
1660, with panelling from the Elizabethan
manor house that previously stood here.
They even kept the old moat but, in the
fashion of the times, it was strictly for
decoration and to blend in with the
original walled garden. The nearby
church of St John the Evangelist is a
charming redbrick chapel; it was constructed by the house owner, John
Packer, to give thanks because Charles I
had not married the Catholic Spanish
Infanta. All was undone when instead he
married Henrietta Maria, also a Catholic.
There are riverside walks, bird displays,
and spooky parts of the forest created by
Ivan Hicks; good fun for children.

Hammerwood Park
☎ 01342 850594
East Grinstead, W Sussex RH19 3QE
Email: latrobe@mistral.co.uk
3m E of East Grinstead on A264
to Tunbridge Wells, 1m S of Holtye
Open *House & park: Easter Mon–Sept Wed*
Sat & BH Mons 2–5.30; guided tour
starts 2.05
The original rockpile, this late 18th-
century hunting lodge was owned
during the 1970s by the group Led
Zeppelin. Designed by Benjamin
Latrobe, who also created the Capitol
Building and the White House in Washington DC, it is one of Sussex's most
charming destinations.

Marble Hill House EH
☎ 020 8892 5115
Richmond Road, Twickenham,
Middlesex TW1 2NL
On A305 between Richmond
& Twickenham
Open *Apr–Sept 10–6, Oct 10–5,*
Nov–Mar Wed–Sun 10–4; closed early Jan
A breathtaking display of the 18th
century's love of symmetry and propor-
tion, built in 1724–9 in the Palladian
style. It was used as a location in the
TV drama, *Longitude*.

Milton's Cottage
☎ 01494 872313
21 Deanway, Chalfont St Giles,
Buckinghamshire HP8 4JH
½m W of A413, 3m N of M40 junction 2
Open *Mar–Oct Tues–Sun 10–1 & 2–6;*
closed Mon except on BHs
John Milton's small cottage, where he
finished his epic *Paradise Lost* and
started *Paradise Regained*, includes
three museum rooms containing first
editions of his poetry and prose works.
There is a garden featuring plants
mentioned in his poetry.

Milton Manor House
☎ 01235 862321
Milton, Abingdon, Oxfordshire OX14 4EN
9m S of Oxford off A34
Open *Aug & BH weekends 2–5; groups*
(15 or more) by arrangement all year
Bought in 1764 by a Catholic lace-maker,
Bryant Barrett, this is a particularly
charming house even by the standards
of the period. It is 17th-century in style
with two Georgian wings. The library
was finished in the so-called 'pastry-
cook's' 'gothick' style, one of the best of
its kind. There is 18th-century Catholic
memorabilia on display, as well as the
telescope of John Benbow, Vice-Admiral
of the *Blue* in 1701. There are gardens
and stables.

Princes Risborough Manor House NT
☎ 01494 528051 (Regional Office)
Princes Risborough,
Buckinghamshire HP17 9AW
Website: www.nationaltrust.org.uk/
regions/thameschilterns
Opposite church, off market square
Open *House (hall, drawing room*
& staircase) & front garden: only by
written appointment with the owner,
Apr–Oct Wed 2.30–4.30
A fine 17th-century redbrick house
with a Jacobean oak staircase, and
18th-century wainscoting.

Spencer House
☎ 020 7514 1964;
Infoline 020 7499 8620
27 St James Place, London SW1A 1NR
Website: www.spencerhouse.co.uk
Tube Green Park
Open *Sun 10.30–5.30; closed Aug & Jan.*
1-hour guided tours approx every 25 mins
The most spectacular 18th-century town
house in London has its great formal state
rooms at full volume in the Neoclassical
style, with paintings and furniture lent

by the Victoria & Albert Museum and the Queen. This was the Spencers' London home (Althorp, p181, is their country seat), which was recently superbly restored. Not a reticent house – just look at the florid bow window in the Palm Room.

Squerryes Court
☎ 01959 562345
Westerham, Kent TN16 1SJ
Email: squerryescourt@pavilion.co.uk
½m SW of Westerham,
leave M25 junction 6, E along A25
Open *Apr–Sept Wed Sat Sun & BH Mons,*
grounds 12–5.30 & house 1.30–5.30
A fine William and Mary redbrick house, plain, handsome and beautifully appointed. There is plenty of art and furniture worth seeing, and landscaped gardens. They were re-landscaped in the 18th century but the more formal, original one is being restored.

Stansted Park
☎ 01705 412265
Rowlands Castle, Hampshire PO9 6DX
Email: stansted@athene.co.uk
Website: www.stanstedpark.co.uk
Follow brown heritage signs from A3
(Rowlands Castle) or A27 (Havant)
Open *July–Sept Sun–Wed 2–5*
The Carolinian revival-style house (of which it is an eminent example) is surrounded by 1750 acres of park and woodland, including walled gardens and conservatories.

Strawberry Hill
☎ Infoline 020 8240 4224;
020 8240 4114
St Mary's College, Waldegrave Rd, Twickenham, London TW1 4SX
Off A310 between
Twickenham & Teddington
Open *Easter–Oct Sun tours only 2, 2.45*
& 3.30; phone for other times

The ultimate 'Gothick' house was created (as an alteration to an existing house) by Horace Walpole and his 'Committee of Taste' (which included Robert Adam, John Chute, Richard Bentley and Thomas Gray) from 1749–76. It was the model for the great vogue in Gothic Revival architecture that followed. It is now a college.

Eastern MAP 3
233 Audley End EH
☎ 01799 522399
Saffron Walden, Essex CB11 4JF
1m W of Saffron Walden on B1383;
M11 junctions 8 & 9 (from S) & 10
Open *House: Apr–Sept Wed–Sun*
& BHs 12–5, Oct Wed–Sun 11–3
Grounds: Apr–Sept Wed–Sun & BHs 11–6,
Oct Wed–Fri 11–4 Sat–Sun 11–5
One of the great Jacobean houses, huge by the standards of the day; only Hampton Court was bigger when the house was rebuilt early in the 17th century to replace a Tudor house belonging to Sir Thomas Audley. What we see today is only half of what was originally there. James I wryly commented that it was 'too large for a king, but might do well for a Lord Treasurer' – apt, because the Lord Treasurer who had built it was Thomas Howard, 1st Earl of Suffolk, who was charged with embezzlement and accused of corruption; obviously a man with ideas well above his station. No wonder that in the 18th century some of the house was demolished to save on the upkeep.

The house comprises two large courtyards, whose buildings slowly gain in size, though later demolition work ruined the effect. The great hall is a key feature, and is dominated by a huge two-storey screen in the Jacobean style. The interior was redesigned in 1760s by Robert Adam, and the grounds were transformed by 'Capability' Brown. Sweeping changes were made in the 19th century too. The house was used in the Second World War to train Polish special agents before English Heritage took over and began the extensive restoration.

234 Blickling Hall NT

☎ 01263 738030
Blickling, Norfolk NR11 6NF
*1m NW of Aylsham on B1354;
signposted off A140 Norwich (15m)
to Cromer (10m)*
Open *House: Apr–Oct Wed–Sun
& BH Mons 1–4.30 (closes 3.30 in Oct)
Garden: Apr–Oct Wed–Sun, also Tues in
Aug, 10.15–5.15. Nov–Dec Thurs–Sun
11–4, Jan–Mar Sat & Sun 11–4*
Built at almost the same time that Inigo Jones was putting the finishing touches to his Banqueting House in Whitehall, this house has a very different Jacobean feel. Remodelled for Sir Henry Hobart by Robert Lyminge from 1616–28, it has one of the finest redbrick façades to have survived from the period. Lyminge, a veteran of Hatfield House (p112), favoured the use of a more turreted look.

The former house was the property of Anne Boleyn's father and her spirit still suffuses the place.

Some of its most celebrated features are its ceilings: elaborately carved plasterwork, created by a genius of stucco, Edward Stanyan. The long gallery displays this to best effect. What makes this ceiling even more attractive is its ambition; it is packed with the kind of detail expected on a painted allegorical ceiling, only here it is in three-dimensional white. There are evocations of the Five Senses, and 20 symbols and emblems derived from Henry Peacham's 1612 volume, *Minerva Britannia.*

The house's fortunes were in the ascendant during the 18th century, hence the number of features borrowed from the newly fashionable taste in Strawberry Hill 'Gothick' (Horace Walpole's London house which was an influential example of the Gothic Revival). There are two major rooms designed entirely in the 18th-century style – the Peter the Great Room and the state bedroom next door. It passed into the care of the National Trust in 1940, one of the first of a number of great country houses to do so.

The rose-pink south front of **Blickling Hall**.

Cromwell's House *where he lived with his family from 1636 to 1647.*

235 Cromwell's House

☎ 01353 662062
St Mary's St, Ely, Cambridgeshire CB7 4HF
Email: tic@eastcambs.gov.uk
W of Ely Cathedral
Open *Apr–Sept daily 10–5.30,*
Oct–Mar Mon–Sat 10–5 Sun 11.15–4
This 13th-century house is where Oliver Cromwell lived with his family from 1636 to 1647. He inherited the house from an uncle, an inheritance which brought with it the position of local tax collector.

236 Holkham Hall

☎ 01328 710227
Wells-next-the-Sea, Norfolk NR23 1AB
Website: www.holkham.co.uk
2m W of Wells-next-the-Sea off A419
Open *Easter Sat & Sun, May Sun & Mon*
11.30–5, June–Sept Sun–Thurs 1–5
Just up the road from Houghton Hall and if anything even more spectacular. This mix of Italianate grandeur and English pragmatism is designed to show the best Italianate/Palladian style possible, on land reclaimed from the dunes and salt marshes.

Holkham Hall has been the home of the Coke family for nearly 250 years. It was built to designs by Lord Burlington and William Kent, though heavily influenced by the man who paid for it all and whose Grand Tour had inspired it – Thomas Coke, 1st Earl of Leicester. It is constructed on an H-plan, with four wings leading to a central section. The exterior remained austere while the interior became ever more lavish. The rooms, corridors and saloons are all hymns to 18th-century grandeur in their furniture, oil paintings and tapestries. A pair of contrasting portraits of Coke tell us much about how 18th-century 'milords' saw themselves: one has hunting gear, plain, sensible and brown; the other the full finery of an Italian peacock.

The design was intended to create long internal vistas, through an endless succession of doors and hallways, to be promenaded through just like the garden outside. The Marble Hall, faced with pink English alabaster, is particularly spectacular, as are the views over nearly 3000 acres of surrounding parkland and lake set out in the flowing natural style loved by 18th-century British aristocrats.

Holkham makes the perfect visit for those who like *big* stately homes. It is the highwater mark of British national and imperial self-regard. It did not last forever but, while it did, it inspired some fantastic architecture. This has some of the best.

237 Houghton Hall*
☎ 01485 528569
King's Lynn, Norfolk PE31 6UE
Website: www.houghtonhall.com
13m E of King's Lynn, 10m W of Fakenham, 1m N of A148
Open *Apr–Sept Sun Thurs & BH Mons 12–5.30. House: 2–5.30. Grounds: 1–5.30*
One of the finest examples of the Palladian style in Britain, the house was built to designs by Colen Campbell, revised by Thomas Ripley, for 'Cock Robin' – Sir Robert Walpole – who was in effect Britain's first Prime Minister. Holkham was where Walpole, the great architect of British 18th-century political life, went to savour the rewards of high office at a safe distance from the dirt, squalor and crowds of London. Situated in beautiful parkland, the house is full of magnificent furniture and pictures, and has interior decoration by William Kent. As at Chatsworth, a nearby all-too-visible village had to be dismantled, lock, stock and barrel, and moved to an alternative location so that Walpole could look at Nature unsullied by any sniff of the riffraff.

Elton Hall
☎ 01832 280468
Elton, Peterborough, Cambridgeshire PE8 6SH
3m from A1 in the village of Elton, off A605 Peterborough–Oundle Road
Open *Late spring BH Sun & Mon, June Wed, July–Aug Wed Thurs Sun & Aug BH Mon, all 2–5*
A gatehouse and crypt have survived from a 15th-century house. A Restoration-era house was built on the site by Sir Thomas Proby. Its most notable feature was the fine library containing 12,000 books, and a number of important volumes including early English Bibles and Henry VIII's Prayer Book. There is also a collection of paintings by Reynolds, Constable and other Old Masters. The gardens are spectacular too, with a newly built orangery.

Felbrigg Hall NT
☎ 01263 837444
Felbrigg, Norwich, Norfolk NR11 8PR
Email: afgusr@smtp.ntrust.org.uk
Near Felbrigg village, 2m SW of Cromer; entrance off B1436, signposted from A148 & A140
Open *House: Apr–Oct Sat–Wed 1–5, BH Suns & Mons 11–5. Garden: Apr–Oct Sat–Wed 11–5.30*
An earlier manor house was remodelled in 1621–4 by Robert Lyminge. It was added to in 1680, and much remodelled again between 1749 and 1756 by the architect James Paine. The library contains books once owned by one of the great figures of the 18th century, Samuel Johnson. The walled garden provided fruit and vegetables for the house. There are hundreds of acres of surrounding landscape.

Gunby Hall NT

☎ 01909 486411 (Regional Office)
Gunby, nr Spilsby, Lincolnshire PE23 5SS
Website: www.gunbyhall.ic24.net
2m NW of Burgh le Marsh,
7m W of Skegness off A158
Open *House (ground floor & basement):*
Apr–Sept Wed 2–6. Gardens: Apr–Sept
Wed & Thurs 2–6

An exquisite example of William and
Mary architecture, with later strong
associations with the poet Tennyson,
being his 'haunt of ancient peace'. It has
good examples of English furniture, a fine
staircase, gardens and stable block.

Peckover House and Garden NT

☎ 01945 583463
North Brink, Wisbech,
Cambridgeshire PE13 1JR
Email: aprgjx@smtp.ntrust.org.uk
On B1441 in Wisbech
Open *House: Wed Sat Sun & BH Mons*
Apr–Sept 12.30–5.30, Oct 12.30–4
Garden: as house but also Apr–Oct
Mon Tues & Thurs

A town house dating from around
1722, it has fine interior decorations,
particularly the wood and plaster
Rococo decorations. There is a lovely
2-acre Victorian garden which has
been recently restored, complete
with orangery.

Saxtead Green Post Mill EH

☎ 01728 685789
Post Mill Bungalow, Saxtead Green,
Suffolk IP13 9QQ
On A1120, 2½m NW of Framlingham
Open *Apr–Sept Mon–Sat 10–1 2–6,*
Oct Mon–Sat 10–1 2–5

There has been a mill on this site for
over 700 years. It is still in working order,
though it ceased production just after
the Second World War. It is as good an
example of a post mill as you will find.

Wimpole Hall NT

☎ 01223 207257
Arrington, Royston,
Cambridgeshire SG8 OBW
Email: aweusr@smtp.ntrust.org.uk
Website: www.wimpole.org
8m SW of Cambridge on A603,
6m N from Royston
Open *Hall: mid-Mar–July & Sept–Oct*
daily except Mon & Fri (open Good Fri
& BH Mons), Aug daily except Mon
(open BH Mon), Nov Sun only 1–4
Park: dawn to dusk. Farm & garden:
mid-Mar–June, Sept–Oct daily except
Mon & Fri (open Good Fri & BH Mons),
Jul–Aug Tues–Sun (open BH Mon)
10.30–5, Nov–Mar Sat & Sun 11–4

Cambridgeshire's largest stately home
has a surrounding 'Capability' Brown
and Humphry Repton landscape, while
James Gibbs and later Sir John Soane had
a hand in creating the house. The large
gardens include parterres and a rose
garden, a grand folly and a Chinese
bridge. There are also splendid avenues
and walks that go on for miles.

Woolsthorpe Manor NT

☎ 01476 860338
23 Newton Way, Woolsthorpe-by-
Colsterworth, nr Grantham,
Lincolnshire NG33 5NR
Email: ewmxxx@smtp.ntrust.org.uk
7m S of Grantham, 1m W of A1 (not to be
confused with Woolsthorpe near Belvoir).
Leave A1 at Colsterworth roundabout via
B676, at second crossroads turn right
Open *House & Science Discovery Centre:*
Mar & Oct–Nov Sat & Sun 1–5, Apr–Sept
Wed–Sun (open BH Mons but closed Good
Fri) 1–5 (closes at 6 in July & Aug)

Isaac Newton's birthplace has an early
edition of his masterpiece on mathe-
matics, *Principia*, on display; and yes,
the orchard outside did contain *that*
apple tree.

Central MAP 4

238 Althorp

☎ House 01604 770107;
Booking line 0870 167 9000
Althorp, Northampton NN7 4HQ
Website: www.althorp.com
5m NW of Northampton on A428
Open *July–Aug daily 9–5*
Tickets for the Diana Princess of Wales Memorial must be bought in advance
The house (the family seat of the Spencers) hit the headlines with Diana's death, and she is buried in the grounds. It had been the home of her family since 1508 when it was bought by John Spencer, a sheep farmer. In 1765 one of his descendants became the 1st Earl Spencer. The 2nd Earl, Robert Spencer, added the long gallery and helped fill it with its pictures. The house (of Tudor origins) was much altered during the 18th century by Henry Holland. It is now one of England's loveliest stately homes with grounds and a collection of art to match (there are many Reynolds and Gainsboroughs), though Diana famously hated it, calling it 'Deadlock Hall'.

239 Belvoir Castle

☎ 01476 870262
Nr Grantham, Lincolnshire NG32 1PD
Email: info@belvoircastle.com
Website: www.belvoircastle.com
7m SW of Grantham off A607
Open *Mar–Sept Wed Thurs Sat Sun & BHs, Oct Sun only, all 11–5*
There can be few houses with so many different incarnations, and what exists today is largely an early 19th-century reconstruction. Once a late-Norman castle held by the Lancastrians during

Belvoir Castle, *part-Baroque, part-Gothic fantasy.*

the Wars of the Roses, it has been owned by the Rutland family since the days of Henry VIII. It was damaged in the Civil War and later by fire. 'Capability' Brown was going to work on the gardens, but the plans were never realized. Today it is a Romantic mock-Gothic mansion full of art treasures, with an Elizabethan saloon built in the east tower, designed by Sir John Thornton. The entrance hall is over-the-top Gothick, dripping with arms and armour, in perfect keeping with the house's exuberant sense of excess. There are fabulous views over the Vale of Belvoir and it is not at all surprising to learn how popular the place is with movie makers – *Little Lord Fauntleroy* was made here starring Alec Guinness.

240 Blenheim Palace*

☎ Infoline 01993 811325
Woodstock, Oxfordshire OX20 1PX
Website: www.blenheimpalace.com
8m NW of Oxford on A44

Open *Mid-Mar–Oct 10.30–5.30*
Belonging to that small club of Very Biggest Stately Homes, more like palaces than houses, this is Sir John Vanbrugh's masterpiece, though it has the finger-prints of his assistant, Nicholas Hawksmoor, all over it.

Blenheim was given by the nation to John Churchill, 1st Duke of Marlborough, to commemorate his victory over Louis XIV at Blenheim in 1704. This gives the house its triumphalist feel in terms of scale and features. There are statues of British lions mauling French roosters, golden cannon balls held aloft at the top of the theatrically ornate southern façade and, most telling of all, a bust of Louis on the southern façade like some kind of hunting trophy. Actually Louis probably had the last laugh because so much of Blenheim's style seems a direct lift from Versailles, especially the layout

of the ornamental garden, a universe away from what later became the 18th-century landscape style.

Inside, too, no expense was spared to the bitter resentment of Churchill's wife who mounted a campaign of complaints and digs at poor old Vanbrugh, moaning at the rising costs. Later, the wife of another Churchill described the place as 'the dump'. The spectacular promenade through its huge interior proceeds from the great vaulted entrance hall, with its allegorical ceiling by Sir James Thornhill depicting the Duke of Marlborough victorious in battle, through saloons decorated with floor-to-ceiling murals by Louis Laguerre, corridors and libraries. The house was designed to take your breath away first, and make you feel at home second.

Today, it is the connection with Winston Churchill that draws the crowds and the walks through the acres of landscaped park ('Capability' Brown's masterpiece), designed to create (very successfully) the illusion that you are in an oil painting. Many visitors, especially those who return time and again, are perfectly happy to stay outside, walk, picnic, and admire the house from all angles. And then there is Woodstock the town, a perfect little parade of teashops and restaurants, and the nearby village of Bladon where Sir Winston Churchill lies buried.

Though Blenheim now has all the accoutrements of the successfully exploited, large stately home, the model train, mazes and restaurant do not mean it has become a theme park.

241 Chastleton House* NT
☎ 01608 674355; Infoline 01494 755560; Bookings 01494 755585
Chastleton, nr Moreton-in-Marsh, Oxfordshire GL56 0SU
Email: tchgen@smtp.ntrust.org.uk

3m SE of Moreton-in-Marsh off A44
Open *Apr–Oct Wed–Sat 1–5; closes at 4 in Oct. Admission by advance booking only*
An exquisite 17th-century house, it was built and lived in by Walter Jones, a Royalist sympathizer during the Civil War who made his money from wool. What makes this house so special is that it has hardly been touched since then. It is obvious from a house inventory dating back to 1633 that much of the original furniture is still here. There is an authenticity about it that more polished houses lack. Especially beautiful is the long gallery on the top floor, with its barrel roof and creaking floorboards. There are fine ceilings, panelling, glass and tapestries. It is a house full of atmosphere, as intriguing for the myriad of small and overlooked things as for any overwhelming desire to impress. The garden contains the lawn on which the rules of croquet were developed, and has a charming mix of topiary and trees.

242 Chatsworth House

☎ 01246 565300
Bakewell, Derbyshire DE45 1PP
Email: visit@chatsworth-house.co.uk
Website: www.chatsworth-house.co.uk
8m N of Matlock off B6012, 16m from M1 junction 29
Open *House: mid-Mar–Oct 11–5.30 (last entry to Scots Rooms in house 4.30). Garden: 11–6 (June–Aug opens 10.30)*
One of the most familiar of all the great stately homes, if only because the owners have made many (many) television appearances. Their family, the Dukes of Devonshire, have lived here since the late 17th century.

This Classical mansion was built between 1687 and 1707 by William Talman for William Cavendish, the first Duke, with subsequent additions by later Devonshires. The gardens also retain features from distinct historical periods, and for one a nearby village was removed because it spoiled the view. The first and most formal part dates to 1688 and was the work of George London, who laid out the canals, fountains and orangery. The cascade, unmatched anywhere in Britain, was added in the 18th century by Thomas Archer, and 'Capability' Brown landscaped much of the surrounding parkland. In the 19th century Joseph Paxton added the sensational glasshouses and the great fountain, as well as many plants and conifers.

Inside, the house matches its scale with an abundance of artwork including the fabulous painted ceilings by Verrio, Thornhill (William Hogarth's uncle) and Laguerre, and the Painted Hall also by Laguerre. There are paintings by Rembrandt, Hals, Van Dyck, Tintoretto, Veronese, Landseer and Sargent. And there are contemporary works by artists like Lucien Freud and Elizabeth Frink which helps save the whole thing from becoming rather mummified, as happens in some over-preserved stately homes.

Chatsworth owes much of its enormous popularity to its setting, a blissful marriage of formal gardens and the great sweep of rolling countryside. There is a commercial side too (never oppressive), and the house makes a spectacular pair with nearby Hardwick Hall (p128), a 40-minute drive away on the other side of Chesterfield.

243 Church of St John the Baptist, Burford*

☎ 01993 822275
Burford Rd, Burford, Oxfordshire OX18 4SD
18m N of Swindon, 18m W of Oxford, off A40 between Witney & Northleach
Open *9.30–5*

A beautiful church in a beautiful Cotswold town, and well worth a visit. It is also the site of one of the most dramatic episodes in British history. Oliver Cromwell executed three of his soldiers in the churchyard as an example to the rest. Their crime? To mutiny against him, as part of a sect called the Levellers. The Roundhead army was the radical party during the Civil War, and the Levellers were the most radical part of the army, too radical even for Cromwell. He was appalled by their desire for sweeping social reform, and for giving the vote to all property-owning men (but not women, and definitely not servants). The name of one of the men kept prisoner there (though not finally shot) is still visible, scratched into the font: 'Antony Sedley 1649 Prisner'. Cromwell then spent the day receiving an honorary degree from Oxford University. He let off the other 300 or so soldiers with a reprimand, before sending them to Ireland to fight a pro-Royalist army.

244 Convocation House, Oxford*

☎ 01865 277216 for information
on Bodleian Library tour
Radcliffe Square, Oxford OX1 3BG
On Broad St in centre of town

Open *Viewed only as part of Bodleian Library tour. Weekdays 10.30 11.30 2 & 3, Sat 10.30 & 11.30. Nov–mid-Mar no weekday mornings; closed for degree ceremonies. Over 14s only.*
Part of the Bodleian Library, and today used by the University of Oxford for various ceremonies, this interior is close to what the interior of the 17th-century parliament would have looked like (apart from the later Gothic Revival ceiling). The makers of the film *The Madness Of King George III* had the brainwave of using this as a stand-in for the House of Commons.

245 Edgehill*

Edgehill, nr Banbury, Warwickshire
Near Kineton, off B4086 between Stratford-upon-Avon & Banbury
Site of the first great battle in the Civil War (23 October 1642). The spot where Charles first raised his standard on the ridge above the battlefield is now marked by an 18th-century folly, an octagonal stone tower which has been turned into a pub and hotel (The Castle Inn Hotel).

There are fabulous views of the ridge at various points along the road, with great swathes of English countryside laid out below. You can follow the course of the battle from contemporary accounts.

*Looking up to the ridge from the site of the battlefield at **Edgehill**.*

246 Kedleston Hall* NT

☎ 01332 842191
Kedleston, Derby, Derbyshire DE22 5JH
Email: ekdxxx@smtp.ntrust.org.uk
*5m NW of Derby, entrance off
Kedleston Road & signposted from
roundabout where A38 crosses A52*
Open *House: Apr–Oct Sat–Wed 12–4.30
Garden: as house, 10–6. Park: Apr–Oct
daily 10–6, Nov–Dec 10–4, Jan–Mar
Sat & Sun 10–4*
The mansion, built in 1759–65 for Sir
Nathaniel Curzon, stands on the site of a
Queen Anne house. Three architects
worked on it, the most famous being
Robert Adam, who was responsible for
much of the interior and the central
block of the main façade. The 800 acres
of surrounding parkland are a classic
example of English landscape gardening,
full of Adam's touches, surviving in pretty
much their original form. The building
formed the model for the great Governor's
Palace in Calcutta, built by Lord Wellesley
in 1799–1805, and has the same preten-
sions: it proclaims lavish supplies of
money and reflects the power and glory
of 18th-century Britain.

247 Moseley Old Hall* NT

☎ 01902 782808
Moseley Old Hall Lane, Fordhouses,
Wolverhampton, Staffordshire WV10 7HY
Email: mmodxl@smtp.ntrust.org.uk
*4m N of Wolverhampton, S of M54
between A449 & A460*
Open *Late Mar–Oct Wed Sat & Sun
& BH Mons & following Tues,
mid-Nov–mid-Dec Sun (guided tours only),
Mar–Oct 1.30–5.30, garden & tea-room
from 1 (BH Mons 11–5), Nov–Dec 1.30–4*
A fine medium-sized Elizabethan/
Jacobean house, beautifully restored
by the National Trust. It is particularly
associated with Charles II who slept here
after his defeat at the hands of Oliver
Cromwell at the Battle of Worcester in
1651 (his dramatic escape is the subject
of an exhibition). Charles's bed and
hiding place are on display, in addition
to a chapel, bedrooms, and a lovely
dining room and hall.

The building gives an evocative
sense of 17th-century living space;
its scale is much more familiar to us
than the bigger mansions of this and
later periods which, for all their impres-
siveness, can be a bit alienating. The
grounds contain one of the best-kept
examples of a knot garden, with topiary,
and using only 17th-century plants.

248 Radcliffe Camera

Radcliffe Square, Oxford OX1 3BG
Near All Souls College in centre of city
Open *Exterior only*
Part of the Bodleian Library and
therefore not open to the public
(although there are organized tours
round other bits of the building), this is
arguably Oxford's most stunning architectural feature; it deserves to be seen
from the tower of the adjacent University church. Designed by James Gibbs
(probably his masterpiece) it takes pride
of place in the spiritual heart of Oxford
University, in an open piazza bordered
on all four sides by other university
buildings. It is full of Italian touches
with the dome echoing St Peter's in
Rome, and the curved buttresses echoing
Santa Maria della Salute in Venice. It is
one of those buildings that it is impossible to take your eyes off.

249 Ragley Hall

☎ 01789 762090
Alcester, Warwickshire B49 5NJ
2m SW of Alcester off A435/A46
Open *House: Apr–Oct Thurs & Fri Sun
12.30–5 Sat 11–3.30
Park: as house, Thurs–Sun 10–6*

Designed by the scientist and mathe-matician Robert Hooke in 1680, there were later additions – plasterwork by James Gibbs in 1750 and a giant portico by James Wyatt in 1780. The Red Saloon is papered in silk and the ceilings were painted by Angelica Kauffmann. The hall is magnificent with a 40ft(13m)-high ceiling and beautiful plasterwork; it is quite simply one of the great rooms of Europe. Its glowing pink walls were designed to accommodate the most lavish of aristocratic pleasures – balls, concerts and games – and endless dis-cussions. All its furniture was specially designed for this space.

Ragley supported a particularly luxurious lifestyle for its inhabitants. The surviving kitchen accounts paint an incredible picture of the quantities and varieties of food wolfed down. There was an ice-house to keep up a flow of ice cream to which the well-heeled were becoming addicted. And then there are surrounding acres of 'Capability' Brown parkland. One of the earliest houses in the country to adopt the Palladian style, it still radiates an air of casual opulence.

250 Rousham House
☎ 01869 347110
Nr Steeple Aston, Bicester, Oxfordshire OX6 3QX
12m N of Oxford, E of A4260; 7m W of Bicester, S of B4030
Open *House: Apr–Sept Wed Sun & BH Mons 2–4.30*
Gardens: daily all year 10–4.30
The house was home to a Royalist garrison during the Civil War, but today is more famous for its landscaped gardens laid out by William Kent, the only example of his work which survives almost unchanged. The gardens are smaller than at Stourhead and Stowe, but they have their own unique charm.

There is the delight of continual visual stimulation created by the combination of natural features and small monu-ments and buildings. Rousham is a gentle garden rather than a self-conscious, bombastic 'Great Garden'.

251 Sheldonian Theatre, Oxford*
☎ 01865 277299
Broad Street, Oxford OX1 3AZ
In the centre of Oxford
Open *Mon–Sat 10–12.30 2–4.30, mid-Nov–Feb closes at 3.30, closed at Xmas & Easter, & for degree ceremonies that take place all through the year*
Wren's first building (1664–9), fabulously ornate, is where the university performs its graduation and other ceremonies. The shiny white cupola dates from the Victorian era. The surrounding stone pillars bearing the heads of Roman emperors had to be replaced in the 1970s because the originals fell victim to air pollution and erosion.

252 Stowe House and Gardens* NT
☎ House 01280 818282; Gardens 01280 822850; Infoline 01494 755568
Nr Buckingham, Buckinghamshire MK18 5EH
Email: enquiries@stowe.co.uk
3m NW of Buckingham via Stowe Avenue, off A422 Buckingham–Banbury road
Open *House: late Mar–mid-Apr & early July–Aug Wed–Sun 12–5, also a few days late Oct, early Nov & late Dec 11–3 Gardens: Mar–Oct Wed–Sun & BH Mons 10–5.30, Nov & Dec Wed–Sun 10–4*
The gardens are the product of just about every gardening genius of the 18th century, with temples and follies designed by the likes of Vanbrugh, Gibbs, Kent and Leoni. They cover over 300 acres, and contain six lakes and over 30 temples and follies making Stowe the pre-eminent British example of the

'natural' landscape garden, built for philosophical contemplation. One of the key features was the 'Elysian Fields' laid out during the 1730s by William Kent, setting the style that dominated 18th-century landscaping. 'Capability' Brown was a head gardener here for ten years, and he was married in the little church hidden behind a screen of trees.

There is no better place in Britain to get an idea of what the enlightened 18th-century aristocrat thought a house and garden should achieve. It is not just the beauty of the way the landscape and architecture have blended (virtually every spot is designed to produce a vista) but the wit with which it has been done. Even if you do not immediately pick up the allusions to classical literature and contemporary politics you get the sense that this is an intelligent garden, not just a luxurious one.

The Temple of British Worthies is deliberately built at the foot of a slight slope, crowned by a Temple to Ancient Virtue, an early example of British self-deprecation! The busts of the Worthies are split between the 'thinkers' and 'doers' (how British is that?), and line up in a gallery of small alcoves reflected in the water of a small lake. There are also columns devoted to Captain Cook, trade, and exploration. And look for the small shell-laden grotto, the Palladian Bridge and Folly Lodge (now run by the Landmark Trust). Much of the grounds have now been turned into a small golf course, the 20th-century answer to the philosophical garden.

The house has a great domed hallway (said to have provided the model for the Washington Capitol building), rounded by a magnificent sequence of bas relief classical figures. Just to walk across its echoing floor is to feel a mixture of Virgil and Alexander Pope coursing up through the soles of your feet. The house is now a public school.

The Temple of British Worthies by William Kent in **Stowe Gardens**.

ADDITIONAL PLACES TO VISIT

Attingham Park NT

☎ 01743 708162; Infoline 01743 708123
Shrewsbury, Shropshire SY4 4TP
Email: matsec@smtp.ntrust.org.uk
4m SE of Shrewsbury,
on N side of B4380 in Atcham village
Open *House: Apr–Oct daily except Wed*
& Thurs 1–4.30, BH Mons 11–5.
Deer park & grounds: daily Mar–Oct 9–8,
Nov–Feb 9–5
The mansion was built in the classical
style in 1783–5, and the grounds were
later landscaped by Humphry Repton.
The front of the house has a columnar
portico and symmetrical wings containing an earlier building dating from about
1700. There is also a picture gallery
designed by John Nash, state rooms, and
Regency interiors with masses of books
and Italian furniture collected by the sons
of the first owner while on a Grand Tour.

Aynho Park

☎ 01869 810636
Aynho, Banbury, Oxfordshire OX17 3BQ
M40 junction 10, then 3m NW on B4100
Open *May–Sept Mon–Sat Wed & Thurs*
2–5; groups by arrangement all year
The 17th-century country mansion was
built on the remains of a Norman castle
and was remodelled by Sir John Soane in
the 18th century. The house contains
collections of paintings and glass.

Belton House NT

☎ 01476 566116
Grantham, Lincolnshire NG32 2LS
Email: ebehah@smtp.ntrust.org.uk
3m NE of Grantham on A607
Open *House: Apr–Oct Wed–Sun & BHs*
12.30–5.30. Garden: as house 11.30–5.30
(opens 10.30 in Aug)
Built in the style of Christopher Wren by
an unknown architect, possibly William

Winde, from 1685–8, Belton is now
acknowledged as one the best examples
of its kind. The house is H-shaped with
a hipped roof, dormer windows and an
elegant cupola. James Wyatt altered the
house in about 1776, and his nephew
added the orangery in 1811. The house
has a good collection of paintings, fine
furniture, tapestries and European
Old Masters. There is also an exhibition
devoted to the Duke of Windsor, including
the only known portrait of him while
he was Edward VIII.

Berrington Hall NT

☎ 01568 615721
Nr Leominster, Herefordshire HR6 0DW
Email: berrington@smtp.ntrust.org.uk
Website: www.ntrustsevern.org.uk/
berrington.htm
3m N of Leominster,
7m S of Ludlow on W side of A49
Open *House: Apr–Sept Sat–Wed*
& BHs 1–5, Oct Sat–Wed 1–4.30
Garden: as house, 12–5; closes 4.30 in Oct.
Park walk: as house, July–Oct
Built on a site recommended by
'Capability' Brown (he then went on
to design the grounds), it has a rather
brutally plain external façade designed
by Henry Holland, Brown's son-in-law.
The interiors are much more grandiose.

Bolsover Castle EH

☎ 01246 822844
Castle St, Bolsover, Derbyshire S44 6PR
6m E of Chesterfield on A632; leave M1
junction 29 or 30
Open *Apr–Sept 10–6, Oct 10–5,*
Nov–Mar Wed–Sun 10–4
When Sir Charles Cavendish built
his 'Little Castle' here in 1613–46 to
resemble a late medieval tower house,
he probably had no idea it would ever
actually see the sort of warfare that had
destroyed the original castle on the site.

But in 1644 the Parliamentarian forces severely damaged it. They did not destroy its powerful atmosphere though, reinforced by its craggy setting and intricate carvings. The site commands fabulous views over the surrounding area, and is clearly visible from the nearby M1, especially at night when floodlit.

Boscobel House EH

☎ 01902 850244
Nr Bishop's Wood, Brewood,
Staffordshire ST19 9AR
On minor road between A41 & A5,
8m NW of Wolverhampton.
3m NE of M54 junction 3
Open *Apr–Sept 10–6, Oct 10–5,*
Nov Wed–Sun 10–4, early/mid-Dec
Sat & Sun 10–4; closed Jan–Mar.
Admission by guided tour only
A beautiful, early 17th-century hunting lodge built by a Catholic already conscious that the mood of the nation was turning against his faith. The biggest attraction, however, is the oak that grows on the spot once occupied by the tree that Charles II is supposed to have hidden in while the Roundheads scoured the grounds searching for him, after they had beaten his Scottish army at Worcester. Various parts of the house and the farmyard have now been restored, and there is an exhibition.

Boughton House

☎ 01536 515731
Kettering, Northamptonshire NN14 1BJ
Email: llt@boughtonhouse.org.uk
Website: www.boughtonhouse.org.uk
3m N of Kettering off A43;
signposted through Geddington
Open *House: Aug daily 2–4.30. Grounds:*
May–July daily except Fri, Aug daily 1–5
Accreted round a Tudor manor house is this attempt at an English Versailles mounted by the Duke of Montagu in

the dying years of the 17th century. The French theme is reflected in much of the furniture and art collected inside.

Calke Abbey* NT

☎ 01332 863822
Ticknall, Derbyshire DE73 1LE
10m S of Derby, on A514 at Ticknall
between Swadlincote & Melbourne
Open *House, garden & church:*
Apr–Oct Sat–Wed. House & church: 1–5.30
(ticket office opens 11). Garden: 11–5.30.
Park: daily all year until 9 (dusk if earlier)
Like Chastleton in Oxfordshire, this is a wonderful example of a house that has barely been touched since its 18th-century heyday. It is filled to bursting with cases stuffed with miscellaneous artefacts and curiosities. There is also surrounding parkland, with gardens, orangery and chapel.

Chillington Hall

☎ 01902 0850236
Codsall Wood, Wolverhampton,
Staffordshire WV8 1RE
Email: info@chillingtonhall.co.uk
Website: www.chillingtonhall.co.uk
2m S of Brewood off A449;
4m NW of M54 junction 2
Open *July Thurs 2–5, Aug Thurs Fri &*
Sun 2–5; groups by arrangement all year
Another stopping place for the fugitive Charles II, since rebuilt as a Georgian hall. 'Capability' Brown laid out the surrounding parkland including the largest lake he ever attempted.

Cottesbrooke Hall and Gardens

☎ 01604 505808
Cottesbrooke,
Northamptonshire NN6 8PF
Email: hall@cottesbrooke.co.uk
Website: www.cottesbrookehall.co.uk
10m N of Northampton near Creaton
on A5199, off A508

Open *Easter–Sept House: Thurs 2–5.30 Gardens: Tues Thurs & Fri 2–5.30*
A perfect, medium-sized gem of a Queen Anne-style house, which apparently gave Jane Austen her model for *Mansfield Park*. There is a large collection of sporting art, an enthusiasm of the current owner, and surrounding formal areas of garden with topiary and statues, and beautiful open countryside beyond. Slightly off the beaten track, but all the more attractive because of it.

Deene Park
☎ 01780 450278
Corby, Northamptonshire NN17 3EW
4m NE of Corby off A43
Open *June–Aug Sun 2–5, also spring & summer BH Sun & Mon; winter by arrangement only*
Painstakingly restored since 1945, this house retains major elements from its Elizabethan and Georgian incarnations. The same attention has been paid to the gardens. The house was once the home of the 7th Earl of Cardigan, who led the Charge of the Light Brigade during the Crimean War.

Eyam Hall
☎ 01433 631976
Eyam, Hope Valley, Derbyshire S32 5QW
Email: nicwri@globalnet.co.uk
Website: www.eyamhall.co.uk
Approx 10m from Sheffield, Chesterfield & Buxton, off A623
Open *Apr–May Sun 11–4, June–Aug Tues Thurs Sun & BH Mons 11–4*
Built on a more intimate scale than many stately homes it has fascinating kitchens, staircases, wall hangings, furniture, china and glass. It is in Eyam village, the site of one of the most moving Black Death stories – the village locked itself in when plague struck to try to prevent the plague spreading.

Frampton Court
☎ 01452 740267
Frampton-on-Severn, Gloucestershire GL2 7EU
Email: clifford.fce@farming.co.uk
At Frampton, ¼m SW of B4071, 3m NW of M5 junction 13
Open *By arrangement*
Frampton is the perfect showcase of the Vanbrugh style, so popular in the early 18th century. An ornamental canal leads to a Gothick orangery in the style of Strawberry Hill (p176).

Hanbury Hall NT
☎ 01527 821214
School Road, Droitwich, Worcestershire WR9 7EA
Email: hanbury@smtp.ntrust.org.uk
Website: www.ntrustsevern.org.uk/hanbury.htm
4½m E of Droitwich, 4m SE of M5 junction 5
Open *House: Apr–Oct Sun–Wed & Good Fri 1.30–5.30. Garden: as house, 12–5*
The William and Mary-style redbrick house has ceilings and staircases painted by Sir James Thornhill (who painted the ceilings in the Royal Naval College in Greenwich) and a fine collection of porcelain. The gardens have an orangery, ice-house and Moorish gazebos. The house is surrounded by gardens and parkland totalling 400 acres.

Lamport Hall
☎ 01604 686272
Lamport, nr Northampton, Northamptonshire NN6 9HD
Email: admin@lamporthall.co.uk
8m N of Northampton off A508; 3m S of A14 (A1/M1 link)
Open *Easter–Sept Sun & BH Mons 2.15–5.15*
The Hall developed in two major bursts; the central block was completed by John

Webb around the 1650s, and the wings were added later by Francis Smith. Inside there is plasterwork, oil paintings, an 18th-century library and a Victorian refreshments room. The gardens date to the mid-17th century.

Lydiard House
☎ 01793 770401
Lydiard Tregoze, Swindon,
Wiltshire SN5 9PA
4m W of Swindon, 1m N of M4 junction 16
Open *Mon–Fri 10–1 2–5, Sat & school summer hols 10–5 & Sun 2–5;
Nov–Feb closes at 4*
The beautiful *c*1740 Palladian façade conceals an earlier medieval house. There are also the remains of three great avenues of trees which give a hint of the kind of 18th-century parkland that predated the present one. The house remains a jewel with an exceptional complement of paintings, furniture and family accoutrements. The nearby church has a number of monuments relating to the St John family who lived here.

Pitstone Windmill NT
☎ 01494 528051 (Regional Office)
Ivinghoe, Buckinghamshire
Website: www.nationaltrust.org.uk/
regions/thameschilterns
S of Ivinghoe, by B488 to Tring
Open *June–Aug Sun & BHs 2.30–6*
One of the earliest surviving post mills (a mill built around a central post which can be turned enabling the sails to catch the wind). It dates back to 1627 and was restored by a team of volunteers.

Shugborough NT
☎ 01889 881388
Milford, nr Stafford,
Staffordshire ST17 0XB
Signposted from M6 junction 13, 6m E of Stafford on A513; entrance at Milford

Pitstone Windmill, *one of the earliest surviving post mills in Britain.*

Open *House & County Museum, Farm & Gardens: Apr–Sept Tues–Sun (open BH Mons) 11–5, Oct Sun 11–5, Oct–Mar Mon–Fri 10.30–4*
Once owned by the Earl of Lichfield, the house passed into the hands of the National Trust in 1960. Its façade has a disarming simplicity. The kitchens and the Georgian Park Farm have been carefully restored for visitors to enjoy.

The grounds are full of replica classical monuments, including the Lanthorn of Demosthenes, Tower of the Winds, Triumphal Arch and a 20ft(6m)-high monument to a pet cat, many by James 'Athenian' Stuart, commissioned by the designer of the garden Thomas Anson. Anson belonged to the 18th-century society, the Dilettanti, devoted to the study and love of all things classical and Italian. The Staffordshire County Museum is based here.

Stanford Hall

☎ 01788 860250
Lutterworth, nr Rugby,
Leicestershire LE17 6DH
Email: enquiries@stanfordhall.co.uk
Website: www.stanfordhall.co.uk
2m from M1 junction 19 (from/to north),
2m from M6 exit/access at A14/M1(N)
Open *Easter–Sept Sat Sun & BHs 1.30–5.30*
An outstanding mansion in the William
and Mary style, it was commissioned in
the 1690s by Sir Roger Cave on the site
of an old Tudor manor hall, and built
by the Smiths of Warwick between 1697
and 1703. There is a well-stocked library
including old manuscripts, a big collection
of paintings, among them a number
of portraits of the Stuart royal family,
and Elizabethan furniture and fittings.
There is a walled rose garden and lake
in the grounds.

Upton House NT

☎ 01295 870266, Infoline 01684 855365
Banbury, Warwickshire OX15 6HT
Email: upton_house@smtp.ntrust.org.uk
Website: www.ntrustsevern.org.uk/
upton.htm
7m NW of Banbury on A422
Open *House: Apr–Oct Sat–Wed &*
Good Fri 1–5. Garden: as house
(opens at 11 on Sat Sun & BHs & 12.30
Mon–Wed), Nov–Dec Sat & Sun 12–4
This William and Mary country mansion
was built in 1695. It is packed with art
including Brussels' tapestries, Sèvres
porcelain, Chelsea figures, 18th-century
furniture and nearly 200 paintings by
European Old Masters. The grounds
contain fine old terraced gardens.

Winslow Hall

☎ 01296 7123239
Winslow, Buckinghamshire MK18 3HL
In Winslow on N side of A413
Open *By appointment only*

The house is most famous for being one
of the few remaining examples of Christopher Wren's architecture outside London
that has been spared later alteration.

Wales MAP 5

253 Carew Castle

☎ 01646 651782
Nr Tenby, Pembrokeshire SA70 8SL
3m E of Pembroke off A477
Open *Apr–Oct 10–5*
Another Cromwell punchbag, this fine
old Norman castle became a ruin in 1644,
partly thanks to alterations made in the
15th and 16th centuries when, naively, the
owners stripped out some defences to
make it more comfortable. More fool them.
There is also a good example of a tidal
mill which eliminated the daily chore of
grinding grain into flour. As the tide enters
the basin, the lock gates open, closing
again at high tide; the entrapped salt water
is allowed to return to the sea through the
mill-race, which supplies several horse-
power. Invented by the later Romans, tidal
mills were common before the invention
of windmills in the 12th century.

254 Tredegar House

☎ 01633 815880
Newport, Monmouthshire NP1 9YW
Email: tredegar.house@newport.gov.uk
2m SW of Newport town centre;
M4 junction 28 then signposted
Open *House: Easter–Sept Wed–Sun & BHs*
11.30–4; rest of year groups by appoint-
ment only. Park: daily all year 9–dusk
A house that is not as famous as it
deserves to be; a classic of late-17th-
century redbrick construction, slightly
reminiscent of Ham House (p163) in
London (they have similar dark great
staircases). There is no particular
architect associated with it. It was a
school from the 1950s but was recently

taken over by Newport County Council and restored to something like its former eminence. It is surrounded by 90 acres of parkland, complete with formal gardens.

ADDITIONAL PLACES TO VISIT

Erddig NT

☎ 01978 355314; Infoline 01978 315151
Erddig, Wrexham LL13 0YT
Email: erddig@smtp.ntrust.org.uk
*2m S of Wrexham, signposted A525
Whitchurch, or A483/A5152 Oswestry*
Open *House: Apr–Oct Sat–Wed
& Good Fri 12–5 (closes at 4 in Oct)
Garden: Apr–June & Sept 11–6,
July–Aug 10–6, Oct 11–5*
This 17th–18th-century house has a range of fascinating exhibitions concentrating equally on life 'below stairs' and above in the great saloons and drawing rooms. The gardens combine the best of the 18th and 19th centuries.

North-west MAP 6

255 Astley Hall

☎ 01257 515555
Astley Park, Chorley,
Lancashire PR7 1NP
Email: astleyhall@lineone.net
Website: www.astleyhall.co.uk
*2m W of Chorley off A581;
5 mins from M61 junction 8*
Open *Easter–Oct Tues–Sun & BH Mons
12–5, Nov–Easter Fri–Sun 12–4*
Large mansion whose earliest parts date from the late 16th century. Oliver Cromwell is said to have stayed here after beating the Scots at Preston in 1648 (ending the Second Civil War).

The long gallery contains a shovel-board table over 20ft (6m) long (for a game a bit like shove ha'penny). The interior has fine furniture and features, and interesting collections of art, glassware and textiles.

Carew Castle *overlooking an inlet in the Milford Haven estuary.*

256 Lyme Park NT

☎ 01663 762023;
Infoline 01663 766492
Lyme Park, Disley, Stockport,
Cheshire SK12 2NX
Email: mlyrec@smtp.ntrust.org.uk
6m SE of Stockport off A6
Open *House: Apr–Oct Fri–Tues 1–5*
Garden: daily 11–5 (Wed & Thurs 1–5)
Many of us know Lyme as 'Pemberley'
from the BBC's adaptation of Jane
Austen's *Pride and Prejudice*. In reality it
is an Elizabethan house transformed
into a Georgian mansion. The interior
details span four centuries and the
surrounding gardens are ravishing.

ADDITIONAL PLACES TO VISIT

Levens Hall

☎ 01539 560321
Kendal, Cumbria LA8 0PD
Email: email@levenshall.fsnet.co.uk
Website: www.levenshall.co.uk
5m S of Kendal on A6,
leave M6 junction 36
Open *House: Easter Sun & Mon*
Apr–mid-Oct Sun–Thurs 12–5
Gardens: as house, 10–5
Beautifully and rather coyly concealed
behind its bizarre, eccentric topiary,
this is a particularly attractive Elizabethan
mansion. The topiary belongs to the late
17th century and and remains largely
unchanged to this day.

Tatton Park NT

☎ 01625 534400;
Infoline 01625 534435
Tatton Park, Knutsford,
Cheshire WA16 6QN
Email: tatton@cheshire.gov.uk
Website: www.tatton.park.org.uk
3m N of Knutsford, 5m from M6
junction 19; 3m from M56 junction 7,
well signposted on A556

Open *Mansion & Tudor Old Hall:*
Mar–Sept Tues–Sun & BH Mons 1–4,
Oct Sat & Sun 1–4. Gardens: (days as house)
Mar–Sept 10.30–6, Oct–Mar 11.30–4
The National Trust is rightly proud of its
work making this more than just a house
and a garden. The building is Neoclassical,
designed by James Wyatt, with Victorian
kitchens for the 'below stairs' experience.
There is also the Tudor Old Hall and an
extensive array of gardens with deer park.

North-east MAP 7

257 Castle Howard

☎ 01653 648444
Nr Malton, N Yorkshire YO60 7DA
Email: mec@castlehoward.co.uk
Website: www.castlehoward.co.uk
15m NE of York; A64 to Malton, then
Castle Howard road via Coneysthorpe
Open *House: Mar–Oct 11–5.30*
Grounds: all year 10–dusk
Another of Sir John Vanbrugh's masterpieces, it is probably the most spectacular
house in Yorkshire or even the North
of England. It is also an exercise in scale
for the sake of scale – it is absolutely vast.
The front drive is 5 miles long and is
heavily punctuated by architectural
treats including monuments, gates
with pyramids, and an obelisk.

Amazingly, this was Vanbrugh's first
ever house. He came to architecture
having been a playwright, and there
remains something endearingly theatrical
about his creations – not just in their
excess, and their desire to overwhelm
the eye and create a space full of action,
but because both Castle Howard and
Blenheim actually look like backdrops.
Their interiors work like framed stages,
with wings to make an entrance and exit.
But there is nothing fake about the
achievement. Vanbrugh was canny
enough to know that his architectural

Castle Howard, *the first house built by Sir John Vanbrugh.*

aspirations needed all the help they could get, and he got sound advice from Nicholas Hawksmoor.

There is refreshing lack of inhibition about Vanbrugh in general, and Castle Howard in particular. He didn't let his lack of experience stop him giving his new creation a central dome – something no other private house had ever had. It also has a marble hall, one of the first of its kind in Britain, that works like an epic preface; the walls are covered by tapestries and oil paintings (not least the fabulous picture of Henry VIII by Holbein); and the sheer audacity of the scale is utterly overwhelming. The central block, crowned by the great dome, is straddled by two wings and inside is a long gallery and chapel. There is an adjacent building which

houses an exhibition of hundreds of historical costumes.

The gardens are no mere after-thought, being created as the house was built and decorated. With their brace of lakes, they include other great features from Vanbrugh's imagination including the Temple of the Four Winds, the New River Bridge, water features and cascades, as well as the Mausoleum by Hawksmoor.

258 Harewood House
☎ 0113 218 1010
Harewood, Leeds, W Yorkshire LS17 9LQ
Email: info@harewood.org
Website: www.harewood.org
On A61 between Harrogate & Leeds
Open *House & bird garden: early Mar–Oct 11–5. Grounds: 10–dusk*

Another of the Great British 'Piles' offering a microcosm of 18th-century grandeur. There is lavish scale, 'Capability' Brown gardens, Robert Adam's Neoclassical interiors, great art, Chippendale furniture and surrounding parkland studded with rhododendrons. Adam was called in to lend some of his magic to the house, whose exterior (designed by John Carr of York in 1759) was robust but a little plain; in the words of Adam's brother, 'he tickled it up so as to dazzle the eyes of the squire'. Robert Adam's success was toasted in 1939 when a great marble statue of the archictect by Jacob Epstein was unveiled in the hall. There are panels painted by the 18th-century artist, Angelica Kauffmann, and some fabulous examples of Baroque *trompe l'oeil* draperies of the state bed that are actually carved out of wood (probably by Chippendale's workshop). There is also a famous bird garden. There are reminders that the Harewood family are cousins to the Queen (HRH Princess Mary, daughter of George V, lived here for many years).

259 Oakwell Hall Country Park*
☎ 01924 326240
Nutter Lane, Birstall, Batley,
W Yorkshire WF17 9LG
On A652 in Birstall; take A62 junction 27 towards Huddersfield
Open *All year Mon–Fri 11–5, Sat & Sun 12–5*
An Elizabethan manor house displayed as 17th-century merchant's home, it is now fully kitted out for education and recreation. Oakwell Hall is a particularly user-friendly historical house. It allows you to get a little closer to the nitty gritty of past experience than is usually the case with more gilded stately homes.

Built in 1583 by John Batt, a local landowner, this is a wonderful example of a late Tudor/Jacobean house with a large entrance hall, kitchen, bedroom, and surrounding grounds. Its middling size means it is big enough to give you an impressive sense of life here (the smooth and rough and ready), especially in the mid-to-late 17th century. The kitchen really looks like people cooked and baked in it, the bedrooms like places where people slept, yawned and scratched.

ADDITIONAL PLACES TO VISIT

Beningbrough Hall NT
☎ 01904 470666
Beningbrough, N Yorkshire YO30 1DD
Email: ybbrgb@smtp.ntrust.org.uk
8m NW of York, 2m W of Shipton,
Open *House: Apr–June & Sept–Oct Sat–Wed & Good Fri, July–Aug daily except Thurs, all 12–5.*
Grounds: as house, 11–5.30
This large redbrick house was built around 1716 and has a very impressive Baroque interior. It is now used by the National Portrait Gallery as home for over 100 of its finest 18th-century portraits, which share the building with some of the best wood carving found anywhere in the North of England.

Bramham Park
☎ 01937 846002
Bramham, Wetherby,
W Yorkshire LS23 6ND
Email: lucy.finucne@bramhampark.co.uk
5m S of Wetherby, 10m NE of Leeds, & 15m SW of York
Open *House: groups by appointment only 1.15–5.30. Garden: Apr–Sept 10.30–5.30*
The house was built in 1698 by Lord Bingley, Chancellor of the Exchequer to Queen Anne. It is thought that he was the one who laid out its fabulous 66-acre garden with water features, follies and ornaments in the style of André Le Nôtre's design at Versailles.

East Riddlesden Hall NT

☎ 01535 607075
Bradford Rd, Keighley,
W Yorkshire BD20 5EL
Email: yorker@smtp.ntrust.org.uk
*1m NE of Keighley on S side of
Bradford Road in Riddlesden*
Open *Apr–Oct Tues Wed Sat & Sun (also
Good Fri, BH Mons & Mon in July & Aug)
12–5 (opens at 1 on Sat)*
Built in 1640 by the Murgatroyd family
who were clothiers and such famously
depraved ne'er-do-wells that local
legend says 'the River Aire changed
course in protest at their doings'.

Look for the magnificent kitchen
with a fine collection of pewter. Other
features include mullioned windows,
plasterwork, panelling, a collection of
textiles, and a delightful garden and duck
pond. The site also has one of the finest
oak-timbered tithe barns in the North
of England.

Fairfax House

☎ 01904 655543
Castlegate, York, N Yorkshire YO1 9RN
Website: www.fairfaxhouse.co.uk
*In central York between
Castle Museum & Jorvik Centre*
Open *Mon–Thurs 11–5, Fri guided tours
only at 11 & 2, Sat 11–5 Sun 1.30–5;
closed early Jan–mid-Feb*
A fabulous example of Georgian town
architecture. It has one of the finest
displays of Georgian furniture and
accoutrements anywhere in the country.

Raby Castle

☎ 01833 660202/660207
Staindrop, Darlington,
Co Durham DL2 3AH
Email: admin@rabycastle.com
Website: www.rabycastle.com
*1m N of Staindrop, 6m NE of Barnard
Castle & 19m SW of Durham*
Open *May & Sept Wed & Sun, June–Aug
daily except Sat, BHs Sat to following
Wed. Castle: 1–5. Park & gardens: 11–5.30*
A dramatically imposing pile of a castle,
built as a fortified house, it played a key
role in both the Wars of the Roses and
the Civil War. It was converted for gentler
living in the 18th century, but still has a
brooding presence. Some great medieval
rooms rub shoulders with later ones
from the 18th and 19th centuries.

Seaton Delaval Hall

☎ 0191 237 1493/0786
Seaton Sluice, nr Whitley Bay,
Northumberland NE26 4QR
3m N of Whitley Bay on A190
Open *June–Sept Wed–Sun 2–6 & Aug BH*
It is not Vanbrugh's biggest work but
it is widely seen as his finest, although it
had to be completed after the architect's
(and first owner's) death. Begun in 1718,
it was built for Admiral George Delaval, a
member of a powerful Border family. The
great central block, flanked by two wings,
was destroyed by fire in 1822, but has
been partially restored, most recently in
the 1960s. The furniture and the garden
features, including the orangery and
obelisks, are as exceptional as you
would expect.

Sledmere House

☎ 01377 236637
Sledmere, Driffield, E Yorkshire YO25 3XG
Off A166 between York & Bridlington
Open *Easter, May–Sept Tues–Fri Sun
& BH Mon 11.30–4.30*
The Georgian mansion was built in the
1750s on the site of an ancient manor.
Inside there is an Adam-style long library,
a feast of French 18th-century furniture
and some of the finest plasterwork in the
North of England, The gardens are also
striking with a 'Capability' Brown park,
knot garden and walled rose garden.

Scotland MAP 8

260 Braemar Castle
☎ 013397 41219
Braemar, Aberdeenshire AB5 4EX
Email: invercauld@freenet.co.uk
Website: www.braemarcastle.co.uk
½m NE of Braemar on A93
Open *Apr–Oct Sat–Thurs 10–6;
closed Fri except in July & Aug*
A classic example of the 17th-century Scottish style of fortress with its distinctive, rounded castellated turrets rising straight up out of the Grampian soil. It was built by the Earl of Mar, an early supporter of the Old Pretender (James II's son, James Stuart, father of Bonnie Prince Charlie) which meant it spent a number of years in the hands of Hanoverian soldiers after the Battle of Culloden. This accounts for a large variety of military additions and embellishments which take the rub off an otherwise romantic castle. The pit prison, for example, is not some throwback to the days of Macbeth and was still used in the 19th century. Still, it is good to know that some things never change; soldiers get bored, and bored soldiers scratch graffiti, and Braemar's garrison has plenty of that. Braemar has been owned by the Farquharson family since the late 18th century.

261 Culloden* NTS
☎ 01463 790607
Culloden Moor, Inverness,
Highland IV2 5EU
Website: www.nts.org.uk/culloden.html
5m E of Inverness on B9006
Open *All year. Visitor centre: Apr–Oct daily 9–6, Nov–Dec & mid-Jan–Mar daily 10–4*
The moorland site of the bloodiest modern battle on the British mainland still has an essential bleakness. It was where on 16 April 1746 the great Stuart dream finally perished; 1200 of Bonnie Prince Charlie's army were annihilated by the Duke of Cumberland (known as the Butcher for obvious reasons) and his Redcoats, who lost only 76. It was the moment when the bayonet-armed musket-wielding Redcoats held off the Highland charge and then routed the Scots. Hundreds were later finished off where they lay bleeding in the heather, or were captured and executed. A cairn, erected in 1881, marks the spot where it is thought the fiercest fighting took place.

262 Drummond Castle Gardens
☎ 01764 681257
Muthill, Crieff, Perth & Kinross PH5 2AA
2m S of Crieff off A822
Open *Easter, May–Oct 2–6*
Anyone seeing Liam Neeson in the film *Rob Roy* will have been struck by the extraordinary gardens featured, and here they are, rightly acknowledged as among the finest in Europe. They are an explosion of Renaissance symmetry, colour, precision and exuberance. Features include a beautiful sundial, and an approach through a mile of beech-lined avenue.

263 Edinburgh New Town*
The First New Town, developed between 1767 and 1830 originally to plans by James Craig, runs N from Princes St to Queen St, and from Charlotte Sq to the W to Leith St to the E: the Northern New Town, begun in 1801, goes from Queen St to Fettes Row to the N, India St to the W & Broughton St to the E; the Western New Town, begun in 1822, including the Moray Estate to the NW, is bounded by the Water of Leith. From the air, the sheer artistry and audacity of the town planning take your breath away. The pattern of circuses and thoroughfares, all shrouded in parks and town gardens, in one of Europe's hilliest cities is impressive enough, but there is

also the stature and the fabric of the beautiful Georgian houses and street fronts. Many have been cleaned up in the last 20 years, and have lost their grim Scottish sooty blackness regaining their honey golden colours.

Anyone thirsting to know what the inside of one of these fabulous houses looks like, should nip round to the Georgian House at 7 Charlotte Square (p200). No 28 Charlotte Square (NTS) is also open to the public: it has 20th-century Scottish paintings on display as well as Regency furniture.

Afterwards look round the New Town, particularly Heriot Row, Moray Place and the surrounding streets and circuses, which give a powerful sense of the scale of what was achieved, and possibly never bettered. It is easy to see why few addresses in Edinburgh are as prestigious. And those interiors that have survived being transformed into dull law and accountancy offices are spectacular, with great high ceilings and, for some, fantastic views over Edinburgh's great romantic chasm, the Water of Leith and Dean Village.

264 Fyvie Castle NTS

☎ 01651 891266
Fyvie, Aberdeenshire AB53 8JS
Website: www.nts.org.uk/fyvie.htm
8m SE of Turriff off A947,
25m N of Aberdeen
Open *Castle: mid-Apr–May & Sept*
1.30–5.30, June–Aug 11–5.30,
Oct Sat & Sun 1.30–5.30.
Grounds: all year 9.30–sunset
One of the most imposing of the Scottish Baronial castles, with five towers (apparently for the five families who have lived here). The towers and central gatehouse are full of swagger, as is the huge

Fyvie Castle, *a fine example of Scottish Baronial architecture.*

stairwell inside the house – wide enough for one generation of owners to ride their horses up and down it.

265 Georgian House NTS

☎ 0131 226 3318
7 Charlotte Square, Edinburgh EH2 4DR
Email: thegeorgianhouse@nts.org.uk
Website: www.nts.org.uk/georgian.html
2 mins from west end of Princes Street
Open *Mar–Oct Mon–Sat 10–5 Sun 2–5, Nov–Dec Mon–Sat 11–4 Sun 2–4. Other times by appointment*

On the north side of Charlotte Square, proudly seated in the middle of the finest terraced façade the entire Edinburgh New Town has to offer, is this masterpiece by Robert Adam with its distinctive Neoclassical 'palace front'. The house is decorated and furnished as it would have been in its heyday in the late 18th century.

266 Glencoe* NTS

☎ 01855 811307 (summer only)
or 01855 811729
Glencoe, Ballachulish, Argyll PA49 4HX
Website: www.nts.org.uk/glencoe.html
17m S of Fort William on A82
Open *Site: all year.*
Visitor Centre: Mar–Apr & Sept–Oct 10–5, May–Aug 9.30–5.30

Glencoe is worth seeing for two reasons. It is a spectacular slice of Scottish Highland landscape, bordering the equally impressive Rannoch Moor which contains a number of Scotland's most photographed peaks. And it is the site of the infamous massacre on 13 February 1692 when 38 of the MacDonald clan were slaughtered by the Campbells, who were loyal to William and Mary. The murder was even worse because the Campbells had been guests of the MacDonalds for over twelve days.

Charlotte Square, *designed by Robert Adam a year before his death in 1792.*

This 'murder under trust' earned the Campbells many years of opprobrium in Scotland. The episode played a pivotal role in the future Acts of Union which merged Scotland and England.

267 Glenfinnan Monument* NTS

☎ 01397 722250
Glenfinnan, Highland PH37 4LT
Website: www.nts.org.uk/
glenfinnan.html
18m W of Fort William on A830
Open *Site: all year*
Visitor centre: Apr–mid-May & Sept–Oct 10–5, mid-May–Aug 9.30–6
The site marks the spot where Bonnie Prince Charlie raised his standard on 19 August 1745 and launched the '45 Rebellion, the last great moment of Catholic Jacobite resistance to the Protestant Hanoverians. (Jacobite comes from the Latin for James, *Jacobus*; their loyalty was to the deposed James II.) Located at the spectacular junction of three glens at the head of Loch Shiel, it is a magnificent spot irrespective of its powerful historical connotations.

268 Greyfriars Kirk*

☎ 0131 225 1900
Candlemaker Row, Edinburgh EH1 2QQ
Email: administrator@greyfriarskirk.com
Website: www.greyfriarskirk.com
South end of George IV bridge
Open *Apr–Oct Mon–Fri 10.30–4.30*
Sat 10.30–2.30, Nov–Mar Thurs 1.30–3.30.
Churchyard: any reasonable time
The National Covenant (with which the 17th-century Presbyterians pledged to maintain their form of worship and church government in Scotland) was signed in front of the pulpit in 1638. With over 40,000 signatories, the Covenant guaranteed that what had begun as a spasm of religious rebellion would lead to war. Sure enough, within months,

Charles I was embroiled in the first of two 'Bishops' Wars', the precursor to the Civil War.

This church was the first one built in Edinburgh after the Reformation, in 1620, and was subsequently greatly altered. The interior, for example, has long lost the austerity of the churchyard, which is still very impressive, full of suitably bleak gravestones and with a wonderful view of old Edinburgh. There is a former Franciscan friary garden, a good collection of 17th-century monuments, the Martyrs' Monument and the Covenanters' Prison.

Greyfriars is also home to 'Bobby', the dog who guarded his master's grave for 14 years in the 19th century. There is a famous little statue of him outside the church gate.

269 Hopetoun House

☎ 0131 331 2451
South Queensferry, W Lothian EH30 9SL
Email: dayvisits@hopetounhouse.com
Website: www.hopetounhouse.com
12m W of Edinburgh,
off M9 at junction 2 for A904
Open *Apr–Sept daily 10–5.30, groups by arrangement*
Close to the Forth Bridge, this is one of William Adam's great achievements, and is generally regarded as one of the finest stately homes in Scotland. Adam worked on it for 20 years (adding to the work of the man who had preceded him, Sir William Bruce), before his sons, Robert and John, took over on his death. The interior work is stunning, as one would expect. The Red Drawing Room has as its crowning feature a masterpiece of chimney-piece sculpture, by Michael Rysbrack, one of the masters of the art. The ceilings are especially fine, and there are paintings by Titian and Canaletto. The furniture is all original. There are also acres of surrounding parkland full of deer.

270 St Giles High Kirk*

☎ 0131 225 9442
Royal Mile, Edinburgh EH1 1RE
Email: stgiles@hotmail.com
Website: www.stgiles.net
Halfway along Royal Mile
Open *Mon–Sat 9–7 Sun 1–5*
(closes at 5 mid-Sept–Easter Mon)
Edinburgh's most famous church was
founded in the 12th century. Its great
sceptred tower acts as a city landmark,
visible over the high rooftops from a surprisingly wide area. It is actually one of
those churches that is far more memorable from the outside than from within.

Largely rebuilt in the 15th and 16th
centuries, the new church was presided
over by John Knox, the Scottish Protestant leader after the Reformation, a man
who burned with contempt for the
authority of bishops. And that makes it
rather ironic since this is technically a
cathedral. He is buried in what was the
old churchyard.

The anti-episcopalian streak in
Scottish Protestantism flared up in 1637
with momentous consequences for
Britain, and for Charles I in particular.
One of the first acts of hostility in what
became the Civil War took place here
when Jenny Geddes hurled a stool at the
Dean for having the nerve to read from
the new Prayer Book that Charles I was
trying to foist on Scotland. The subsequent riots mushroomed over the next
few months into open insurrection,
which in turn helped precipitate a chain
of events culminating in the Civil War.

There are fine examples of late
medieval architecture and plenty of
stained glass from various periods. In the
south-east corner is the Thistle Chapel,
built in 1911, containing the beautiful
carved wooden stalls of the Order of
the Thistle, Scotland's oldest order of
chivalry, designed by Robert Lorimer.

271 St Monan's Parish Church*

☎ 0131 665 2894
Braehead, St Monance, East Neuk, Fife
15m S of St Andrews off A917
Open *Apr–Oct all daylight hours*
If you want a picture of the Scottish Kirk
in all its uncompromising severity, then
visit this church. There are few more
imposing. Perched on the edge of the sea
and protected by sea walls (that fail to
prevent it being lashed by the spray at
high tide), this was a fisherman's church,
the spire used as a navigation aid by
local boats. But it clearly demonstrates
the gulf that separated the Protestant
Church in Scotland from the High
Anglican world, represented by William
Laud, Archbishop of Canterbury, that
Charles tried to impose on it.

Built by Sir William Dishington in 1370,
with later Victorian and 20th-century
alterations, it contains a 14th-century
sedilia (minister's seat) and piscina
(stone basin) and medieval consecration
crosses. And, most fun, there is a large
model ship symbolizing the close ties
with the maritime community.

ADDITIONAL PLACES TO VISIT

Argyll's Lodging HS

☎ 01786 431319
Castle Wynd, Stirling FK8 1EG
In Stirling just below castle
Open *Apr–Sept 9.30–6, Oct–Mar 9.30–5*
This beautiful and fascinating example
of a grand 17th-century Scottish town
house has a number of impressive
rooms, as would have befitted the Dukes
of Argyll, who used it while carrying out
royal duties in Stirling Castle.

Arniston House

☎ 01875 830515
Gorebridge, Midlothian EH23 4RY
Email: henrietta.d.bekker@btinternet.com

Website: www.arniston-house.co.uk
1m W of junction with A7 on B6372
Open *July–mid-Sept Sun Tues & Thurs 2–5;*
rest of year groups by arrangement
Beautiful example of William Adam
architecture dating from the 1720s.
It has a gorgeous setting, fine furniture
and a collection of Scottish portraits.

Castle Fraser NTS

☎ 01330 833463
Sauchen, Inverurie,
Aberdeenshire AB51 7LD
Website: www.nts.org.uk/fraser.html
4m N of Dunecht off A944,
16m W of Aberdeen
Open *Castle: mid-Apr–May & Sept*
1.30–5.30, June–Aug 11–5.30,
Oct Sat & Sun 1.30–5.30.
Garden: all year 9.30–sunset
With its round pointed towers, it is a
classic example of the Scottish Baronial-
style stately home. It is considered the
largest and most complex example of the
Z-plan castle, and has a particularly
impressive great hall.

Drum Castle NTS

☎ 01330 811204
Drumoak, Banchory,
Aberdeenshire AB31 5EY
Website: www.nts.org.uk/drum.html
3m W of Peterculter off A93,
10m W of Aberdeen
Open *Castle: Apr–May & Sept 1.30–5.30,*
June–Aug 11–5.30, Oct Sat & Sun
1.30–5.30. Garden: as castle, 10–6.
Grounds: all year 9.30–sunset
Strikingly white and high walled (rising
up 70ft/21m), this 17th-century mansion
with a medieval tower and numerous
19th-century additions has been lived
in by the Irvine family for 650 years.
There was a rocky patch in the mid-
17th century when it was attacked and
ransacked, but not destroyed.

Dunnottar Castle

☎ 01569 762173
The Lodge, Stonehaven,
Aberdeenshire AB39 2TL
2m SE of Stonehaven just off A92
Open *Easter–Oct Mon–Sat 9–6 Sun 2–5,*
Nov–Easter Mon–Fri 9–sunset;
closed weekends when clocks change
A great Highland ruin now, but in the
years after the Civil War this was where
Scottish Royalists stowed the Scottish
Crown Jewels. They were smuggled out
when Cromwell laid siege to it. A photog-
rapher's dream, perched on an isolated
coastal outcrop.

Haddo House NTS

☎ 01651 851440
Ellon, Aberdeenshire AB41 7EQ
Website: www.nts.org.uk/haddo/html
4m N of Pitmedden off B999
19m N of Aberdeen & 10m NW of Ellon
Open *Mid-Apr–Sept 1.30–5.30, Oct Sat &*
Sun 1.30–5.30. Garden: Mar–Oct 9.30–6,
Nov–Feb 9.30–4
A classic, 1730s' example of the work of
the Scottish architect William Adam. The
style is plain but highly elegant with
lavish decorations, mostly dating from
the late 19th century. Particularly
impressive is the curving flight of steps.

Inverary Castle

☎ 01499 302203
Cherry Park, Inverary, Argyll PA32 8XE
Email: enquiries@inverary-castle.com
Website: www.inverary-castle.com
Just NE of Inverary on A83;
W shore of Loch Fyne
Open *Apr–June & Sept–Oct Mon–Thurs*
& Sat 10–1 2–5.45, Sun 1–5.45, July–Aug
daily 10–5.45, Sun 1–5.45
Built by the Dukes of Argyll in 1745–90,
by which time castle design had become
slightly more fanciful. It is particularly
noted for its great display of armoury.

Paxton House

☎ 01289 386291

Nr Berwick-upon-Tweed,
Scottish Borders TD15 1SZ
Email: info@paxtonhouse.com
Website: www.paxtonhouse.com
*3m W of Berwick-upon-Tweed off A1
on B6461*
Open *House: Apr–Oct 11.15–5.
Grounds: as house, 10–sunset*
As well as being worth visiting in its own
right, this Georgian house (built in 1758
by the Adam brothers) has a good range
of art and furniture. The Chippendale
pieces are among the best in the north,
and much of the art is loaned by the
National Galleries of Scotland.

Thirlestane Castle

☎ 01578 722430

Lauder, Scottish Borders TD2 6RU
Email: admin@thirlestanecastle.co.uk
Website: www.thirlestanecastle.co.uk
28m S of Edinburgh off A68 at Lauder
Open *Apr–Oct daily except Sat 10.30–4.15*
Old and beautifully situated castle
which is still lived in. It has peerless
17th-century ceilings and portraits, and
a room slept in by Bonnie Prince Charlie.

Winton House

☎ 01875 341309

Pencaitland, E Lothian EH43 5AT
Email: info@wintonhouse.co.uk
Website: www.wintonhouse.co.uk
*14m SE of Edinburgh off A1 at Tranent;
lodge gates S of New Winton (B6355)
& in Pencaitland (A6093)*
Open *First weekends of June July &
Aug 12.30–4.30; rest of year groups by
appointment*
Winton has the very best of Scottish
'twisted' chimneys, which rise out of the
roof of this classic Scottish Renaissance
house. There is also art, fine furniture,
and good gardens.

Northern Ireland MAP 9

272 Florence Court NT

☎ 028 6634 8249

Enniskillen, Co Fermanagh BT92 1DB
Email: ufcest@smtp.ntrust.org.uk
8m SW of Enniskillen via A4 & A32
Open *House: Easter, Apr–May & Sept
Sat Sun & BH Mons (weekdays groups
only by arrangement), June–Aug daily,
all 12–6 (opens at 1 in June)*
One of the most bucolic and important
houses in Ulster, it was built by John
Cole in the mid-18th century. There
is fabulous interior plasterwork and
furniture, and a ravishing setting outside
including an ice-house, and views over
the distant mountains.

273 Monea Castle

Nr Enniskillen, Co Fermanagh
*6m NW of Enniskillen & 1m E of
St Molaise's Church approached along
a beech avenue through Castletown*
Open *Public access*
Fermanagh's best preserved 'Plantation'
era castle is set back from the south-west
shore of Lower Lough Erne. Building
commenced in 1616 by the Rector of
Devenish, the Revd Malcolm Hamilton.
In 1619, it was described as 'a strong
castle of lime and stone being 54ft (16m)
long and 20ft (6m) broad.' The castle is
rectangular, with two circular towers
with Scottish-style corbelled (or supporting) projections. Nearby are two other
historically interesting farmhouses from
the 18th and 19th centuries.

274 Mount Stewart NT

☎ 028 4278 8387/8487

Greyabbey, Newtownards,
Co Down BT22 2AD
Email: umsest@smtp.ntrust.org.uk
*15m SE of Belfast on Newtownards–Porta-
ferry road A20, 5m SE of Newtownards*

The octagonal hall at **Mount Stewart**.

Open *House: Easter, Apr & Oct Sat Sun & BH Mons, May & Sept daily except Tues, June–Aug daily, all 12–6*
Garden: Late Mar, Apr & Oct Sat Sun & BH Mons, May–Sept daily, all 11–6 (or dusk if earlier)
The childhood home of Lord Castlereagh is an 18th-century house with Victorian additions. It now houses one of the greatest paintings by a British artist, George Stubbs' *Hambletonian*, a picture of an exhausted racehorse, which has just won a gruelling race, being swabbed down. Almost lifesize and mounted somewhat awkwardly halfway up a rear staircase, it attracts scores of visitors.

The gardens are among the finest anywhere in Ireland, with their series of outdoor 'rooms' and the Temple of the Winds, a banqueting pavilion built by James 'Athenian' Stuart, a genius of Neo-classical design.

275 Mussenden Temple NT
☎ 028 7084 8728
42 Mussenden Rd, Castlerock, Coleraine, Co Londonderry BT51 4RP
Email: uncwaw@smtp.ntrust.org.uk
1m W of Castlerock on A2 coast road, in Downhill Castle estate
Open *Apr May & Sept Sat Sun & BHs, June–Aug daily, all 11–6*

The small domed rotunda juts out of a headland on the Londonderry coast. It was built in 1783 by Frederick Augustus Hervey as a memorial to Frideswide Mussenden, his cousin. The design deliberately echoes the famous Temple of Vesta at Tivoli on the outskirts of Rome.

ADDITIONAL PLACES TO VISIT

Ardress House NT
☎ 028 3885 1236
64 Ardress Road, Portadown,
Co Armagh BT62 1SQ
Email: uagest@smtp.ntrust.org.uk
5m from Portadown on B28,
3m from M1 junction 13
Open *House & farmyard: Apr–May & Sept*
Sat Sun Good Fri & BH Mons,
June–Aug daily except Tues, all 2–6
This 17th-century farmhouse had major additions made to it in the 18th century by the owner, George Ensor, who was also the main architect. Note the beautiful plasterwork and fascinating display of farm implements.

Barons Court
☎ 028 8166 1683
Newtonstewart, Omagh,
Co Tyrone BT78 4EZ
3m SW of Newtonstewart
Open *By appointment only*
Originally an 18th-century house, it was reworked by Sir John Soane in 1791, completely remodelled by William and Sir Richard Morrison in 1819–41, and again altered in the 20th century.

Castle Coole NT
☎ 028 6632 2690
Enniskillen, Co Fermanagh BT74 6JY
Email: ucasco@smtp.ntrust.org.uk
1m SE of Enniskillen on A4
Belfast–Enniskillen road

Open *House: Easter, Apr–May & Sept*
Sat Sun & BH Mon (weekdays groups
by arrangement), June–Aug daily
except Tues in June, all 12–6
Park: May–Sept 10–8 Oct–Apr 10–4
This James Wyatt-designed Neoclassical mansion has colonnaded wings. Both within and without it remains a stunning example of Georgian architecture and landscape design.

Castle Ward NT
☎ 028 4488 1204
Strangford, Downpatrick,
Co Down BT30 7LS
Email: ucwest@smtp.ntrust.org.uk
7m NE of Downpatrick,
1m W of Strangford village on A25,
on S shore of Strangford Lough
Open *House: Easter, Apr & Sept–Oct*
Sat Sun & BHs, May daily except Tues,
June–Aug daily, all 12–6 (opens at 1
in May & June)
Grounds: all year dawn to dusk
It is not often that the two conflicting styles so popular in the 18th century are found jostling for supremacy in the same house, but that is what makes Castle Ward so interesting. On one side is a perfect Palladian façade, on the other a rambling Gothick extravagance. Added to its almost perfect setting on the shores of Strangford Lough (with extensive walks, and a Wildlife Centre), the house also has a number of attractions, notably a Victorian laundry, and a Pastime Centre.

Hezlett House NT
☎ 028 7084 8567
107 Sea Rd, Castlerock, Coleraine,
Co Londonderry BT51 4TW
Email: uncwaw@smtp.ntrust.org.uk
5m W of Coleraine on A2 coast road
Open *Easter, Apr–May & Sept*
Sat, Sun & BHs, June–Aug daily
except Tues, all 12–5

Mussenden Temple, *perched on a cliff edge overlooking the Atlantic.*

A thatched house from the 17th century with 19th-century furniture and a curious roof. One of only a handful of pre-18th-century Irish buildings still surviving.

St Columb's Cathedral

☎ 028 7126 7313
London St, Derry,
Co Londonderry BT48 6RQ
Email: stcolumbs@ic24.net
Website: www.stcolumbscathedral.org
Open *Easter–Sept 9–5, Oct–Easter 9–4*

One of the first cathedrals built anywhere in the British Isles in the years after the Reformation, it retains a distinctive 'Planter'-style appearance. It was constructed in the southern part of the town from 1628–33. The west tower was capped in 1778 by a graceful spire, courtesy of Frederick Augustus Hervey, though the tower and spire were substantially rebuilt in the 19th century. On the roof of the cathedral are stone corbels with the heads of past bishops of Derry carved upon them.

CHAPTER FIVE

Grime, Soot, Steel and Glass

Until now the great architectural and landscape locations we most associate with British history are also monuments to permanence and continuity, an illusion reinforced by the accident of their survival. Cathedrals, castles and country houses are almost by definition symbols of buildings that have weathered the centuries, and of a larger history which we like to tell ourselves is characterized by the long term. But from the Victorian period this all changed. Everything changed, and did so with greater speed and profundity than at any moment before.

For many this was the age which definitively reinvented British history. The Victorian image is now almost always the starting point for any imagining of the past. Think of anyone or anywhere in British history and the long flowing grey beard, the perfect round turreted castle, the cloak laid across the puddle, the medieval virgin at the palace window, the monarch of the glen, you name it, they are all Victorian. And what an effort it takes to leave them behind, to move on and replace them with something sharper, edgier, more likely to have a vestige of truth. Nobody engineered history (or anything else) as powerfully as the Victorians.

Always the Victorians make us wonder: what would it have been like to be part of the world's most powerful nation, as the USA is today? But for many the Victorian period will always be the 'in-between' era; not as pure as what came before it and not as interesting as what came after – 'The poor old Victorians stuck right in the middle.' Whichever line you take, this was an era of great designers and writers about design, with an explosion in new styles, redis-covered older styles such as the Gothic, and above all, hybrid styles. It was also the birth of that other great modern institution, the heated, public, political, no-holds-barred argument over the virtues of different designs – arguments in which John Ruskin and A.W.N. Pugin often saw their words reach the status of literature.

The Victorian period was also when whole new types of institution had great buildings constructed for them. Besides the usual mix of stately homes and churches came the new 'palaces' – the insurance company headquarters, railway stations, bridges, sewage works, teacher training colleges, art galleries, libraries, swimming pools, music halls and seaside piers – the list is endless. And at the top of that list, of course, were the new **Houses of Parliament** and the great new state departments bloated by empire, like the **Foreign Office**. They are textbook examples of a nation creating a model of itself in stone.

The High Gothic front of **St Pancras Station and Hotel** *designed by Sir George Gilbert Scott.*

*Part of the model estate at **Saltaire** designed by the industrialist Titus Salt.*

In style, too, we look at the Victorian period and see excess in size, ambition and decorative detail piled up in endless layers just waiting for the Modern Movement to sweep it all away. Victorian architecture is like the Victorian novel, a huge, exhausting, endless, baggy monster containing the whole of life in its teeming and inexhaustible profusion. Like the novels too, these buildings were suffused with moral purpose. The Victorians liked to believe that human society was on the brink of making a vault ahead in human and moral affairs, as well as in technological and imperial ones.

We admire their energy, zeal and enthusiasm, and recognize that we still live largely in their world, particularly in cities underpinned by Victorian achievements such as terraced housing and sewage systems. And the Victorians gave us smaller domestic virtues which, while not being anywhere near as heroic or as inspiring as the values we find in earlier periods of history, nevertheless help to make our world tolerable. They shaped our notions of the domestic, the comfortable and the bourgeois.

The Victorian period was the time when class entered the political scene. The labouring masses were no longer simply part of the background, they now noisily occupied the centre stage, indispensable to the creation and the stoking of this new world largely built out of manual labour. They created all kinds of new demands. What sort of housing should they live in? What sort of education did they deserve? What recreations could they have? The great Utopian projects of **New Lanark** in Scotland and **Saltaire** in Yorkshire still challenge us today to organize life better. The great housing schemes of the local authorities and individual housing associations set important trends.

The Victorians handed down their love affair with the huge and the impressive, and the use of new materials with which, for example, to build ever bigger bridges and railways. The **Forth Railway Bridge** is still more awesome than its 1960s' neighbour, the Road Bridge. And the use of iron and glass in the Great Exhibition, and in the **Palm House** at Kew Gardens, opened a great chapter in the use of materials besides stone and wood.

This, too, was the age of municipal, not just aristocratic, power: just think of all those new town halls and civic institutions. It was an age of faith troubled by doubt, and also of enormous optimism. Visitors describe places such as the **Natural History Museum** in South Kensington, London, as resembling cathedrals, and they are right because the spirit soars there as much as in any of the era's great churches. And these impulses carry on into the 20th century; the range of buildings with historical significance has mushroomed (like radio telescopes, department stores and bus terminals) as have the types of material with which buildings are made.

South-west MAP 1

276 Castle Drogo NT
☎ 01647 433306

Drewsteignton, nr Exeter, Devon EX6 6PB
*5m S of A30 Exeter–Okehampton road
via Crockernwell or A382 Moretonhampstead–Whiddon Down road*
Open *Castle: Mar Wed–Sun, Apr–Oct
daily except Fri, all 11–5.30; guided
tours during summer holidays
Garden: all year daily 10.30–dusk*

One of Sir Edwin Lutyens' most imposing
if severe creations, it is a full-scale baronial
castle built out of granite and oak with a
full complement of 20th-century rooms.
It was commissioned by Julius Drewe who
had made his fortune by the age of 33,
having founded the Home and Colonial
Stores. He was convinced that he was
descended from a Norman nobleman
called Drogo de Teigne (after whom the
castle was named).

Clifton Suspension Bridge *leaps some
700ft (210m) across the Avon Gorge.*

277 Clifton Suspension Bridge
☎ 0117 974 4664

Bridge House, Sion Place, Clifton,
Bristol BS8 4AP
Email: visitinfo@clifton-suspension-
bridge.org.uk
Website: www.clifton-suspension-
bridge.org.uk
2m NW of city centre
Open *Bridge: open access
Visitor centre: Apr–Oct 10–5,
Nov–Mar 11–4 (closes at 5 on Sat & Sun)*

Spanning the Avon Gorge, this is a
perfect example of elegant technology
and Isambard Kingdom Brunel's ability
to blend engineering with the surrounding landscape. At a height of over 245ft
(77m) above the gorge, and necessitating
a wider span (some 700ft/210m) than
had ever been attempted before, this
was Victorian technology taken to its
limits. Unfortunately Brunel had been
in his grave for five years when it was
completed, with some modifications
by Sir John Hawkshaw and W.H. Barlow.
It opened in 1864.

ADDITIONAL PLACES TO VISIT

A La Ronde NT
☎ 01395 265514
Summer Lane, Exmouth, Devon EX8 5BD
2m N of Exmouth on A376
Open *Apr–Oct Sun–Thurs 11–5.30*
The 35ft(10.6m)-high octagonal hall
from which all the other rooms radiate
was inspired by the Byzantine Church
of San Vitale in Ravenna. On their
return from a grand tour of Europe,
two cousins, Mary and Jane Parminter,
had the house built to their instructions
*c*1796. They created the extraordinary
mosaic of shells and the feather frieze,
both still on display.

Clouds Hill NT
☎ 01929 405616
Wareham, Dorset BH20 7NQ
9m E of Dorchester,
1½m E of Waddock crossroads (B3390)
Open *Apr–Oct Thurs Fri & Sun*
& BH Mons 12–5 (dusk if earlier)
A brick cottage bought by T.E. Lawrence
(of Arabia fame). While returning here
on his motorbike he was killed in a road
accident in 1935. The cottage is pretty
much as he left it, including his foil-
lined bedroom.

Hardy's Cottage NT
☎ 01305 262366
Higher Bockhampton, nr Dorchester,
Dorset DT2 8QJ
3m NE of Dorchester, ½m S of A35;
10 mins walk from car park
Open *Apr–Oct Sun–Thurs*
& Good Fri 11–5 (dusk if earlier)
The perfect little cottage and garden
have mementoes of the life and career
of the novelist and poet Thomas Hardy,
including the desk and pens he used
writing some of his greatest works.
He was born here in 1840.

Lacock Abbey, Fox Talbot Museum and Village NT
☎ 01249 730227; Museum 01249 730459
Lacock, nr Chippenham,
Wiltshire SN15 2LG
3m S of Chippenham, E of A350
Open *Museum, cloisters & garden:*
Mar–Nov 11–5.30; closed Good Fri;
Museum also open winter weekends
Abbey: Apr–Oct 1–5.30; closed Tues
& Good Fri
Although primarily a 13th-century
nunnery which was converted into a large
country house in 1539, it is most famous
for being where William Henry Fox Talbot
conducted his early experiments in photography. An oriel window in the south
gallery was the subject, in August 1835, of
the world's oldest surviving photographic
negative, now on display inside the house.

Lanhydrock NT
☎ 01208 73320
Bodmin, Cornwall PL30 5AD
Email: clhlan@smtp.ntrust.org.uk
2½m SE of Bodmin, overlooking valley
of River Fowey; follow signposts from
either A30, A38 or B3268
Open *House: Apr–Oct daily except Mon but*
open BH Mons 11–5.30 (closes at 5 in Oct)
Garden: all year 10–6
Overlooking the River Fowey, in 450
acres of woods and parkland, this is a
stunning example of Victorian interior
styling. The Cornish house was built
on the fire-destroyed ruins of an earlier
Jacobean mansion, whose gatehouse
is about all that has survived; 50 rooms
are on show.

Royal Albert Bridge
Saltash, Plymouth, Devon
4m NW of Plymouth; runs parallel with
A38 crossing River Tamar at Saltash
Built by Isambard Kingdom Brunel, this
is a classic Victorian cantilever railway

suspension bridge that runs alongside the Tamar River road bridge carrying the A38 into Cornwall. Like the Forth Railway Bridge it had to be built to quite a height to allow room for ships passing underneath. It comprises two 461ft (140m) curved, oval, wrought-iron tubes on massive stone piers to carry the railway track which is suspended underneath. Brunel's name is proudly inscribed on the side of one of the towers.

St Andrew's Church

☎ 01297 560610 (keyholder)
Monkton Wyld, Dorset DT7 3RN
3m W of Charmouth off A35
Open *Key on request from house next door*
Built in 1848 by R.C. Carpenter, this is a Pugin-style church which shows just how pervasive Pugin's church design orthodoxy had become. It has a fine broad spire, placed right over the church crossing, with interior details to match. There is a stencil-decorated chancel, and fine stained glass by G.E. Cook from the late 19th century.

Sheldon Bush Lead Shot Tower

☎ Bristol tourist info 0117 9260767
Cheese Lane, Bristol
On corner of Temple Way & Passage Plain
Open *Exterior only*
If anyone denies there is something Freudian about towers, then they have not seen this one. The shape of this utterly phallic pinnacle was determined by its industrial purpose. You make lead shot by dropping molten lead from a great height though a screen of perforations, landing in cold water, perfectly spherical in shape. The present tower is a post-war replacement of the original, though it still serves the same purpose. It is 140ft (42m) high, and one of only two towers still serving this purpose. The other, dating from 1799, is in Chester.

Tate Gallery St Ives

☎ 01736 796226
Porthmeor Beach, St Ives,
Cornwall TR26 1TG
Email: information@tate.org.uk
Website: www.tate.org.uk
Open *Mar–Oct 10–6.30,*
Nov–Feb Tues–Sun 10–4.30
The beautiful modern gallery was built close to one of the centres of modern British painting. There is a regularly changing programme of exhibitions, with particular emphasis on 20th-century paintings and sculptures. The Tate also manages the Barbara Hepworth gallery in St Ives.

Truro Cathedral

☎ 01872 276782
St Mary's St, Truro, Cornwall TR1 2AF
Email: visitor@trurocathedral.org.uk
Website: www.trurocathedral.org.uk
In centre of town
Open *Daily 8–5 or until last service*
Built from 1880–1910 to designs by J.L. Pearson, this is the first Anglican cathedral built in Britain since Christopher Wren finished St Paul's in London. The cloisters and chapter house were added in 1935–67. It does not have the same outstanding site as some of its Gothic counterparts, but more than makes up for it with its three great spires. Tall and narrow, it makes a considerable impact.

White Mill NT

☎ 01258 858051;
White Mill, Sturminster Marshall, nr Wimborne, Dorset BH21 4BX
On River Stour, N of Sturminster Marshall
Open *Apr–Oct Sat Sun & BH Mons 12–5,*
pre-booked groups at other times
Although it no longer operates, this is a wonderful example of an 18th-century mill with much of its original machinery.

South-east MAP 2

278 Albert Memorial EH

☎ 020 7298 2117;
Tour bookings 020 7495 0916
Kensington Gardens, Kensington Rd,
London W2 2UH
Tube Kensington High St
Open *Any reasonable time;*
guided tours Sun 2 & 3

Sir George Gilbert Scott's memorial to
Prince Albert was constructed between
1863 and 1872 and is modelled on the
design of the Eleanor Crosses (p66). It is
a good acid test about the high point of
Victorian Gothic: cloying and excessive
or magisterial and exuberant? Thanks
to recent restoration, at least we get to
judge pretty well what Scott intended.

Typical of Victorian hagiography,
the memorial is heaving with a horde of
contemporary luminaries (the Victorian
world is full of crowds, even on its
monuments). Albert is seen holding a
brochure from the 1851 Great Exhibition.
The memorial is also an echo of the Scott
Monument (p245) in Edinburgh, with
its seated figure beneath a towering
Gothic-style canopy, but this is much
more delicate. There is an Italian feel
to it, the metalwork motifs reminiscent
of the tombs in Verona which Ruskin
so loved. At each corner are sculptural
groups evoking the four great continents,
as well as podium statues symbolizing
(what else?) Agriculture, Manufacture,
Commerce and Engineering. The bronze
statue was the work of John Henry Foley.

279 All Saints Church

☎ 020 7636 1788
7 Margaret Street, London W1W 8JG
Tube Westminster
Open *Daily 7–7*

Built by William Butterfield from 1850–9,
this masterpiece combines simple
Victorian forms with a wealth of stunning
colours inside. No surface is too small to
escape being emblazoned. But then it
had to be pretty good because it was built
for the Ecclesiological Society, the Tractari-
ans, who were propagandists for church
design. Butterfield was further challenged
by having to do it on a tight urban site.
The result is quite spectacular.

280 Dimbola Lodge
(Julia Margaret Cameron Trust) *

☎ 01983 756814
Terrace Lane, Freshwater Bay,
Isle of Wight PO40 9QE
Email: admin@dimbola.co.uk
Website: www.dimbola.co.uk
A3054 to Totland, then A3055
Open *Tues–Sun & BH Mons 10–5*

This was the home of one of the great
Victorian pioneers of early photography,
Julia Margaret Cameron. There is a
museum and a gallery dedicated to
her life and work.

281 Freud Museum

☎ 020 7435 2002
20 Maresfield Gardens, London NW3 5SX
Email: freud@gn.apc.org
Website: www.freud.org.uk
Tube Finchley Road
Open *Wed–Sun 12–5*

A piece of early 20th-century Vienna
transplanted into leafy London: the
museum of the life and work of one of
the century's most influential thinkers.
Sigmund Freud arrived in London,
fleeing the Nazis after they had annexed
Austria. The main room is his study,
preserved intact, containing a collection
of antiquities, and his library. The house
is decked out in fine Biedermeier and
Austrian furniture, all brought with him
from Austria. The most famous piece of
furniture is the couch, on which his
patients revealed their dreams and fears.

The Houses of Parliament by A.W.N. Pugin and Sir Charles Barry.

282 Highgate Cemetery*

☎ 020 8340 1834
Swains Lane, London N6 6PJ
Tube Archway
Open *Western Cemetery: view by tours only Apr–Oct Mon–Fri 12, 2 & 4 Sat & Sun 11–4 (on hour), Nov–Mar weekends only 11–3 Eastern Cemetery: Mon–Fri 10–5 Sat & Sun 11–5 (Nov–Mar closes at 4) Closed during funerals*

One of the most famous cemeteries in the world, this Gothick adventure is London's answer to Père Lachaise in Paris. It is split into two: a Western and an Eastern cemetery. The Western is older, dating back to 1839, and is particularly famous for its elaborate statuary and headstones overgrown with ivy. It is a perfect monument to the Victorian desire to put a face on death. The Eastern Cemetery (most famous resident Karl Marx) is plainer and more ordered.

283 Houses of Parliament*

☎ House of Commons info 020 7219 4272;
House of Lords info 020 7219 3107;
Guided tour bookings 020 7344 9966
(through Ticketmaster); for tours of
Palace of Westminster contact local MP,
overseas visitors contact 020 7219 2105
(Parliamentary Education Unit)
Parliament Square, London SW1A 2PW
Website: www.parliament.uk
Tube Westminster
Open *To listen to debates from public gallery, queue at St Stephen's Entrance: both Houses sit Oct–July Mon–Wed 2.30–10 Thurs 1.30–7.30 Fri (most) 9.30–c2.30am Guided tours: Aug–Sept Mon–Sat 9.15–4.15*

Probably the most famous Victorian building in the world, although many are (as slightly intended) fooled into thinking it belongs to the Middle Ages. The product of the combined geniuses of A.W. N. Pugin and Sir Charles Barry –

a showcase to the world of the Britishness of Gothic architecture – was necessitated by the catastrophic fire that destroyed almost all of the original parliament building in 1834. Fortunately Westminster Hall survived the fire. Built in 1097–9, it was remodelled by Richard II in 1394–1402 when the fabulous hammerbeam roof was made.

The delight of the building is its lack of symmetry; there is the clock tower with Big Ben at one end (designed by Pugin), and the Victoria Tower at the other. For anyone curious about what lies inside, you have to join a queue for the public gallery.

284 Knebworth House

☎ 01438 812661
Knebworth, Hertfordshire SG3 6PY
Email: info@knebworthhouse.com
Website: www.knebworthhouse.com
Off M1 at junction 7 near Stevenage
Open *Easter–June Sat Sun & BHs,*
July–Aug daily; Sept–Apr pre-booked
groups only. House: 12–5
Park & Gardens: 11–5.30

The Victorian writer Edward Bulwer-Lytton transformed this family mansion (it had been in his mother's family since 1492) into the Gothic mansion you see today, with its mock battlements, heraldic symbols and gargoyles. Many of the great writers of the day came here to be entertained, including Charles Dickens (there is an exhibition of letters from Dickens to Bulwer-Lytton) and Wilkie Collins. It later became home to Lord Lytton, the Viceroy of India, who organized one of the most expensive meals in history, a banquet for 68,000 to celebrate Queen Victoria's durbar (court) in India in 1877, while hundreds of thousands, even millions, of Indians were dying of famine. The interior is a satisfying mix of styles, and the surrounding gardens are full of idiosyncratic details.

285 London Eye

☎ 0870 5000 6000
Jubilee Gardens, South Bank,
London SE1
Website: www.ba-londoneye.com
Tube Waterloo, or Embankment
& then walk over Hungerford Bridge
Open *Jan–May 10–9.30,*
June–Aug 9.30–10, Sept–Dec 10–8

The London Eye is an unlikely masterpiece, delicate yet bold, a fairground attraction, but elegant, even rather sublime. At 135ft (41m) it is the world's largest observation wheel. The cigar-shaped capsules and the knock-out views combine to make this an unbeatable triumph – reminding us how often historical significance resides in the playful and the useless – like the Eiffel Tower or the Asahi Beer Hall in Tokyo.

286 Osborne House * EH

☎ 01983 200022
East Cowes, Isle of Wight B32 6JY
1m SE of Cowes
Open *House: Apr–Oct 10–5, Nov–early Dec*
& Feb–Mar Sun Mon Wed & Thurs 10–2.30;
pre-booked tours only. Gardens: as house,
but closes at 6 Apr–Sept

Victoria and Albert's beloved rural retreat was the scene of many of her happiest times. She described it as 'a place of one's own, quiet and retired [where] we can walk anywhere without being followed and mobbed.' It was a house much more geared for family life than the more forbidding Buckingham Palace or Windsor Castle, something Victoria exploited to the full. The building, and its surrounding gardens, were very much Albert's own project. There are two towers, one for decoration, the other hiding the water tank (a common feature in Victorian houses getting used to the luxury of running water). Victoria died here in 1901, and much has been preserved as it was then.

The Palm House *at Kew Gardens, a masterpiece of 19th-century functionalism.*

287 Palm House, Kew Gardens

☎ 020 8940 1171

Royal Botanic Gardens, Kew Road,
Richmond, Surrey TW9 3AB

Website: www.rbgkew.org.uk

Tube Kew Gardens

Open *Gardens: Apr–Oct Mon–Fri 9.30–6.30
Sat & Sun 9.30–7.30, Nov–Mar daily 10–4*

A Victorian masterpiece sits in the middle of Kew Gardens. The great glasshouse was built in the late 1840s, designed by Richard Turner and the creator of the Athenaeum Club, Decimus Burton. It may well be plain and functional, but at 330ft (100m) long, 100ft (30m) wide at the centre and 66ft (20m) high, it has genuine scale and impact, and its grace is made possible by the brilliant handling of this new technology, glass and wrought iron. One of the key functions of English greenhouses at the time was to display the range of exotic plants and flowers which flourished in the British Empire.

288 Royal Festival Hall

☎ 020 7921 0600

South Bank Centre, Belvedere Road,
London SE1 8XX

Website: www.sbc.org.uk

*Tube Waterloo, or Embankment
& then walk over Hungerford Bridge*

Open *Daily 10–10*

The great majority of London's lets-finally-bury-the-war Festival of Britain buildings and structures were supposed to be temporary and disposable, with one major exception: the concert hall to replace the Queen's Hall in Langham Place that had been destroyed by bombs. The result is one of the world's great auditoria, and London's classiest concert hall.

Designed by Sir Leslie Martin and Robert Matthew, it had a number of key innovations and technological challenges, the most pressing being that of noise from nearby Hungerford Bridge with trains thundering over it, out of

Charing Cross Station. Their answer was an ingenious 'egg in the box' design that insulated the performance area from the outside noise. It was also one of the first cultural buildings to provide a place for meetings and relaxation during the day.

The rest of the South Bank complex offers a variety of modernist cultural experiences, including the Hayward Gallery, which defies you to like it and then you realize that, for all its brutal in-your-face concrete, you really do. Further along is Sir Denys Lasdun's Royal National Theatre, built to resemble a great ocean liner. With its three auditoria, it has been a great success with the theatre-going public.

289 Royal Mausoleum, Frogmore*
☎ 01753 868286
Windsor, Berkshire SL4 1NJ
In Windsor Great Park, S of Castle
Open *A few days in May & Aug BH*
In Windsor Great Park, surrounding Windsor Castle (p55), are two locations of particular significance to the Royal Family: Frogmore House, still used as a royal retreat, and the Royal Mausoleum, built in 1862–71, where Queen Victoria and Prince Albert are buried. The mausoleum was much influenced by Albert's tastes in architecture and design (it echoes his family vault in Coburg). It draws its inspiration from the Italian High Renaissance, a passion of his. Much of the interior, an overwhelming mix of marble, wall painting and statuary, was the work of German artists. The centrepiece is the granite tomb where he and Victoria lie interred, built from the largest block ever cut in Britain and topped by marble effigies of the couple, with bronze angels standing guard.

290 Royal Pavilion
☎ 01273 290900
4–5 Pavilion Buildings, Brighton, E Sussex BN1 1EE
Website: www.royalpavilion.brighton.co.uk
In centre of Brighton
Open *June–Sept 10–6, Oct–May 10–5*
The fanciful folly was built as a seaside extravaganza for George IV, courtesy of John Nash (on the site of two earlier structures). Recently extensively restored, this is the place to go for architectural fun. A real treat, with plenty of treasures within.

291 St Pancras Station and Hotel
☎ 020 7304 3900 (to book tour)
Euston Road, London NW1 2QP
Tube King's Cross
Open *Station: open access*
Hotel: Mon–Fri 11.30–3.30 tours only
One of the three great North London railway stations (with Kings Cross and Euston), only St Pancras survives in anything like its original, spectacular 19th-century form. Designed by Sir George Gilbert Scott, and unmatched in its Gothic Revival extravagances, spires and pinnacles, it remains to this day one of London's most spectacular silhouettes. A major refurbishment is planned, starting in late 2002.

292 Sir John Soane's Museum
☎ 020 7405 2107
13 Lincoln's Inn Fields, London WC2A 3BP
Website: www.soane.org
Tube Holborn
Open *Tues–Sat 10–5 & 1st Tues of each month 6–9; closed BH Mons*
This is one of the most extraordinary houses you can visit in London, or Britain for that matter. Built and lived in by the great architect Sir John Soane, it is

*The interior of **Sir John Soane's Museum** crammed with antiquities.*

a perfect 3-dimensional monument to his fertile romantic imagination, full to bursting with utterly fascinating objects, particularly antiquities, statues and paintings. In the Picture Room, you can also see Hogarth's masterpiece, *The Rake's Progress*, a sequence of eight paintings depicting the life and downfall of an 18th-century ne'er-do-well.

293 Sissinghurst Castle Gardens NT

☎ 01580 710700;
Infoline 01580 710701
Sissinghurst, nr Cranbrook,
Kent TN17 2AB
Email: ksixxx@smtp.ntrust.org.uk
16m W of Ashford (A28 & A262),
1m E of Sissinghurst village (A262)
Open *Apr–mid-Oct Tues–Fri 1–6.30*
Sat Sun & Good Fri 10–6.30
It is more famous today for its garden and its associations with Vita Sackville-West and Harold Nicolson (the horti-cultural co-creators) than as a mansion that once entertained Queen Elizabeth I. The gardens are intimate rather than landscaped, a sequence of beautifully co-ordinated spaces, and are full of atmosphere. The study where Vita worked can also be visited.

294 South Kensington Museums*

Victoria & Albert Museum

☎ 020 7942 2000
Cromwell Road, London SW7 2RL
Website: www.vam.ac.uk/Infodome/
Tube South Kensington
Open *10–5.45 Wed also 6.30–9.30,*
last Fri in month 6.30–10.

Natural History Museum

☎ 020 7942 5011
Cromwell Road, London SW7 5BD
Website: www.nhm.ac.uk
Tube South Kensington
Open *Mon–Sat 10–5.50 Sun 11–5.50*

'Albertopolis' is a whole postal code of great Victorian institutions and even greater buildings to house them, the Victoria & Albert and the Natural History Museums being the most spectacular. A little further away in Kensington Gore is the Royal Albert Hall, a vast elliptical concert hall designed by Captain Francis Fowke and completed in 1871. The museums best exemplify British self-esteem at its peak. The Natural History Museum was built from 1873–81 by Alfred Waterhouse. It is as interesting to visit just to savour the Victorian interiors as the state-of-the-art child-friendly animatronic dinosaurs. The Victoria & Albert (1856–1908), originally called the Museum of Science and Art, was designed and built with the intention of improving the technical and art education of designers and manufacturers at a time when Britain was beginning to lose her industrial supremacy. It was renamed in 1899 in memory of Prince Albert.

295 Tate Modern

☎ 020 7887 8000;
Infoline 020 7887 8008
Bankside, London SE1 9TG
Website: www.tate.org.uk
Tube Southwark or Blackfriars
Open *Sun–Thurs 10–6 Fri Sat 10–10*
Modern art has a very powerful effect on its surrounding space. The Tate Modern – astonishingly popular with visitors, native and foreign alike – proves this tenfold. Sir Giles Gilbert Scott's power station has been transformed into a power house art gallery. People seem particularly drawn to its immensity – especially the former Turbine Hall which runs the whole length of the building and makes a breathtaking entrance to the gallery. It has revivified a moribund bit of the Thames.

Tate Modern, *formerly Bankside Power Station and now transformed into a vast modern art gallery.*

296 University of Sussex
☎ 01273 606755
Falmer, Brighton BN1 9RH
Website: www.sussex.ac.uk
2m W of Lewes on A27
Open *Exteriors only, except the Gardner Arts Centre (01273 685861), which hosts plays & concerts*
It stands right at the forefront of the last generation of university building, and is one of architect Sir Basil Spence's great works. He began preparing for this new university in 1959, and ended up producing a series of buildings with echoes of Le Corbusier, the patron saint of uncompromisingly modern continental architecture (so much easier to do when students are the residents and not young families).

Spence was responsible for a number of the key campus buildings, various faculty departments and the large arcade courtyard. It was the first of seven similar greenfield campuses across the country built during the 1960s, the so-called 'Plate Glass' universities.

297 Waddesdon Manor NT
☎ 01296 653212;
Infoline 01296 653211
Waddesdon, nr Aylesbury,
Buckinghamshire HP18 0JH
Website: www.waddesdon.org.uk
6m NW of Aylesbury on A41
Open *House: Apr–Oct 11–4 Wed–Sun & BH Mons. Grounds: Mar–Dec 10–5*
A stately home that gloriously decided to disobey the great English rule of display by understatement. Everything about its Frenchified excess (it looks like a French Renaissance château) goes against the English notion about the propriety of

house and garden. Gladstone's daughter 'felt much oppressed with the extreme gorgeousness and luxury' (in those days they were terms of abuse).

It was built in 1874–89 by G.H. Destailleur for the Rothschild family (possessors of a large collection of French art in need of a home), who fully entered into the spirit of the landowning past. The nearby village of Waddesdon is full of buildings which they helped restore or build. A good antidote to all that Palladian restraint.

ADDITIONAL PLACES TO VISIT

Apsley House, The Wellington Museum
☎ 020 7499 5676
Hyde Park Corner, London W1J 7NT
Website: www.vam.ac.uk/Infodome/
Tube Hyde Park Corner
Open *Tues–Sun 11–5 & BH Mons (except May); closed Good Fri*
The Duke of Wellington's magnificent London residence, originally designed by Robert Adam, is filled to bursting with stunning art. There are paintings by Velazquez, Goya, Rubens, Thomas Lawrence, David Wilkie, and many Dutch masters.

Broadlands
☎ 01794 505010
Romsey, Hampshire SO51 9ZD
Email: admin@broadlands.net
Website: www.broadlands.net
S of Romsey on A3090 Romsey bypass
Open *June–Aug 12–5.30*
The beautiful Palladian manor house was once the country residence of Lord Palmerston, the Victorian Prime Minister. It was later owned by Lord Mountbatten, and contains an exhibition documenting his life and work, plenty of art and high-quality furniture. Outside are beautiful landscaped gardens.

Buckingham Palace
☎ Infoline 020 7799 2331 (24-hr);
Pre-bookings 020 7321 2233;
General enquiries 020 7839 1377
Buckingham Palace Rd, London SW1A 1AA
Email: buckinghampalace@
royalcollection.org.uk
Website: www.the-royal-collection.
org.uk
Tube Green Park or St James's Park
Tickets can be bought on the day
at office in Green Park
Open *State Rooms: Aug–Sept 9.30–4.30*
Royal Mews: Mon–Thurs 12–4
The most famous of the official royal residences used by the Queen. Originally built as a town residence by John Sheffield, newly created Duke of Buckingham in 1703, and purchased in 1762 by George III for his bride Charlotte. The building was extended by John Nash for George IV in the 19th century and work continued on it into the 20th century. The State Rooms are opened during August and September, royal commitments allowing. The Royal Mews houses the Queen's coaches and horses.

Centre Point
101 New Oxford St, London W1
Tube Holborn or Tottenham Court Rd
Open *Exterior only*
One of those buildings where exterior viewing only barely seems a handicap, apart from missing out on the views. Built by Richard Seifert in 1963–7, the 398ft(121m)-high 35-storey skyscraper was famously empty for years after completion, a classic white elephant for all its self-consciously swinging self-esteem, though now it is fully occupied.

It rises straight up out of an otherwise dull corner, at the nothing end of Oxford Street, like a great silver tombstone. It was one of the first modern buildings to be totally clad in pre-cast concrete in inverted T-shaped sections, and one of the few best examples in the world of a building bearing its own name in large capital letters above the penthouses. A true landmark missing one thing, a restaurant or bar at the top.

Chartwell* NT
☎ 01732 866368
Nr Westerham, Kent TN16 1PS
Email: kchxxx@smtp.ntrust.org.uk
2m S of Westerham off B2026
Open *House & garden: Apr–June & Sept–Oct Wed–Sun, July–Aug Tues–Sun, open BH Mons, all 11–5*
The beloved private retreat owned by Winston Churchill from 1924 until the end of his life. The interior has been left largely untouched, and is full of mementoes, papers and artefacts that chronicle his life. There is also the garden studio where the great statesman would barricade himself with his paints and his easels. There is a lovely garden, much of it planted by Churchill.

Chiddingstone Castle
☎ 01892 870347
Edenbridge, Kent TN8 7AD
4½m E of Edenbridge off B2027
Open *June–Sept Wed–Fri 2–5.30, Oct–Apr pre-booked groups only*
Website: www.chiddingstone.net
This is a recently restored, grand example of an early 19th-century, 'castle style' mansion. The rooms are full of art and artefacts, including Japanese lacquer and Egyptian antiquities.

Cliveden NT
☎ 01628 605069
Taplow, Buckinghamshire SL6 0JA
Email: tclmrg@smtp.ntrust.org.uk
2m N of Taplow; leave M4 junction 7 on to A4, or M40 junction 4 on to A404 to Marlow
Open *House (part): Apr–Oct Thurs & Sun 3–5.30. Octagon temple (chapel): as house. Estate & garden: mid-Mar–Oct 11–6, Nov–Dec 11–4*
The ultimate 19th-century Victorian mansion was built for the Duke of Sutherland from 1850–1 by Sir Charles Barry, who designed the new Houses of Parliament. It sits on the site of earlier mansions, and was where George III first heard a performance of 'Rule Britannia' while still a prince. Later, in the 1890s, the Astors took possession and Cliveden became a thriving political and literary centre where many of the early 20th-century great luminaries were entertained. In the 1930s it became home to the 'Cliveden Set', presided over by Nancy Astor, the first woman to serve in Parliament. Cliveden also became associated with 'appeasement' in the years before World War II. Although it is now a hotel, three of its rooms, and its grounds, remain open to the public.

Clock Tower and Pool
Stevenage, Hertfordshire
Website: www.stevenage.gov.uk
Town square in centre of Stevenage
Open *Open access*
Nothing quite symbolizes post-war Britain as dramatically as its new towns – and nothing symbolizes them as well as this clock tower. Stevenage was designated a New Town in November 1946 when the word 'New' meant so much, with the war only months over, and people's gaze suddenly looking to the future. In their attempt to rekindle the idealism of the earlier 'garden cities' movement at the turn of the century, architects and ministers did contribute something new and significant. In Stevenage's case, it was the pedestrianized city centre, the first in Britain. Now such a familiar feature, it is hard

to remember a time when this seemed a daring borrowing from the Continent; the model was De Lijnbaan (shopping centre) in Rotterdam.

Crossness Pumping Station
☎ 020 8311 3711
Engine House, Belvedere Rd, Abbey Wood, London SE2
Website: www.tanton.ndirect.co.uk/crossness
A2016 from Woolwich, leave at junction with A2041, then take Belvedere Road to Thames Water; 1m from Abbey Wood railway station
Open *Sun & Tues once a month; visits must be booked in advance*
Built out of yellow brick, in a Romanesque style, this is a wonderful example of Victorian industrial engineering, a masterpiece of cast-iron grandeur, and a reminder that dealing with sewage was the great Victorian contribution to British civilization. There are four beam-engines designed by James Watt and son.

Dickens House Museum
☎ 020 7405 2127
48 Doughty St, London WC1N 2LX
Website: www.dickensmuseum.com
Tube Russell Square or Chancery Lane
Open *Mon–Sat 10–5*
In the spirit of *A Christmas Carol*, the museum is even open at Christmas itself. The great novelist lived here from 1837–9, and wrote *The Pickwick Papers* and *Oliver Twist*. There is a comprehensive exhibition of documents and artefacts relating to his life and career.

Down House EH
☎ 0870 6030145
Orpington, Kent BR6 7JT
Off A21 near Biggin Hill
Open *Apr–Sept Wed–Sun 10–6,*

Oct Wed–Sun 10–5, Nov–23 Dec & Feb–Mar Wed–Sun 10–4; closed 24 Dec–early Feb
This is where Charles Darwin wrote *On the Origin of Species by Means of Natural Selection* in 1859; he lived here for 40 years, until his death in 1882. There are many Darwin relics on display.

Dymchurch Martello Tower EH
☎ 01304 211067
Dymchurch, Kent
Website: www.martello-towers.co.uk
Access from High St only
Open *Phone for times*
The tower has been fully restored, making it the most impressive example of the great drum-shaped fortifications built along the coast as strongholds to counter any Napoleonic invasion. There is a 24lb (10kg) cannon for inspection on the roof.

Foreign and Commonwealth Office
☎ 020 7270 1500
King Charles St, London SW1A 2AH
Website: www.fco.gov.uk
Tube Westminster
Open *Exterior only; occasional open days publicized on website*
After numerous battles with various Prime Ministers, Sir George Gilbert Scott was persuaded to abandon his earlier Gothic Revival plans and replace them with what we see today. This is more of a 16th-century, Italianate Renaissance building, with square towers and inner courtyards. There is a spectacular double staircase, but the building is rarely open to the public.

Harrods
☎ 020 7730 1234
Brompton Rd, Knightsbridge, London SW1X 7XL
Website: www.harrods.com

Highclere Castle *built by Sir Charles Barry in the 1830s.*

Tube Knightsbridge
Open *Mon–Sat 10–7*
Bear in mind that Harrods is an
architectural extravaganza as well as
a department store. The entire front
and dome are covered by a triumph of
Doulton's terracotta. Inside, only the
meat hall retains any real connection
to the building's 1901–5 origins with
its Art Nouveau tile decoration. The
explosion in shopping and, in particular,
the provision of department stores,
created a number of wonderful shops;
Selfridges in Oxford Street, Peter Jones
in Sloane Square and Jenners in
Edinburgh are all top-quality examples.

Highclere Castle and Gardens
☎ 01635 253210
Nr Newbury, Hampshire RG20 9RN
Email: theoffice@highclerecastle.co.uk
Website: www.highclerecastle.co.uk
7m S of Newbury on A34
Open *July–Aug Tues–Sun 11–5 (closes at
3.30 on Sat)*

One of Sir Charles Barry's wonderful
creations, it was built in the 1830s on
an enormous and grandiose scale for
one of Queen Victoria's most lavish hosts,
the 3rd Earl of Carnarvon. There is a
flamboyant cocktail of styles in the
interior, lots of fine works of art and
Napoleonic memorabilia, as well as
relics from the tomb of Tutankhamun.
The surrounding gardens are by
'Capability' Brown.

Hitchin British Schools
☎ 01462 420144
41–42 Queen Street, Hitchin,
Hertfordshire SG4 9TS
Email: brsch@britishschools.freeserve.
co.uk
Open *Feb & Nov 10–4, Apr–Oct Tues
& Sun 2.30–5*
Unique examples of the sort of school-
rooms found in Victorian England, dating
from 1837 to 1905. They include the
only surviving example of a galleried
classroom (1853) and an infants' school.

Hughenden Manor NT

☎ 01494 755573; Infoline 01494 755565
High Wycombe,
Buckinghamshire HP14 4LA
Email: thdrxl@smtp.ntrust.org.uk
1½m N of High Wycombe on W side A4128
Open *Mar Sat–Sun, Apr–Oct Wed–Sun &*
BH Mons, all 1–5. Garden: as house, 12–5
Park & woodland: all year 12–5
The redbrick Gothic-style mansion was
once the home of the Victorian Prime
Minister, Benjamin Disraeli. It contains
many of his books and mementoes, and
is surrounded by beautiful gardens.

Jane Austen's House

☎ 01420 83262
Chawton, Alton, Hampshire GU34 1SD
Email: enquiries@janeausten.demon.
co.uk
Website: www.janeausten.demon.co.uk
At junction of A31 & A32 just S of Alton
Open *Mar–Dec 11–4.30,*
Jan–Feb Sat & Sun 11–4.30
For anyone interested in the life and
works of Jane Austen, this charming two-
storey redbrick house is a real treat. She
revised her early novels and wrote her
final novels here, and the house is full
of items relating to her life and writing.

Keats House

☎ 020 7435 2062
Keats Grove, Hampstead,
London NW3 2RR
Email: keatshouse@corpoflondon.gov.uk
Website: www.keatshouse.org.uk
Tube Hampstead or Belsize Park
Open *May–Oct Tues–Sun 12–5,*
Nov–Apr phone for details or check website
The beautiful Regency house, the home
of the poet John Keats, is where he fell
in love with Fanny Brawne. And he wrote
here at least two of his best poems, the
'Ode to a Nightingale' and 'The Eve of
St Agnes'.

Kensal Green Cemetery *

☎ 020 8969 0152;
Guided tours info 020 8969 1030
Dissenters' Chapel 020 8960 1030
Harrow Rd, London W10 4RA
Tube Kensal Rise
Open *Cemetery: Mon–Fri 9–5 Sat & Sun*
10–5. Dissenters' Chapel: daily
Guided tours Sun pm
London's oldest public cemetery dates
back to 1832, and has a number of
famous graves, including those of some
members of the Royal Family (one of
George III's daughters was buried here).
It also contains the Dissenters' Chapel,
designed in the Greek Revival style by
John Griffith in 1834 (today restored
and in regular use as a visitor centre
and exhibition space).

London Zoo

☎ 020 7722 3333
Outer Circle, Regent's Park,
London NW1 4RY
Website: www.zsl.org/londonzoo
Tube Camden Town
Open *Mar–Oct 10–5.30, Nov–Feb 10–4*
Home to all those animals, and to three
of Britain's most interesting structures.
There is a wonderful aluminium-framed,
geometrically intense tent of netting
which is the aviary designed in 1963
by Lord Snowdon, with Cedric Price
and Frank Newby; Berthold Lubetkin's
penguin enclosure of 1934 has pearly
white walkways and a pool; and there is
Sir Hugh Casson's concrete elephant and
rhino house (1965).

Rhinefield Bridge

☎ New Forest tourist info 02380 282269
New Forest, nr Brockenhurst, Hampshire
On A337, leave M27 junction 13
Not every landmark has to be gargan-
tuan or imposing and not all bridges
have to span gorges or estuaries; some

delight by their modesty and subtlety. One of a number of lovely footbridges in the New Forest, the Rhinefield Bridge is an early example of the Freyssinet system of pre-stressing concrete. The bridge was built by Edwin W.H.Gifford using the French technique and was the first pre-stressed concrete bridge of its type in England.

Royal Courts of Justice (Law Courts)
☎ 020 7947 6000
The Strand, London WC1 2LL
Tube Chancery Lane or Temple
Open *Mon–Fri 9–5*
There are few finer examples of Victorian Gothic than the Law Courts on the Strand, built from 1868–82, just when the style was falling out of vogue. The architect George Edmund Street died before being able to complete his plans, and his son took over. The appeal is in the detail and the lack of bombast.

Royal Geographical Society
☎ 020 7591 3000
1 Kensington Gore, London SW7 2AR
Website: www.rgs.org
Tube High St Kensington
Open *Members only;*
some events open to general public;
details on website
Originally a private society, it was founded in 1830 and dedicated to the exploration, discovery and dissemination of geographical knowledge. The house includes a library and map room, open to the public, with tens of thousands of maps, as well as mementoes of famous explorers.

Royal Holloway College (University of London)
☎ 01784 443004
Nr Egham, Surrey TW20 0EX
Website: www.rhul.ac.uk
Off A30 nr Egham
Open *Tours by arrangement;*
for open days & public events phone
or try website
Possibly the most remarkable university building anywhere in the country. It is a French château extravaganza in red brick and white stone, built as London University's first college for women, thanks to a hefty donation from a drugs millionaire (named Holloway). The architect was W.H. Crossland and it was built in 1879–87.

Royal Society of Arts
☎ 020 7930 5115
8 John Adam Street, London WC2N 6EZ
Website: www.rsa.org.uk
Tube Embankment or Charing Cross
Open *First Sun of the month 10–1;*
lectures open to public but pre-book
Designed by Robert Adam in the early 1770s, the building hosts a spectacular 360-degree wall painting in the Lecture Hall, James Barry's mad but brilliant *The Progress of Human Knowledge* which traces the evolution of human wisdom from ancient to contemporary times. It is full of cameo portraits and is a stunning window on the mind of the British Romantic artist.

Saint Hill Manor
☎ 01342 326711
Saint Hill Rd, East Grinstead, W Sussex RH19 4JY
2m SW of East Grinstead, off A22
Open *2–5*
Gibbs Crawford designed the mansion, and built it with lovely pale sandstone in 1792. It was later owned and fully restored by L. Ron Hubbard, the man who invented Scientology. There is a library full of his works. There are 59 acres of landscaped gardens and woodlands to enjoy.

Shaw's Corner NT

☎ 01438 820307

Ayot St Lawrence, nr Welwyn,
Hertfordshire AL6 9BX
Website: www.nationaltrust.org.uk/
regions/thameschilterns
*2m NE of Wheathamstead,
leave A1 junction 4 or M1 junction 10*
Open *Apr–Oct Wed–Sun 1–5;
closed Good Fri but open BH Mons*
The Edwardian villa home of George
Bernard Shaw, until his death in 1950,
is full of relics from his life and career.
It is very much as when he lived and
worked here.

Stratfield Saye House

☎ 01256 882882

Nr Basingstoke, Hampshire RG7 2BZ
Email: info@stratfield-saye.co.uk
Website: www.stratfield-saye.co.uk
*1½m W of A33,
between Reading & Basingstoke*
Open *June–Aug Wed–Sun 11.30–5,
Sept Mon–Fri pre-booked groups only*
Just as Blenheim was given to the Duke
of Marlborough as a reward for his great
Continental victory, so this was donated
to the Duke of Wellington by a grateful
nation for his victory at Waterloo. There
is an embroidered Tricolour in the hall,
given to him after his entry into Paris in
1815. The Duke left his mark by covering
the wallpaper in a number of rooms
with prints, and by introducing central
heating, some of which is still in use.
The library even contains a lock of
Wellington's horse's hair. There is an
exhibition in the stable block dedicated
to Wellington's life.

Taplow Court

☎ 01628 591209

Taplow, Buckinghamshire SL6 0ER
*1m from Burnham,
6m from M40 junction 2*
Open *Spring & summer Sun & BHs;
phone for details*
Ornate house remodelled in the middle
of the 19th century with exhibitions
and lovely grounds. It is now a Buddhist
cultural centre.

Trellick Tower

5 Golborne Rd, London W10
Tube Westbourne Park
Open *Exterior only*
It is the second of London's great
once-reviled-now-revered tower block
skyscrapers. When built, in 1973, these
were the tallest flats in London. The
public can only see the outside but the
flats inside are stunning. Like Centre
Point, it is a building potent enough to
shape the surrounding cityscape. It is the
masterpiece of Ernö Goldfinger's career
with the similar, but stumpier, Balfron
tower block he designed in Blackwall,
East London.

Walmer Castle EH

☎ 01304 364288

Walmer, Deal, Kent CT14 7IJ
*On coast S of Walmer, on A258;
leave M20 junction 13 or M2 to Deal*
Open *Apr–Sept 10–6, Oct 10–5,
Nov–Dec & Mar Wed–Sun 10–4,
Jan–Feb Sat & Sun 10–4*
This was once a Tudor fort but it was
converted into a stately home. Originally
built for Henry VIII, and suffering damage
during the Civil War, it finally became
the official residence of the Lord Warden
of the Cinque Ports in the 18th century.
(Holders of this office have included
the Duke of Wellington and Winston
Churchill). Even Wellington's boots are
on display. The gardens are beautiful.

Westminster Cathedral

☎ 020 7798 9055

Victoria St, London SW1P 1QW

Website: www.westminstercathedral.
org.uk
Tube Victoria
Open *Mon–Fri 7–7 Sat & Sun 8–7*
The spectacular Byzantine red and
white striped building in the heart
of London's Victoria is Westminster's
Roman Catholic Cathedral. Designed
by J.F. Bentley and opened in 1903,
it is gaudy and magnificent.

2 Willow Road NT

☎ 020 7435 6166
Hampstead, London NW3 1TH
Website: www.nationaltrust.org.uk/
regions/thameschilterns
Tube Hampstead or Belsize Park
Open *Mar Sat 12–5, Apr–Oct Thurs–Sat
(closed Good Fri), entry by guided tours
every 45 mins 12–5, Nov–Dec Sat 12–5*
The former home of the architect Ernö
Goldfinger (most famous for the 1970s
Trellick Tower in London), designed and
built by him in 1939. This is a three-storey
masterpiece of modern domestic design
filled with his furniture, and paintings.

Eastern MAP 3

298 Harlaxton Manor

☎ 01476 403000
Harlaxton, nr Grantham,
Lincolnshire NG32 1AG
Website: www.ueharlax.ac.uk
3m SW of Grantham off A1 or A607
Open *Groups by appointment only*
Designed by Anthony Salvin in the
1830s and modelled on a Jacobean house,
Harlaxton was intended to rival nearby
Belvoir Castle. Moderation went straight
out the window: it is a volcanic eruption
of bays, oriels, turrets, curved gables,
pierced balustrades, chimneys and
cupolas. Luckily, Salvin was a genius and
pulled it off with aplomb. Inside (mostly
by William Burn from 1838 on) is a
similar story culminating in the utterly
magnificent cedar staircase. This masterpiece of Baroque illusion ascends three
storeys up into a painted sky, adorned at
the top by the figure of Father Time
looking down from a precarious ledge.
Unique in Britain it is safe to say.

The grandiose façade of **Harlaxton Manor** *seen from the mile-long drive.*

American Cemetery
☎ 01954 210350
Madingley, Cambridge CB3 7PH
A1303, 3m W of Cambridge city centre
Open *Mid-Apr–Sept 8–6, Oct–mid-Apr 8–5*
Stunning and surprisingly exuberant, this war cemetery and memorial is dedicated to the American service men and women based in Britain who died in Europe during the Second World War. 3811 are buried here and a further 5127 are remembered who have no grave. The cemetery is sited here because the majority of American bomber bases during the war were in the eastern counties. The memorial has bright and dynamic ceiling murals, interweaving flights of bombers and angels, culminating in a memorial altar. The dead are commemorated either by marble crosses and Stars of David, or by names carved into a memorial wall.

Bridge Cottage NT
☎ 01206 298260
Flatford, East Bergholt, nr Colchester, Suffolk CO7 6OL
1m S of East Bergholt off B1070
Open *Mar–Apr & Oct Wed–Sun 11–5.30, May–Sept daily 10–5.30, Nov–Dec Wed–Sun 11–3.30, Jan–Feb Sat & Sun 11–3.30*
After visiting Flatford Mill, the subject of Constable's famous painting *The Haywain* and once owned by the artist's father, you can reach this cottage by a short walk upstream. There is an exhibition of several paintings by the great landscape artist.

Newbury Park Bus Shelter
Eastern Avenue, Ilford, Essex
In forecourt of Newbury Park tube station
The railways were not the only form of transport to spawn their own breed of architecture; so too did buses. Newbury Park Bus Shelter, designed by Oliver Hill, is a wonderful blend of brute post-war austerity and stark geometry (in this case a long barrel-shaped garage, glorying in its simplicity and lack of ornamentation). It won a Festival of Britain Merit Award in 1951, and you can see why.

Sir Alfred Munnings Art Museum
☎ 01206 322127
Castle House, Dedham, nr Colchester, Essex CO7 6AZ
Off A12, on B1029 to Dedham
Open *Easter Sun–1st Sun in Oct Sun Wed & BH Mons, Aug Thurs & also Sat, all 2–5*
An Edwardian house with attractive garden now serves as a museum to the life and work of Sir Alfred Munnings, the equestrian painter and one-time President of the Royal Academy. He was famous for drunkenly and blimpishly abusing modern art in general, and Picasso in particular, in a speech given to the Royal Academy. His works are absolutely unfashionable – though undeniably popular – so make up your own mind. His old studio is also open for inspection at the bottom of the garden.

Central MAP 4

299 Coventry Cathedral
☎ 02476 227597
Priory Row, Coventry, Warwickshire CVI 5ES
Email: information@coventrycathedral.org
Website: www.coventrycathedral.org
In town centre
Open *9.30–4.30, services permitting*
Sir Basil Spence's spectacular cathedral was built on the site and retains elements of the medieval Gothic cathedral that was destroyed by German bombs on 14 November 1940. Work began in 1954, finishing in 1962. Its great power derives from being uncompromisingly of the

moment – a confident, modern cathedral. The works of art, inside and out, are powerful evidence that even a secular age can produce religious sublimity. Note Sir Jacob Epstein's bronze sculpture of St Michael (the patron saint of the cathedral), Graham Sutherland's tapestry of Christ in Glory, the largest tapestry woven in one piece in the world; and the baptistry window, containing 200 panels designed by John Piper and made by Patrick Reyntiens.

300 Iron Bridge EH

☎ 01952 432166
Ironbridge, Shropshire TF8 7AW
Email: info@ironbridge.co.uk
Website: www.ironbridge.org.uk
5m S of Telford, off A4169
Open *Bridge: open access*
Museums: 10–5 (some closed Nov–mid-Feb)
Ironbridge Gorge has the first large iron bridge ever built in the world. It was cast in Coalbrookdale by the local ironmaster, Abraham Darby, and erected over the River Severn from 1777–9. It is not only a powerful icon of the early industrial age, but a work of art.

It has a single soaring arch with a 100ft (30m) span, rising 45ft (14m) above the water. Because the original builders had little idea what iron's structural properties would be, the bridge has no rivets or bolts. Instead it was constructed as though the iron were timber, fitted together with dovetail and shoulder joints. Nearby is the Blists Hill Museum, with a pair of blast furnaces known as the Bedlam furnaces. The museum offers a wonderful display covering the four main industries associated with the area, iron, coal, pottery and transport. Other museums include the Coalport China Museum, the Jackfield Tile Museum, the Museum of Iron and Darby Furnace and the Museum of the Gorge.

The graceful single span arch of the **Iron Bridge** *over the River Severn.*

301 Jodrell Bank Science Centre, Lovell Telescope

☎ 01477 571339
Jodrell Bank, nr Macclesfield,
Cheshire SK11 9DL
Email: visitorcentre@jb.man.ac.uk
Website: www.jb.man.ac.uk
5m W from Macclesfield on A537, M6 junction 18, 3m SW on A535
Open *Visitor centre: mid-Mar–Sept 10.30–5.30, Oct–mid-Mar Tues–Sun 11–4.30; closed early Jan*

One of the precursors to what has become a key late 20th-century structure is the radio telescope. Jodrell Bank's 250ft (76m) parabolic dish, based on wartime radar technology, was designed by Professor Sir Bernard Lovell and Charles Husband in the mid-1950s, and there can be few more beautiful structures anywhere in the country.

It can be tilted and moved on a circular track to be aligned with any part of the sky. The precision involved in casting the dish – it has to be close to perfect in order to stand any chance of picking up tiny radio frequencies – was achieved by welding 7100 panels together, none thicker than a couple of millimetres. It remains the third largest such telescope in the world, after Effelsberg in Germany and Green Bank in West Virginia. A new, and even more precise, dish surface is currently being developed.

ADDITIONAL PLACES TO VISIT

Buxton Opera House

☎ 01298 72050
Water St, Buxton, Derbyshire SK17 6XN
Email: admin@buxton-opera.co.uk
Website: www.buxton-opera.co.uk
Open *Some tours Sat am; performances all year*

The centrepiece to this lovely Derbyshire spa town is its opera house built in 1903. Buxton contains a number of great Victorian buildings which all spas demanded, geared for genteel pleasures and remarkable for their cast iron work.

Hidcote Manor Garden NT

☎ 01386 438333;
Infoline 01684 855370
Hidcote Bartrim, nr Chipping Campden, Gloucestershire GL55 6LR
Email: hidcote_manor@smtp.ntrust.org.uk
Website: www.ntrustsevern.org.uk
4m NE of Chipping Campden, 1m E of B4632 off B4081
Open *Apr–May Aug–Oct Sat–Wed, June–July daily except Fri, all 10.30–6.30 (closes at 5.30 or dusk if earlier in Oct)*

This Cotswold garden has regularly been dubbed the most beautiful 20th-century garden in England. In 1907 an American officer, Major Lawrence Johnston, decided to transform what had been little more than a wilderness; the result is a masterpiece which helped set the trend for a sequence of compartmentalized 'rooms'.

Kelmscott Manor

☎ 01367 252486
Kelmscott, nr Lechlade, Gloucestershire G17 3HJ
Email: admin@kelmscottmanor.co.uk
Website: www.kelmscottmanor.co.uk
2m E of Lechlade off A417
Open *Apr–June Wed 11–1 2–5 & 3rd Sat of month 2–5, July–Aug 1st & 3rd Sat 2–5, Sept Wed 11–1 2–5 & 3rd Sat 2–5*

William Morris, the poet, craftsman, forefather of the Arts and Crafts movement and socialist, turned this 16th-century manor into his home from 1871 until his death in 1896. The house contains many examples of his work and those of his close associates.

St Giles Church*

☎ 01538 753130
Charles St, Cheadle,
Staffordshire ST10 1ED
Open *8.30–4.30 (except when services)*
Designs were begun in 1840 for a church in Cheadle, commissioned and paid for by the 16th Earl of Shrewsbury who lived in nearby Alton Towers. Completed in 1846, this was Pugin's most expensive and most elaborate project, one of the few churches with sufficient funds behind it to allow the architect to give full rein to his architectural passions. The result is a building whose interior is bathed in colourful excess. The patterns adorning the walls, piers and roofs are all beautifully stencilled (though it is reported the Earl liked the ceilings more than the architect ever did). The tower and the spire are regarded as Pugin's finest, with delicate canopy work embellishing the spire's base.

St Michael and All Angels Church

☎ 01902 751622 (Church Cottage)
Church Rd, Tettenhall,
Wolverhampton WV6 9AJ
Off A41 west of town centre
Open *Mon–Fri 10–12*
(access from Church Cottage)
Old churches remain vulnerable all through their lives, and making it to living memory is good but not good enough. This medieval church had survived but was badly ravaged by fire in 1950. The result, though, was a fascinating attempt to rekindle the spirit of a traditional church but in the Arts and Crafts 20th-century style. Particularly fine is the great timbered roof (1950), a wonderful echo of the 15th century.

Walcot Hall

☎ 01568 610693
Lydbury North, Bishop's Castle,
Shropshire 5Y7 8AZ
Email: enquiries@walcothall.com
Website: www.walcothall.com
4m SE of Bishop's Castle on B4385
Open *By appointment only*
This Georgian mansion was bought and added to by Robert Clive, or Clive of India as he became known. He is the man who, as an East India Company clerk and soldier, helped lay the foundations for the British in India, turning them from traders to conquerors.

Wales MAP 5

302 Pontcysyllte Aqueduct

Nr Llangollen, Denbighshire
4m E of Llangollen off A5
The masterpiece of Britain's great canal system carried its barges over 120ft (36.5m) above the River Dee. Even more radical was Thomas Telford's design of an iron trough to carry the water and the water-borne traffic. The trough is over 1000ft (304m) long, and at its highest is 121ft (37m) above the water below. The base of the trough is a series of 19 cast-iron arches, each 53ft (16m) wide and supported on pillars of stone. It was built from 1795–1805, and is still as impressive as the day it was opened. It is visible from the A5, but a quick walk down the towpath gives you the chance to stand and admire.

303 Tintern Abbey CADW

☎ 01291 689251
Tintern, nr Chepstow,
Monmouthshire NP6 6SE
5m N of Chepstow on A466,
Open *Apr–May & Oct 9.30–5,*
June–Sept 9.30–6, Nov–Mar 9.30–4
(opens 11 on Sun)
Tintern Abbey became the first and most famous example of the Romantic Movement's love-affair with ancient ruins. The inspiration for one of the most

The ruins of **Tintern Abbey** *on the banks of the River Wye.*

moving poems ever about landscape and memory, by William Wordsworth, it is set in a beautiful swathe of wooded valley, and is Wales' best-preserved ruined abbey. Unusually, it stands almost to roof level. Tintern was founded in 1131 by the Cistercians, though the ruins here by the River Wye date mainly from the 13th century. Needless to say, it was 'dissolved' in the mid-16th century. To the north of the cloister are the remains of the 'warming house', so-called because it was the only room, apart from the kitchen, allowed to keep a fire.

ADDITIONAL PLACES TO VISIT

Blaenavon Ironworks CADW
☎ 01495 792615; Torfaen Co Borough Council 01633 648082 (winter only)
North St, Blaenavon, Torfaen NP4 9RQ
Email: blaenavon-tic@tsww.org.uk
6m N of Pontypool, on W edge of town

Open *Apr–Oct 9.30–4.30*
Wales' best-preserved ironworks had furnaces and nearby homes for 350 workers at the height of its activities, the nucleus of the present town. The surviving ironworks occupy three sides of a square, built to follow the contours of the land. Two of the casting houses still stand but work ceased in the 1860s.

Bodelwyddan Castle
☎ 01745 584060
Bodelwyddan, Denbighshire LL18 5YA
2m W of St Asaph off A55
Open *July–Aug daily 10–5,
Oct–Apr Tues–Thurs Sat & Sun 10–3.30;
closed Dec*
The Victorian mansion set in acres of rolling parkland houses an impressive exhibition of paintings and artefacts, many on loan from the Victoria & Albert Museum and the National Portrait Gallery in London.

Castell Coch CADW

☎ 029 2081 0101
Tongwynlais, Cardiff CF1 1PC
5m NW of Cardiff off A470
Open *Apr–May & Oct 9.30–5,*
June–Sept 9.30–6, Nov–Mar 9.30–4 (opens
11 on Sun); closed Jan–mid-Feb
There was nothing here but the total
ruin of a 13th-century castle, when the
Marquis of Bute, owner of Cardiff's
docklands, commissioned William
Burges to restore it in 1875. The result
is a persuasive attempt at re-creating
what a medieval castle might have
looked like, although the many appealing
eccentricities within are entirely of the
19th century.

Penrhyn Castle NT

☎ 01248 353084
Bangor, Gwynedd LL57 4HN
1m E of Bangor, at Llandygai on A5122
Open *House: Apr–Oct daily except Tues*
12–5 (opens at 11 in July–Aug)
Garden: as house but opens 1 hour earlier
You would expect to find some of the
world's finest medieval castles in Wales,
so it comes as no surprise to find that
some of the best 19th-century fantasy-
castles are there too. It was built by
Thomas Hopper for the Penrhyn family,
who had made their fortune out of the
local slate quarry and Jamaican sugar.
No expense was spared in providing the
house with an interior to match its gargantuan exterior. There are 40 acres of
parkland, and a museum of locomotives.

Portmeirion Village

☎ 01766 770228
Portmeirion, Gwynedd LL48 6ET
Email: enquiries@portmeirion-village.com
Website: www.portmeirion.wales.com
3m E of Porthmadog on A487
Open *9.30–5.30*
Usually follies are single buildings,
but in Portmeirion's case, it is a whole
hamlet. It was the brainchild of Welsh
architect Clough Williams-Ellis who
conceived the plan of an outdoor architectural museum and holiday coastal
village, combined in a kind of living
exhibition (inspired by the Italian
village of Portofino). Begun in 1926
and completed in the 1930s, it is a mix
of various buildings and monuments
from different moments in history with,
for example, a barbican gatehouse,
campanile, lighthouse and cloisters.
There are ornate and complex gardens
woven through Portmeirion with sculptures, murals and ironwork, as well as
acres of trees, rhododendrons, palms,
cypresses, eucalyptus and magnolias.

Severn Bridge

Linking England & Wales
over the River Severn
Approach via M4 then M48 to Chepstow;
for new Severn bridge stay on M4
This landmark bridge, built in 1961–6
in a bid to help regenerate South Wales,
was based on technology developed
and first used by the Forth Road Bridge.
It incorporates one key refinement –
the deck on which the road is based is
much thinner, being only 9ft (3m) deep
against the 24ft (8m) of the Forth Bridge.
This was to minimize the bane of all
suspension bridges, the impact of side
winds. The result is a structure even
more elegant than the Forth's. Despite
some strengthening work in the late
1980s, the bridge remains a powerful
testimony to a brilliant technological
innovation. The volume of traffic was
such that a second Severn crossing,
sited downsteam from the suspension
bridge, has now been built. It is 3 miles
long and has as its main span a cable-
stayed bridge approached by viaducts
of varying heights.

North-west MAP 6

304 Dove Cottage and Wordsworth Museum*

☎ 01539 435544
Grasmere, Cumbria LA22 9SH
Email: enquiries@wordsworth.org.uk
Website: www.wordsworth.org.uk
Immediately S of Grasmere village on A591
Open *9.30–5.30*

The poet William Wordsworth lived here from 1799–1808. The cottage has been preserved as a museum with both permanent and temporary exhibitions exploring his life and work, and those of the Romantic poets. There are lovely gardens to explore as well.

305 Liverpool's Cathedrals

Liverpool Cathedral (Anglican)

☎ 0151 709 6271
St James' Mount, Liverpool L17 AZ
Website: www.merseyworld.com/cathedral
Open *8–6*

Liverpool Metropolitan (Catholic)

☎ 0151 709 9222
Mount Pleasant, Liverpool L35 TQ
Website: www.merseyworld.com/metcath
Open *May–Oct 9–6, Nov–Apr 9–5*

Liverpool boasts two 20th-century cathedrals, the gargantuan red sandstone Anglican cathedral and the even more contemporary Roman Catholic one. The former is the second largest in the world, topped only by St Peter's in Rome. At its heart is the High Altar, Sir Giles Gilbert Scott's masterpiece (his grandfather, Sir George Gilbert Scott, was the architect of the Albert Memorial and the St Pancras Hotel). The construction was plagued by financial problems and endless delays, and Scott was dead long before it was finished.

The Roman Catholic cathedral was consecrated in May 1967. There had been two previous attempts to build one on this hilltop site, but finally a design by Sir Frederick Gibberd was chosen after earlier ones by Sir Edwin Lutyens and, before him, Pugin, had failed to materialize. Designed completely in the round, it has no conventional east or west end. Its dominant feature is the circular central lantern with stained glass by John Piper and Patrick Reyntiens.

306 Manchester Town Hall*

☎ 0161 234 5000;
Manchester tourist info 0161 234 3157
Albert Square, Manchester,
Lancashire M60 2LA
Open *Mon–Fri 9–5; tours Sat*

This stunning piece of Gothic Revival architecture, designed by Alfred Waterhouse, was built from 1868–77. It is proof that the great municipal buildings of the Victorian era won the same sort of architectural detail previously found mainly in cathedrals – in this case, the tall clock-tower with its pinnacles and flying buttresses supporting a spire. Inside are Ford Madox Brown's 12 murals celebrating the history of Manchester.

It is a brilliant use of a triangular site, and an impressive monument to Manchester's Victorian credentials as the seedbed of Liberal and Nonconformist thinking.

307 Quarry Bank Mill* NT

☎ 01625 527468
Wilmslow, Cheshire SK9 4LA
Email: msyrec@smtp.ntrust.org.uk
Website: www.quarrybankmill.org.uk
1½m N of Wilmslow off B5166,
2½m from M56 junction 5,
10m S of Manchester

The Gothic Revival clock-tower and spire of **Manchester Town Hall**.

Open *Mill: Apr–Sept 10.30–5.30, Oct –Mar 10.30–5 (closed Mon).*
Park: daily during daylight hours
Situated in Styal Country Park in a beautiful corner of the River Bollin valley is a fully working cotton mill from the late 18th century. Built by the industrialist Samuel Greg, it has been restored to provide a living model of what conditions in a cotton mill would have been like during the early years of the Industrial Revolution. There is also an Apprentice House, once home to the impoverished young children later indentured to the mill, and still looking pretty grim. At the heart of the complex is a 50-tonne waterwheel which more than anything symbolizes the trans-formation of textile manufacture from a rural cottage activity into an industrial behemoth. The Steam Power Gallery contains an 1830 beam engine which steams daily. There are numerous displays and audio-visual exhibits that catalogue the changes which would have taken place here over the fifty years or so that saw the textile industry at its peak.

308 Runcorn Bridge
Runcorn Gap, Cheshire
A533 linking Runcorn & Widnes over River Mersey
When built it was the largest steel-arch bridge anywhere in Europe, and the third largest in the world. It has a main span of 1082ft (330m) and, with its end cantilevers, a total length of 1626ft (496m). It is built to a design that characterized a number of the great bridges (eg Sydney Harbour), built in the years between the wars. Unlike them it has no stone towers to help take the burden – its span of the river is entirely down to metal and engineering. It is the main route to the south from Liverpool.

Dunham Massey NT
☎ 0161 941 1025
Dunham Massey, Altrincham,
Cheshire WA14 4SJ
Email: mdmjxf@smtp.ntrust.org.uk
3m SW of Altrincham off A56
Open *House: Apr–Oct Sat–Wed 12–5, Sun & BH Mons 11–5, Oct 12–4*
Garden: Apr–Oct 11–5.30
Park: Apr–Oct 8–7.30, Nov–Mar 8–5
Belonging to the early part of the Georgian period, Dunham Massey was extensively reworked in the early years of the 20th century. This helped transform it into one of Britain's most sumptuous Edwardian interiors, housing excep-tional collections of 18th-century walnut furniture, paintings and Huguenot silver, and extensive servants' quarters. The gardens contain a Victorian bark-house and well-house, as well as a bewildering array of plants, and an ancient deer park.

Gawthorpe Hall NT
☎ 01282 771004
Padiham, nr Burnley,
Lancashire BB12 8UA
Email: rpmgaw@smtp.ntrust.org.uk
On A671, E outskirts of Padiham
Open *House: Apr–Oct 1–5; closed Mon & Fri but open Good Fri & BH Mons*
Garden: all year daily 10–6
Another restoration job by 'Mr Houses of Parliament', Sir Charles Barry, on a largely Elizabethan house, probably designed by Robert Smythson. Thanks to Barry, the house has sumptuous Edwardian interiors; it also hosts paintings on loan from the National Portrait Gallery.

Meols Hall
☎ 01704 228326
Botanic Road, Churchtown, Southport,
Merseyside PR9 7LZ

Email: events@meolshall.freeserve.co.uk
Website: www.meolshall.freeserve.co.uk
3m NE of Southport
Open *Mid-Aug–mid-Sept 2–5;*
all other times by appointment
A fascinating experiment – a Palladian
mansion built in post-war Britain. Using
stonework saved from a wing demolished
in a nearby 18th-century house, Roger
Fleetwood Hesketh set out to transform
what had been a family second home
since the Middle Ages. The result is a
pretty convincing facsimile of expensive
18th-century fashion – the super-civilized,
elegant country house

Port Sunlight Heritage Centre

☎ 0151 644 6466
95 Greendale Road, Port Sunlight,
Wirral CH62 4XE
Website: www.portsunlightvillage.com
On B5137 to Bebington;
follow signs from M53, M56 or A41
Open *Apr–Oct daily 10–4, Nov–Mar*
Mon–Fri 10–4 Sat & Sun 11–4
Port Sunlight is another fine example of
the enlightened industrial community,
built to house the families of workers in
the nearby Lever soap factory. The result
is this attractive 19th-century garden
village on the Wirral. The centre tells
the story of the factory, the workers
and the village.

Wordsworth House NT

☎ 01900 824805
Main Street, Cockermouth,
Cumbria CA13 9RX
Email: rwordh@smtp.ntrust.org.uk
Open *Apr–Oct Mon–Fri 10.30–4.30;*
open BH Sats & all Sats June–Aug
This Georgian house in the middle of
Cockermouth is where the poet William
Wordsworth was born in 1770 and lived
as a child. There is an exhibition of his
personal effects.

North-east MAP 7

309 Park Hill

South St, Talbot St & Duke St,
Sheffield, S Yorkshire
SE from Sheffield centre on A616
In the post-war years, one of the great
champions of social housing was Lewis
Womersley, city architect in Sheffield
from 1953–64. Park Hill remains one of
his greatest monuments. It is spectacularly located on the steep hills that
characterize Sheffield, comprising
blocks of flats ranging from 4–13 storeys.
When it was first completed, it attracted
a storm of media attention. A brave new
world? Mass housing has now become
almost totally synonymous with social
problems as awful as those it was
supposed to solve, and Park Hill has
its share (not enough lifts, concrete
degradation, windswept open spaces),
but for all that it works pretty well.

310 Saltaire Model Village

☎ 01274 774993
Saltaire, nr Shipley, W Yorkshire BD18 3LA
Between Bradford & Keighley, off A650;
tourist centre in Victoria Road
Open *Mill: 10–6. Church: Sun 12–4*
Guided walks from tourist centre Sat 11 &
Sun 2; opening & walks by arrangement
at other times
Titus Salt was one of a number of
Victorian industrialists and men of
business pioneering the idea of the
estate village – a community of homes
for his workers built round sound morals
and fine architecture. By 1854 there
were 150 houses, and 20 years later the
number had more than quadrupled.
These are well-built stone terraces with
schools, a Congregationalist church,
library, reading rooms, almshouses, a
park and a boathouse, but no pubs. The
mills for the town to serve were built in

1851 by two Bradford architects, and have a degree of ornamentation (including two Italian style turrets). Today the 1853 mill is the site of a display of works by the locally-born artist, David Hockney. This pioneering village, built at a time when Utopia was not yet a discredited concept, was in startling contrast to the terrible conditions experienced by most workers in post-Industrial Revolution Britain.

311 York Railway Station
Station Rd, York YO21 1AY
Just outside city walls to W

The main arcade over the platforms is a particularly fine example of Victorian engineering originally designed by Thomas Prosser and opened in 1877. The long curving structure, over 800ft (244m) long of four arched, parallel roofs on iron Corinthian columns, with a span of over 80ft (24m) and a height of 48ft (15m), is still most people's idea of what an ideal station should look like (shame that the exterior is so anonymous). However, Newcastle Station entrance is more impressive and Temple Meads in Bristol is more self-consciously designed to echo a cathedral.

The curved iron train shed roof at **York Railway Station**.

Bowes Museum
☎ 01833 690606
Barnard Castle, Co Durham DL12 8NP
Email: info@bowesmuseum.org.uk
Website: www.bowesmuseum.org.uk
E of Market Place in Barnard Castle
Open *11–5*
This is a magnificent French château-style creation containing the country's largest collection of French paintings. Built by J.A. Pellechet in self-conscious Empire style with a fabulous marble hall, it was opened in 1892. Nobody matched this style of house anywhere in the country.

Brontë Parsonage Museum
☎ 01535 642323
Church St, Hawarth, Keighley,
W Yorkshire BD22 8DR
Email: info@bronte.org.uk
Website: www.bronte.org.uk
8m W of Bradford, 3m S of Keighley
Open *Apr–Sept 10–5.30,
Oct–Dec Mar 11–5; closed Jan–Feb*
The Georgian parsonage is now a museum dedicated to the life and works of the three Brontë sisters, who lived here for most of their lives.

High Level Bridge
Newcastle upon Tyne
Carries B1307 & railway linking Newcastle & Gateshead; just to W of Swing Bridge & Tyne road bridge
One of seven bridges spanning Newcastle's River Tyne, this, the oldest, was built by Robert Stephenson in 1849. It is 150ft (45m) high and is built of cast-iron girders on masonry piers carrying road and rail traffic on separate levels. Just upstream is the newest – the Millennium Bridge – a foot and cycleway which opened in Autumn 2001.

St Mary's Church, Studley Royal
EH & NT
☎ 01765 608888
Nr Ripon, N Yorkshire HG4 3DY
*In grounds of Studley Royal Estate,
2½m W of Ripon off B6265*
Open *Apr–Sept 1–5*
Surely one of the most impressive Victorian churches with a highly decorated interior in a rainbow of coloured marble, stained glass, gilding and figurative statues.

Scargill Chapel
☎ 01756 760234 (Scargill House)
Kettlewell, N Yorkshire BD23 5HU
*Off B6180 SE of Kettlewell,
6m N of Skipton*
Open *Daily as part of Scargill House Conference Centre*
A great challenge for modern architects is how to revisit the past, and create modern equivalents to buildings that we venerate because of their indissoluble link to history. Put another way, how do you build a chapel? One beautiful example is Scargill Chapel which was built in the early 60s to blend into the surroundings, and is reminiscent of the great tithe barns of the Middle Ages.

Scotland MAP 8
312 Calton Hill, Edinburgh
☎ 0131 556 2716 (Nelson's Monument)
NE of city centre; Waterloo Place leads from Princes St to Calton Hill
Open *Nelson's Monument: Apr–Sept Mon 1–6 Tues–Sat 10–6, Oct–Mar 10–3*
Edinburgh has an embarrassment of stunning hillside views – Castle Rock, Arthur's Seat and this, the site of more postcard photographs than any, Calton Hill. Here is Nelson's Monument built to celebrate the Battle of Trafalgar, unveiled in 1816. The view from the

top is spectacular. And just behind is the unfinished National Monument (1822), begun by William Playfair to plans by the English architect Charles Cockerell for a temple modelled on the Parthenon. They ran out of money before being able to complete it – though you might argue it offers the skyline a better silhouette for its columns. The City Observatory was also built by Playfair for his uncle John Playfair, the astronomer and mathematician.

313 Forth Railway Bridge

South Queensferry, W Lothian
Forth Road Bridge runs parallel (A90); approach via M90 & M8; good views from shore
The road bridge is all 1960s suspension, sweeping and minimal, while the rail bridge is brute steel with its three great cantilevered arches. And the rail bridge takes the crown. It is red, magnificent, solid and graceful — one of those bridges

you become desperate for a chance to cross. It is even worth a quick train trip north out of Edinburgh to do this.

The bridge was a result of plans by Sir John Fowler and Sir Benjamin Baker, hastily drawn up to replace the original ones which were too close to the design used in the Tay Bridge which had so disastrously collapsed. Work began in 1882 on the two 1700ft (518m) main spans, which for many years remained a world record. It rises 360ft (109m) high above the water, to virtually the same height as St Paul's Cathedral, and was opened in March 1890. It had to be high enough to allow the passage of Navy ships in and out of the yards at Rosyth.

To see a sequence of Victorian photographs chronicling the key stages of its construction is to be astonished at the chutzpah, and the scale of Victorian engineering. And yes, it does need continual rust-proofing, done in an endless Sisyphean cycle.

The tangled steel girders of the **Forth Railway Bridge** at night.

Hill House, *the best example of Charles Rennie Mackintosh's domestic architecture.*

314 Glasgow School of Art
☎ 0141 353 4526
167 Renfrew St, Glasgow G3 6RQ
N of Sauchiehall St, NW of city centre
Open *Guided tours only, pre-booking
advisable: Mon–Fri 11 & 2, Sat 10.30 &
11.30, Sun (July–Aug only) 10.30 & 11.30*
As so often was the case in Victorian
architecture, this building was the
winning entry in a competition to
choose a replacement for an earlier
school of art. Charles Rennie Mackintosh,
then 28, the future champion of Art
Nouveau, was working for a Glasgow
firm and his plan won. Building began
in 1897. The practicality of the design
(all those large windows to let light
flood in) is beautifully lifted by his distinctive flowery decorations. He also
designed much of the building's
interior, fabrics and furniture, such as
the distinctively tall chair backs. The
library is sensational, with oak panelling
and 3-storey-high windows. If you're
hungry for more Mackintosh, then the
Willow Tearoom at 217 Sauchiehall Street
(0141 332 0521) has been restored and
is one of Glasgow's most popular
and stylish cafés.

315 Hill House NTS
☎ 01436 673900
Upper Colquhoun St, Helensburgh,
Argyll G84 9AJ
23m NW of Glasgow off B832
Open *Apr–Oct 1.30–5.30*
A mecca for anyone intrigued by Charles
Rennie Mackintosh. He built the hilltop
house in 1902–4 and then furnished it
as a showcase for all his most forward-
looking notions about design and
comfort. It is his masterpiece. It is
modelled on the type of Baronial manor
house that litters Scotland, but in a
simplified and abbreviated form. The
chimney, windows, L-shaped floor plan,
and softly rounded corner tower are
all intensely attractive. The interior
provides a perfect setting for his furnishings and textile designs.

316 New Lanark
☎ 01555 661345
New Lanark Mills, Lanark,
S Lanarkshire ML11 9DB
Email: visit@newlanark.org
Website: www.newlanark.org
25m SE of Glasgow, 1m S of Lanark
Open *11–5*

The industrial village is remarkable for its planning and virtually nothing has changed since it was built. It exemplified the great social experiment that was pioneered by Robert Owen, a man appalled by the living and working conditions associated with the mills of the Industrial Revolution.

The 2500 workers and their families were housed in tenements (which are still sound) built up the steep hillside. The village was sited round the mill, and close to the river (the water supplied the power). Other buildings include the New Institution for the education of adults and children. Today, New Lanark is a nominated World Heritage Site, and has an award-winning visitor centre, while also being home to about 200 people.

317 Scott Monument
☎ 0131 529 4068
Princes St, Edinburgh EH2 2EJ
In East Princes St Gardens
Open *Mar–May & Oct 10–6, June–Sept Mon–Sat 9–6 Sun 10–6, Nov–Feb 10–4*
It is hard to feel as deeply about Sir Walter Scott as did his contemporaries. For them, he was the last word in epic historical romance, and one of the largest Gothic Revival memorials in Britain was the least they could erect in his memory. It is done in fitting style with over-the-top Gothic excess, looking satisfyingly like Thunderbird 3, and with great views from the top for those who can manage the climb.

318 Scottish National Portrait Gallery
☎ 0131 624 6200
Queen Street, Edinburgh EH2 1JD
Website: www.natgalscot.ac.uk
E end of Queen St, N of Princes St
Open *Mon–Sat 10–5 Sun 12–5*

*The massive statue of William Wallace on the exterior of the **Wallace Monument**.*

This fine Edinburgh gallery is housed in a masterpiece of Scottish Gothic Victoriana. It has a particularly atmospheric foyer and atrium. Inside, there is a wide-ranging collection of archaeological remains, and portraits of Scotland's great and good through the centuries. It boasts a primitive 17th-century Scottish forerunner to the guillotine.

319 Wallace Monument *
☎ 01786 472140
St Ninian's Rd, Abbey Craig, Stirling FK8 2AP
2m N of Stirling
Open *Mar–May & Oct 10–5, June–Sept 9.30–6.30, Nov–Feb 11–4*
Until Hollywood arrived to do the job properly with *Braveheart*, William

*The red sandstone exterior of the **Scottish National Portrait Gallery**.*

Wallace, who led the Scots to victory over the English at the battle of Stirling Bridge in 1297, had to make do with this as his monument. Designed by J.T. Rochead, this 220ft (67m) crown-topped Scottish tower (built 1862–69) had a massive statue of Wallace by David Watson Stevenson added in 1887. Inside is Wallace's sword and a hall of Scottish heroes, with a row of white marble busts of, among others, John Knox and Adam Smith.

ADDITIONAL PLACES TO VISIT

Abbotsford
☎ 01896 752043
Melrose, Scottish Borders TD6 9BQ
*3m from Melrose between
the Tweed & B6360*
Open *3rd Mon in Mar–Oct 9.30–5
(opens 2 on Sun, Mar–May & Oct)*
As you would expect of a house lived in and greatly extended by Sir Walter Scott, it is a wonderful place. It is crammed with relics and historical artefacts (particularly armour and weapons), as well as having Scott's library of thousands of rare volumes. This was where Scott died in 1832, having spent the final six years of his life desperately trying to get out of debt.

Ayton Castle
☎ 018907 81212
Ayton, Eyemouth,
Scottish Borders TD14 5RD
*7m NW of Berwick on A1;
2m SW of Eyemouth*
Open *May–Sept by appointment*
Built in 1846 by James Gillespie Graham, this is an imposing red sandstone house with a huge central tower, from which sprout a host of smaller round towers. It has recently been totally restored. There is surrounding parkland.

Balmoral Castle
☎ 01339 742334
Crathie, Aberdeenshire AB35 5TB
Email: info@balmoralcastle.com
Website: www.balmoralcastle.com
Off A93 between Ballater & Braemar
Open *Apr–July 10–5
(grounds & exhibitions only)*
This has been the Royal Family's Highland holiday home since the days of Victoria (Albert bought it in 1852).

Bonawe Iron Furnace HS
☎ 01866 822432
Taynuilt, Argyll PA35 1JQ
12m E of Oban off A85
Open *Apr–Sept 9.30–6.30*
This remote spot on the banks of Loch Etive is one of the most impressive industrial locations in Britain. It is the site of an iron works that was founded in 1753, and one of the last to use charcoal as its fuel. The furnace is a square stone structure built into the slope of the hill and is in three sections; the charge house, a short bridge and the furnace itself with a squat chimney. It could produce about 2 tonnes of pig iron a day.

Burns' Cottage
☎ 01292 441215
Burns National Heritage Park,
Alloway, S Ayrshire KA7 4PY
Email: heritage.park@robertburns.org
Website: www.robertburns.org
2m S of Ayr on B7024
Open *Apr–Oct 9–6,
Nov–Mar Mon–Sat 10–4 Sun 12–4*
The modest thatched cottage was the birthplace of the great Scottish poet, Robert Burns, in 1759.

Burrell Collection and Pollok House NTS
☎ Burrell Collection 0141 287 2550;
Pollok House 0141 616 6410

Pollok Country Park, 2060 Pollokshaws Rd, Glasgow G43 1AT
3m SW of city by M77, junction 21 or 22, follow signs for Burrell Collection
Open *Burrell: Mon–Sat 10–5 Sun 11–5*
Pollok: Apr–Oct 10–5, Nov–Mar 11–4
Two for the price of one. This wonderful modern building houses one of Scotland's finest collections of historical artefacts and works of art, with a distinct leaning to the medieval, but going right the way back to Roman times. It was amassed by Sir William Burrell, and donated to the city during the war. The award-winning gallery has become one of Glasgow's major cultural attractions. Deeper in the park is the beautiful 18th-century Pollok House, designed by William Adam, which also contains a collection of Old Masters, particularly Spanish artists such as El Greco, Goya and Murillo.

Carlyle's Birthplace NTS
☎ 01576 300666
The Arched House, Ecclefechan, Lockerbie, Dumfries & Galloway DG11 3DG
5½m S of Lockerbie off M74
Open *Apr–Sept Fri–Mon 1.30–5.30*
The Arched House is where the great polemicist, historian and Romantic crusader Thomas Carlyle was born in 1795. It now contains a museum with many original documents and other artefacts relating to Carlyle.

David Livingstone Centre NTS
☎ 01698 823140
165 Station Rd, Blantyre, S Lanarkshire G72 9BY
In Blantyre, leave M74 junction 5
Open *Apr–Oct 10–5.30, Nov–Mar 10.30–4.30; opens 12.30 on Sun*
Livingstone, the quintessence of great Victorian exploration, was born here in 1813. The house has been transformed into a museum celebrating his life.

Dean Gallery
☎ 0131 624 6200
73 Belford Rd, Edinburgh EH4 3DS
Email: deaninfo@natgalscot.ac.uk
Website: www.natgalscot.ac.uk
In West End, nr Dean Village
Open *Mon–Sat 10–5 Sun 12–5*
The Baroque-style building was originally built as an orphanage in 1833. It used to be a teacher training college, until transformed into a stunning art gallery which opened in 1999. It has a collection of Dali, Duchamp, Ernst, Giacometti, Magritte, Man Ray and Miro. The gallery is also home to a significant collection of works by the Scottish sculptor, Sir Eduardo Paolozzi, as well as a mock-up of his studio. But above all it is a wonderful example of how well old institutional buildings adapt to modern purposes. No attempt has been made to disguise its origins, and the overlay of art gallery over what is still clearly a school environment (helped by its beautiful stone work) is deeply impressive.

Floors Castle
☎ 01573 223333
Kelso, Scottish Borders TD5 7SF
1m NW of Kelso off A6089
Open *Apr–Oct 10–4.30*
In the heart of the Scottish Borders, this great red pile (claimed to be the largest inhabited castle in Scotland) had a multitude of extravagant features added in the mid-19th century to the basic Robert Adam structure. It is surrounded by parkland overlooking the River Tweed.

Hutchesons' Hall NTS
☎ 0141 552 8391
158 Ingram St, Glasgow G1 1EJ
In city centre, near SE corner of John St
Open *Mon–Sat 10–5; closed BHs & early Jan*

The elegant Neoclassical building was designed by David Hamilton in 1802 as a hospital. It is now a visitor centre, and used by the National Trust for Scotland as an office.

Manderston

☎ 01361 883450
Duns, Scottish Borders TD11 3PP
Email: palmer@manderston.demon.co.uk
Website: www.manderston.co.uk
12m W of Berwick-upon-Tweed off A6105
Open *May–Sept Thurs & Sun 2–5.30*
This stately home was restored from floor to ceiling in the first years of the 20th century, and now offers one of the most vivid pictures of the contrasting worlds of Edwardian 'upstairs' and 'downstairs'. There are grand state rooms, and an exhibition of Huntley and Palmer biscuit tins (the source of the fortune behind it all).

Mount Stuart House

☎ 01700 503877
Mount Stuart, Isle of Bute PA20 9LR
Email: contactus@mountstuart.com
Website: www.mountstuart.com
Open *House: May–Sept 11–5*
Gardens: 10–6
The ancestral home of the Marqesses of Bute is a High Gothic extravaganza with sumptuous interiors and extensive woodland grounds (over 300 acres).

Museum of Scotland and Royal Museum

☎ 0131 225 7534
Chambers St, Edinburgh EH1 1JF
Email: info@nms.ac.uk
Website: www.nms.ac.uk
On Old Town, next to University
Open *Mon–Sat 10–5 Tues 10–8 Sun 12–5*
Edinburgh's great museum now boasts a stunning new addition, but for many it is the Victorian atrium that continues to amaze – possibly one of the best

examples of its kind in the country. It is a great airy tent of metal and glass, its delicate iron columns and walkways the last word in Victorian elegance; more Art Deco Paris, than Calvinist Edinburgh. Opened in the mid-1860s, it is still home to a wonderful variety of exhibits drawn from the worlds of natural history, industry and anthropology. The new museum, which opened in 1998, houses the Museum of Scotland. It has a great pink and yellow rotunda exterior, although inside things are a little more hushed.

National Gallery of Scotland and Royal Scottish Academy

☎ 0131 624 6200
The Mound, Edinburgh EH2 2EL
Website: www.natgalscot.ac.uk
In E Princes St Gardens
Open *Mon–Sat 10–5 Sun 12–5*
This pair of Greek temples at the base of the Mound (the hill that links Princes Street to the Royal Mile) are at the heart of 'The Athens of the North', as Edinburgh used to be called. The National Gallery is Edinburgh's equivalent to London's National Gallery. Opened to the public in 1859, it has a collection of Old Masters including Raphael, Titian, Poussin, Degas and Cézanne, as well as 18th- and 19th-century Scottish artists. The Royal Scottish Academy closed in 2001 for refurbishment which is expected to take about 3 years.

St Vincent Street Church

☎ 0141 221 1937
St Vincent St, Glasgow G2 7LA
In city centre
Open *Phone to arrange a visit; services Sun 11 & 6.30*
This 1859 church was built by the hero of 19th-century Glasgow architecture, Alexander 'Greek' Thomson. It has a wonderful tower which also serves as a powerful hilltop landmark, while the

Grecian-style church is set on an imposing podium. The outside has spectacular Ionic porticoes. Inside it is all spaciousness and colour, with galleries and two tiers of strange columns decked out in Pompeiian red, blue, white and gold.

Scottish National Gallery of Modern Art
☎ 0131 624 6326
75 Belford Road, Edinburgh EH4 3DR
Email: gmaininfo@natgalscot.ac.uk
Website: www.natgalscot.ac.uk
In West End, near Dean Village
Open *Mon–Sat 10–5 Sun 12–5*
Right opposite the Dean Gallery is a school converted (in 1984) into a gallery. The building is a Palladian-style two-storey affair with portico and symmetrical flat front. The space works perfectly because, like many Palladian buildings, the long corridors and sequence rooms were built to display art. The collection is magnificent, absorbing all the major movements in art since the 1890s, and includes a large number of masterpieces, from Matisse and Picasso to Hockney and Hirst. It also has a strong collection of contemporary Scottish art.

Tenement House NTS
☎ 0141 333 0183
145 Buccleuch St, Garnethill, Glasgow G3 6QN
NW of Sauchiehall St
Open *Mar–Oct 2–5*
An old tenement house has been turned into a museum. It was occupied from 1911–65 by Miss Agnes Toward who spent a lifetime amassing the detritus of ordinary life. Set in a wonderful red sandstone building that dates from 1892, it is an example of the type of architecture that used to dominate Glasgow, and much of Edinburgh. Though lacking the genuine tang of poverty, it is still an eye-opener.

Northern Ireland MAP 9
320 The Argory NT
☎ 028 8778 4753
Moy, Dungannon, Co Armagh BT71 6NA
Email: uagest@smtp.ntrust.org.uk
4m from Moy, 3m from M1 junction 13
Open *House: Apr May & Sept Sat Sun & BHs, June–Aug daily, all 2–6 (opens at 1 on weekdays in June)*
Grounds: daily May–Sept 10–8, Oct–Apr 10–4
This early Victorian Neoclassical house is almost unchanged since 1900. It is full of fascinating treasures gathered from all over the world and feels much more like a home than a museum. There is a huge barrel organ which is played once a month for musical tours. In the grounds are stables and a coach house, also a acetylene gas plant. Surrounded by woodland and overlooking the River Blackwater, it has pleasant riverside and woodland walks.

ADDITIONAL PLACES TO VISIT
Belfast Castle
☎ 028 9077 6925
Antrim Rd, Belfast BT15 5GR
Website: www.belfastcastle.co.uk
2½m N of city centre
Open *Mon–Sat 11–10 Sun 9–6*
Built in 1870 in the Scottish Baronial style (its six-storey tower, with gables and turrets, is modelled on Balmoral), the castle stands above the city on the slopes of Cave Hill. It has a renowned Italian-style serpentine staircase created in 1894 which leads from the main reception rooms to the garden terrace below. An easy climb to the top of Cave Hill offers spectacular views over the city and Belfast Lough. There are earthworks and caves that have historical associations with the 1798 rebellion.

Map 1 SOUTH-WEST

1

Woodbridge
Haverhill
Sudbury
Ipswich
Royston
Baldock
Saffron Walden
Manningtree
Felixstowe
Halstead
Harwich
Stevenage
ESSEX
Braintree
Colchester
HERTFORDSHIRE
Bishop's Stortford
Welwyn Garden City
Hertford
Witham
West Mersea
Clacton-on-Sea
Hatfield
Harlow
Chelmsford
149
Maldon
Waltham Abbey
Enfield
Burnham-on-Crouch
Barnet
Chigwell
Brentwood
Rayleigh
Foulness Island
2 63 215 221 227 230 278 279
Southend-on-Sea
81 282 283 285 288 291 292 294 295
Basildon
LONDON
Canvey Island
218
Woolwich
Tilbury
222 225
Dartford
Sheerness
Minster
Margate
Swanley
Gravesend
60 156
Isle of Sheppey
Herne Bay
Croydon
14
Rochester
Whitstable
Gillingham
20
Caterham
18
Chatham
Sittingbourne
Ramsgate
Faversham
Canterbury
Sandwich
Sevenoaks
56 61
147
Oxted
153 152
Maidstone
Deal
Reigate
154
151
Tonbridge
KENT
16 57
155
Ashford
Dover
East Grinstead
Tunbridge Wells
293
Crawley
Folkestone
Cranbrook
145 Hythe
Crowborough
Tenterden
Haywards Heath
EAST SUSSEX
New Romney
Uckfield
144
Hurstpierpoint
Heathfield
Rye
55 Battle
290 296
Lewes
150
Hailsham
Hastings
59
Bexhill
Brighton
Newhaven
Seaford
Eastbourne
Beachy Head

E N G L I S H   C H A N N E L

2

Map 3 EASTERN

3

Map 5 WALES

5

Map 6 NORTH-WEST

6

IRISH
SEA

LANCASHIRE

CHESHIRE

STAFFORDSHIRE

WREXHAM

FLINTSHIRE

DENBIGHSHIRE

CONWY

GWYNEDD

ISLE OF ANGLESEY

Caernarfon
Bay

Great Ormes
Head

Carmel
Head

Holy Island

Bardsey
Island

MANCHESTER

LIVERPOOL

STOKE-ON-TRENT

Fleetwood
Blackpool
Lytham St Anne's
Southport
Formby
Crosby
Bootle
Wallasey
Hoylake
West Kirby

Skipton
Keighley
Barnoldswick
Clitheroe
Nelson
Garstang
Padiham
Burnley
Preston
Accrington
Kirkham
Blackburn
Oswaldtwistle
Warton
Darwen
Rawtenstall
Leyland
Chorley
Standish
Ormskirk
Skelmersdale
Maghull
Kirkby
Bebington
Birkenhead
Ellesmere
Port

Todmorden
Rochdale
Middleton
Oldham
Bury
Bolton
Wigan
Leigh
St Helens
Sale
Altrincham
Widnes
Runcorn
Frodsham
Northwich
Middlewich
Winsford
Sandbach
Crewe
Nantwich

Glossop
Stockport
Salford
Wilmslow
Knutsford

Whaley
Bridge
Macclesfield
Holmes Chapel
Congleton
Biddulph
Kidsgrove
Newcastle-
under-Lyme

Leek

Stone
Stafford
Rugeley
Cannock

Chester
Buckley
Mold
Flint
Holywell
Denbigh
Ruthin
Wrexham
Ruabon
Llangollen
Wem
Ellesmere
Oswestry
Market
Drayton
Whitchurch
Newport
Telford
Shrewsbury
Welshpool

Rhyl
Colwyn Bay
Conwy
Llandudno
St Asaph

Bangor
Bethesda
Caernarfon
Porthmadog
Criccieth
Pwllheli
Amlwch
Menai
Bridge
Llangefni
Holyhead

River Dee

256
306
307
183
255
308
305

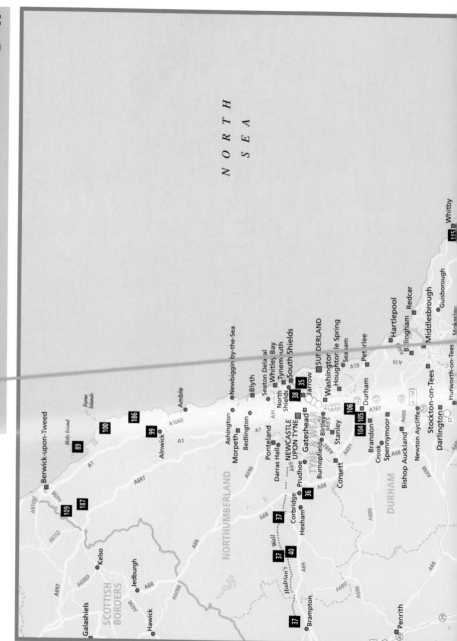

7

Map 8 SCOTLAND

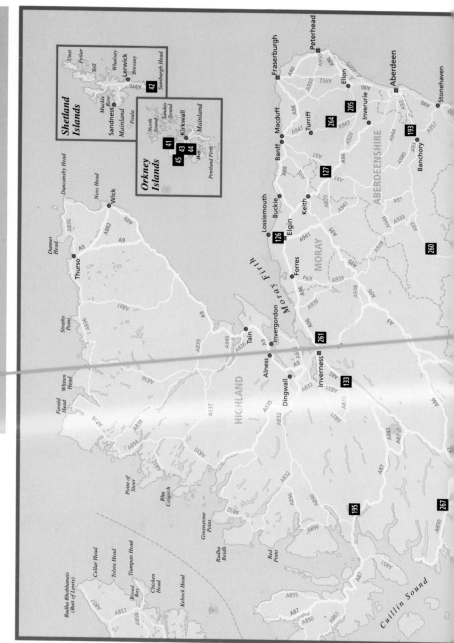

Shetland Islands

Unst
Fetlar
Yell
Whalsay
Muckle Roe
Sandness
Mainland
Foula
Lerwick
Bressay
A970
Sumburgh Head

42

Orkney Islands

North Sound
Sanday Sound
Kirkwall
Mainland
Hoy
Pentland Firth

41
43
44
45

Duncansby Head
Noss Head
Wick
Dunnet Head
Thurso
A836
A882
A9
A99
Strathy Point
A897
A9

Whiten Head
Farraid Head
A838
A838
A894
A835
A837

Point of Stoer
Rhu Coigach

Greenstone Point
Rubha Réidh
Red Point

Rudha Rhobhanais (Butt of Lewis)
Cellar Head
Tolsta Head
Tiumpan Head
Broad Bay
Chicken Head
Kebock Head
A857
A857
A858

A835
A832
A896
A890

Fraserburgh
Peterhead
A950
A90
A98
A90
A952
Ellon
Aberdeen
Stonehaven
A90
A957

Macduff
Banff
Turriff
A947
264
205
Inverurie
A920
A944
193
Banchory
A980
A93
A957

127
A96
A97
A947
ABERDEENSHIRE
A944
A939
A93
A53

Lossiemouth
Buckie
126
Elgin
Keith
A920
A941
MORAY
A95
A941
A939
260

Forres
A96
A939
A95

Invergordon
Moray Firth
A938
A939
A95
A9

Tain
Alness
261
A9
A862
Dingwall
Inverness
133
A832
A831
A833
HIGHLAND
A835
A832
195
267
A87
A887
A87
A82
A830

A855
A87
A850
A863
Cuillin Sound

8

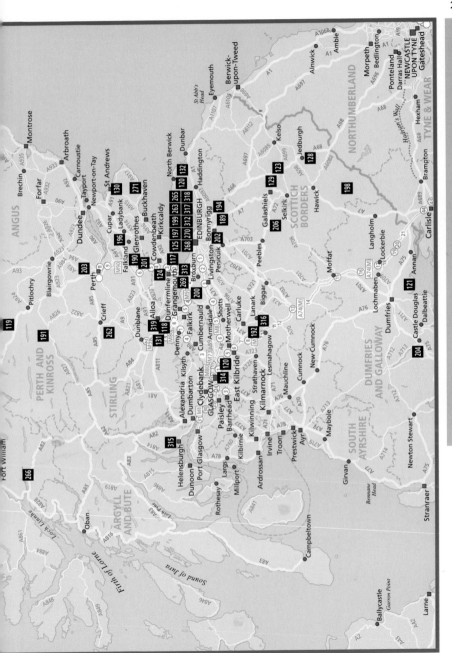

8

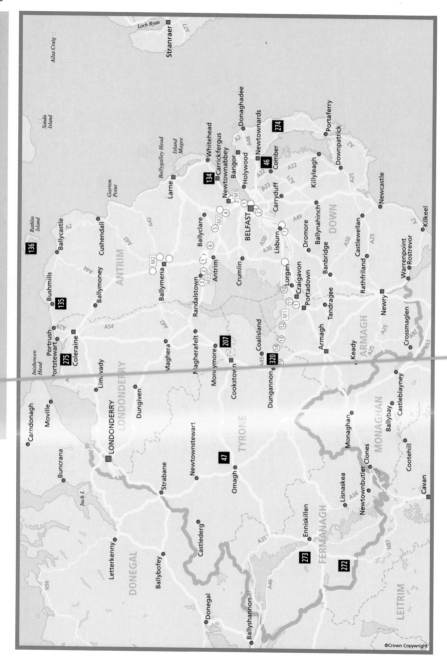

Bibliography & websites

This is a short list of books that go into greater detail than a simple guide book can hope to do. Each has its own substantial bibliography for anyone wanting to delve deeper into Britain's historical locations.

Brabbs, Derry, *Abbeys and Monasteries*, Sterling Publications, 2000

Clayton, Peter, *A Companion to Roman Britain*, Phaidon Press, 1980

Clifton-Taylor, Alec, *The Cathedrals of England*, Thames & Hudson, 1967 & 1995

Dixon, Roger, and Muthesius, Stefan, *Victorian Architecture*, Thames & Hudson, 1997

Girouard, Mark, *The Victorian Country-House*, Yale University Press, 1979

Girouard, Mark, *Robert Smythson and the Elizbethan Country-House*, Yale University Press, 1985

Irvine, Peter, *Scotland the Best!*, HarperCollins, 2000

Jenkins, Simon, *England's Thousand Best Churches*, Penguin, 2000

Johnson, Paul, *Castles of England, Scotland and Wales*, Seven Dials, 2000

*Kerr, Nigel and Mary, *A Guide to Medieval Sites in Britain*, Paladin, 1988

Montgomery-Massingberd, Hugh, and Simon Sykes, Christopher, *Great Houses of England and Wales*, Universe, 2000

Orbach, Julian, *Blue Guide to Victorian Architecture*, Norton, 1988

*Pevsner, Sir Nikolaus (founding editor), *The Buildings of England* series, Penguin, 1950 on (magnificent county-by-county survey, recently updated and re-issued by Penguin)

*Pragnell, Hubert, *Britain: A Guide to Architectural Styles from 1066 to the Present Day*, Ellipsis, 2000

*Scotland's Churches Scheme, *Churches to Visit in Scotland*, St Andrew Press, 2000

*Saul, Nigel (General Editor), *The National Trust Historical Atlas of Britain: Prehistoric to Medieval*, Sutton Publishing, 1997

*Saumarez Smith, Charles, *Eighteenth-Century Decoration: Design and the Domestic Interior in England*, Weidenfeld & Nicolson, 1993

*Thompson, M.W., *The Decline of the Castle*, Cambridge, 1987

Watkin, David, *English Architecture*, Thames & Hudson, 2001

Wilson, Christopher, *The Gothic Cathedral*, Thames & Hudson, 1992

There is a wealth of information available on the internet, not just from the websites of such organizations as the National Trust, CADW or Historic Scotland (all of which have information on individual properties). Many individual properties, especially the larger ones, now have their own website pages and we have included many of these in this book. You can usually access them also by entering the name of the location into a search engine (such as Google or Alta Vista).

In addition, the BBC's own History Website (www.bbc.co.uk/history) has a whole section dedicated to the series *A History of Britain*, with images and information on many of the sites mentioned in the book.

USEFUL WEBSITES

CADW Welsh Historic Monuments
www.cadw.wales.gov.uk
EH English Heritage
www.english-heritage.org.uk
HS Historic Scotland
www.historic-scotland.gov.uk
NT National Trust
www.nationaltrust.org.uk
NTS National Trust for Scotland
www.nts.org.uk
Residences of HM the Queen
www.the-royal-collection.org.uk
Historic Houses Association
www.hha.org.uk
Hudson's Historic Houses & Gardens
www.hudsons.co.uk
Landmark Trust
www.landmarktrust.co.uk

ADDITIONAL WEBSITES TO VISIT

www.aboutbritain.com
www.britain.co.uk
www.castles.org
www.castlesontheweb.com
www.castlewales.com
www.familycastles.com
www.gardenvisit.com
www.information-britain.co.uk
www.irelandseye.com
www.leisurebritain.co.uk
www.palaces.org
www.roman-britain.org
www.theheritagetrail.co.uk
www.ukvillages.co.uk
www.villagnet.co.uk

*UK Edition

Index

A La Ronde, Devon 212
Abbotsford, Borders 246
Aberconwy House, Conwy 135
Aberdour Castle, Fife 91
Albert Memorial, Lon 214
Aldborough Roman Site 38
Alfriston Clergy House 116
All Saints Church, Lon 214
Alnwick Castle, Nrthumb 80–1
Althorp, Northants 181
Ambleside Roman Fort, Cumb 34
American Cemetery, Cambs 230
Ancient High House, Staffs 130
Anne of Cleves House, E Suss 116
Antony House, Corn 158
Apsley House, Lon 222
Arbeia Roman Fort, Tyne 34–5
Arbor Low Stone Circle 30
Arbroath Abbey, Angus 96–7
Arbury Hall, Warwks 130
Ardress House, Armagh 206
Argory, The, Tyrone 249
Argyll's Lodging, Stirling 202
Arniston House, Midl 202–3
Arthur's Round Table, Cumb 34
Arthur's Stone, Herefs 30
Arundel Castle, W Sussex 109
Ascott, Beds 170
Ashby de la Zouch Castle 126
Ashdown House, Oxon 170–1
Ashleworth Tithe Barn, Glos 130
Assembly Rooms, Bath 158
Astley Hall, Lancs 193
Athelhamton House 105–6
Attingham Park, Shrops 188
Auckland Castle, Dur 88
Audley End, Essex 176–7
Avebury Stone Circles, Wilts 15
Avington Park, Hants 171
Aydon Castle, Nrthumb 88
Aynho Park, Oxon 188
Ayton Castle, Borders 246

Baddesley Clinton, Warwks 130
Ballowall Barrow, Corn 18
Balmoral Castle, Abers 246
Balvenie Castle, Moray 148
Bamburgh Castle, Nrthumb 81
Bannockburn Heritage Centre,
  Stir 91

Banqueting House, Lon 160
Bant's Carn Burial Chamber,
  Scilly Is 18
Barons Court, Tyrone 206
Barrington Court, Som 106
Basildon Park, Berks 171
Basing House, Hants 160–1
Bath Abbey, Bath 103
Battle Abbey, E Sussex 50
Bayham Old Abbey, E Sussex 56
Beaulieu Abbey, Hants 56
Beaumaris Castle, Anglesey 71
Beeston Castle, Ches 80
Belas Knap Long Barrow 30
Belfast Castle 249
Belsay Hall, Nrthumb 139
Belton House, Lincs 188
Belvoir Castle, Lincs 181–2
Bembridge Windmill,
  Isle of Wight 171
Beningbrough Hall, N Yorks 196
Benthall Hall, Shrops131
Berkeley Castle, Glos 63–4
Berkhamsted Castle, Herts 62
Berrington Hall, Herefs 188
Berry Pomeroy Castle 106
Berwick Barracks, Nrthumb 139
Bessie Surtees House 139
Beverley Minster, E Yorks 82
Bignor Roman Villa 21–2
Binham Priory, Norfolk 121–2
Bishops' Old Palace, Lincoln 62
Blackness Castle, W Lot 148–9
Blackstone Edge Roman Road,
  Gr Man 38
Blaenavon Ironworks 234
Blair Castle, Per 92
Blenheim Palace, Oxon 182
Blickling Hall, Norfolk 177
Boarstall Tower, Bucks116
Bodelwyddan Castle, Den 234
Bodiam Castle, E Sussex 109–10
Bolsover Castle, Derbys188–9
Bolton Castle, N Yorks 88
Bonawe Iron Furnace, Argyll 246
Borthwick Castle, Midl 140
Boscobel House, Staffs 189
Bothwell Castle, S Lan 92–3
Boughton House, Northants 189
Bourne Mill, Essex 125

Bowes Museum, Dur 241
Bowood House, Wilts 158
Boxgrove Priory, W Sussex 56
Bradford-on-Avon Tithe Barn,
  Wilts 106
Brading, Isle of Wight 22
Bradley Manor, Devon 106
Braemar Castle, Abers 198
Bramham Park, W Yorks 196
Branscombe Manor Mill 106
Bratton Camp & White Horse 18
Brecon Gaer Roman Fort 32
Brenchley, Kent 116
Bridge Cottage, Suffolk 230
Bristol Cathedral 47
Broadlands, Hants 222
Broch of Gurness, Orkn 38–9
Brodick Castle, N Ayr 97
Brodie Castle, Nrthumb 139
Brontë Parsonage Museum 241
Brough Castle, Cumb 78–9
Brougham Castle, Cumb 80
Broughton Castle, Oxon 131
Buckfast Abbey, Devon 47
Buckingham Palace, Lon 222
Buckland Abbey, Devon 106
Buildwas Abbey, Shrops 69
Burgh Castle, Norfolk 27
Burleigh Castle, Per 140
Burleigh House, Lincs 122
Burns' Cottage, S Ayr 246
Burrell Collection & Pollok
  House, Glas 246–7
Burton Agnes Hall, N Yorks 137
Bushmead Priory, Beds 69
Buxton Opera House 232
Byland Abbey, Nrthumb 88

Cadhay, Devon 106–7
Caerlaverock Castle, Dumf 93
Caerleon Roman Fortress 32
Caernarfon Castle, Gwyn 71–3
Caerphilly Castle, S Wales 73
Cairnpapple Hill, W Lothian 41
Caister Castle, Norfolk 122
Caister Roman Site, Norfolk 27
Calanais Standing Stones 41
Calke Abbey, Derbys 189
Calshot Castle, Hants 116
Calton Hill, Edin 241–2
Camber Castle, E Sussex 116

Canterbury Cathedral 50–1
Cardiff Castle, S Wales 75–6
Carew Castle, Pemb 192
Carisbrooke Castle, Isle of Wight 161
Carlisle Castle, Cumb 79
Carlyle's Birthplace, Dum 247
Carn Euny Ancient Village 15
Carrickfergus Castle, Antrim 98
Castell y Bere, Gwyn 76
Castell Coch, S Wales 235
Castle Acre Priory, Norfolk 62–3
Castle Campbell, Clac 149
Castle Coole, Ferm 206
Castle Drogo, Devon 211
Castle Fraser, Abers 203
Castle Howard, N Yorks 194–5
Castle Menzies, Per 140
Castle Rising Castle, Norfolk 58
Castle Ward, Down 206
Castlerigg Stone Circle 34
Cawdor Castle, Highland 149
Centre Point, Lon 222–3
Cerne Abbas Giant, Dorset 18
Charlecote Park, Warwks 131
Charleston, E Sussex 117
Chartwell, Kent 223
Chastleton House, Oxon 182–3
Chatsworth House, Derbys 183
Chedworth Roman Villa, Glos 27
Chenies Manor House 117
Chepstow Castle, Gwent 76
Chester Cathedral 69
Chester Amphitheatre 27–8
Chichester Cathedral 56–7
Chiddingstone Castle, Kent 223
Chillingham Castle, Nrthumb 88
Chillingham Wild Cattle Park 88–9
Chillington Hall, Staffs 189
Chirk Castle, N Wales 76
Chiswick House, Lon 161–2
Christ Church, Spitalfields 171
Christchurch Castle &
      Constable's House 47, 49
Chysauster Ancient Village 15
Cilgerran Castle, Pemb 76–7
Cirencester Amphitheatre 30
Clandon Park, Surrey 171–2
Claydon House, Bucks 162–3
Claypotts Castle, Angus 149
Cleeve Abbey, Som 45
Clifford's Tower, N Yorks 82
Clifton Suspension Bridge 211
Cliveden, Bucks 223
Clock Tower & Pool, Stevenage 223–4
Clouds Hill, Dorset 212

Clun Castle, Shrops 69
Cobham Hall, Kent 172
Cochwillan Old Hall, Gwyn 136
Coggeshall Grange Barn, Essex 58–9
Coity Castle, Bridgend 77
Colchester Castle, Essex 25–6
Compton Castle, Devon 107
Compton Wynyates 126–7
Conisbrough Castle, S Yorks 82
Convocation House, Oxford 184
Conwy Castle, N Wales 74
Corbridge, Nrthumb 35
Corfe Castle, Dorset 45
Corsham Court, Wilts 103
Cosmeston Medieval Village 134
Cotehele, Corn 103–4
Cothay Manor, Som 107
Cottesbrooke Hall 189–90
Coughton Court, Warwks 131
Coventry Cathedral 230–1
Craigmillar Castle, Edin 149
Craignethan Castle, S Lan 140–1
Crathes Castle, Abers 141
Criccieth Castle, Gwyn 77
Crichton Castle, Midl 141–2
Croft Castle, Herefs 64
Crofton Roman Villa, Kent 22
Cromwell's House, Ely 178
Crossness Pumping Station 224
Crossraguel Abbey, S Ayr 97
Culloden, Highland 198

Danebury, Hants 22
Danny, W Sussex 172
Dartmouth Castle, Devon 107
David Livingstone Centre 247
Deal Castle, Kent 111
Dean Gallery, Edin 247
Deddington Castle, Oxon 69
Deene Park, Northants 190
Delgatie Castle, Abers 150
Denbigh Castle 77
Denny Abbey, Cambs 63
Dickens House Museum 224
Dimbola Lodge, Isle of Wight 214
Dirleton Castle, E Lot 93
Doddington Hall, Lincs 125
Donnington Castle, Berks 49
Dorney Court, Berks 117
Doune Castle, Stirling 150
Dove Cottage, Cumb 237
Dover Castle, Kent 51–2
Dover Roman House 22
Down House, Kent 224
Drum Castle, Abers 203

Drummond Castle Gardens 198
Dryburgh Abbey, Borders 93
Dudley Castle 69–70
Dunblane Cathedral, Stir 97
Dunfermline Abbey & Palace, Fife 93–4
Dunham Massey, Ches 238
Dunluce Castle, Antrim 98–9
Dunnottar Castle, Abers 203
Dunstaffnage Castle, Arg 97
Dunstanburgh Castle 137
Dunster Castle, Som 159
Dunvegan Castle, Skye 97
Durham Castle 82–3
Durham Cathedral 83
Dymchurch Martello Tower, Kent 224
Dyrham Park, S Glos 155

Easby Abbey, N Yorks 89
East Riddlesden Hall 197
Edgehill, Warwks 184
Edinburgh Castle 94
Edinburgh New Town 198–9
Edzell, Castle, Angus 150
Egglestone Abbey, Dur 89
Eilean Donan Castle 142
Elgin Cathedral, Moray 94
Elton Hall, Cambs 179
Ely Cathedral, Cambs 59
Englefield House, Berks 117
Erddig, Clwyd 193
Etal Castle, Nrthumb 137–8
Eton College, Berks 117
Exeter Cathedral, Devon 45–6
Eyam Hall, Derbys 190

Fairfax House, N Yorks 197
Falkland Palace, Fife 142
Farleigh Hungerford Castle 107
Farnham Castle Keep, Surrey 52
Felbrigg Hall, Norfolk 179
Finchdale Priory, Dur 83
Fishbourne Roman Villa 22–3
Flint Castle, Flin 74–5
Floors Castle, Borders 247
Flowerdown Barrows, Hants 25
Foreign Office, Lon 224
Forth Railway Bridge, W Lot 242
Fotheringhay Castle 123
Fountains Abbey, N Yorks 83–4
Framlingham Castle 59–60
Frampton Court, Glos 190
Freud Museum, Lon 214
Furness Abbey, Cumb 79–80
Fyvie Castle, Abers 199–200

Gainsborough Old Hall 125
Gawsworth Hall, Ches 136
Gawthorpe Hall, Lancs 238
Georgian House, Edin 200
Gladstone's Land, Edin 142, 144
Glamis Castle, Angus 150
Glasgow School of Art 243
Glencoe, Argyll 200–1
Glenfinnan Monument 201
Gloucester Cathedral, Glos 64
Glynde Place, E Sussex 117, 119
Godolphin House, Corn 107–8
Goodrich Castle, Herefs 64, 66
Goodwood House, W Sussex 172
Great Chalfield Manor, Wilts 108
Great Coxwell Barn, Oxon 66
Great Dixter, E Sussex 119
Great Witcombe Roman Villa 30
Greyfriars, The, Worcester 131–2
Greyfriars Kirk, Edin 201
Greys Court, Oxon 174
Grimes Graves, Norfolk 27
Grimspound, Devon 18
Grimsthorpe Castle, Lincs 63
Groombridge Place 174
Gunby Hall, Lincs 180
Gwydir Castle, Gwyn 136

Haddo House, Abers 203
Haddon Hall, Derbys 127
Hadrian's Wall 35–7
  Birdoswald, Cumb 35
  Chesters, Nrthumb 35, 36
  Housesteads, Nrthumb 36–7
Hailes Abbey, Glos 66
Hailes Castle, E Lot 98
Halloggye Fogou, Corn 18
Ham House, Surrey 163
Hammerwood Park 175
Hampton Court Palace 111
Hanbury Hall, Worcs 190
Hardingstone Eleanor Cross,
  Northants 66
Hardknott Roman Fort, Cumb
  34
Hardwick Hall, Derbys 128
Hardy's Cottage, Dorset 212
Harewood House, E Yorks 195–6
Harlaxton Manor, Lincs 229
Harlech Castle, Gwyn 75
Harrods, Lon 224–5
Hatfield Earthworks, Wilts 19
Hatfield House, Herts 112
Haughmond Abbey, Shrops 70
Hedingham Castle, Essex 60
Hellens, Herefs 70
Helmingham Hall 125–6

Helmsley Castle, N Yorks 89
Hendy Head, Anglesey 32
Hereford Cathedral 66–7
Hermitage Castle, Borders 144
Herstmonceaux Castle 113
Hever Castle, Kent 113
Hezlett House, Londonderry
  206–7
Hidcote Manor Garden 232
High Level Bridge, Newcastle
  241
Highclere Castle, Hants 225
Highgate Cemetery, Lon 215
Hill House, Argyll 243
Hitchin British Schools 225
Hob Hurst's House, Derbys 30
Hod Hill, Dorset 15
Holkham Hall, Norfolk 178–9
Holy Trinity Church, Long
  Melford, Suffolk 122–3
Holyroodhouse Palace, Edin 144
Hopetoun House, W Lot 201
Horton Court, Glos 108
Houghton Hall, Norfolk 179
Houses of Parliament 215–16
Hughenden Manor, Bucks 226
Huntingtower Castle, Per 151
Huntley Castle, Abers 94–5
Hurlers Stone Circles, Corn 19
Hutchesons' Hall, Glas 247–8

Ightham Mote, Kent 113
Inchcolm Abbey, Fife 98
Inchmahome Priory, Stir 98
Innisidgen Burial Chambers,
  Scilly Is 19
Inverary Castle, Argyll 203
Iron Bridge, Shrops 231

Jane Austen's House, Hants 226
Jarlshof Settlements, Shet 39
Jarrow Monastery 36–7
Jedburgh Abbey, Borders 95
Jewel Tower, Lon 57
Jewry Wall & Museum, Leic 30
Jodrell Bank Science Centre 232
Jordan Hill Roman Temple 19

Keats House, Lon 226
Kedleston Hall, Derbys 185
Kellie Castle, Fife 151
Kelmscott Manor, Glos 232
Kenilworth Castle, Warwks 67–8
Kensal Green Cemetery, Lon 226
Kenwood House, Lon 163
Kidwelly Castle, Carm 77
King Alfred's Tower, Som 16

King Doniert's Stone, Corn 19
King's College Chapel, Cam 123
Kingston Lacy, Dorset 155
Kingston Russell Stone Circle 19
Kirby Hall, Northants 128
Kirkham Priory, W Yorks 89
Kit's Coty House, Kent 25
Knaresborough Castle 89
Knebworth House, Herts 216
Knole, Kent 114
Knowlton Church, Dorset 19

Lacock Abbey, Wilts 212
Lamport Hall, Northants 190–1
Landguard Fort, Suffolk 126
Lanercost Priory, Cumb 80
Lanhydrock, Corn 212
Langley Chapel, Shrops 70
Launceston Castle, Corn 49
Lavenham Guildhall, Suffolk 123
Leeds Castle, Kent 114
Leigh Court Barn, Worcs 132
Lennoxlove House, E Lot 151
Levens Hall, Cumb 194
Lewes Castle, E Sussex 57
Lexden Earthworks, Essex 27
Lilleshall Abbey, Shrops 70
Lincoln Castle 63
Lincoln Cathedral 60–1
Lindisfarne Priory & Castle 37
Linlithgow Palace, W Lot 145
Little Moreton Hall, Ches 128
Littlecote House & Villa 25
Liverpool Cathedral 237
Liverpool Metropolitan
  Cathedral 237
Lochleven Castle, Per 145
London Eye 216
London Zoo 226
Longleat, Wilts 104
Longthorpe Tower, Cambs 123
Loseley Park, Surrey 119
Ludlow Castle, Shrops 68
Lullingstone Castle, Kent 119
Lullingstone Roman Villa 23
Lunt Roman Fort, Warwks 30–1
Lydiard House, Wilts 191
Lydney, Glos 31
Lyme Park, Ches 194
Lyveden New Bield 124

MacLellan's Castle, Dum 151
Maes Howe, Orkney 39–40
Maiden Castle, Dorset 16
Maison Dieu, Kent 119
Malmesbury Abbey, Wilts 49
Manchester Town Hall 237

Manderston, Borders 248
Manor, The, Cambs 63
Manorbier Castle, Pemb 77–8
Mapledurham House, Oxon 119
Marble Hill House, Middlx 175
Marker's Cottage, Devon 49
Mayburgh Earthwork, Cumb 34
Medieval Merchant's House,
    Southampton 119–20
Melford Hall, Suffolk 126
Melrose Abbey, Borders 95
Meols Hall, Merseyside 238–9
Merrivale Prehistoric
    Settlement, Devon 19
Middleham Castle, N Yorks 89
Milton Chantry, Kent 120
Milton Manor House, Oxon 175
Milton's Cottage, Bucks 175
Minster Lovell Hall, Oxon 132
Mitchell's Fold Stone Circle 31
Monea Castle, Ferm 204
Montacute House, Som 104
Moreton Corbet Castle 132
Moseley Old Hall, Staffs 185
Mottisfont Abbey, Hants 57
Mount Grace Priory, N Yorks 84
Mount Stewart, Down 204–5
Mount Stuart House, Bute 248
Muchelney Abbey, Som 49
Museum of Scotland & Royal
    Museum, Edin 248
Mussenden Temple,
    Londonderry 205–6

National Gallery of Scotland &
    Royal Scottish Academy 248
Natural History Museum 220
Nendrum, Down 41
Nether Winchenden House 120
Netley Abbey, Hants 120
New Lanark, S Lan 243, 245
Newbury Park Bus Shelter 230
Nine Ladies Stone Circle 31
Norham Castle, Nrthumb 84
North Leigh Roman Villa 28
Notgrove Long Barrow, Glos 31
Nunnington Hall, N Yorks 139
Nympsfield Long Barrow 31

Oakham Castle, Rutland 70
Oakhurst Cottage, Surrey 120
Oakwell Hall Country Park 196
Offa's Dyke, Glos 28–9
Okehampton Castle 49–50
Old Royal Naval College,
    Greenwich 165
Old Sarum, Wilts 16

Old Soar Manor, Kent 120
Old Wardour Castle, Wilts 159
Orford Castle, Suffolk 61
Osborne House, Isle of Wight
    216
Osterley Park, Middx 165
Owlpen Manor, Glos 132

Palm House, Kew Gardens,
    Surrey 217
Parham House, W Sussex 120
Park Hill, S Yorks 239
Paxton House, Borders 204
Peckover House, Cambs 180
Pembroke Castle 75
Pencarrow, Corn 159
Pendennis Castle, Corn 105
Penrhyn Castle, Gwyn 235
Penrith Castle, Cumb 80
Penshurst Place, Kent 114–15
Peterborough Cathedral 62
Petworth, W Sussex 165–6
Pevensey Castle, E Sussex 52
Peveril Castle, Derbys 70
Pickering Castle, N Yorks 84
Pitstone Windmill, Bucks 191
Plas Mawr, Conwy 134
Pontcysyllte Aqueduct, Den 233
Port Sunlight, Wirral 239
Portchester Castle, Hants 23
Portmeirion Village, Gwyn 235
Powderham Castle, Devon 108
Powis Castle, Powys 134–5
Preston Mill, E Lot 151
Princes Risborough Manor
    House, Bucks 175
Priory Cottages, Oxon 70
Prudhoe Castle, Nrthumb 89

Quarry Bank Mill, Ches 237–8
Queen's House, Greenwich 166

Raby Castle, Durham 197
Radcliffe Camera, Oxford 185
Raglan Castle, Gwent 135
Ragley Hall, Warwks 185–6
Rathlin Island, Antrim 99
Reculver Towers & Fort 25
Restormel Castle, Corn 46
Rhinefield Bridge, Hants 226–7
Rhuddlan Castle, Den 78
Richborough Roman Fort 23–4
Richmond Castle, N Yorks 84
Rievaulx Abbey, N Yorks 84–5
Ring of Brodgar, Orkn 40
Ripon Cathedral, N Yorks 89–90
Roche Abbey, S Yorks 90

Rochester Castle, Kent 53
Rochester Cathedral, Kent 57
Rockbourne Roman Villa 19
Rockingham Castle, Leics 132
Rollright Stones, Oxon 31
Roman Baths, Bath 16
Roman Wall, Herts 25
Rosslyn Chapel, Midl 145, 147
Rough Castle, Falkirk 41
Rousham House, Oxon 186
Row 111 House, Great Yarmouth
    126
Royal Albert Bridge 212–13
Royal Citadel, Devon 159
Royal Courts of Justice, Lon 227
1 Royal Crescent, Bath 156
Royal Festival Hall, Lon 217–18
Royal Geographical Society 227
Royal Holloway College 227
Royal Mausoleum, Frogmore 218
Royal Pavilion, Brighton 218
Royal Society of Arts, Lon 227
Rufford Old Hall, Lancs 137
Runcorn Bridge, Ches 238
Rushton Triangular Lodge 132–3
Rycote Chapel, Oxon 133

Saint Hill Manor, W Sussex 227
Salisbury Cathedral, Wilts 46
Saltaire Model Village 239–40
Saltram House, Devon 156–7
Sanctuary, The, Wilts 20
Saxtead Green Post Mill 180
Scarborough Castle, N Yorks 90
Scargill Chapel, N Yorks 241
Scone Palace, Per 147
Scott Monument, Edin 245
Scottish National Gallery
    of Modern Art, Edin 249
Scottish National Portrait
    Gallery, Edin 245
Seaton Delaval Hall 197
Segontium Roman Fort,
    Caernarfon 34
Selby Abbey, N Yorks 85
Severn Bridge 235
Shakespeare Houses, Stratford-
    upon-Avon 133
Shaw's Corner, Herts 228
Sheldon Bush Lead Shot Tower,
    Bristol 213
Sheldonian Theatre, Oxford 186
Sherborne Castle, Dorset 157
Sherborne Old Castle, Dorset 46
Shugborough, Staffs 191
Silbury Hill, Wilts 16–17
Silchester Roman Walls 24

Sir Alfred Munnings Art
  Museum, Essex 230
Sir John Soane's Museum,
  Lon 218–20
Sissinghurst Castle 220
Sizergh Castle, Cumb 136
Skara Brae Prehistoric Village,
  Orkn 40
Skipton Castle, N Yorks 86
Sledmere House, E Yorks 197
Snowshill Manor, Glos 133
South Kensington Museums:
  Natural History Museum 220
  Victoria & Albert Museum
    220
Speke Hall, Merseyside 137
Spencer House, Lon 175–6
Spofforth Castle, N Yorks 139
Springhill House, Londonderry
  151
Squerryes Court, Kent 176
St Albans Roman Theatre 24
St Andrew's Castle, Fife 95
St Andrew's Church, Aller 19–20
St Andrew's Church, Didling 166
St Andrew's Church, Monkton
  Wyld, Dorset 213
St Augustine's Abbey, Kent 53
St Breock Downs Monolith 20
St Briavel's Castle, Glos 71
St Columb's Cathedral,
  Londonderry 207
St David's Cathedral, Pemb 78
St Edmundsbury Cathedral 63
St George's Guildhall,
  King's Lynn 126
St Giles Church, Cheadle 233
St Giles High Kirk, Edin 202
St John the Baptist Church,
  Burford, Oxon 183–4
St Leonard's Church, Hythe 110
St Mary the Virgin Church,
  Wallingford, Oxon 110
St Mary's Church, Studley Royal,
  N Yorks 241
St Mary's Priory Church,
  Abergavenny, Mon 136
St Mawes Castle, Corn 108
St Michael and All Angels
  Church, Wolverhampton 233
St Monan's Parish Church 202
St Pancras Station & Hotel 218
St Paul's Cathedral, Lon 167–8
St Paul's Church, Jarrow 36–7
St Peter-on-the-Wall Chapel,
  Essex 26
St Vincent Street Church,
  Glas 248–9

Stafford Castle, Staffs 71
Stanford Hall, Leics 192
Stansted Park, Hants 176
Stanton Drew Circles, Som 20
Stanton Harcourt Manor 128–9
Stanwick Iron Age Fortifications,
  N Yorks 38
Stirling Castle, Stirling 95
Stockbridge Down, Hants 25
Stokesay Castle, Shrops 129–30
Stoneacre, Kent 120–1
Stonehenge, Wilts 17
Stoney Littleton Long Barrow 20
Stowe House & Gardens, Bucks
  186–7
Stourhead, Wilts 157
Stratfield Saye House, Hants 228
Strawberry Hill, Lon 176
Sudeley Castle, Glos 130
Sutton House, Hackney, Lon 121
Syon Park, Middlx 168

Tamworth Castle, Staffs 71
Tantallon Castle, E Lot 96
Taplow Court, Bucks 228
Tate Gallery, Corn 213
Tate Modern, Lon 220
Tattershall Castle, Lincs 124
Tatton Park, Ches 194
Tenement House, Glas 249
Thirlestane Castle, Borders 204
Thornton Abbey, N Lincs 90
Threave Castle, Dum 147
Titchfield Abbey, Hants 58
Tintern Abbey, Mon 233–4
Tolquhon Castle, Abers 147
Tomen y Mur, Gwyn 34
Totnes Castle, Devon 50
Tower of London 53–4
Traquair House, Borders 147–8
Tredegar House, Mon 192–3
Tregiffian Burial Chamber 20
Trellick Tower, Lon 228
Trethevy Quoit, Corn 20
Trewithen, Corn 159
Truro Cathedral, Corn 213
Tutbury Castle, Staffs 133
Tynemouth Priory, Tyne 90

Uffington Castle, Oxon 29
Uley Long Barrow, Glos 31
Ulster History Park, Tyrone 41
University of Sussex 221
Upnor Castle, Kent 115
Uppark, W Sussex 167–9
Upper Plym Valley, Devon 20
Upton House, Warwks 192
Urquhart Castle, Highland 96

Valle Crucis Abbey, Den 78
Victoria & Albert Museum 220
Vindolanda, Nrthumb 37–8
Vyne, The, Hants 115–16

Waddesdon Manor, Bucks 221–2
Walcot Hall, Shrops 233
Wall Roman Site, Staffs 31–2
Wallace Collection, Lon 169
Wallace Monument, Stir 245–6
Walmer Castle, Kent 228
Walsingham Abbey, Norfolk
  124–5
Waltham Abbey Church
  & Gatehouse, Essex 125
Warkworth Castle 139–40
Warwick Castle 68
Wayland's Smithy, Oxon 32
Wells Cathedral, Som 47
Wenlock Priory, Shrops 68
West Kennet Avenue, Wilts 20
West Kennet Long Barrow 18
West Stow Anglo-Saxon Village,
  Suffolk 26
West Wycombe Park, Bucks
  169–70
Westminster Abbey, Lon 54
Westminster Cathedral 228–9
Wharram Percy, N Yorks 138
Wheeldale Moor Roman Road,
  N Yorks 38
Whitby Abbey, N Yorks 86
White Castle, Mon 78
White Mill, Dorset 213
Whithorn Priory, Dum 98
2 Willow Road, Lon 229
Wilton House, Wilts 157–8
Wimpole Hall, Cambs 180
Winchester Cathedral 54–5
Windmill Hill, Wilts 32
Windmill Tump Long Barrow,
  Wilts 20
Windsor Castle, Berks 55–6
Wingfield Manor, Derbys 133
Winslow Hall, Buckingham 192
Winterbourne Poor Lot Barrows,
  Dorset 21
Winton House, E Lot 204
Woburn Abbey, Beds 170
Wolfeton House, Dorset 108
Wolvesey Castle, Hants 121
Woolsthorpe Manor, Lincs 180
Worcester Cathedral 68–9
Wordsworth House, Cumb 239
Wroxeter Roman City, Shrops 29

York Minster 86
York Railway Station 240